THE

EARLY SESSIONS

Book 6 of The Seth Material

SESSIONS 240-280

3/9/66–8/24/66

THE EARLY SESSIONS

The Early Sessions consist of the first 510 sessions dictated by Seth through Jane Roberts, and are expected to be published in a total of 8-10 volumes. For information on expected publication dates and how to order, write to New Awareness Network at the following address and request the latest catalogue.

New Awareness Network Inc.
P.O. BOX 192
Manhasset, N.Y. 11030

Internet Address: http://www.sethcenter.com

THE SETH AUDIO COLLECTION

Rare recordings of Seth speaking through Jane Roberts are now available on audiocassette. For a complete description of The Seth Audio Collection, write to New Awareness Network Inc. at the above address.

(Further information is supplied at the back of this book)

THE

EARLY SESSIONS

Book 6 of The Seth Material

SESSIONS 240-280

3/9/66–8/24/66

Published by New Awareness Network Inc.

New Awareness Network Inc.
P.O. Box 192
Manhasset, New York 11030

Opinions and statements on health and medical matters expressed in this book are those of the author and are not necessarily those of or endorsed by the publisher. Those opinions and statements should not be taken as a substitute for consultation with a duly licensed physician.

Cover Design: Michael Goode
Photography: Cover photos by Rich Conz and Robert F. Butts, Sr.
Editorial: Rick Stack
Typography: Juan Schoch, Joan Thomas, Michael Goode

Library of Congress Cataloging-in-Publication Data

Seth (Spirit)
The early sessions: volume 6 of the seth material / [channeled] by Jane Roberts ; notes by Robert F. Butts.
p. cm.–(A Seth book)
ISBN 0-9652855-6-1
1. Spirit writings. 2. Self–Miscellanea
I. Roberts, Jane 1929–1984. II. Butts, Robert F. III. Title
IV. Series: Seth (Spirit), 1929–1984 Seth book.
Library of Congress Catalog Number:96-70130

ISBN 0-9652855-6-1
Printed in U.S.A. on acid-free paper

I dedicate The Early Sessions
to my wife, Jane Roberts,
who lived her 55 years
with the greatest creativity
and the most valiant courage.
-Rob

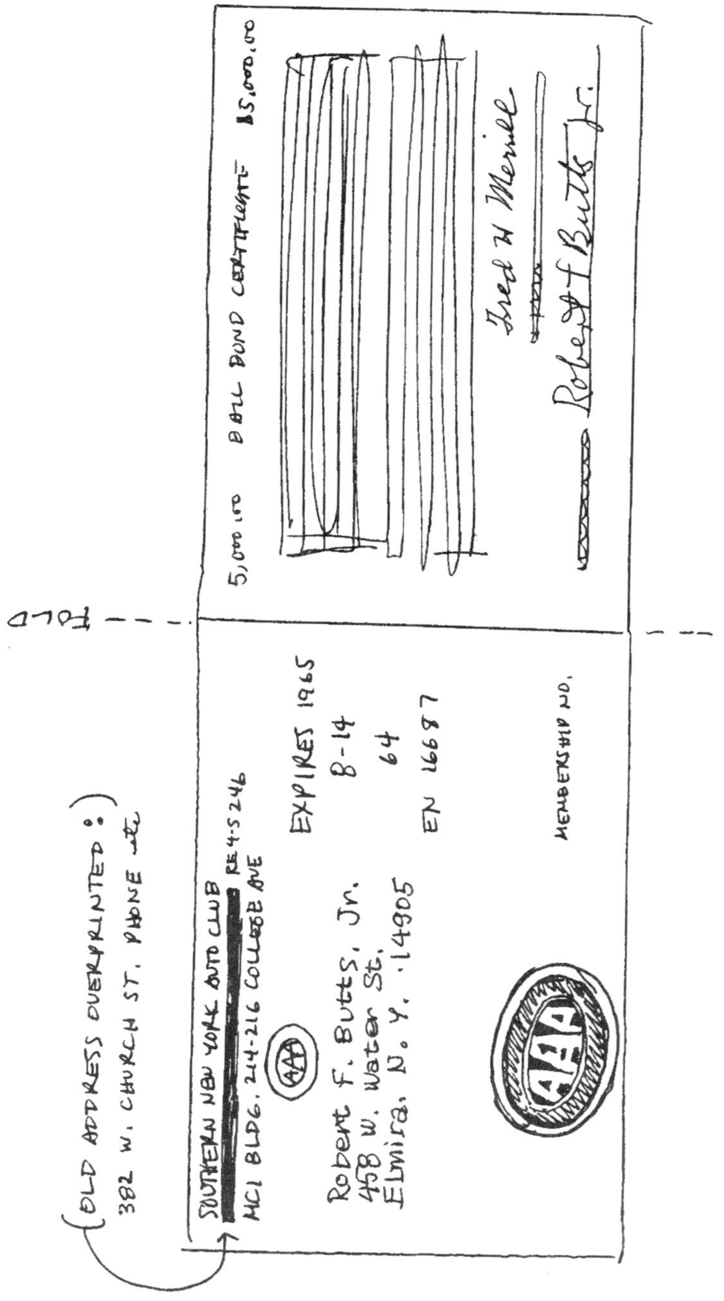

(Tracing of the front and back of the AAA membership card used as the object in the 39th envelope experiment, in the 240th session for March 9, 1966.)

SESSION 240
MARCH 9, 1966 9 PM WEDNESDAY AS SCHEDULED

(The 39th envelope experiment was held during the session; see the tracing of the AAA membership card used as the object on page 1. Some interesting and hilarious results were obtained in the connections made by Seth/Jane.

(Before this evening's session I was at work typing up the envelope data for last Monday's session. I stopped at 8:30 PM to get ready for this session at 9 PM. I began to be aware of a rather stiff pain growing in the back of my neck. By 8:45 it was quite bothersome, so I returned to the studio in the back of the apartment, to use the pendulum for a quick check to see if I could learn the cause. I did not think it physical.

(I became absorbed in the task, and had just obtained the answer when Jane called me from the front room at 8:55. I hadn't mentioned the pain to her, deciding on the spur of the moment to see if Seth could also pinpoint the trouble during the session. Nor did Jane know I was using the pendulum. When I took my seat at our table in the living room just before 9 PM Jane told me she had felt surprisingly nervous at my absence so close to the session; hence her calling to me. She also felt a definite irritation, but did not know its source, or who or what the target was.

(The session was held in our front room. Jane began speaking while sitting down. She was not smoking and her eyes were closed. Once again her pace was quite slow, and broken by some long pauses.)

Good evening.

("Good evening, Seth.")

Now. Sooner or later we are going to have to discuss the ways in which what would appear to be sensual perception is made available to an individual when the physical body, with its senses, perceives an event at which it cannot be said to be present.

Unfortunately this will be somewhat complicated. More so than is at first apparent.

I have told you that each individual creates physical matter, including objects, that he constructs his own physical image. Coherence, the illusion of permanency, placement in space, color and mass, all these are arrived at and agreed upon, in ways that I have clearly explained.

(In Volume 2, see the 60th to 73rd sessions, given during the summer of 1964, plus many others.)

Telepathic communication is one of the methods by which such agreement is reached. Long ago, primary and secondary constructions were explained. I emphasized that each individual only perceives his own physical constructions.

Basically there is no difference between precognition and telepathy. The apparent difference is the result of an inadequate understanding of the nature of time. The important fact is, in both cases, that information is received by an individual that does not come through recognized sense systems.

This main issue is frequently overlooked, while emphasis is placed instead upon whether or not the information seems to be perceived from the present or future. When an individual—in quotes—"clairvoyantly sees"—end quotes—an event, this is what happens.

First of all, he forgets the concept of continual moments, which usually hampers his perception. His perception changes focus so that he is aware of an event that would otherwise be future for him. He constructs subconsciously, as always, material objects in line with the data that is available to him. It goes without saying then that he helps to construct the clairvoyantly perceived physical event, just as he helps to construct any physical event in the present.

The agreement as to physical dimensions and so forth is reached precisely in the same manner that it usually is. The only unusual issue, to you, should not be that the event has not yet occurred, but that John Jones for example, from his chair, has been sensually aware of a situation that is obviously beyond the reaches of his physical senses.

The self does not remain as permanently attached to the physical body as you imagine, during physical existence.

The ego is much more dependent upon the physical self than are other portions of the personality. The physical body is more like a home station, from which frequent excursions are made. The ego is like a guardian who is left at home, as watchdog.

Sensual data is not basically—underlined—dependent upon the physical body. The individual can receive sensual data in other ways. The senses are indeed often used by the inner self as a constant method of acquainting it with circumstances pertinent to the survival and interests of the physical body, but the inner self is not entirely dependent on them for its entire data by any means. The mind can bypass the senses, and receive its data in a more direct manner, translating what it perceives as automatically as it translates sensual data.

I suggest your first break.

(Break at 9:30. Jane was dissociated as usual. Her eyes had opened but once, when she sipped some wine. Her pace had been better as the delivery progressed.

(I now told Jane that as the session progressed I had more and more difficulty keeping "awake." Actually I began to notice a heavy lassitude, although I kept writing without trouble, and I recognized that I seemed to be in a trance state. At the

same time, as I looked about the room, everything seemed to be in a sharper focus, and I had a feeling of more light in the room, although it was well lit to begin with. I began to wonder if I was responding to the material Seth was presenting; I had found it very interesting.

(I then remembered that in the 232nd session Seth had said I was in a light trance myself during sessions, as I made "certain automatic adjustments in order to perceive what little of my presence that you do perceive. And I also have a calming effect on you, which is most beneficial to you." See Volume 5, page 277. Recalling this, I wondered if I was not making a strong effort to perceive Seth, perhaps in apparition form, this evening; which meant that possibly he was present to a stronger degree than usual.

(Jane said she too has experienced the seemingly contradictory effects of sleepiness or lethargy, and the sharper vision, during trance. Needless to say, I saw nothing unusual in my frequent glances about the room, nor did I notice any change in Jane's features. The sensation was pronounced by the time break came, yet during break it disappeared. I have been aware of something like it, on a must reduced scale, many times during sessions.

(Jane once again resumed with her eyes closed, and at a little faster pace, at 9:37. A reminder: Seth calls for all underlined words.)

Now. Under so-called usual circumstances, data is received through the physical senses, and is <u>then</u> interpreted by the brain.

When a clairvoyant event is perceived the data is received by the <u>mind</u> and given to the brain, which then interprets it as it does usual data. The physical body becomes aware of it in other words, but the senses have been bypassed.

The interpretation is made however in the same way as it is usually made. Otherwise the data would make no sense to the physical organism, and would not register. Actually much data perceived directly by the mind bypasses the physical organism completely.

The physical organism is not aware of it. The subconscious does receive the information however, in some of these cases. In other cases the experience is simply not recorded in any way within the physical organism, but it is recorded to deeper layers of the self that are divorced to a large degree from any physical manipulations.

(Once again the lassitude began to creep over me, while I looked about the room with sharp eyes. I had a little trouble focusing on my writing paper, but none looking away from the table. Jane's eyes were closed, her manner as usual.

(Shortly after this my familiar old thrilling sensation began to creep over me. I have not been aware of it much recently, although in the early sessions both Jane and I experienced such effects often. It is, briefly, a rich tingling or thrilling that is

very pleasant. It can appear in any limb or part of the body, remain localized or sweep the whole organism. Deeper stages of this are what Jane has called ecstasy in her psychological time experiments.

(This time it began in both my feet and moved up my legs to my hips, then manifested itself in the back of my head. It did not interfere with my writing. It was not overwhelming by any means, yet most definite, and lasted in residue until next break. See Volume 1, page 172 for a description of my first experience with this sensation, which was at first frightening to me, and accompanied by visual internal data which was quite vivid. Seth went into the experience in detail in the 24th session, explaining how at times it represented my attempts to perceive him, and at other times my attempts to perceive other data outside the usual sense channels.)

This physically unrecorded material is available to the subconscious however, if the need for it arises. Before it can be used by the physical organism it must then be taken from the deeper layers of the self to the brain for interpretation, as if it were new sensual data received through the methods with which you are more familiar.

In the dream state you smell odors that are not in your room. The memory of the odors is imprinted and registered by the physical body as faithfully and realistically as any—quote—"real"—end of quote—odor is in the waking state.

The odor experience becomes a part of memory and can be recalled through hypnosis. Sometimes it will arise spontaneously, as any memory may. The odor is as legitimate to the physical organism as any odor smelled in the waking condition. This is fairly important.

It makes no difference basically, underlined, whether or not the sense data is real in your terms or not. If it is recorded and registered by the physical organism it becomes a part of, and an equal part of, memory. In the case of the odor smelled in a dream, the mind experiences, and then the experience is interpreted precisely as if the senses had been used to perceive it. It is then incorporated with other experience by the physical organism.

You may take your break.

(Break at 9:56. Jane was dissociated as usual. Her eyes had remained closed, her pace had been better, her voice average.

(Again toward the end of the delivery I had felt the pleasant lethargy, coupled with the sharp vision as I looked about the room. I noticed nothing unusual at break once more. I described my feelings to Jane once more, and she then surprised me by saying that she had a subjective feeling while speaking that her features had changed.

(We wondered if Jane's feeling was due to suggestion. During the week she had been referring to the 68th session as she did some work on the book on the Seth

material; these sessions have to do with the construction of physical matter by each individual. This particular session was witnessed by Bill Macdonnel, and during it he made two pen and ink drawings of an apparition he claimed to see in a doorway of our apartment. The effect lasted for about an hour; during this session Bill and I together saw a distinct change in Jane's features. This occurred at a break, without warning, and lasted for at least a minute, so that we had time for observation.

(Seth told us at the time that the apparition was of him, and that Bill could see it but that Jane and I could not because we were too "fussy" about what we allowed ourselves to see. He said that in the future—time unspecified—we should be able to see his apparition at times, but by no means regularly.

(Bill's drawings of Seth show an extremely high cranium—according to Seth Bill's graphic translation of Bill's feeling of high intelligence on Seth's part—and a pointed chin. While pointed the chin is not long. Jane said, this evening, that her subjective feeling was one of elongation of the chin, to a point. She also felt her head was down onto her shoulders, and this is another attribute of Bill's drawings.

(Note above that the apparition and the feature change in Jane are two distinct and separated effects, both occurring in the same session. The one was visible to me, the other was not. Again, this evening I saw no change in Jane's features.

(It was now time for the 46th Dr. Instream experiment. Jane had smoked only at break. Her eyes were now closed, her hands raised to her face, her pace broken by many short pauses and a few long ones. Resume at 10:05.)

Now. Give us a moment for our Instream material.

He has received today a parcel bound in string, with string.

The object is made of glass. A tumbler, partially filled with water. A transparent tumbler, with a stem, and chalice-shaped.

The package has to do with the initials M. Minnesota, I do not know except for the initial. The number four is also connected with the package. It was addressed on both sides, and cost 43 cents, I believe, to mail.

The address was in ink, and printed. A W also connected with the sender of the package. Perhaps something like Winnip, but I am only sure of the W. The number 16 after the city in which the sender lives. Perhaps a connection with some kind of cards, and a scoop, using the word as a news scoop.

Also a letter or note having to do with mileage. Perhaps in connection with a trip.

Do you have an envelope for me, Joseph?

("Yes."

(Jane paused at 10:15. Her eyes still closed, she reached out to take the envelope for our 39th experiment from me. She held it to her forehead for a few sentences, then lowered it to her lap.)

Give us a moment, please. These are impressions.

A connection with the letter M, and with an occasion in which something was not appreciated. A connection with four here also. A rectangular shape, and a rather large X-shape mark.

(With the hand holding the envelope, Jane reached out to make a large vigorous crossing-out gesture, or X-shape, with her full arm. Her eyes remained closed.)

This sort of thing, you see, in dark color, the X-shape mark in dark color, as something canceled.

Connection with an error. Connection with music, and with an ace. With something not known, and with 4 people. With a pole. Ruburt thinks of telephone pole, this leading him to a connection with a telephone pole.

A sun shape, or yellow in the upper right hand corner. Perhaps like rays.

The number 12, and perhaps 3 with this. December, I do not know.

Do you have any questions?

(I have been trying out different kinds of questions. This was my third opportunity. The first time I had asked Seth for data on a category not mentioned, namely color. The second time I asked him to start over the whole thing. This time I tried something else.

("How about elaborating on your reference to something that was not appreciated?")

All I have is the feeling that something was not appreciated, and that an error might have been somehow responsible.

A Saturday here. It seems the letters D and C, and something to do with grace, and an appointment.

I suggest your break.

(Break at 10:25. Jane was dissociated as usual. Her eyes had remained closed, her pace had gradually speeded up somewhat.

(It seems to be the rule now that Jane has some visual data, whether faint or stronger, during the envelope experiments. She said she may have had such data in the earlier experiments, also, but hadn't been quick enough to catch it. It is tricky. The point is, Jane explained, that such data often needs interpretation. Seth gives her the information visually; it is then up to a part of Jane to correctly interpret this. Jane believes that in the early experiments her failure to appreciate this, to interpret correctly, led to many errors in the material; that actually, through Seth, she had received the correct data to begin with, but needed the practice in fine discrimination to even be aware that the problem existed. And of course needs more. A case in point here is the X-shape data explained later.

(See the tracing of the envelope object on page 1. As stated it is a membership card in the AAA, purchased by me on August 14,1964, and good for one year. It is

printed entirely in dark blue ink on glossy white heavy paper. The exception is the large AAA seal affixed by hand beneath my typed address; this is in black, embossed on foil. The back of the card is covered by fine print, giving detailed instructions re the procedure after an accident, etc., calling Western Union, bail bond procedure, etc.

(Strangely enough, some of tonight's envelope data is corroborated by earlier session material—something I did not anticipate when using the card as object. The notes in the 81st session for August 28,1964, explain some connections made this evening. I was about to throw the card away this week when I thought of using it for the envelope tonight, and consciously had forgotten many of the 1964 connections.

(Seth did not go over each connection with us, but does agree with the ones Jane and I were able to make.

("A connection with the letter M", referred, I thought, to the initials, MCI, which are used to designate the modern new office building here in Elmira, at which I bought my membership in the AAA. Later note by RFB: Signed by Merrill. Note on the object that the address of this new building was added later to the card, beneath the old address which was blocked out. This building was barely in operation at the time I joined AAA, in August 1964; the top floors were not yet finished.

("and with an occasion in which something was not appreciated." This at once reminded me of a most definite event, involving Jane and me, that was not appreciated. It took place at the same time I purchased membership in AAA, and the locale of this unappreciated event was a gasoline station directly across the street from the MCI building. Our car was the subject, and this material is well covered in the notes in the 81st session for August 26,1964. See Volume 2.

(I bought the membership in AAA on Friday, August 14,1964, at about 1 PM. We were both on vacation beginning that day, and were due to leave for York Beach, Maine, the next day, Saturday, August 15. Jane and I drove downtown Friday. Jane had a couple of hours work to finish at the art gallery where she then worked. I dropped her off there, then left the car at the station in question for an oil filter change and a general checkup. I went across the street to the MCI building, joined AAA, then walked home. I was due to return to the station for the car at 5 PM that same day. I would pick up Jane and we would be free.

(When I walked back downtown to the station at 5 PM to pick up the car, I was dismayed to be told that the mechanic there was having much trouble replacing the oil filter cap, that it persisted in leaking no matter how much force he used trying to tighten it. I was afraid the threads on the cap would be stripped; if the part in question had to be replaced, it meant dismantling the steering gear on our particular make of car, and thus a delay starting our vacation until next week.

(Watching the mechanic struggle with the car, I felt sure he was not familiar enough with the work to know what he was doing. I made my feelings known, then

left for the gallery to tell Jane. This was at a time when Seth was beginning to fill us in on the power of expectation; Jane insisted that the car would be ready when we went back for it. We ate in a diner, and Jane concentrated on the car being ready. When we went back for it an hour later it was indeed ready. The station mechanic told us he was surprised that he had been able to fix it. The incident had upset me considerably, in a way that would not bother me now.

("A connection with four here also." We could not see any such connection, other than the number four appearing several times on the object.

("A rectangular shape", The membership card is rectangular in shape, whether opened up as shown on page 1, or folded as indicated. It was folded in the usual double sealed envelope this evening.

("and a rather large X-shape mark. This sort of thing, you see, in dark color, the X-shape mark in dark color, as something canceled." As mentioned on page 7, this is an instance where Jane received internal visual data from Seth, and had the responsibility of interpreting it correctly. Note that she feels her way through this data, finally arriving at something more specific in the last three words. On the membership card it is plainly printed that the coverage expires in 1965.

(Jane said that when giving this bit of data she plainly had the feeling that the visual X-shape was to show her that something was canceled. The card expired in 1965. Jane also saw the large X on a rectangular card shape, within, but saw no detail on this card shape that would have enabled her to identify the envelope object specifically.

("Connection with an error." An error is prominent here. When I filled out my application for the insurance policy that went with the AAA membership, I inadvertently made a mistake in my license number. I did not discover this until I returned home, so when I went back downtown to pick up the car at the station, I dropped in at the MCI building to the AAA office. I was told the mistake did not matter.

("Connection with music", reminds me that I heard music while in the AAA office; the music was piped throughout the new building by a public address system. Jane and I are well aware of this because a friend of ours worked in another office in the MCI building, and remarked often on this piped music, which she disliked but was forced to listen to all day on the job. In addition, the AAA office was below ground level and without windows, and my personal opinion was that the music was some kind of compensation for not being able to see daylight.

("and with an ace." Jane said this is a personal derivation of hers from the prominent black seal of the AAA, affixed to the bottom of the card, below my name, as described. Another interpretation of this seal follows later.

("With something not known, and with 4 people." Jane and I have an idea as

to a connection here, but since we cannot support it we decided not to list it.

("With a pole. Ruburt thinks of telephone pole, this leading him to a connection with a telephone pole." On the back of the envelope object shown on page 1, there are many references to using the telephone, in the detailed instructions given by the AAA as to procedures after involvement in an auto accident. Many of the instructions have to do with using the telephone, Western Union, etc., as indicated on the card itself.

("A sun shape, or yellow in the upper right hand corner. Perhaps like rays." See the bottom of page 9. Jane said this is another reference to the heavy, glossy, or shiny black AAA seal affixed to the membership card below my name. To her, the design of the three A's can represent the conventional lines of radiation around a circle, or sun, shape. She often used this symbolism in her own oil painting, thus:

(The yellow or sun references may come from the design of the letters A, but perhaps also from the shiny surface foil texture of the seal itself. It can be seen that if the object was held upside down while sealed in the double envelope, it would appear to the percipient to be in the upper right hand corner.

("The number 12, and perhaps 3 with this. December, I do not know." My membership in AAA was good for twelve months, which could have led Seth to the December, or twelfth month, data, but we are not sure here. Nor do we come up with anything for the number 3.

("All I have is the feeling that something was not appreciated", followed my request for Seth's elaboration on this data. See the original interpretation on page 7.

("and that an error might have been somehow responsible." My own idea is that the error here mentioned refers to my error in my license number, as explained on page 9. Seth also says "might have." I think an error can enter into the car adventure, possibly, in that at the time I felt the mechanic servicing the car did not go about the job properly, and nearly delayed our leaving on vacation by several days as a result.

("A Saturday here." It can now be seen that my question for elaboration on Seth's part did lead to a little more data. Saturday is involved with the envelope object, through our car. I obtained the actual object on Friday, August 14,1964; while doing this the car was left at the station for servicing, and the events developing at the station very nearly prevented our leaving on vacation the following day, Saturday, August 15.

("It seems the letters D and C", offered no connections to us.

("and something to do with grace", Jane burst out laughing when she made a connection here. At first we thought her idea did not apply, but then she felt it did, and Seth agrees. Note that on the AAA membership card the old address was blocked out. This was done with thin ink and we could read the old address, 382 W. Church Street. Jane at once made the connection between church and grace.

(More, the new MCI building is but a couple of blocks from the old AAA location; the new address is on the corner of College Avenue and Church Street. And the Grace Episcopal Church is two blocks up Church Street.

("and an appointment." As noted in the car data on pages 8 and 9, I had an appointment to pick up the car at the service station at 5 PM Friday, August 14,1964, the same day I bought membership in AAA. The station was located across the street from the AAA office, and the car was at the station while I was in the AAA office.

(Before she resumed I told Jane I hoped Seth would say something about my sensations earlier in the session. They had all but disappeared by now. I felt but a light lingering of the thrilling effect, mainly in the back of my head; the lethargy was gone. Also gone was the neck pain that I had experienced before the session began. Jane did not know about this.

(Jane resumed with her head resting on her crossed arms as they lay upon the table. Her eyes were closed, her pace average. 10:48.)

Now. I will not keep you.

Your feelings were quite legitimate. You did sense my presence, and I came through rather strongly earlier.

Ruburt has been concerned already, thinking in advance of some of the criticisms that will be made concerning his book, and he has been somewhat disturbed. Not in a severe manner however. For this reason I hovered about rather closely.

Intuitively he will arrive at the proper balance between intellectual concerns and inner spontaneity.

Now, I will leave you unless you have any questions.

("How about the connections we made with the envelope data? Were we correct?")

You were indeed.

("Does this include Jane's connections about the church and grace data?")

This was correct. He is learning to interpret the inner images which become available to him.

Now, I am quite prepared to speak as long as you would like. It is your convenience that I am thinking of.

("How about saying something about the pain in the neck I had, just before the session?"

(Jane, now sitting upright, smiled. Her eyes were still closed.)

You were concerned because of the poor test results in your last session. Did not admit it. You think, occasionally, that your <u>own</u> tests are a pain in the neck, even while you admit their necessity.

("That's what the pendulum told me, just before the session.")

Is there anything else?

("No, I guess not. It's been fun.")

My best regards to you both.

("Will I ever get to see you, or your apparition?")

If you keep your eyes open. You have come close in the past.

("But not close enough.")

Again, use the right set of eyes.

("I'll keep trying. Jane wants me to tell her to open her own eyes, when I do see you.")

We shall see.

("Good night, Seth."

(End at 11:00 PM. Jane was dissociated as usual. Her eyes had remained closed.

(Jane was pleased to learn Seth's answer about my neck pain agreed with the answer I had obtained through the pendulum. See the notes on page 2.

(Seth got to the point quicker than I did with the pendulum, although I was somewhat handicapped through lack of time. I did not begin using it until fifteen minutes before the session, and then began by eliminating categories in Monday's session until I found the one I was reacting to physically. This proved to be Monday's envelope experiments, and my fear, or concern, that perhaps I was pushing Jane on such matters.

(The pendulum told me Jane did not feel this way, and after the session she agreed. Nevertheless the pendulum told me I felt some anger at myself on this score, hence the stiff neck. I had not reached any such neat conception as "a pain in the neck" before Jane called me. Jane now said the irritation she felt quite strongly just before the session, was her sensing of my own irritation at myself. As stated on page 2, she was aware of the irritation before the session, but puzzled as to its source. She did not know of my pain in the neck, or that I was using the pendulum.)

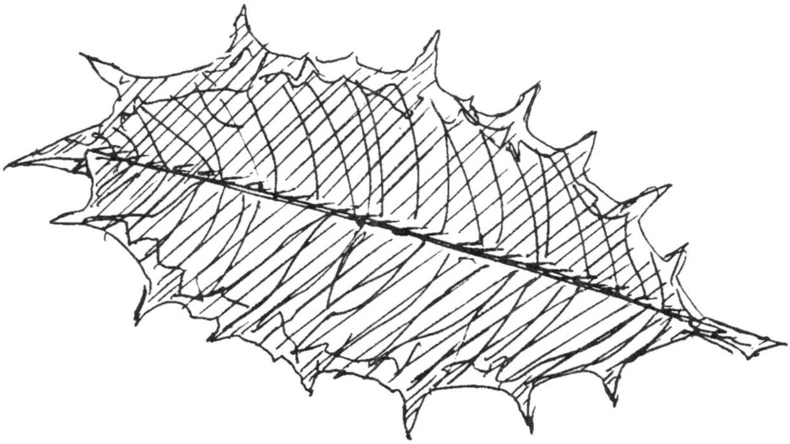

(Tracing of the holly leaf used as the object in the 40th envelope experiment, in the 241st session for March 14,1966.)

SESSION 241
MARCH 14, 1966 9 PM MONDAY AS SCHEDULED

(The 40th envelope experiment was held during the session. See the tracing above. The envelope object was a dried holly leaf. This gray-brown leaf had been taped to the shade on my lamp at work for well over a year; originally I had used it as a model in doing some artwork for a Christmas card. I saved it because of its interesting color and shape, and the fact that its points were as sharp as ever. It was sealed in the usual double envelope, between two pieces of Bristol. Jane had never seen it, nor did she know I had brought it home.

(Last night Peggy Gallagher told us that she is following the suggestions given by Seth in the unscheduled 238th session, but hasn't noticed any improvement yet in the "bursitis" in her neck and left shoulder and arm. She is continuing to follow the suggestions however. Seth has linked her difficulty to improper yoga exercises, and tension between the third to fifth vertebrae.

(The session was held in our front room. Once again Jane smoked very little during the session. Her pace was again slow, with many pauses of varying length. She spoke while sitting down, and with her left hand raised to her lowered head. Her eyes were closed; she maintained this position until break.)

Good evening.

("Good evening, Seth.")

Now. There are indeed psychological frameworks that operate in communications such as ours, and I shall attempt to explain their function and composition.

I will first discuss our own particular circumstances, and then proceed to a more general discussion. There is Ruburt's ego, and his subconscious, as you know. There are also other areas or levels that are part of his whole personality. In our case a gestalt personality or a psychological bridge

(Jane and I were at once very intrigued by Seth's term, "psychological bridge"—one most natural and evocative, it seemed to us.)

This psychological framework obviously must be receptive. It must also be formed by portions of my <u>own</u> essence, and by portions of Ruburt's personality. It can be thought of almost as a psychological <u>protrusion</u>, though this is not precisely the word to explain it.

Bridge perhaps is better. This psychological framework is in itself capable of growth, in terms of development. It represents on Ruburt's part a psychological expansion, and indeed on my own part also. It is formed partially by abilities inherent within all personalities, psychic abilities, and it is composed of energy. It is not a secondary personality, for it exists in quite a different dimension than secondary personalities.

Now. This psychological framework is the medium through which we can communicate. It is purely a psychic organization that telepathically transmits concepts from me to Ruburt. We have always preferred the light trance state over a deeper trance for several reasons.

I am interested mainly in education, and with Ruburt's training by me through our present methods, the processes themselves are more clearly seen and understood. Some information comes to Ruburt fairly automatically, in that he speaks for me without having to consciously translate for me.

At the same time, because of the methods we use, some translation is often necessary. In many cases this translation is done by the intervening psychological framework, which is simply the psychological point closest to the meeting of Ruburt's personality and my own, for he does not fade out as a personality. He extends himself in an expansion. The psychological expansion on his end, and the psychological expansion on my end, form the gestalt, the psychological bridge, of which I have spoken.

As he is learning it is, however, often up to him to interpret the images that I send him. The psychological bridge can transmit, you see, and to some extent translate, but not interpret.

This psychological gestalt is a connector. I am dependent in a large measure upon Ruburt's own knowledge, and lack of it, in that I cannot force for example from him, from his speech mechanism, concepts with which he is entirely unfamiliar. I must introduce them step by step.

I could not have explained moment points to you, for example, until I had clearly given the idea of the spacious present. It is not as simple a thing as it might seem, for there is no coercion involved, Ruburt always consenting to let me push concepts at him, which he interprets speech-wise with my assistance.

Often I give him an internal image, or experience, of a whole concept, but unless it could be vocalized it would have no meaning except to him.

Now I suggest your first break.

(Break at 9:30. Jane had been dissociated as usual for a first delivery. She had maintained her original position—eyes closed, head resting on her left upraised hand, for the whole delivery. She did not know why. She hadn't smoked and her pace had been a little faster toward break.

(Seth began talking about moment points in the 149th-152nd sessions. He began on the spacious present in session 44 in Volume 2.

(Jane has been reading G.N.M. Tyrrell's book, Science and Psychical Phenomena & Apparitions, *lately, and she now told me she had hoped that Seth might discuss his relationship with her this evening.*

(Jane resumed in the same manner and in the same position, with pauses, at 9:39.)

Now, in some cases this is what happens.

Ruburt is of course much more familiar with sense impressions than he is with internal data, or with impressions that do not come to him through the physical senses. Therefore in our experiments, often, I will give him an impression, and he will automatically translate it into visual terms, although his eyes are closed. And then he is tempted to interpret it literally, as he would an ordinary visual image.

A beautiful example of this occurred in our last session, with the X image.

(See page 7 of the 240th session for the envelope data on the AAA card used as the object. The card bears the expiration date, and Jane got at the idea of this by gesturing boldly with her arm, finishing up the several lines of data with "as something canceled." See also page 9, where Jane describes the internal visual data accompanying her vocal data.)

For simplicity's sake, I say that I gave him the image, but actually I gave him the impression, which he translated into an image, so that he could deal with it in a more familiar way.

As a result in such instances, it is up to him to interpret the image correctly. The words that you hear are my words and not Ruburt's. However, they are representations of my thought, as they are sifted through various layers, first of all of our composite psychological framework, and then through layers of Ruburt's own personality.

There is often at his end a final tug and pull, so that the vocal mechanism will finally speak the correct interpretation. Of course Ruburt's own associations are used by me, with his consent, up to a certain point, to enable me to lead him to the proper subject or image.

Then when we are successful there is a divergence from his associations so that he says the correct word, even though the correct word, for him personally, would be the wrong word as far as his personal associations are concerned.

This point is fairly important, for it shows how the personal associations are utilized up to a certain point, and then sometimes quite suddenly dispensed with, for they have served our purposes.

On Ruburt's part this can sometimes be disconcerting. We must always work with psychological organizations however. The emotions always follow associative lines in this regard.

The trick is to allow Ruburt's associations free reign to a certain point, and then expertly insert the correct data. This is sometimes difficult. Ruburt's associations may go for example from C, D, E, and F, but precisely where he would say G, we must insert X or Y, and do it so smoothly that he is quite unaware.

He consents for me, he consents to let me use his associations in such a manner. Nevertheless there is a small sense of alienation when the associations do not follow through, but are diverted to the desired end.

Here is a very brief example. Suppose I am trying to give him the impression of a glass of water. It is fairly easy to insert the idea of water, but this may lead him personally to think of the Gulf of Mexico, or the ocean off of Marathon, or even of the Atlantic at York Beach. I will use his associations until I am certain that he has the concept of the word water, but precisely where he is about to say the ocean for example, and after having made use of his associations to get him to this point, I must suddenly make him say a glass of water.

Now I suggest your break.

(Break at 9:59. Jane was dissociated as usual. Her pace had picked up considerably. Once again she sat in the same position for the entire delivery—her head lowered, her left hand raised to her closed eyes. Her eyes had remained closed and she had not smoked.

(It was now time for the 47th Dr. Instream experiment. Once more Jane used the same position, with the difference that now her pace slowed once again. Resume at 10:06.)

Now. Give us a moment, please, for our Instream material.

We will give the object shortly.

First of all, a formal affair of some kind. It has to do mainly with a group of men. It is their affair, or it is to honor them. But women I believe are also present.

There is also a dinner connected here.

Now, the object is something very small, like a thimble. Metallic, hollow, with very small holes in it. It is a shade of green, on the grayish side, with a patina. Perhaps with initials on it.

He holds it in his hands. Nervously, I believe. At least, tossing it from one hand to the other.

Gray threads, does he wear a gray suit? It would not seem so at a formal affair, yet I pick up that connection. And a connection with something round and red, of apple shape.

Music. He meets a woman who was a close friend of a male friend of his, who has since died. I believe the initial W here.

Something about a margin of safety, perhaps concerning health, and a recent doctor's appointment. A <u>mental muddle</u>. I do not know to what this refers.

Do you have an envelope for me, Joseph?

("Yes."

(Jane paused at 10:17. She still sat in the same position, her eyes closed, her head lowered to rest on her left hand. Without opening her eyes, she reached out with her right hand to take the sealed 40th envelope from me. She then held it against her forehead.)

Give us a moment, please. These are impressions.

A connection with something deep. A hole underground, as a mine or a grave. The number 6.

Something fairly remarkable. A phone call. Gray and brown. Stripes. A G and H. A miscellany of shapes arranged in a row. A note from a man in connection with an achievement.

A reference to four people. A connection with an appointment made but not kept, or not kept yet.

Do you have any questions?

(This was my fourth chance to ask a question about envelope data. I had an idea about the first bit of data.

("Will you elaborate on the something deep, or underground, data?")

Give us a moment.

Ruburt's impression now is of a basement. Mine is of something steep, downward, with rock. Rock walls, and hard rather than soft beneath. And perhaps water.

I suggest your break. Unless you have any more questions.

("No, that's okay.")

(Break at 10:28. Jane was dissociated as usual, and once again maintained the same position throughout the delivery. Her eyes had remained closed.

(See the tracing of the envelope object, the holly leaf, on page 13. Some of Seth's points were good. I thought another group of them tried to get at the origin of the envelope object—namely my place of employment—hence the reason I chose the question I asked. I also thought the hole and grave data referred to an earlier envelope experiment dealing with my place of employment.

(Jane and I made connections, and Seth briefly concurred regarding some of them.

("A connection with something deep. A hole underground, as a mine or grave." Seth had been talking about association regarding envelope data in the earlier part of the session, and I thought this data a good example of it. My idea was that this data referred to my place of employment, from where I obtained the object, by calling upon the death of a friend, Ezra Havens, in 1964. Ezra had worked at my place of employment, Artistic Card Co., for many years.)

(In Volume 5, see the 232nd session for Feb. 9,1966. In that session Ezra is dealt with in the envelope data with the same type of data; Seth gave Jane the grave data, signifying Ezra's death, but at that time Jane, who did not like the idea of graves, did not use the word. This time, Jane now said, she came out with it when Seth gave her the data. We believe the grave data was to refer to Ezra, who worked at Artistic before he died, and that this in turn was to lead Jane to identify Artistic as the source of the envelope object.

("The number 6." A lengthy article on Jane's ESP book was published in the local Elmira Star-Gazette on July 6,1965. This can be a possible connection but we are not sure since I did not ask Seth to speak on this point. The article however is involved with some of the following data.

("Something fairly remarkable." Nor did I follow up on this item, although we believe it referred to the ESP book also, as dealt with in the above newspaper article.

("A phone call." The newspaper article led to a note to Jane from the wife of my boss, Harry Gottesman, inviting us to the Gottesman home for an evening. Jane answered the note, received in July 1965, by phone. All of these oblique references are attempts to tie in my boss, Harry, with the envelope object itself.

("Gray and brown." These are the colors of the envelope object; the holly leaf is very dry and brittle, and faded out to a gray-brown.

("Stripes." I believe these refer to the pronounced pattern of the veins on the leaf. They are more pronounced than indicated on my sketch, having a three

dimensional quality as they branch out in roughly parallel lines from the central stem.

("A G and H." I thought this an inverted reference to the fact that the envelope object came from my place of employment, presided over by my boss, Harry Gottesman. Harry noticed the holly leaf in particular when it was first given to me about a year ago; and like I did, he pricked his finger on the exceedingly sharp points.

("A miscellany of shapes arranged in a row." I call this a good reference to the location of the holly leaf at work. I have a Dazor lamp, a standard piece of equipment, fastened to my drawing table at work. It is a fluorescent lamp with a shade about 18 inches long. I have a habit of sticking various objects on the shade for easy reference—small pictures, drawings, pieces of tape, stickers of various kinds, and other objects. One of these was until recently the holly leaf; I had taped it there after finishing with it close to a year ago. Due to the long narrow shape of the lamp shade, the objects fastened thereon end up arranged in a row.

("A note from a man in connection with an achievement." Jane said she believed she meant to say woman here instead of man, and that this data is another oblique reference to the connection of my boss with the source of the envelope object. See the notes after "phone call" above. My boss's wife actually wrote the note.

("A reference to four people." We were not sure here, unless this was a reference to the evening Jane and I spent with my boss and his wife, after the note and the phone call, etc. We call these kind of impressions twice-removed from the actual object.

("A connection with an appointment made but not kept, or not kept yet." We were not sure.

("Ruburt's impression now is of a basement. Mine is something steep, downward, with rock. Rock walls, and hard rather than soft beneath. And perhaps water." This is the data obtained after I asked Seth to elaborate upon the underground, or grave, data. It adds a little to the first impression given tonight. See page 17 also. Jane said now that because she hadn't given the word grave in the envelope data in the 232nd session, involving a death, she made it a point to speak it aloud this evening when she obtained a similar impression.

(Yet note that above she has an impression of a basement instead, personally, and when speaking for Seth does not use the word grave, as she did the first time. One point I am curious about. Is water somehow involved with Ezra's grave? Is Seth clairvoyantly aware of water in, or near, the grave? I wasn't quick enough to ask the question after break.

(Jane said she had no images that she could remember, during this experiment.

(She resumed once again in the same position, sitting with her eyes closed, her head lowered to her upraised left hand. Resume, with pauses, at 10:37.)

Now. We will shortly end our session.

The initial grave association was meant to lead Ruburt to your place of work, since in another experiment the test item was connected with a man who had died.

The color was correct, and the miscellaneous shapes, as you see. The initials were inverted, and applied to your Harry Gottesman, to the note from his wife. Ruburt misinterpreted here. To the four people in the Gottesman family, at your visit there.

(Since the data hadn't been specific enough, Jane and I had thought of ourselves and Harry and his wife, as making up the four people.)

The appointment made but not kept refers to the fact that you all said you would get together again in the near future, and you did not.

(As has happened before, I remembered this as soon as Seth mentioned it. As did Jane, even while she spoke in trance.)

All in all, hardly our best. However the color and the initials—the initials particularly—were quite specific.

I wanted to add a brief note, to the effect that neither of you have any health worries at this time. You may insert this in the record or not, as you prefer.

We will then end this evening's session. My heartiest regards to you both. If you wish we can continue, or end the session as you prefer.

("We'll end it then. Good night, Seth."

(End at 10:48. Jane was dissociated as usual. Her eyes had remained closed, as they had all evening with the exception of one instance.)

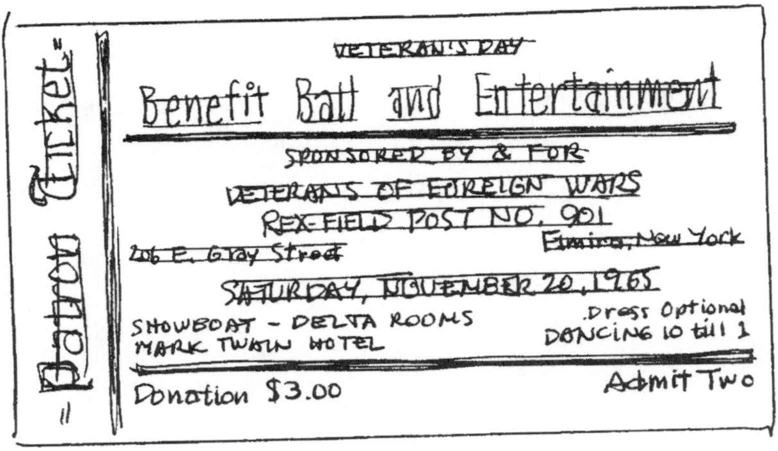

(Tracing of the ticket used as the object in the 41st envelope experiment, in the 242nd session for March 16,1966.)

SESSION 242
MARCH 16, 1966 9 PM WEDNESDAY AS SCHEDULED

(The 41st envelope experiment was held during the session. See the tracing on page 20. The object was an unused ticket to a VFW ball and entertainment. It is printed in heavy black type on yellow card stock; the back is blank. It was given to us on the evening of Saturday, November 20,1965, by a friend of our neighbor across the hall. Our neighbor is Leonard Yaudes. As Jane and I were leaving our place to go dancing that evening Leonard called us into his place to meet two friends of his, a man and a woman, not married; we have forgotten their names. The man, who was also planning to attend the VFW affair later that evening, gave Jane and me a free ticket.

(We preferred not to go, but took the ticket to avoid explanations, without making promises. We thought the affair would be dull. I forgot about the incident until a couple of days ago, when I found the ticket in a coat pocket. Jane hadn't seen it since last November. I sealed it in the usual double envelope, between two pieces of Bristol.

(The session was held in our front room. There was a chance that Peggy Gallagher would be present with a press camera, to take some pictures of Jane while she was in trance. Jane's publisher has written requesting some photos, drawings, etc., in connection with the book Jane is now writing on the Seth material. Peggy is a writer for Elmira's newspaper, the Star-Gazette, and has access to the necessary equipment.

(For the session Jane and I looked more presentable than usual, but by 8:30 Peggy had not appeared. In my daily predictions for today, made yesterday, I had noted that Peggy would not make it. The predictions were made at 3 PM, March 15; Seth has something to say about the hour and day later in the session.

(Once again Jane began speaking while sitting down and with her eyes closed. Her head rested on her left hand, but she soon became quite restless in her Kennedy rocker and began to shift about. She used some pauses. Her voice was average.)

Good evening.

("Good evening, Seth.")

I would like to continue the discussion we began in our last session.

Now. As I have told you in the past, the individual does indeed survive physical death, but there is a reorganization of psychological elements that compose the personality. The personality, even as you know it, is never static, always changing, and even the ego is not the same from one day to the next.

The child's ego is not the adult's ego. As a rule you perceive the similarity, and overlook the differences of psychological patterns of this sort. The ego is not the most powerful or the most knowledgeable portion of the self. It is simply a well-specialized portion of the personality, well equipped to operate under certain circumstances.

When these circumstances no longer exist, then other layers of the self take over the dominant position, and the personality realigns its psychological components. The ego does not disappear, however. It merely takes a back seat in some respects, as your own subconscious does during physical existence.

When you sleep the ego becomes unfocused, but still present, and its goals and attitudes to some extent do color dream experiences. The survival personality has somewhat the same relationship to the ego as the dreaming personality has to it now.

It is a great mistake to imagine that the human being has but one ego, however. The ego represents merely any given pattern of characteristics, psychological characteristics, that happen to be dominant at any given time. If any kind of a thorough investigation were to be carried on, it would become apparent that during one lifetime any given individual will display several, sometimes quite different, egos at various times, each one quite honestly seeing itself as the permanent I.

A survival personality in many respects is psychologically much different from the individual that he was. The ego is now under the control of what may be loosely called the inner self. When communications take place between a survival personality and a personality who exists within the physical system, then this involves a reshuffling, again, on the part of the survival personality, where the ego is momentarily given greater reign.

There is the same sort of disorientation that the ego experiences within physical reality when an individual dreams. The same sort of psychological reshuffling occurs. If it did not occur, then in most cases communication would not be possible, simply because the survival personality would have such difficulty in impressing the personality who was still ego-oriented within the physical system.

The survival personality for example relies mainly upon telepathic communication. The survival personality does not think in terms of words, but experiences concepts in a much more direct manner. This sort of thing simply could not be understood by the physically-oriented individual.

(Seth began talking about these points in the very early sessions. By the 15th session he was explaining Jane's role as a translator for him, putting concepts into words, etc. See Volume 1.)

The survival personality therefore momentarily inserts his ego in its old position. It can then interpret this data in terms that can be received and understood. This reassembly however does cause some disorientation on the part of the survival personality. The ego, back in its dominant position, finds the circumstances difficult to deal with. It is being asked to manipulate in a manner unfamiliar to it. The survival personality's inner self gives this reassembled ego concepts in the same way that, often, the subconscious gives the ego concepts in physical existence.

This reassembled ego then attempts to perceive these concepts in terms of sense perceptions, which are sent as communications to the physical individual at the other end. Sometimes the communications are made directly, though they must be sifted through the subconscious of the physical individual. When the physical individual is trained along these lines however, he helps in this process, and a psychological framework, like a bridge, is erected that serves to connect the two personalities.

I suggest your break.

(Break at 9:31. Jane was dissociated as usual for a first delivery. Her eyes had opened once briefly, when she sipped wine. She did not smoke. Her pace had picked up considerably and her restlessness in her chair had continued. She hadn't been aware of this. See Seth's psychological-bridge material on page 14.

(Jane resumed in the same manner at 9:40.)

Now. When you consider that in sleep the ego is not dominant, then it should not seem strange to you that it is not dominant after death.

In sleep there is no need for it to be dominant, nor is there under survival conditions. In sleep other areas of the self are being trained through their own kind of experience, and psychic organizations are built up, dispensed with, and built up again in a sort of practice maneuver.

These levels of the self have known self-consciousness in other existences, before the present one. But they cannot be allowed to remain completely dormant, but must continually reassert their characteristics and abilities.

They share physical life with you therefore, whether the ego realizes this or not. After this existence the ego will not remain dormant either. It simply will not be the dominant psychological entity that it is during physical existence.

I am aware of the various egotistical selves that I have been. I am still each of these selves, but the whole self that I am is dominant now. The psychological structure has changed, but it has changed not only in realignments but in quality. For I am aware of all my selves.

(Seth began on this material in the 13th session. See Volume 1.)

In my communications to you, I speak as my whole self, and not on the part of any one of the egos which have been dominant in other existences. If I had known either of you as contemporaries within your physical time in your present existence, then after death I would have assumed, once again, the dominant ego by which you had known me. I am not tied to physical existence by any strong emotional bonds however, and my personality structure is more advanced than is usual for communicators from other systems.

I do not need therefore to adopt a past ego. Perhaps because this is not necessary, the psychological bridge of which I have spoken is necessary in order to make my communications comprehensible to Ruburt.

(Jane's pace had now slowed considerably. Her restlessness had also subsided. She took a long pause before continuing.)

This connecting psychological framework does some of the translating for me, that a reassembled ego would do for me. It delivers information to Ruburt in a way which he can understand. Occasionally I do communicate without this psychological framework, as when I impress him directly, telepathically, with a concept.

When he receives data in the form of images, the psychological framework is operating. On my end this framework projects imagery, and with my direction it uses Ruburt's own personal associations to direct his impressions toward the correct point. Then when we are successful I insert the correct data.

I am a communicator. The control personality, so-called, in our case, is entirely passive, the psychological framework to which I have referred, and shall remain so.

Now you may take a brief break before our Instream material.

(Break at 9:59. Jane was dissociated as usual. Her eyes had remained closed and her pace had been slow toward the end of the delivery.

(It was now time for the 48th Dr. Instream experiment. Jane spoke with her eyes closed once more; her pace, although broken by many short pauses, was good overall. Resume at 10:05.)

Now. Give us a moment please. We will give the object shortly.

First of all, I have the impression of a cycle. Perhaps a delivery boy on a bicycle.

The impression of a birthday cake.

The object is a small round object in a small square box. There is also cotton in the box. The object is shaped somewhat like a ring, but it is not a ring. The circle is not complete. It is of a grayish color, like stone. Perhaps somewhat speckled, and it is very old.

The initial P seems to be connected with it, and it has a connection with another country also, and has passed through many hands. It is worn down, and somewhat triangular, in that—

(Jane now took a long pause, sitting with her right hand raised to her closed

eyes at 10:11.)

—where the circle area is not complete, it is distorted down to a point, and I believe broken or open at the opposite side. This way, you see.

(Her eyes still closed, Jane now made a full-armed gesture in front of herself. I made a quick drawing of what I thought she was indicating, with both hands. My sketch is below on the left. Jane's is on the right, made at next break:)

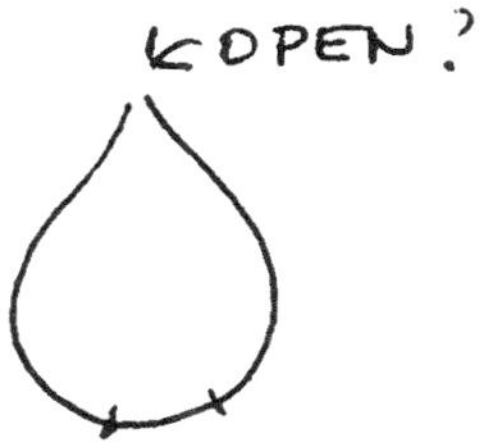

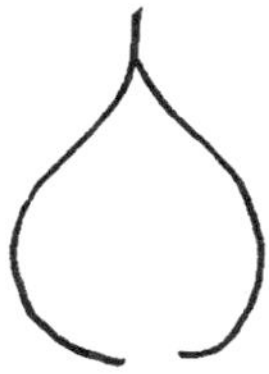

It is heavier than a ring.

There have been a variety of circumstances lately, with which Dr. Instream is not pleased. One having to do with a man with a mustache, and a change of locations.

Do you have an envelope for me?

("Yes.")

(Jane paused at 10:15. Her eyes still closed, she took the usual double envelope from me. This time she did not hold it to her forehead but in her lap. Her left hand was raised to her eyes. This was our 41st such experiment.)

Give us a moment please.

The number four in the center of a square. A connection with a turn-about, and a street or avenue, as an <u>avenue</u> of escape.

White paper with small implied border. A July date. A note, short, that does not take up all the available space.

Symbols or initials in the lower left hand corner. Having something to do with a house, or residence.

The appearance of a neat, even, script, with small letters. The main paragraph forming a neat rectangular form, but neatly squared off. A block of matter.

Color at the top, like strips. Connection with a dog.

Do you have any questions, Joseph?

(My fifth opportunity to question Seth concerning envelope data. See the second paragraph of the data above.

("I'm wondering about part of the early data here; you seem to be talking about a letter or note. What's the connection with the envelope object?")

Give us a moment, please.

A note was sent, I believe, concerning the object.

I have the impression of a solid-appearing rectangular shape, in the center of a larger white object. The smaller one made up of small shapes which have been interpreted as script.

I suggest your break.

(Break at 10:25. Jane was dissociated as usual, and her eyes had remained closed. We made what connections we could, but missed some that Seth later pointed out; these then seemed to be rather obvious. It also developed that we had some conflict of terminology, as will be seen, and as Seth hints at in the last data above.

(See the tracing of the envelope object on page 20. The ticket is printed in bold black type on yellow card stock. On page 24 Seth stated that when Jane receives images, the psychological framework between Seth and Jane is operating; in these instances Seth is not giving Jane envelope data by way of concepts, directly and telepathically. Jane had some images this evening.

("The number four in the center of a square." We made no connection here, although Seth points out an interesting one, somewhat distorted, after break.

("A connection with a turnabout", refers we believe to our accepting the ticket from Leonard's friend—see page 21—then not going to the affair.

("and a street or avenue, as an avenue of escape." A street, Gray Street, is printed on the object. Our thought also is that the escape data here refers to our not wishing to attend the affair represented by the ticket.

("White paper with small implied border. A July date. A note, short, that does not take up all the available space." This is the data I asked Seth to connect with the envelope object. His answer was that a note was sent, presumably to our neighbor across the hall, Leonard Yaudes, concerning the object. Jane and I do not know if this is so, and probably will not ask Leonard; he does not know of these sessions.

("Symbols or initials in the lower left hand corner. Having something to do with a house, or residence." Near the lower left hand corner of the object is printed the name of the hotel in which the VFW affair was to be held, along with the specific rooms. We wonder if Seth/Jane mentioning a house or residence referred to a hotel, via a close distortion.

("The appearance of a neat, even, script, with small letters. The main paragraph forming a neat rectangular form. But neatly squared off. A block of matter." Jane said this data referred to the printed envelope object, even though she used the word script instead of type. I was wondering if her use of the word script was a reference to the note sent in connection with the object, but Jane said no. She is not aware of the difference between the terms script, lettering, and type, for instance. She had an image here, of small even words on a rectangular shape; but my questioning

could not elicit whether she could distinguish, here, between type, script, etc., on this rectangular shape. She merely knew there were words present.

(After we had discussed this point, Jane added that it is possible she also had an image, very vague, of the note referred to earlier in the data. This seemed to return to mind after our discussion; she didn't mention it during the session, but when I was typing up these notes. This could account for the reference to a "main paragraph" above. But in giving the above data, Jane had the image of a rectangular form and block of matter with neat borders.

("Color at the top, like strips." The object is yellow, so the color reference could be somewhat distorted. Jane said she believed the strips referred to the black printed lines of the object. Another color, Gray Street, is also mentioned in the data, and indirectly.

("Connection with a dog." I drew a blank here. Jane offered a connection perhaps twice removed from the object. Leonard Yaudes has a girlfriend who has a dog; occasionally they leave the dog in Leonard's apartment when they go out on a date. The connection would be that the object came from Leonard's apartment. It is a weak one, in that the girl in question is not the girl who was present in the apartment on November 20,1965, when Jane and I were given the object. Jane didn't know whether her interpretation was correct.

("A note was sent, I believe, concerning the object." This was Seth's answer to my question about the "white paper, July, note," data. See page 26.

("I have the impression of a solid-appearing rectangular shape, in the center of a <u>larger</u> white object. The smaller one made up of small shapes which have been interpreted as script." As stated, by script Jane meant print, or type. Jane said this is another reference to the object.

(Jane said it is possible that the "<u>larger</u> white object" referred to the inside envelope used as a matter of course in our experiments. This envelope is perhaps half again as large as the largest dimension of tonight's object, and is almost square. I put the object in this envelope, place it between two pieces of heavy Bristol board which are cut to just fit inside the second, or outside, envelope. I did not think to ask Seth to clear up this point.

(Jane resumed, with her glasses still on but with her eyes closed, at 10:42.)

Now. I do not know if it was worthwhile to go into this test in detail.

A good deal was legitimate, but not precisely-enough interpreted. Whether or not a test such as this were involved, Ruburt's terms and your own would not agree as to the printed material and so forth.

The house or residence had to do with the words "room" and "hotel" clearly written on the object.

The street or "avenue of escape" should have been separated. A street was mentioned on the object, and you wished to escape attending the event referred to on the object.

The color mentioned was not clear, and the connection was to the street, which was Gray Street. The—shall I say printed material—was neatly blocked off by strips of black.

The four, unfortunately, went completely astray. I was trying to get the word war to Ruburt. I wanted the word war in the plural; however the plural gave him the idea of the number, which was blended with the sound of war, into four.

(Check the printed copy in the center of the object. Beside the word "wars" there, we see the words "for" and "foreign." Seth mentioned "the number four in the center of a square." The envelope object is rectangular rather than square. We wondered whether the square reference was to the "larger white object," mentioned at the end of the envelope data. See page 27. The inside envelope used in these experiments is almost square.)

The dog was legitimate, but too far afield. You received the card in a friend's apartment. The friend has a girlfriend with a dog. She takes the dog with her on her visits there.

("Was this the girl who was visiting Leonard the night we were given the object?")

No. Ruburt can explain the connection here now. It is now apparent to him.

Unless you have further questions we will end the session.

("Why didn't Peggy Gallagher show up tonight?"

(See the notes on page 21.)

A change of plan. Having to do with a disturbance.

("She did intend to come, though?")

She did earlier, yes. It became apparent then that she could not.

("At what time did it become apparent to her that she couldn't come?")

A connection with 3 o'clock, I believe this afternoon.

("Good night, Seth."

(End at 10:53. Jane had been dissociated as usual. Her eyes had remained closed. In my daily predictions for today, made yesterday, I had noted down that Peggy would not appear this evening. I made them at 3 PM.)

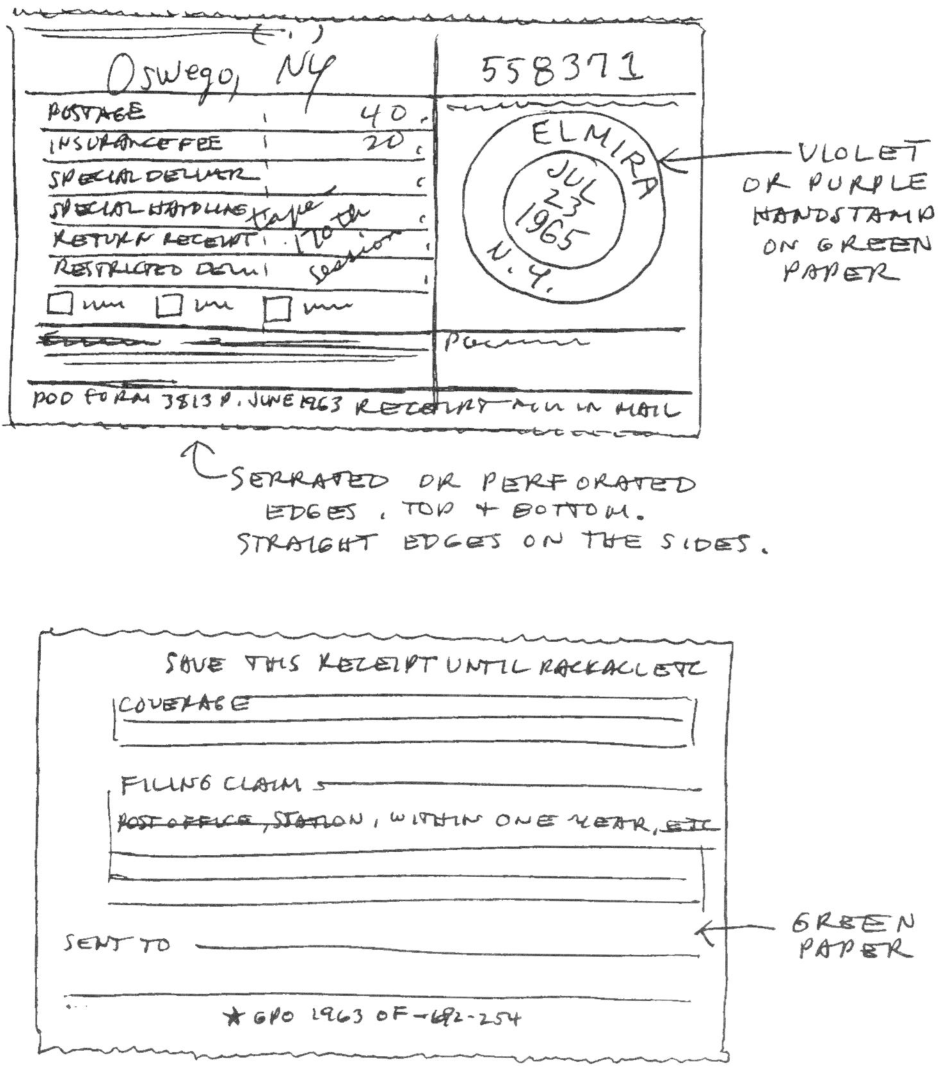

(Tracings of the insurance receipt used as the object in the 42nd envelope experiment, in the 243rd session for March 21,1966.)

SESSION 243
MARCH 21, 1966 9 PM MONDAY AS SCHEDULED

(The 42nd envelope experiment was held during the session. See the tracing on page 29. The object is the insurance receipt for the tape of the 170th session, which was sent to Dr. Instream on July 23,1965. The tape was made with the Gallaghers as witnesses, at their home outside Elmira, NY, on July 19,1965.

(Peggy Gallagher was due this evening, to photograph Jane while in trance. Peg was also due for the 242nd session but did not appear. In that session Seth told us she did not come because of "A change of plans. Having to do with a disturbance. A connection with 3 o'clock, I believe this afternoon."

(We checked with Peggy this weekend. As Seth said, she did not appear; her planned activities at the newspaper where she works were changed unexpectedly; she was taken out of town Wednesday night, the time of the 242nd session. Peggy was given the assignment in the afternoon, she said, and it could have been around 3 PM; she does not know the exact time. Seth, or Jane, was incorrect on the day however. Peggy was given the out-of-town assignment one day earlier, Tuesday, March 15.

(There was no disturbance at the newspaper through Wednesday of last week, Peggy said, but there was a most definite one, involving the manager and the city editor, on Thursday, March 17. This shook up the whole staff and resulted in a suspension. Since Seth was a day late regarding the change of plan, we wondered if he was a day early regarding the disturbance.

(At supper time this evening we were notified that once again Peggy could not appear tonight. Since we do not have a phone, she called a neighbor who relayed the information that Peggy could not come because "something urgent" had developed.

(Last Friday Jane received word that her article on the envelope experiments was rejected by Fate Magazine. *In the 233rd session Seth said the article would sell, without naming the buyer, "providing Ruburt follows the way which has been set out for him." See Volume 5, page 287.*

(Since we wanted Seth to discuss this prediction, this gave us the idea of checking up on some other recent session material. I wrote up the notes on these and read them to Jane just before session time, thinking that if Seth didn't cover all the points this evening, at least a beginning could be made.

(See the notes on page 269, Volume 5, of the 232nd session, dealing with Jane's recent poetry book and the request by Jane's publisher, F. Fell, that she send it to him along with a tape of some of the poems, also by Jane. In the 277th session Seth said this book would be published. F. Fell returned the book a couple of weeks ago, and it is now in the hands of another publisher. Jane did not seriously expect Fell to accept

this book, but still wants to hear from Seth about it. Playboy Press has also rejected the poetry book. See the notes on page 312, Volume 5. Seth hasn't named any specific publishers in his predictions, nor have we asked.

(In the 210th session for November 22,1965, Seth stated that he had picked up an "incipient malignancy" in Helen Dyer, who is a friend of our landlady, Marian Spaziani. See Volume 5, page 81. This data was given after the two women had visited us. We have heard nothing more on this, either from Seth or the two women. Last weekend Marian's husband Jimmy told us that Marian herself must have an operation to remove a tumor on an ovary. Since Seth mentioned the abdominal region in connection with Helen, we wonder about possible distortion on Jane's part here. The material in the 210th session was focused strongly on Helen however.

(In the 229th session Seth went into some detail concerning the tax problems of our landlord, Jimmy Spaziani. If Jimmy is having tax troubles we know nothing about it, and have heard no rumors. Since we have seen Jimmy a few times recently we wonder if Jane has picked up any telepathic information. Seth mentioned legal difficulties for Jimmy in connection with a March 15 date. Seth also saw a possible future illness for Jimmy.

(In the 234th session, Seth dealt with predictions and free will. On page 293, Volume 5, he stated that he is hardly omnipotent—"Nor, strictly speaking, is such omnipotence possible." See other recent sessions, on probabilities also. Jane and I wondered what part probabilities might have played in any of the above dates.

(The session was held in our front room. Jane began speaking while sitting down and with her eyes closed. She was not smoking; her voice was average, her pace again slow, with many pauses.)

Good evening.

("Good evening, Seth.")

Now. A few general remarks following our last discussion, concerning our sessions.

A fine tuning of focus takes place here, where Ruburt's abilities are focused in new directions, directions that are unfamiliar to the ego. A focusing is involved on my part also, and a kind of synthesis formed that allows us to bridge the gap that separates our fields of action.

The training involved on Ruburt's part does result in a utilization of abilities, and for his <u>conscious</u> use. That is, the abilities are not being developed haphazardly, despite his own inclinations, but in answer to his inclinations. The personality therefore is being highly developed.

Now this development helps me, for I need his development in order that my communications be more clearly presented and received. Basically however <u>all</u> of this takes place in deeply unconscious layers. Abilities and energies are released. These cannot be willed however, on a conscious level.

Consciously Ruburt can learn to note various circumstances that seem to facilitate or inhibit his abilities, and our communications, but the abilities themselves develop in accordance with unconscious principles. I can take advantage of these principles, and to some extent use them, but I cannot ignore them.

I am obviously also directed by my own unconscious, for there is always a principle that does not become conscious. This is a reserve, represents an overabundance, it is eternally inexpressible.

Now. I am not going to discuss many of your points this evening. However, the poetry book will indeed sell.

The material concerning your landlady's friend was legitimate. The material concerning your landlord was legitimate. Probabilities are involved in this case, however.

(Jane now paused. Her eyes were still closed. She leaned forward in her rocker, elbows on knees, head down. The pause was rather long, and her voice was quieter when she resumed at 9:14.)

Give us a moment, please.

Now, let us go at our own pace here. These are impressions.

Four. The word Marguerite, I believe. A crisis involving health. A doctor. Initials R G. The words monosodium, and a long word that begins with a G or has the sound of a G.

Eight, perhaps eight o'clock, but I am not certain here.

The second letter of the long word, or the third, is I believe an L. Perhaps there is a connection with eyes, e-y-e-s.

A connection with a man who can be considered an outsider to a group. He is connected with the crisis.

I suggest your break.

(Break at 9:21. Jane was well dissociated for a first break, she said. Her eyes had remained closed. Her pace had been slow at the end of the delivery. She was surprised at the early break, but more so at the impressions given, since she hadn't expected them.

(We did not know who they referred to particularly, but thought of the Gallaghers, since Peggy had canceled her date for tonight's session because of "something urgent." Peggy's first name is Margaret, incidentally, rather than Marguerite.

(I thought the second of the two long words Seth had been groping toward might be glutamate, after the common food preservative monosodium glutamate. I thought that once I had read the chemical also had a medical use, but could not recall much here.

(As Jane sat resting during break, staring absently at the floor, she received the

word "mine." She doesn't know if this was from Seth or is a production of her own. In two recent envelope experiments Jane has used the word mine, or the underground image thus conjured up, to refer to a grave, meaning death.

(Jane began speaking at a much faster pace. Her eyes opened as soon as she began, widely, and remained so for some little time. The rapid delivery was interspersed with short pauses. Resume at 9:30.)

Now. The physical body often and consistently acts upon subconscious knowledge, but in order to impress consciousness, such information must be carried by some kind of sense impression, whether this be a pseudosense impression, or a more normal one.

Some sense impressions fall beneath the threshold of consciousness, these impressions coming from the outside environment. Some impressions however have their origin within inner reality, and the personality is receiving information not available to the egotistical self. If such inner data is to become at all conscious, it must be translated into terms that the ego can recognize. In other words, into sense data.

Sense data therefore may be the result of perception of outer <u>and</u> inner environment. It is simpler to translate information from the outer environment into sense data. It is more difficult to translate inner data in this manner. There are frequent distortions but there are also frequent distortions in more ordinary sense perceptions. Inner data so translated must be built up from scratch, so to speak. There is in the physical world an illusion of continuity, against which sense data can be checked. There is no like sense of continuity, <u>as a rule</u>, against which to check sense perceptions which are translations of inner data.

There is a significant similarity between sense perceptions that are translations of inner data, and the sense perceptions that take place in dreams, in that both are relatively fleeting. Both are highly symbolic. Both are methods of bringing deep knowledge closer to the realms of the egotistical self.

Both involve culminations formed by various levels of the self, and yet are impressed into the physical organism. They must be registered by the physical self in one way or another, if the information is to become at all conscious.

Now. In the earlier impressions that I gave you this evening, I was trying something new, and we will give you what further information we can, when we can. We were throwing our net of awareness in a large circle, so to speak, to see what we could catch, and the results should prove rather interesting.

I suggest a very brief break, and we shall continue.

(Break at 9:48. Jane had again been well dissociated. She felt Seth rather strongly tonight, she said, and did not remember much of the material. Her eyes, after being open wide after break, closed and remained so for the rest of the delivery.

(It was now time for the 49th Dr. Instream experiment, although as it developed this came a bit later than usual. Once again Jane spoke slowly, with her eyes closed and her voice rather quiet. Resume at 9:59.)

Now. The material that I gave you earlier, concerning your finances, was quite approximately correct.

(We had asked Seth to comment on some of his material this evening, but this question hadn't been included. See the 217th session in Volume 5.)

The trip to New York should be made, and if made will be important to you. I advise you strongly to make the journey.

I believe there will be further changes at your own place of employment.

("What kind?")

Changes that may allow you to insist upon bettering your own position there. Now do not rush me.

(Once again Jane bowed her head. She paused, her eyes closed. There have been changes at my place of employment, due to the retirement of management, the consolidation of some departments and the elimination of others, etc.)

Changes that would involve, on your part, <u>if</u> you see the opportunity, <u>not</u> more time, but payment and recognition of responsibility that you already assume in the main. Some sort of a change involving your boss, I believe. Not one that will take him from the firm, but one which might take him <u>further</u>, in some way, from his immediate department, while he still remains connected with it.

The situation can be used to your advantage if you recognize it. The initiation might be up to you. I am not clear on this.

(As far as I know, no such change is contemplated at Artistic Card Co. I have heard no talk or even rumors to this effect. Our department was recently moved but there has been no change in personnel. But as stated there have been many changes lately, and there could be more. My boss has held his present position for about fifteen years. Offhand I cannot think of how he could advance within the firm, unless he moved into the selling end of it. He is presently art director, and a member of the board.

(Jane now took another pause, at 10:06.)

Now, give us a moment for our Instream material.

I will give an object shortly. First, an impression of several small packages—<u>many</u>, I believe, all of the same size, coming to him or being sent from him through the mails. Perhaps they involve cards for scoring. Or a survey.

I also have the impression of an object that looks like a toothbrush, but is used for cleaning something else. I do not know to what this refers.

Another separate connection, or separate impression, with a celebration of some kind.

Now for the object. A book, or an object resembling one. It could be a box of book shape. The space between either the covers of the book or the covers of the box being colored, and patterned. *(Long pause.)* The patterns resembling imperfect circles—shapes—perhaps red, orange or yellow, but more than one color.

The top of the book or box a shade of brown. Brown, yellow, or deeper—that is, darker. Perhaps a clasp on the side, to keep it shut. *(Pause at 10:12.)*

These are impressions. He writes in the margin. A purple fabric, nubby, with a resemblance to upholstery fabric.

Do you have an envelope for me?

("Yes.")

(Jane paused at 10:14. Without opening her eyes she took the envelope for the 42nd experiment from me. She pressed the envelope to her forehead briefly, then lowered it to her lap.)

Give us a moment, please. These are impressions.

Nine. A miscellany of shapes. A connection with a light or a round bright object that suggests light.

A motor. A forgotten item. Something spilled. Copy in the center of the bottom of a paper item. Elmira, NY, connected with this copy.

Ruburt for his own reasons connects this with the announcement of your niece's marriage. I mention this for your edification. His connection also here—keep this separately from mine—is of the old house used by the Christian Science church.

A door which is dark, or opens into darkness. Twelve. A river or water connection. Perhaps this is no more than Water Street. I do not know here, so check it.

Circular shapes. Perhaps four heads.

Do you have any questions?

(This is my sixth opportunity to question Seth concerning envelope data.

("Will you elaborate on the four heads data?")

Give us a moment. Four heads came from the impression of circle shapes. Here interpreted as being connected with four people. Perhaps at a table.

(Jane paused once more, and seemed to wait expectantly. This was my first shot at a second question during an experiment. We hadn't discussed the possibility of more than one question yet, but evidently Seth—or Jane—is getting used to the idea of envelope questions so rapidly that soon questions may be asked at leisure.

(To date I have picked general questions. I do not believe they are leading ones, and usually they bring forth more data.

("Do you want to say something about the color of the object, if any?")

White, it seems, with a large oval darker shape. A date connected with it. Black, rather clear lines, one on the top, bottom, and two sides. Vertical. That is, vertical lines, on the top and bottom, and horizontal on the sides.

(Jane gestured rather strongly with the envelope while giving this data. Her eyes remained closed.)

A white border, with <u>un</u>even edges, or slightly scrolled edges.

(Once more Jane paused, sitting quietly with her eyes closed. I waited a moment to see if she would resume.)

If you have a question you may ask it. Otherwise we may take a break.

("How about more on the motor reference?")

Something beats like a motor. I suggest your break.

(Break at 10:25. Once again Jane said she was well dissociated; she didn't recall much of what she had said. Her eyes had remained closed since last break, and her pace had been fair.

(See the tracing of the envelope object on page 29. As stated, it is the insurance receipt for the tape of the 170th session, made on July 19,1965 at the home of the Gallaghers, with them as witnesses. The receipt is handstamped July 23,1965, the day the tape was mailed to Dr. Instream.

(The receipt is rectangular in shape; in connection with this shape, Jane said she had an image within, of a whitish color. It was rectangular and of the approximate proportion of the object. She was aware of black lines upon it. She saw it standing on a narrow end. This is quite possible, since I noticed during the experiment that she held the sealed envelope at various angles. Remember also that she gave white in connection with the object's color, in answer to my second question. The receipt is green.

(Jane and I made quite a few connections ourselves, and did not ask Seth for more since he went into other material.

("Nine." We are not sure, since we did not ask Seth. The sessions usually begin at 9:00 PM on the dot. The 170th session, represented by the envelope object, actually began at 8:57.

("A miscellany of shapes." This phrase crops up often in the data in describing words, numbers, other small repetitive printed matter. The object is covered with printed matter on both sides.

("A connection with a light or a round bright object that suggests light." Jane said this is her interpretation of Seth's first data regarding the circular handstamp on the object. Later in the data she becomes more specific.

("A motor." A reference to the motor of our tape recorder. Jane said this is tied in with the last reference: "Something beats like a motor," in answer to my third

question.

("A forgotten item." I left my favorite pen at the Gallaghers the night we recorded the 170th session. Peggy found it later and returned it. I am attached to that particular type of pen, finding them easy to take the notes with for sessions.

("Something spilled." Both Jane and I have vague memories of something being spilled at the Gallaghers' that evening, when the 170th session was recorded. We believe it was a drink. We will check with Bill and Peggy.

("Copy in the center of the bottom of a paper item." No matter which side of the envelope object was facing up, there would be copy in the center of the bottom side. Jane changed the position of the envelope frequently, as she held it while giving the data.

("Elmira, NY, connected with this copy." Elmira, NY, is included in the handstamp on the receipt. This data would indicate then that while Jane held the envelope "this copy", including the handstamp, was on the underside.

(The next paragraph of envelope data does not apply to the envelope object. These are Jane's impressions, as Seth noted, and referred to my niece's marriage, and the Christian Science Church.

("A door which is dark, or opens into darkness." Jane and I had the same thought, independently, before mentioning it: that this impression referred to the layout of the Gallagher's house, where the 170th session was recorded. The session was held in their living room. A hall opens off this and leads back to the kitchen. Other rooms open off the hall on either side. Usually when we visit there we see a light on in the kitchen.

(I recall that on the particular night of the recording session, we did not want to be interrupted. Therefore we had the curtains pulled in the living room, and all other lights out. Thus the hallway leading from the living room to the kitchen was dark. Since we did not ask Seth we cannot be sure our interpretation is correct.

("Twelve." See the back of the envelope object. As indicated on the tracing there are instructions about filing claims for lost objects. A time limit of one year is mentioned.

("A river or water connection. Perhaps this is no more than Water Street. I do not <u>know</u> here, so check it." There are many connections with the object and our residence of West Water Street, Elmira, NY.

("Circular shapes. Perhaps four <u>heads</u>." Four people were present when the 170th session, represented by the envelope object, was recorded: Jane and I, and Bill and Peggy Gallagher. Four heads of course could have referred also to coins or cabbages. I knew four people were present at the 170th session. I did not think I would be giving Jane information when I asked my first question, pertaining to elaboration of the four heads data. As far as she was concerned, I could have picked either a bit

of data I knew to be wrong, or about which I knew nothing, as well as something that was correct.

("Give us a moment. Four heads came from the impression of circle shapes. Here interpreted as being connected with four people. Perhaps at a table." Seth/Jane gave this data in answer to the first question, and it is more specific in that people as such are mentioned. None of us sat at a table however during the recording, or the evening; the Gallaghers do not have such a table in their living room.

(Until otherwise noted, the following data resulted from my second question.

("White, it seems, with a large oval darker shape." As stated on page 36, Jane had a mental image of a rectangular object that was whitish in color, with lines upon it. Hence the persistent references to a white object instead of the actual green color. The handstamp is round; does oval mean round, or something nearly round? Perhaps the meaning is subjective, as well as the size of the handstamp in relation to the size of the whole object.

("A date connected with it." The handstamp on the receipt bears a date.

("Black, rather clear lines, one on top, bottom, and two sides. Vertical, that is, vertical lines, on the top and bottom, and horizontal on the sides." The insurance receipt contains clear black printed lines, both horizontal and vertical on the front, and horizontal only on the back. As stated, Jane changed the position of the envelope frequently while she was giving the data. Thus lines that were vertical at one time would become horizontal, and it seems this would apply whether in relation to her as the clairvoyant observer, or the floor or whatever. I also wonder if some of this data might refer to the black lines formed by the printed matter on the object, and its neat-appearing edges, top, sides and bottom.

("A white border, with <u>un</u>even edges, or slightly scrolled edges." In giving this data Jane emphasized <u>un</u>. See the tracing of the object on page 29. The top and bottom edges of the object are serrated or perforated; several receipts are contained on one page in the book at the post office, and are torn off as used. The sides of the object are straight.

(Seth now prodded me into asking the third question, so I asked for elaboration on the motor data given early in the experiment.

("Something beats like a motor." Jane said this use of the word beats reminded her of the hum of the motor on our recorder. We didn't get enough information here, but she believes it a reference to the recorder motor rather than a reference, say, to our car.

(More and more, it appears that questions can bring out much data during these experiments that might otherwise remain hidden.

(Jane resumed at an average pace and with her eyes closed at 10:43.)

Now we shall indeed close our session.

Our friend Ruburt is picking up again, and in his own work as well. Now. If you are tired we will close immediately.

("No, I'm all right.")

Then I have a few personal remarks which you may or may not include in the records, as you prefer. From now on I will give such information at the <u>end</u> of a session, because you can delete it if you want from the record.

(In the 232nd session for February 9,1966 Seth suggested that a portion of a session a month be devoted to our psychic and physical circumstances. He agreed with my suggestion that we try the first session after the first of each month. We haven't been this faithful but have decided to make stronger efforts here. There will thus be more deletions in the future. None of this evening's material is cut. I regard it as illuminating and a good example of the way Seth presents such material. On but two or three occasions in the past we have eliminated personal material from these records. This material is on file and available to anyone studying these sessions.

(The personal material we have received in the sessions has been psychologically sound. Jane and I feel this way because whenever we have put Seth's suggestions to the test through practice, the results have been excellent.)

You are now out of the woods, physically speaking. You have passed the period where in the past illness was most probable. The afternoon at your parents' home could have initiated an illness, but did not because of your more rational reactions.

(Jane and I visited my parents at their home in Sayre, PA, last Sunday, March 20,1966. We got along well. Following Seth's recent suggestions, usually given in unscheduled sessions, I have been making conscious efforts concerning my reactions to my parents. The results have been very good.)

I did not tell you this earlier since I did not want negative suggestion to operate. If you maintained good health up to and including March 20 of this year, you were in the clear, and so you are. And for the first time in three years, you are <u>completely</u> in the clear.

In the past a virus operated of a peculiar kind. There was a subconscious bargain made, and your dream of the other evening is connected here. Whether or not we have time to discuss it this evening I do not know.

(On March 19,1966 I had a long, vivid and involved dream that I thought probably quite significant. Jane agreed and we made what interpretations we could on our own. The dream is noted in my regular notebook.)

You were upset psychically for all of the reasons that I have given you in the past. The subconscious bargain was this: For relative freedom the <u>rest</u> of the year, you settled for a virus that would hit you any time between January and March 20.

March 21st, you see, meant spring to you, and because of your peculiar makeup the illness would only be permitted to attack during winter, or your conception of winter.

(Last year I fell ill on March 24,1965. See the 143rd session in Volume 3. Thus my idea of spring did not coincide exactly with the calendar's.)

Now there are pills I believe that once taken become activated again within given time periods. This is how your virus acted, and you yourself triggered it. Now there was a connection here with a vaccine, I believe taken by you and Ruburt, that should not have affected you at all.

("Do you mean the polio vaccine?")

I do.

(Cards given to Jane and me at the time show that we received Type I Sabin oral polio vaccine in October 1962, and Type II in November 1962. The card for Type II contained a notice to the effect that information about Type III would be available in the spring of 1963, but if memory serves correctly Type III never was available for public free distribution in this area. In any event Jane and I never did receive Type III.)

You activated it yourself, and I would not tell you this until you had completely conquered it. Ordinarily it would not have been dangerous at all, and it was not dangerous to Ruburt.

(While speaking, Jane opened her eyes and then got up briefly to get a cigarette from a nearby stand. She had been quite restless in her chair.)

A negative suggestion given you by your mother allowed you to activate it. However, you would have found ways of your own in any case. And even though you activated it, you fought it.

(Strange as it may seem—or perhaps not so strangely after all—I remember my mother giving me this negative suggestion quite clearly. There had been a good deal of radio and newspaper publicity concerning the oral vaccines at that time. When we happened to mention to my parents that we had taken it, my mother was rather emphatic in emphasizing the dangers in taking "such things; you might get polio," etc.

(Remember that this episode took place just before, or just as, these sessions began. At the time Jane and I knew little about the power of suggestion. We received Type II in November 1963, the month in which we began experimenting with matters psychic. We did not get to work, really, with the Ouija board until later in the month; Seth made his appearance in December 1963.

(As stated I fell ill with the virus in March 1965. I was also troubled by a virus in 1964, sometime between January and March; I was not in the habit of noting such things in the sessions then, so have no accurate record. I remember that I was

sick three times that winter, each time to a lesser degree. The first two episodes cost me work time of several days each. I do not remember having any thoughts, at any time, connecting my illnesses to the polio vaccines.)

It represented, the illness, the last of a rather long-term and somewhat exaggerated distaste for your position in the world financially, that began when you left the field of comics.

You struck out at yourself because in the past you found pleasure in doing something, and you were well paid to do it. Then you turned to something, painting, for which you were not well paid. You were caught between two reactions. One, resentment against the world in general, hence you listened to the news and picked out purposely the most blatant of your fellow mans' transgressions, deriving from them perverse pleasure.

(This I well remember doing. Seth goes into the situation in some detail in the 143rd session.)

The other was to hurt yourself. Now, it has taken you this much time to recover completely, and without our sessions recovery would have been slower. Now, your energy can indeed bubble up freely in your work.

You may take a break, or end the session.

(Break at 11:04. Jane was well dissociated, she said. Her pace had become fairly good, her eyes opening often. I left the well-paying field of comics just about at the time I met Jane, in the spring of 1954. Jane now resumed in the same manner at 11:06.)

We will end our session.

I wanted to congratulate you however, you personally, Joseph. Now your next line of endeavor will involve good health in the late summer, and this can be arranged. We will work on it, and shortly give you some specific suggestions that will be of practical benefit.

My heartiest regards to you both.

("Good night, Seth."

(End, presumably, at 11:08. Jane was again well dissociated.

(Here Seth refers to my fall hay fever. In the unscheduled 182nd session for August 28,1965, Seth said my father gave me his hay fever when I was about three years old. It is true my father lost his hay fever when I was very young.

(Seth has discussed hay fever a few times; with these bits and pieces of information, plus knowledge of and use of suggestion, I managed to maintain myself in fairly good condition during last fall's season; for me this is from mid-August to about the third week in September. I have already begun telling myself I will feel very good this fall.

(Jane resumed briefly at 11:09.)

Now. Whenever you find time, we will hold sessions in which definite diet suggestions are given for you both, for there are allergies that operate here, and you are not taking advantage of the information that I have in this regard.

("Good night, Seth."

(End at 11:10. Jane, again well dissociated, said Seth "could go on for hours," but by now we were getting tired. We have often wondered whether food allergies might be influencing us. Seth had some information for us on our diet, in a general way, in the 185th session. See Volume 4.)

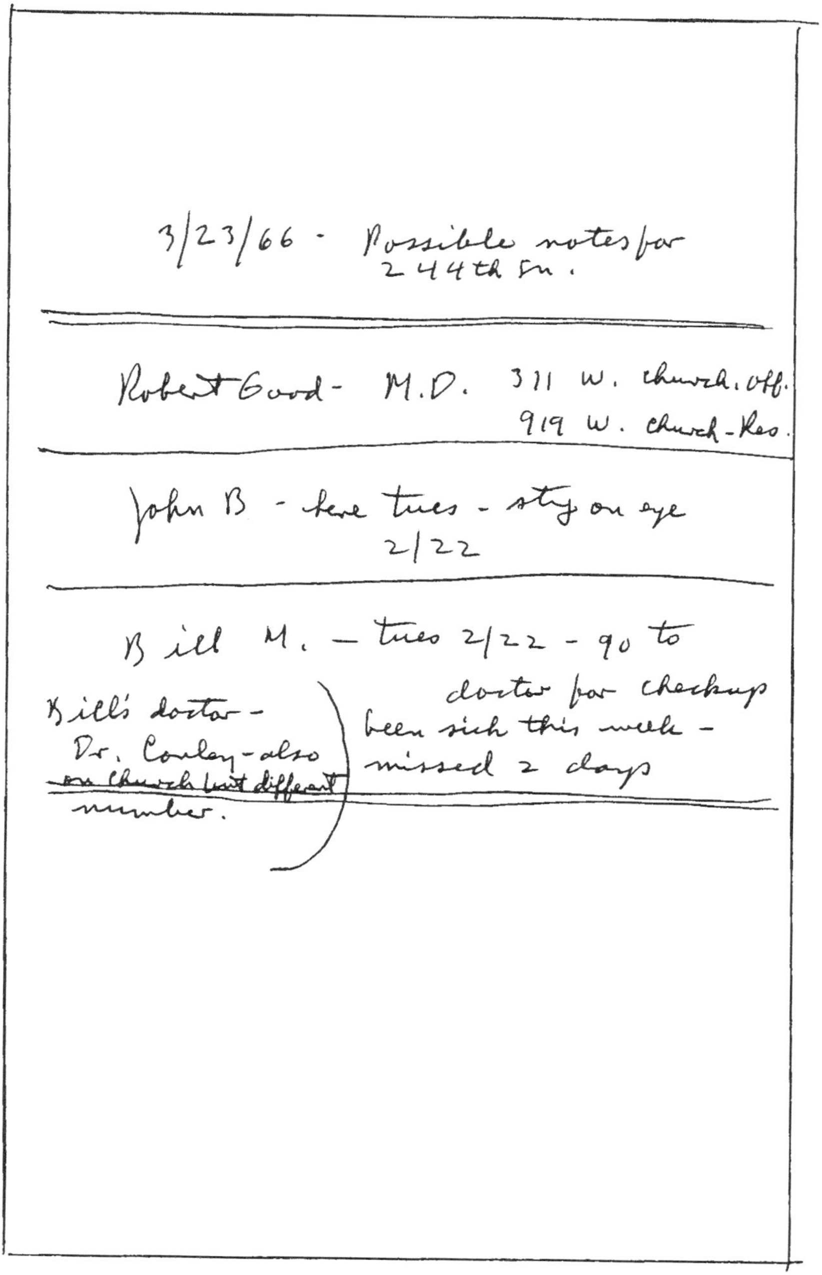
3/23/66 - Possible notes for 244th Sn.

Robert Good - M.D. 311 W. Church. Off.
919 W. Church - Res.

John B - here tues - sty on eye 2/22

Bill M. — tues 2/22 - go to doctor for checkup
been sick this week - missed 2 days

Bill's doctor - Dr. Conley - also on Church but different number.

(Reduced tracing of the page from my notepad, used as the object in the 43rd envelope experiment, in the 244th session for March 23, 1966.)

SESSION 244
MARCH 23, 1966 9 PM WEDNESDAY AS SCHEDULED

(The 43rd envelope experiment was held during the session. The tracing on page 43 is a reproduction of the envelope object, a page of notes from my pad. The notes concern the efforts of Jane and myself to pin down Seth's impressions given on page 32 of the last session.

(Sometimes Jane has seen envelope objects, and sometimes she has not. Sometimes she has seen them but a few days before, sometimes months or years before. Whatever the case may be, it apparently makes no difference in the results as far as time goes, or previous visual contact. Seth does respond to emotional charges; these charges we have learned need not stem from Jane or myself or a friend; they can be related to a total stranger and still be detected. Someday perhaps these envelope experiments can be correlated with various factors, sensual and otherwise. For some time now we have kept a weather record, taken just before session time, and there are probably correlations here. This record includes time, temperature, humidity, barometric pressure, rainfall to date, wind velocity and wind direction. Soon I will make a copy of the chart to include with these sessions.

(There may also be correlations via dreams but we haven't made any effort to study this, nor has Seth been asked.

(The approach was a little different this evening, in that Jane had seen the envelope object perhaps two hours before the session. She helped me compile it for future checking against page 43. At this time I had no idea of using it for the experiment; the idea occurred later, some time after Jane had left the studio. I sealed it up in the usual double envelope, between two pieces of Bristol.

(Bill and Peggy Gallagher were due to witness the session. Peggy was going to take flash pictures of Jane while she was in trance; Jane's publisher had asked to see some material of this kind. We had no idea of the success of this venture—whether Jane would be distracted while delivering the regular material, or during the envelope experiment; if possible we wanted to cover both categories.

(The Gallaghers arrived just before 9 PM, when we were about to begin the session. Peggy had her press camera. We took a few minutes to make our witnesses comfortable. Peggy was to prowl around, seeking out compositions, etc., and to take pictures whenever she chose. Jane and I were to go on as usual.

(The session began at 9:06. Seth was in a very good mood at its opening but quickly became serious. Jane's pace was good from the beginning. Her eyes were closed, her manner brisk and with many gestures, her voice average in timbre.)

Good evening.

("Good evening.")

And I welcome our friends, as always, to this very formal occasion when we have a family portrait taken.

Indeed, Ruburt was correct before our session. He said that I might speak about dream locations, since he has been working on this subject for his <u>own</u> book.

He wants to know in what dimension dream locations have their reality, and indeed he has considered all of the possibilities save the correct one. The correct one is the most simple one.

Now. He has taken it for granted that dream locations do not exist within physical space.

(Peggy now took her first picture. The flash startled me more than it did Jane, for she continued on, unperturbed.)

Dream locations exist in so-called physical space as <u>truly</u>, or as falsely, as physical objects exist in physical space. As you should know by now, physical objects are only the results of your own perception, and this perception is based upon your psychological makeup, your physical structure, certain combinations of nerves and chemical reactions. As <u>any</u> physicist will tell you, <u>you</u> perceive objects, and you perceive solid objects—

(Peggy took her next picture, and once again Jane did not pause. Her eyes remained closed as before.)

—in a dimension where neither solidity nor objects exist. You perceive certain patterns of energy <u>as</u> solid objects, <u>and that energy which you do not perceive as solid, you call space</u>.

Because of other procedures which I have explained, including the existence of constant telepathy, there is some agreement as to the placement of these objects, or if Ruburt prefers, locations, in space. Now this gives rise to what you may call mass-perception, with a hyphen between the two words.

When you are dealing with dream locations you are not dealing with mass-perceptions, but with personal perceptions. There is no need therefore for any complicated arrangements calculated to insure agreement between persons as to location in space.

(Seth has dealt with the problem of mass-perception in the sessions on the creation of matter: 60-73, among others. See Volume 2.)

Each dream location is created by the individual precisely in the same way that I have explained to you; that is, they do not differ basically from physical locations, but in one degree. The difference is mainly that they need not be perceived by others.

The question however, in what dimensions do dream locations exist, was simply based. Nevertheless it is one that has many implications, for which you need more background. I will attempt a simplified explanation then. Do you remember some of the material that I gave concerning the expanding universe?

("Yes."

(See sessions 42-45. But as early as the 15th session Seth was discussing these problems as related to dreams. All in Volume 1.)

I said then that the universe expands in a way that has nothing to do with space. Now. A dream location exists, contracts or expands also in a way that has nothing to do with space as you understand it.

I suggest a brief break, and we shall continue.

(Break at 9:22. Jane had been dissociated as usual for a first delivery. Her pace had been good, her voice a bit stronger than usual, her eyes had remained closed. Jane said she had noticed the flash but had not been bothered by it when Peggy took the pictures.

(Peggy was having trouble composing a picture, she said, so for the next delivery she had Jane and me seat ourselves in another part of the room. We also moved about later in the session, but Jane kept using her favorite session chair, our Kennedy rocker.

(Seth, or Jane had been engrossed in the material. Jane's manner remained most emphatic when she resumed, again with her eyes closed, at 9:32.)

Now. I wish to congratulate Ruburt.

There is a rather important section in the work he did today. He hit upon something, and if he had continued working, then he would not have needed to ask me in what dimension dream locations exist. He was close to the answer. In this particular section he told the reader that he suspected that Freud's terms, the ego, or the conscious and the subconscious, had in themselves led you seriously astray. Such is indeed the case.

For you see, you think that you are only conscious when you are focused in physical reality. You assume yourselves unconscious while you are sleeping. In Freud's terminology, the dice are indeed loaded, on the side of the conscious mind.

Pretend, all of you for a moment, that you are looking at this situation from the other side. Pretend that while you are in the dream state, you are concerned with the problem of consciousness and existence. From that viewpoint the picture is entirely different, for you are indeed conscious while you sleep.

The locations that you visit while dreaming are as real to you then as physical locations are to you in your waking state.

What you have is this. Let us speak no more of a conscious self and a subconscious or unconscious self. There is one self, and it focuses its consciousness in various dimensions, and that is all.

In the waking state the whole self is focused toward physical reality. In the dreaming state the whole self is focused within a different dimension. It is every bit as conscious and aware.

Now. If you have little memory of your dream locations while you are in the waking state, then remember you have as little memory of waking locations when you are in the dream state. Both are legitimate, and both are realities.

For Ruburt then: When the physical body lies in bed, that physical body is separated by a vast distance from the dream location in which the dreaming self may dwell. But this distance, dear friends, has nothing to do with space. For the dream location exists simultaneously with the room in which the body dwells.

(Jane was most emphatic in giving this material, speaking in a good voice and with many gestures. Her pace was also good. Once in a while her eyes opened briefly. Peggy had been taking pictures, and as far as I could tell Jane was not bothered.)

The dream locations are not superimposed upon the chest and bed and chair. They exist composed of the very atoms and molecules that in the waking state you perceive as bed and chest and chair.

In the first place, the chest and bed and chair are only the results of your perception, and of your physical perception. From energy you form patterns which you recognize, and give names to and use, but the utility of these objects is useless to you unless you are focused within the dimension for which they were specifically formed.

When, in the dream state, you are focused in a different dimension, then you see you form from these same atoms and molecules the environment in which you will operate. Yet while you dream you cannot find the bed nor chest nor chair, and when you wake you cannot find the room or city or location which was there moments before.

It cannot be too strongly stressed that these dream locations are actualities. But as a rule they are personal actualities, without a general (underline general) mass framework. However mass dreams do occur (underlined). There are dreams that you share with others. There are dream environments that you share, as you share your physical environment. These are not as limiting however as that framework that holds together your physical reality. Nevertheless it does exist.

You may take a break, and then we shall turn to our Dr. Instream material.

(Break at 9:52. Jane was dissociated as usual, she said. Her eyes had been closed for the most part, her manner and gestures very emphatic. Peggy's flashgun hadn't bothered her. A total of seven pictures had been taken by now.

(It was time for the 50th Dr. Instream experiment. Jane's pace and voice now

changed to a slower tempo. Once more she sat with a hand raised to her closed eyes. Resume at 10:05.)

Now. Give us a moment, please. *(Long pause.)*

A brown object, small, of wallet size, containing plastic partitions. I do not believe it belongs to Dr. Instream, but to another male.

I have the impression of four. Now I believe that this refers to four photographs. One taken many years ago, in a location near a body of water. Four people in this photograph, parents and two children.

An old-type photograph, and a connection with the year 1901. A connection with this photograph, and a two-or-three-story house, a frame house with brick or stone stairs at the front.

Another photograph of a nephew who was in college, or of college age, when the photograph was taken.

Another single photograph of a child; also a photograph of a woman who is now the wife of the man to whom these photographs and the object belong.

I believe Dr. Instream chose this object precisely because it did not belong to him. A university connection is very strong here. The object belongs to another professor.

Now for some general notes, still concerning Dr. Instream. He is working on, now, the next symposium. There is still some disagreement even as to rather general plans. This makes more specific details difficult to work out.

There is some connection here also with a young girl, a child connected with Dr. Instream, but not with the symposium.

Do you have an envelope for me, Joseph?

("Yes."

(Jane paused at 10:15. She took the usual sealed double envelope from me without opening her eyes. This was our 43rd experiment. Peggy was ready for more pictures. Jane pressed the envelope to her forehead briefly, then lowered it to her lap—possibly because she knew pictures were to be taken of the experiment. I wondered about the results this evening in the face of possible distractions.)

Give us a moment again, please. These are impressions.

(Peggy took a picture. Jane did not appear to be bothered.)

A switch. A statement. A bright color suggesting sunlight. A plan. The number three, the number six, though not necessarily in that order. (And a photograph—for your edification, not my impression; Ruburt thinks of the word bizarre, since he is thinking of published photos—

(Peggy took another picture, and again Jane continued unperturbed; her eyes remained closed.)

—regarding published photos of your flying saucers, in parenthesis.)

A cross shape. A paper item. Three of a kind here, perhaps three strong parallel lines on the object. If so they are contrasted colorwise, or much darker.

Seven. A miscellany of shapes that all point toward one direction. 2 o'clock. A connection with a March 13 or 15 date, I believe.

Do you have any questions, Joseph? Strong diagonals also.

("How about some more information on the switch data?")

Give us a moment again. The switch seems to be involved with a change of plans, or a switch of dates.

Now. I will end our session, so that you have some time for social discourse, and I myself thank our cat lover for the time and energy expended.

If I am not too humorous this evening, it is because in our regular sessions I am too concerned with their education. My heartiest regards to all.

("Good night, Seth."

(End at 10:23. Jane was dissociated as usual, she said. Her eyes had begun to open toward the end of the delivery, and her voice became humorous. Peggy Gallagher had taken ten photographs in all, and the taking of them had not seemed to bother Jane. I did think the envelope data had probably been shortened somewhat.

(Jane and I made what connections we could, and did not ask Seth for any clarifications. See the tracing of the envelope object on page 43. As stated it is a reproduction of a page of notes I had made, concerning the efforts of Jane and myself to pin down Seth's impressions given on page 32 of the last session.

(We believe we have made some progress checking Seth's impressions in this case, and they involve Bill Macdonnel, John Bradley, and Peggy Gallagher among others. It isn't necessary here to go into these points in detail one by one, either in the data on page 32, or on the envelope object. But we do believe these excerpts from page 32 apply to Peggy and her place of employment, the local newspaper: "A crisis involving health. A doctor... A connection with a man who can be considered an outsider to a group. He is connected with the crisis."

("A switch." This we believe involves Peggy's failure to appear at the two previous sessions, 242 and 243, to take photographs of Jane. This is borne out also by Seth's last statement, where I asked him to elaborate: "The switch seems to be involved with a change of plans, or a switch of dates." The change of plans was on Peggy's part, twice, and the somewhat involved mechanics of the situation here are explained in the notes on page 30 of the 243rd session.

(The connection with the envelope object is that the object concerns an investigation of Seth's data on page 32; this data involves Peggy's involvement in a crisis at her place of employment. The change of plans came about when Peggy was ordered out of town on assignment for March 16,1966, Wednesday night, the time she had planned to photograph Jane during the 242nd session. Peggy was given this change

of plans on Tuesday, March 15, and as shown Seth mentions March 15 in the data this evening.

(The crisis involving health concerns Peggy's employer, the general manager of the paper, who was in the hospital with heart trouble for several days last week. The general manager was also responsible for sending Peggy out of town on assignment. In addition, there was another crisis involving the general manager at the paper last week, and this material is also to be found on page 30. This upset concerned the general manager and the city editor, and the whole newspaper staff was present on request.

("A statement." The envelope object is a statement of various possibilities to be checked out concerning the impressions on page 32.

("A bright color suggesting sunlight." We don't know. A reference to the flashgun? Peggy took three shots of Jane during the envelope data. The sunlight reference is one occurring once in a while in the envelope data, and sometimes involves circles of bright colors. The object tonight is white paper, but then many objects are.

("A plan." The envelope object can also be a plan for checking the impressions on page 32, as well as a statement.

("The number three, the number six, though not necessarily in that order." The object contains the date in this fashion—March 23,1966—as well as the number three one other time, with some other numbers.

(Now follows Jane's impressions concerning a news photo of a drawing of flying saucers, which we had discussed recently. As Seth said, these were Jane's impressions and not his.

("A cross shape." There is a large cross shape toward the bottom left corner of the envelope object:

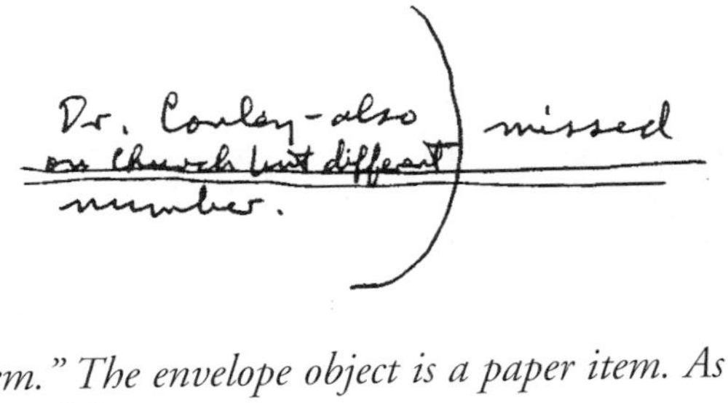

("A paper item." The envelope object is a paper item. As mentioned by me at various times, many of them are.

("Three of a kind here, perhaps three strong parallel lines on the object." We regard this as a good reference to the parallel lines dividing the subject matter on the object. The object contains four lines, rather than three, however.

("Seven." We don't know.

("A miscellany of shapes that all point toward one direction." This is one of

Seth/Jane's favorite ways to refer to writing, whether handwritten or printed. The pointing reference we think a reference to the uniform direction of the verticals in my script.

("2 o'clock. A connection with a March 13 or 15 date, I believe." This is quite possible, we think, although we did not check with Seth. See the notes again on pages 30, and 50, concerning Peggy's failure to appear as scheduled to photograph Jane during the 242nd session. As stated the 242nd session was held on Wednesday March 16. Peggy did not appear because she was given an out-of-town assignment for Wednesdsay evening. She was actually given the assignment on Tuesday, March 15, in the afternoon. On page 30 it is stated Peggy does not recall the exact time she was told about the assignment except that it was not too late in the afternoon. Seth had mentioned 3 PM during the 242nd session, and Peggy said it was possible. Does 2 o'clock apply here? We do not know since we did not check with Seth. Peggy is sure however that she was given the assignment no later than 3 PM.)

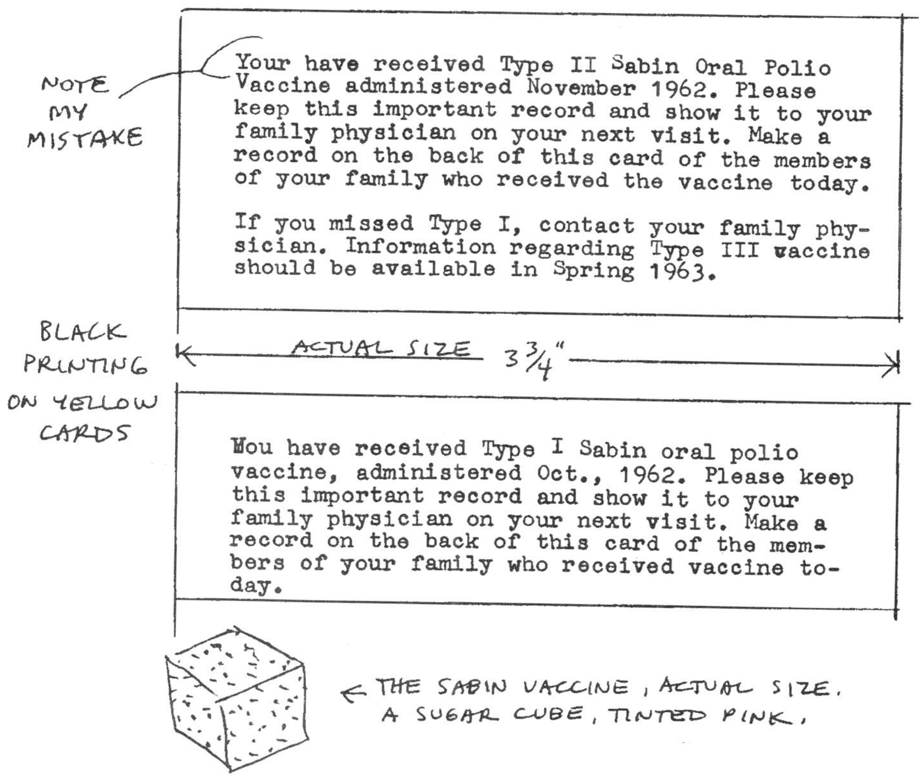

(My typed front copies of the two cards used as the objects in the 44th envelope experiment, in the 245th session for March 28, 1966.)

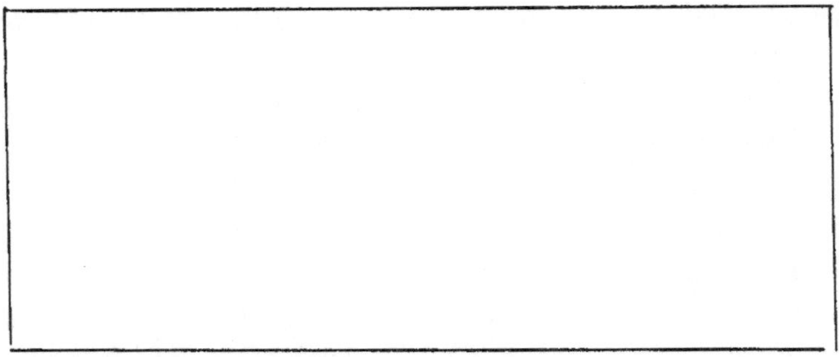

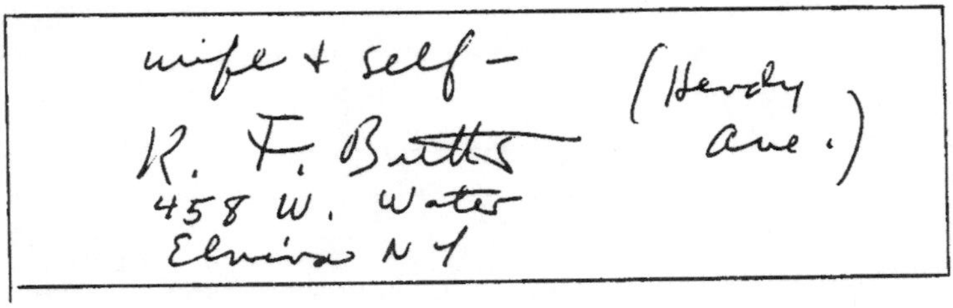

(Copies of the backs of the two cards used as the objects in the 44th envelope experiment, in the 245th session for March 28,1966.)

SESSION 245
MARCH 28, 1966 9 PM MONDAY AS SCHEDULED

(The 44th envelope experiment was held during the session. See the copies of the objects on page 51, and note the copy on the back of one of them, above. These cards are mentioned on page 40 of the 243rd session; this gave me the idea of using them for an experiment. Jane had read the 243rd session recently but had not seen the cards. She hadn't seen them since November 1962, in fact, for they had been in my files. I placed them between two pieces of Bristol and sealed them in the usual double envelope.

(Jane had an unusual experience late last week, and I had one earlier today; we hoped Seth would discuss them this evening. Here follows the material from our notebooks:

(Jane: Thursday night, March 24. I woke up sometime in the middle of the night and saw the form of a woman standing by Rob's side of the bed, not mine. The room was dark but I saw that her dress was blue. She was rather thin and fairly tall.

Her face was not clear at all but her dress was clearly visible—at least the color. It was one-piece, of moderate length. I do not remember her face at all. I do recall that our bookcase, behind her, showed up well; its cream color was clear although the rest of the room was dark. I believe her head was covered. As soon as I saw the figure it disappeared. I had the feeling that something was trying to make me forget what I saw, so I quickly woke Rob and told him what I had seen. The woman did not remind me of anyone I know, or had known.

(Rob: Monday, March 28, 5:45 PM. After doing my daily yoga exercises for about half an hour, I lay relaxed and in a drowsy state. I then became aware that I was hearing voices. They were speaking at a normal rate; I was aware of two men, not old, seated at desks. I think the desks were old and battered, a brown color. I heard their words with exceptional clarity, sentence by sentence, including the timbre of their voices, etc., and retained them briefly. I soon forgot them however. One of the men laughed, in a deep and pleasant, friendly way.

(I then realized I was also "seeing" one of the men, the one who had laughed. I did not see his companion as the voice exchange continued. The one in my vision was a thin man in shirt sleeves, perhaps in his late thirties, with thick straight brown hair combed straight back, a thin very friendly face with a generous mouth. His voice was deep and gentle. I thought the other voice belonged to an older man with glasses and white hair, though I did not see this person. I saw no details of their surroundings, not even walls. End.

(This is the first time Jane has had such an experience in the waking state, although she has seen many things in psychological time experiments. She is positive she was awake when she saw the woman.

(I have long been aware that the yoga exercises have a powerful effect on me personally, and that I evidently end up in a dissociated state at times after doing them. I have neither encouraged or discouraged this effect. I have had the experience of hearing voices before but have not asked Seth to comment. He did mention my hearing music recently. The last time I heard voices they chattered away at a great rate, like a tape played too fast.

(See page 280 for a description of my first experience involving strong visual and bodily data while in the waking state. Seth dealt with this in the 24th session and subsequent ones. See Volume 1.

(The session was held in the front room. Jane began speaking at a slow rate, and with her eyes closed. She was smoking however and her eyes soon began to open for brief periods. Her voice was average.)

Good evening.

("Good evening, Seth.")

Now. We shall have a quiet session. I shall deal with matters that are connected with you both.

We shall start with your experience, Joseph, of this afternoon. You were in a very passive state. This passivity comes rather easily to you under such conditions, as those that existed at the time.

(Jane was speaking leisurely. She took time out to put out her cigarette and sip some wine, her eyes blinking.)

I want to make myself clear here, so I am speaking slowly. Conditions that come about during your exercises bring forth this passive state, with you personally. Now this passivity is good, and you use it well. It also comes more easily to you however, because you have always been given to solitude and introspection.

This is not to be overdone however. The daily exercise period is fine. The tendencies are used and developed for the good of the overall personality. It is important that they continue to be so disciplined. I do not suggest that you give more time to this daily period however, now.

The period should result in a feeling of refreshment. Your energies afterwards however should be directed outward. You are doing very well indeed, and not overdoing it. There is a good balance here. I simply want to point out that here certain characteristics are being well used. They could also be ill-used, and so the energy should then be directed outward, as indeed it is since the supper hour so shortly follows.

Now for today's experience. You tuned in telepathically to a group of people, I believe in the Midwest. Their own abilities are well developed.

(Jane now took a long pause at 9:13. Geography is not one of her strong points, as the next sentence shows, but she has an unerring sense of direction.)

I believe the state was Wyoming. In your passive state you were a receiver. The room in which they sat was simple, and unadorned. No rug upon the floor. The young man whose face you saw is someone much like yourself, as far as personal characteristics and temperament are concerned.

(Our cat Willy had been eating in the kitchen. Ordinarily he pays no attention to the sessions, after his early displays when the sessions first began; at that time, according to Seth, he sensed Seth's presence and reacted strongly. He has since grown used to this.

(Tonight Willy merely wanted to play. I would have preferred that Jane not be interrupted at this point, but Willy lost a toy in back of a bookcase. He made so much noise I had to lay my notes aside to take care of him. Jane waited, her eyes closed.)

Are you ready?

("Yes.")

There was an attraction for this reason. The group sat in a large cabin-type room, in mountainous country, I believe in the northwest portion of the state. The location begins with an S or s sound, but we will try to be more specific shortly.

(This was the question I wanted answered more than any other.)

Because of your state of mind, the people in that room subconsciously felt your presence. Had conditions been better it is possible that they would have sensed you more directly, or even formed a telepathic image of you, as you formed one of them.

It should be remembered here that all physical images of other individuals are basically telepathic images, formed subconsciously by the perceiver.

I suggest your break.

(Break at 9:21. Jane was pretty well dissociated, she said. Her eyes remained closed as the session progressed; they looked heavy and bleary at break. She had taken many short pauses.

(I could think of several Wyoming places beginning with the appropriate sound, but did not mention them to Jane. We had driven through the state several years ago, but Jane did not remember doing so. Nor did she recall any city or town names in the state. She said she had the idea of Cisco for a place name in the state, but thought she had chosen this because it has a western sound. It can qualify however under the S sound mentioned by Seth.

(We were interested in a specific location especially in view of Seth's mentioning people with well-developed abilities. If this referred to psychic abilities I thought we could write them. We know of no such organizations in Wyoming. Perhaps I could include a drawing of the face I saw so clearly. We have an outdated state atlas on a closet shelf, and Jane agreed not to look at it in case we did not get a place name this evening.

(She said she did not think it would help if she did look at a map of the state.

(Jane resumed in the same manner, with pauses and with her eyes closed, at 9:31.)

We are going to confine ourselves this evening to the kind of discussion we have begun.

You, Joseph, are now learning to use your inner intuitions and inner abilities, and to focus them also outward creatively in your work, and also in your own physical activities and environment.

In the past years you had a tendency to use them haphazardly and with no idea as to how they should be directed. They can and will transform your psychic and physical environment. The one main test to be applied to these sessions, to my advice and to the material is this: The sessions, the material and your new knowledge must transform your psychic and physical environment, your health and all aspects of your inner and outer life for the better. And I believe that we are doing this.

The overall state of your health at this time is a direct result of the knowledge that you have gained and used. You are in a good state of health, and as we continue you will be in a state of exuberant health.

Now since this session is a rather personal one I have some comments to Ruburt before I discuss his experience. At least a year ago I suggested that a room divider be kept up to divide his working area. I specifically mentioned the benefits that could be expected from such an arrangement, and I now most strongly repeat my remarks, suggesting that the present arrangement be kept, or another divider substituted.

Either one should be permanent. Your home situation will be much more stable for one thing, and such an arrangement is really necessary for Ruburt's efficiency. It enables him to direct his energy where he wants it, when he wants it. The divider may only be a symbol but it is a necessary one. It is the symbol for a discipline on his part that will enable him to override the vicissitudes of mood, and <u>temporary</u> inclinations.

Now. What he saw was not an hallucination.

I have told you that many other systems coexist with your own, simultaneously. Other fields exist that you do not perceive with your physical senses. Ruburt was not perceiving with his own physical senses, nor was he asleep.

The image had no specific personal meaning for him at all. He simply perceived a woman, a survival personality if you prefer. She was standing motionless within her <u>own</u> system, and momentarily the two systems coincided, which is not at all unusual.

What is unusual is that Ruburt was able to use his perceptions <u>fully</u> to see within the patterns of the physical system, or to see <u>through</u> them to the patterns formed by another system.

Now, both systems exist in actuality. Usually you only perceive your own. Ruburt <u>turned off</u> his usual focus of perception. He focused it differently, and so saw an image of which he would normally not be aware.

The woman <u>left</u> your own physical system not long ago, according to your terms. She had a connection with this <u>house</u>, though not with you. She was a friend of the woman above you. This is the first time that Ruburt has allowed himself such freedom of perception, and he shall have other such experiences.

Now I suggest a break.

(Break at 9:56. Jane was again well dissociated, she said. Her eyes had remained closed. She had spoken with many pauses and gestures.

(A single woman named Lucy lives in a small apartment above our own. A

woman friend of hers died a few months ago. Neither Jane or I had ever met Lucy's friend but we recall hearing about her death through Lucy. We remember in particular because the dead woman's relatives gave Lucy her television set.

(Jane has always wanted to see an apparition, or survival personality, and now has had her wish. She said the experience was not frightening at all.

(I asked Jane to keep these questions in mind, perhaps to be answered by Seth later in the session: Was the survival personality aware of Jane? Can Seth be more specific about the location in Wyoming, and the group's abilities?

(It was now time for the 51st Dr. Instream experiment. As usual Jane sat with a hand to her closed eyes, speaking slowly. Resume at 10:05.)

Now. Give us a moment please for our Instream material.

A shell. A man's hat on a table next to a shell, such as a seashell. A cluttered desk. I believe Dr. Instream is in his own office at the college, now. *(Pause at 10:07.)* He has had a male visitor within the hour.

Earlier this evening there was a meeting which both men attended. The visitor was tall and thin, dark, with glasses. Perhaps the frames were also dark. At least they were thick frames, rather than thin ones. His face narrow.

Either he is dark-complected also, or slightly in need of a shave. The sides of his face appear not smooth, as if stubble, very slight, or poor complexion here. Longish ears. Perhaps the man is Jewish. Quite tall.

They discussed a location in another state, rather distant. Perhaps another college or foundation. I believe to the west rather than to the east however.

The other man is interested also in music. He has an unusual cigarette holder or lighter, which I believe Dr. Instream has noticed. There is a connection with this item and a dog's head, or dog-shaped head. That is, an animal head either symbolized on the item, or in the shape of it. The man also has a dog.

There is a connection with the man and a foreign country. Not a northern one. Some distant connection with the man and Milan, and a parent with an unusual occupation.

Do you have an envelope for me, Joseph?

("Yes."

(Jane paused at 10:16. Without opening her eyes she took the envelope for our 44th experiment from me, and pressed it to her forehead.)

Give us a moment, please. These are impressions.

A connection with a merger, and something spontaneous. A meeting. A connection with a trip. Ornamentation connected with the object. Squares. A date on it. I think of July or April.

A connection with your place of employment. A large circular shape on a rectangular pattern, and movement. The object, the round object, seems to have something to do with motion.

A connection with a family group, of one, five, three and two. A specific address. Connection with a fall, or something falling, and a formal rather than an informal affair.

Do you have any questions?

(I was not at all sure the data on the family group applied to the envelope object, so I picked this subject.

("Will you elaborate on the family group data?")

Give us a moment.

The question, you see, leads Ruburt to think of a letter from your sister-in-law, concerning a change of dates for a family affair.

For some reason I get the impression of the word organization with the family group. More than four members.

Do you have any other questions?

(This is the second time I was able to ask more than one question about envelope material.

("Can you be more specific on the date?")

April 66. Now this is connected with Ruburt's letter image. Personally, I have the impression of Ruburt's father.

If you have no more questions you may take a break.

("Do you want to try naming the object?")

We will say that it is a letter, and we will say that it is from one of Ruburt's parents. Now take your break.

(Break at 10:27. Jane said she was dissociated as usual. Her eyes had remained closed.

(Jane said she knew she was going astray in the data when I asked about the family group, although the envelope objects do mention family groups. But the question confused her; this is the first time this has happened. Jane said she had an image of a "round object", that had to do with motion, but had no idea as to what it represented.

(We made some connections ourselves, and Seth elaborated on others. At times during the data I wasn't sure who was speaking—Jane or Seth. Sometimes when Ruburt was mentioned, I thought it was Jane saying so, rather than Seth. After the session Jane said she had no awareness along these lines, but one of confusion concerning the data. Knowing it was wrong somehow, she tried to be objective, to get back on the right track without knowing how to go about it. There was a confusion of levels, she said, that left her groping.

(See the tracings on page 51-52.

("A connection with a merger," We take this to be a reference to the "wife and self" written on back of one of the envelope objects; marriage, merger.

("and something spontaneous". draws a blank with us. As stated there had been much publicity about the vaccine. I recall that Jane and I decided to take the vaccine more or less on the spur of the moment, without advance planning, but hesitate to claim that here.

("A meeting." We can say that a meeting of many people was involved when we took both types of vaccine; distribution took place in high schools, and many people were there waiting.

("A connection with a trip." The high school we visited was on Water Street, our street, and at first we thought of walking up to it. At the last moment we decided it was too far, so I drove us there.

("Ornamentation connected with the object." We don't see the connection.

("Squares." I thought this a reference to the form in which we received the vaccine on both occasions. See the sketch on page 51. We were each given a small cube—the squares—of pink sugar, containing the vaccine, and we let them dissolve on our tongues.

("A date on it." Both envelope objects contain dates. Note that Jane doesn't distinguish between singular and plural here—one of the points I hoped would be brought out in the experiment.

("I think of July or April." At the bottom of one of the objects is a reference to Spring 1963. Originally both cards were the same size, and contained two paragraphs of information. For some reason I do not recall now I clipped the second paragraph off one of the cards. Whether this contained a July reference, for instance, I cannot say.

("A connection with your place of employment." We made no connections here.

("A large circular shape on a rectangular shape on a rectangular pattern, and movement. The object, the <u>round</u> object, seems to have something to do with motion." Again, we made no connections.

("A connection with a family group, of one, five, three and two." Both envelope objects refer to family groups. We are not sure what the numbers refer to. Types one, two and three polio vaccines are referred to on the cards, but this leaves the five to be explained. Nor do the numbers fit our family groups completely. In the phone book the school at which we received the vaccine on each occasion is listed by avenue, but no number is given.

("A specific address." The back of one of the envelope objects contains our address, 458 West Water Street, Elmira, NY, written there by me when we took Sabin Type I polio vaccine in October 1962.

("Connection with a fall, or something falling," Both Jane and I felt at once

that this referred to my falling ill with the virus, on March 24,1965. Seth discusses the virus episodes that I became involved in, after taking the polio vaccines, in the 243rd session. See pages 40-41. I literally fell ill, falling in a faint upon arising one morning. In addition, Jane had a vivid dream in which I fell ill in the same manner, perhaps a week before the event. In reality I fainted in the bathroom; in Jane's dream I fainted in the kitchen.

("and a formal rather than an informal affair." We suppose that taking vaccine is probably more a formal than an informal affair.

(I now asked Seth to elaborate on the family group data. "The question, you see, leads Ruburt to think of a letter from your sister-in-law, concerning a change of dates for a family affair." This does not apply to the envelope objects. Seth explains somewhat concerning why this data came about however.

("For some reason I get the impression of the words organization with the family group." Family groups are mentioned on the envelope objects, and the vaccine was distributed by the Chemung County Medical Society, an organization.

("More than four members." We made no connection, speculating that this data was somehow related to the sister-in-law data above.

(My second question asked for more specific data on the July or April reference already given. "April 66. Now this is connected with Ruburt's letter image. Personally, I have the impression of Ruburt's father." Again, this material is off. I could feel Jane groping about, trying to right herself. I wondered if I could cut across the confusion here by asking her to name the object, so that was the third question:

("We will say that it is a letter, and we will say that it is from one of Ruburt's parents."

(This is the first time, I believe, that I have asked that the object be named intrinsically. Jane's pace was the fastest of the evening when she resumed, again with her eyes closed, at 10:39.)

Now. Much of the material you have figured out for yourselves.

This time your question led us astray. I did not want Ruburt to get away from the family group idea, you see, but he kept getting specific in the wrong direction. Still keeping however the family group image.

(Jane laughed.)

We got involved finally, with his father, in an effort to get him away from your family. We were trying to lead him to his mother, who is an invalid, to get near the polio connection, but I am afraid we did not succeed here.

Now give us a moment. *(Pause.)*

The April was an attempt to get a spring date, but with the connection with the letter from your family we ended up with the wrong year.

The trip was to be a trip by car. More than four in the family did not come through correctly. I meant many families, you see.

He knew he was off the track, however, and this prevented him from getting more valid information, for he was alarmed.

I will give you information on the location of your experience in your next session, therefore.

(Here Seth refers to the Wyoming data connected with my telepathic experience described on page 53.

("Did the data on the squares refer to the vaccine?")

The squares were the cubes.

(Again see page 51.

("What did the ornamentation data mean?")

Very poor. Ruburt wore a string of beads.

(Jane has no idea as to whether or not she wore beads when we received either of the vaccines.

("How about my place of employment reference?")

It would take too long to explain it. I will if you prefer. Ruburt realizes the connection and he will tell you later.

("Okay.")

The large circle shape was vaguely connected. Ruburt noticed a large orange sun, drawn by a child, in the hallway of the school. Something else here: He equated the cube with a large pill, which would be round and difficult to swallow.

(A note: Jane doesn't like to take pills. She will often put off taking them. I've found her daily vitamin pills in all parts of the apartment at various times.)

The organization data was good. Also the family group.

You may end the session or take a break, as you prefer.

("We'll take a short break then."

(Break at 10:45. Jane was dissociated as usual. Her eyes had remained closed, her pace had been rather fast.

(Jane still didn't remember the children's drawings in the hallway of the school on one of the occasions when we took the vaccine, but I did—again, when Seth mentioned it.

(Concerning my place of employment data: Jane said she had received the word "mine" again. In two recent envelope experiments involving my place of employment, this word had cropped up in connection with the death of an older fellow worker; mine referring to grave, or underground, because Jane instinctively disliked the idea of graves. The older worker had been named Ezra Havens. Jane said she received the word again this evening in connection with Ezra; she felt Seth wanted to connect Ezra with the idea of disease—hence the polio data—followed by

death, etc.

(See page 18 in this volume, and page 275 in Volume 5.

(Jane said she could feel Seth trying to get her away from data involving her father. She knew she was confused, as stated, yet couldn't straighten herself out.

(I reminded Jane that one of the questions we had asked Seth to answer, earlier, still hadn't been dealt with: Whether or not the woman Jane saw, as a survival personality, was aware of Jane.

(I also hoped aloud that Seth would clear up the reference to the numbers given in "A connection with a family group, of one, five, three and two." Unfortunately he did not do so. I didn't catch the oversight until after the session.

(Jane was smoking when she resumed, her eyes opening at times, at 10:59.)

Now. The woman was not aware of Ruburt.

<u>Her</u> abilities are not much further advanced than they were. Death does not automatically bring enlightenment or development. Those that are muddled continue to be muddled. Individual differences always operate.

Death brings a certain knowledge that things have changed, as on earth you know when you have walked from one room to another, but nothing can automatically make the survival personality understand or perceive clearly the new conditions.

A developed personality will perceive them as he would perceive new conditions in the physical environment. An undeveloped personality will keep his characteristic attitude and capabilities. There is <u>some</u> difference, naturally, but the <u>degree</u> of perception is determined by the personality itself.

Some understanding is <u>almost automatic</u>, simply because some elements are unmistakably different. You must understand however that basic characteristics of the personality <u>as a whole</u> operate more fully after death. Subconscious drives for good are liberated from egotistical fears. Do you have any other questions?

("Was the woman Jane saw aware that she had died?")

In this case yes, but this is not always the case. Certainly not immediately.

I will end our session. My heartiest wishes to you both.

("It's been very interesting.")

It has indeed. Whenever you find time I will give you more personal material. And whenever you feel the need to rest from your typing, Joseph, by all means say so. Ruburt worries here.

("I feel all right. Good night, Seth."

(End at 11:06. Jane was dissociated as usual.)

SESSION 246
MARCH 30, 1966 9 PM WEDNESDAY AS SCHEDULED

(No envelope experiment was held during the session.

(Our young friends, Marilyn and Don Wilbur, visited us before the session this evening but did not stay for the session itself. With their young friend Ann Diebler, they have witnessed a very few unscheduled sessions. They have been reading some of the early material and now want to attend a regular session, so arrangements were made whereby they would witness the 247th session. Don plans to bring a camera and flash also. Jane is 37, I'm 46.

(I became acquainted with Marilyn and Ann at my place of employment. Marilyn no longer works there because she has a son, but Ann still does. As stated before, these young people have asked Jane and me many interesting questions about the material, and other related subjects. Some of the questions have been surprisingly acute, and their general reactions have not been what we might have expected. They have become genuinely interested in the ESP field, and this in spite of a rather deliberate lack of pushing on our part. In turn, they have sparked an interest in some of their friends of their own age.

(We wondered whether Seth would be able to come through with the Wyoming location also, in respect to the data given in the last session. This concerned my tuning in telepathically on a small group in that state. According to Seth they have well-developed abilities. My experience took place Monday, March 28 at supper time.

(The session was held in our front room. Jane began speaking at a slow rate, her eyes closed, her voice average.)

Good evening.

("Good evening, Seth.")

Now. I would like to make a few remarks concerning your friends.

<u>You</u> have no idea, Joseph, of your effect upon the young people with whom you come in contact, at your place of employment in particular. You have met them at a crucial period in their lives. Indeed, you are teaching them to think.

Your influence upon them is much stronger than you believe, and you have already <u>changed</u> their lives in rather important and beneficial ways. In the not too distant past you were not able to help others to this degree.

The two who were here this evening, and their friend called Ann, these three are capable of developing in ways that were denied them in their earlier years, mainly because of their environments. Every effort should be made, within reason of course, to stimulate their intellectual curiosity and develop their inner capabilities.

A meeting together once a month for the purpose of answering their questions, explaining our material, would be most beneficial. This would not be a social affair however, per se, and that should be clearly understood. Through these people you have also influenced their circle of relatives and friends, though to a lesser degree.

(Jane and I have met none of the relatives and friends.)

Generally, for the first time, you and Ruburt are bringing the world of books to these people, the young people, for the first time. Your own artistic endeavors have influenced the young woman who was here this evening. You have completely changed and broadened their conception of what adults are like, at a time when they found no mutual correspondence with the adults that they had known.

Both of you also benefit by the encounters, and it is of course up to you to direct the relationships along the lines that are most fruitful. This after all presents no difficulties, since they will follow your lead. The gift given you this evening was given in a wordless attempt to express appreciation.

(This evening Marilyn gave Jane and me a flowerpot that she had made in ceramics class.)

If your Friday get-togethers have become boring, it is to a large extent because you have both allowed them to do so, and not taken the lead in directing the conversations along more responsible lines. For these young people can offer much. They look at things with fresh minds, and their questions can lead both of you along new lines of thought.

("They already have in some respects.")

I do not want to take any more time with this discussion. But I did want to impress you with these facts. The relationship between you and Ruburt also gives the young couple the basis upon which to build their own life together, and such a basis was quite necessary for them.

One more note. These are the people, you see, we want to reach, for they are young and they can learn, and they are not hampered by old theories. Through watching them, you see, you can observe the effect that our material has on their daily lives. This is the material in its functional working dimensions, and that is very important.

You may take a brief break and we shall continue along other lines.

(Break at 9:22. Jane was dissociated as usual for a first delivery. Her pace had begun to pick up finally. Her eyes began to open and she sipped at wine.

(She resumed in this more active manner at 9:37.)

Now. I have some remarks to make. You are taking the first steps toward a much more enjoyable, flexible, and fulfilling existence.

I mean this, in the fullest context of those words. You are acting incidentally not as parents in those terms at all, but more as teachers. To some extent you are a teacher in your painting, Joseph. What you want is a more flexible arrangement. If possible get away from the idea of weeknights and weekends, for this is hampering to some degree.

Make no mistake. You gain also in your relationships with these young people when you direct the relationship along desired lines. If it were allowed to continue as it is, it would have disintegrated on both sides, and to some good extent you would have failed, in that you would not have helped them as much as you could have had you been wiser. And you would have deprived yourselves of what they had to give.

You are simply beginning something new. Make your own arrangements along the lines I have suggested. You will find your daily lives more fulfilling, and will notice it at once. These young people also feel quite legitimately, though subconsciously, that you are beginning to let them down. For the relationship begins to disintegrate into the social discourse they could get anywhere else.

They think very much of you both, and are easily hurt when you are not being honest, for they realize this instinctively. They are not hurt by honesty.

Now let us change the subject. I am pleased with the outline that Ruburt prepared for another book. And that book, when it is written, will be an excellent one, and a major contribution.

(The other morning in a burst of inspiration Jane wrote out a full outline, including chapter breakdown, of the book she intends to write after she finishes the first book on the Seth Material, and the book on dreams that she now has well under way.

(The new book is titled The Expansion of Human Consciousness. *Jane wrote the outline for it in less than an hour, and says the process of intuition responsible for it was much like that which led to her production of the book of poetry discussed in the 227th and 228th sessions in Volume 5.*

(Seth now begins to elaborate on the Wyoming data given in the last session, in connection with my telepathic perception. See pages 53-55.)

I told you that the group of people you saw were well developed psychically. They are not members of a nationally organized group however, but of a small group of five to seven. They were gathered informally when you perceived them.

They were not trying any experiments at the time, but their energies were free, and reaching outward. Often you are trying your psychic wings, so to speak, when you do not realize it. This is rather important.

What you call the astral body does much of its traveling when you are not consciously trying to experiment. Telepathically you receive thoughts when you are not trying to receive them. This does not mean that conscious experimentation will not work however. It simply means that what you are trying to do, consciously, you have been doing without knowing it all the while.

I am still waiting for the day when you become aware of your own dreams while you are awake, and conscious at the same time, fully, of your physical environment, and able to operate normally at the same time in the physical universe.

Now I suggest a brief break and we shall continue.

(Break at 9:55. Jane said she was well dissociated. Her pace had been fast, her eyes open often and very dark.

(Many sessions ago, I believe within the first 50, Seth told us we should one day be aware of our dreams while fully conscious. At the time we did not have enough background material to see how this would be possible. We now believe it possible, and the closing paragraph above struck a chord within me; I think the very passive state I achieve at times after doing hatha yoga might signal a beginning here.

(For while approaching the end of the exercise routine I am quite aware that I will be in an extremely relaxed mood, and that as I lay resting I can count on drifting into a state where dreams reveal themselves. This would include other related material like hypnogogic images, hearing voices, etc. My point is that I am usually aware that such passages are transpiring as I lay quietly; I am not asleep yet some of the material seems to be dreams. This is a long way from being fully and consciously active while such internal data is manifesting itself, but perhaps it is a beginning.

(The images, voices, dreams, etc., disappear when I deliberately bring myself back to the full waking state, but it might be interesting to see what I can do to prolong them through the use of suggestion. Perhaps I can carry them with me briefly as I get to my feet, etc.

(It was now time for the 52nd Dr. Instream experiment. As usual Jane sat with her eyes closed and her head bowed to one hand. Her pace included many pauses; they were short for the most part however and her pace was on the whole good. Resume at 10:06.)

Now give us a moment please for our Instream material.

This is an impression I do not understand: Minnow.

A small fish of some sort.

Now our object is something small and round, quite like a button but with symbols on it, and larger than a button. It resembles a coin, and is dark as if stained or old.

It has a connection with a foreign country. One of the symbols is a snake shape, like a heavy twisted rope. Now the fish impression mentioned earlier may also be connected with the symbols on this object. The symbols on the object seem to represent creatures of the sea, land and air.

There is a connection with a word, not too clear. It sounds like Osis, but this is not it. The sound of an Egyptian god.

(I thought of Isis.)

The object does not belong to Dr. Instream. Something to do with mileage. This is not the object now, but a separate impression. He plans a trip, to a specific location. A connection with Canada. Also I believe with a boat, though this will not be the main method of transportation.

The hypnosis experiments are slumping. There is disagreement about a score. Perhaps the initials R L, having to do with these and something to do with 14. These impressions all concerning the hypnosis experiments.

Also the impression of an illness of a relative. Another connection, separate, with Formosa. I do not know to what this refers.

Now we are finished with the Instream material.

You made rather too much of a point of our location in Wyoming, Joseph. We will see what we can do however, and if we do not get the correct data this evening, we shall do so eventually.

(Jane paused at 10:16, her eyes closed. I hadn't mentioned Wyoming today, although we had discussed it yesterday. But evidently this had been enough to alarm Jane subconsciously.)

This information is to be added to the information given earlier. In the word an l, and I believe two E's, perhaps a double E. The name seems to conjure up an image that is distantly connected—underline distantly—with an animal. There are mines nearby.

Put down the number 91. This may refer to a road number, or such designation. There are high hills or mountains to the northwest, close, and the land juts off to the southeast I believe.

There is a body of water, though not large, nearby. There is a connection with Indians. The image of an Indian is representative, or used as a symbol here. You see, we are trying to speak around the word we want.

(Jane smiled, her eyes closed.)

A connection with salt. I give Ruburt a break after our impressions, and I shall do so now. Then if you are not tired we shall continue. I leave the length of the session to you. Add the number 103 to our information concerning the location, and there is the whistle of wind.

(Break at 10:25. Jane was dissociated as usual. Her eyes had begun to open occasionally after the impressions for Dr. Instream, and her pace had quickened.

(Jane knew that after Monday's session I had looked at a road map of

Wyoming; she had not done so. She said she had grown used to the envelope experiments, and missed them now when we didn't have them. We had been busy with our visitors before session time and I hadn't had my mind on preparing an envelope.

(Jane began speaking in an active manner again, and her eyes opened almost at once. Her voice was, briefly, quite loud when she resumed at 10:31.)

If you use your head my friend, you can end up with a week that is well balanced, will meet both of your needs, will allow you to operate more effectively for this reason in <u>all</u> your endeavors. You will have a framework in your existence which is truly refreshing. The challenge and the opportunity is yours, but now is the time to initiate such a procedure.

I cannot stress this too strongly.

Also, I believe that there is a pleasant surprise in store for <u>you</u>. We shall let you wait and see what it is.

Give us a moment, please. I have a few suggestions.

For Ruburt, with the longer afternoon now, a clear break with perhaps a walk and a small snack in the middle of the afternoon, will allow him extra and most enjoyable working time before dinner. He has not been flexible enough here.

You should both think of time in different ways. Remember what I have told you, and you will not be tempted to treat time in a rigid manner. I suggest—this is something new—grapefruit to be substituted for oranges. I strongly suggest at least a short walk for you, Joseph, daily, and Ruburt as well.

In our next session we will return to our basic material. However this information, such as tonight's will be most beneficial.

You have both been so consciously concerned with your Ouija board pointer that it is difficult for me now to get much information through. The conscious demands inhibit inner information. However give us a moment and we shall see what we can do, despite the difficulty.

(Jane paused and closed her eyes. Both of us had almost forgotten that we wanted Seth to help us locate the little three-legged pointer that goes with the Ouija board. Last weekend we had discovered the pointer was missing, and had been trying to find it ever since.

(We haven't used the Ouija board for perhaps two years. It will be recalled that the board helped these sessions get under way, in December 1963, but it was soon dispensed with when Jane began to speak the material. The pointer's loss however was quite embarrassing because the board did not belong to us, but to our landlord, James Spaziani. We never did get around to buying our own.

(When we discovered the pointer was lost, I remarked to Jane that now Jimmy would probably want the board back. Two days later, Jimmy visited us and asked us

if he could take the board back; he and his wife wanted to experiment with it. They had never used it after Jimmy bought it. Jimmy now told us it had been on his mind in recent days. Jane and I looked for the pointer again while Jimmy waited. We didn't find it and all three of us ended up embarrassed. Jane and I decided it was time to ask Seth for help.)

Low. A connection with magazines or papers. An earlier connection with the top of your filing cabinet, Joseph. I believe that it is in a dark rather than bright place. I suggest that you try your back porch. In any case at one time the object was between papers.

You might also check the papers on your floor, because I am only certain of the low impression and the papers. In any case that is all I can get through now.

(As of the time I type this, Saturday, April 2, we haven't yet found the pointer. We used to keep it on a low bookcase shelf; we used to keep newspapers on the same shelf also. We tie the papers in bundles and put them on an outside back porch for collection. Jane searched the papers there but didn't find the pointer. But collections have been made recently and the pointer, if there, could be gone easily enough by now.)

I will answer any questions that you have, personal or otherwise, or you may end the session as you prefer.

("Sometime soon we'd like you to discuss the quasars, but we haven't got the time now."

(Recently several magazines and newspapers have printed articles on the newly-discovered quasars, or quasi-stellar radio sources. These objects are at the limits of our observable universe according to our instruments, yet are many times too bright and emit much too much energy for their size, according to the laws of physics. See the Time Magazine *article for March 11,1966.)*

If you prefer we can devote a session to the subject. Or you may take a break and we will continue. I leave it to you.

(I was sorely tempted, but concerned lest Jane be tired. The situation was like having a book before you that you were very interested in, yet you didn't open the cover.

("I guess we'll end it then.")

My best wishes to you both. If it were not for the labor involved on your part, Joseph, I would speak to you both more often. There is personal material that we do not seem to have time for, as I want to continue developing our basic material. You may always call upon me whenever you wish, however.

("Yes.")

And once more, I am with you both more often than you realize, and I help you when I can.

("Thank you. Good night, Seth."

(End at 10:51. Jane was dissociated as usual. Her eyes had opened often and her pace had been faster. She ended the session with a broad smile, and explained now that she'd had a strong feeling of rapport with Seth. He would, she said, be only too pleased to speak to us and be of help; he would speak now for hours, Jane said, were it not for the work involved on our parts.)

SESSION 247
APRIL 2, 1966 APPROXIMATELY 10 PM
SATURDAY UNSCHEDULED

(These notes are written on April 4 from memory.

(A long unscheduled session was held at the home of our landlord, James Spaziani, on the above date. It was attended only by Jane, myself and Marian Spaziani, the wife of our landlord, although others were present in the house.

(The session was entirely unplanned and spontaneous. An unusual feature was that Jane spoke in either a very low voice or a whisper for the whole session. It ended at 1:30 AM. The session came about after the three of us had spent some time discussing a recent vivid dream of Marian's, and her telepathic adventure described in the 234th session. See Volume 5.

(Marian and Jimmy have known about the sessions since they began; indeed it was with their Ouija board that we began to experiment. They have read some of the early material but never attended a session. Marian said frankly that the idea made her "scary" so we did not insist, and rarely mentioned this material unless she brought up the subject herself. Seth has said both Marian and Jimmy possess strong undeveloped abilities.

(Saturday evening the three of us sat in the living room discussing Marian's recent dream, which she thought might presage her own death. Marian is 50, and in June must undergo an operation to remove an ovarian tumor which has been diagnosed as benign. She has been worrying about the operation, and later Jane and I learned that this made her more receptive to a session than she had been previously.

(After we had talked for some time Jane told me that she felt Seth "buzzing around," and that he could explain Marian's dream to her should she be willing to listen. Marian surprised us by agreeing, after we had explained to her that there was nothing to be alarmed about. Otherwise, Jane said, she would prefer to leave; she had no trouble keeping Seth from speaking, yet felt it would be better to change her surroundings should no session be held.

(Marian has five children and they were all home. Her husband was at work and did not get home until after the session. The living room can be closed off by old-fashioned glass doors, so we closed those and had relative privacy even though the children passed back and forth on the other side. We could also hear the TV set faintly. The children did not know the session was taking place; from their viewpoints we must have appeared like three adults who sat talking, and closed the doors because they didn't want to be bothered.

(Seth reassured Marian that should a child enter the room unexpectedly Ruburt would instantly "be himself," and nothing would be noticed by the child. No interruptions took place however. Seth began to speak in a loud whisper or a very soft voice, however one chooses to define it, and maintained this aspect throughout the evening, with frequent breaks. I have not heard him speak in this manner before. Jane's eyes opened at times, and she smoked an occasional cigarette. We had had a couple of drinks apiece before the session began and the atmosphere was warm and easy. I suppose that the session being held in her own home added to Marian's confidence, and at first break she said she was "fascinated."

(The session was a long one and will not be described in detail here, except for a couple of points I would note for possible future reference. It dealt only with personal material regarding Marian and her family, with some reincarnational data added.

(Seth reassured Marian about the dream involving her dead mother, explaining how it was a case of Marian projecting her own subconscious fears, among other things. Marian's concern over her approaching operation entered in here, and Seth used this concern to make his main points of the evening. Marian loves children deeply. Seth explained that the ovarian tumor represented her subconscious attempt to grow something, since she has now almost gone through menopause and cannot grow children. Seth stressed that if Marian could learn to channel her energies outward, perhaps in helping underprivileged children, the subconscious need to be wanted would be satisfied and the tumor would shrink by itself.

(Seth said he did not know whether Marian could learn rapidly enough how to do this; but if she could get herself on the right track soon, he said, she would not need the operation in June; a medical examination then would show that the tumor was shrinking, and would continue to shrink. Since Marian is a deeply religious person also, Seth tied his ideas on positive thinking and suggestion in with the religious theme, stressing the positive use of faith. He went to considerable length in all of this, repeating himself often in an effort to teach Marian as much as possible.

(Should she not be able to master the use of suggestion and positive religious faith quickly enough, Seth reassured Marian that the operation would then take care of the tumor, and that Marian had no worries here. Seth also included suggestions

for Marian regarding therapeutic dreams; at breaks Jane and I explained what we could, but left feeling there was much we didn't have time to include. The last part of the session involved reincarnational data. According to Seth two of the Spaziani children are psychically older than their parents. There has been much complicated switching of roles and sex among the family members. Marian herself has been twice a male and twice a female. The last time she was a female she was childless; Seth stressed quite often that this subconscious memory had much to do with her strong desire for children in this life.)

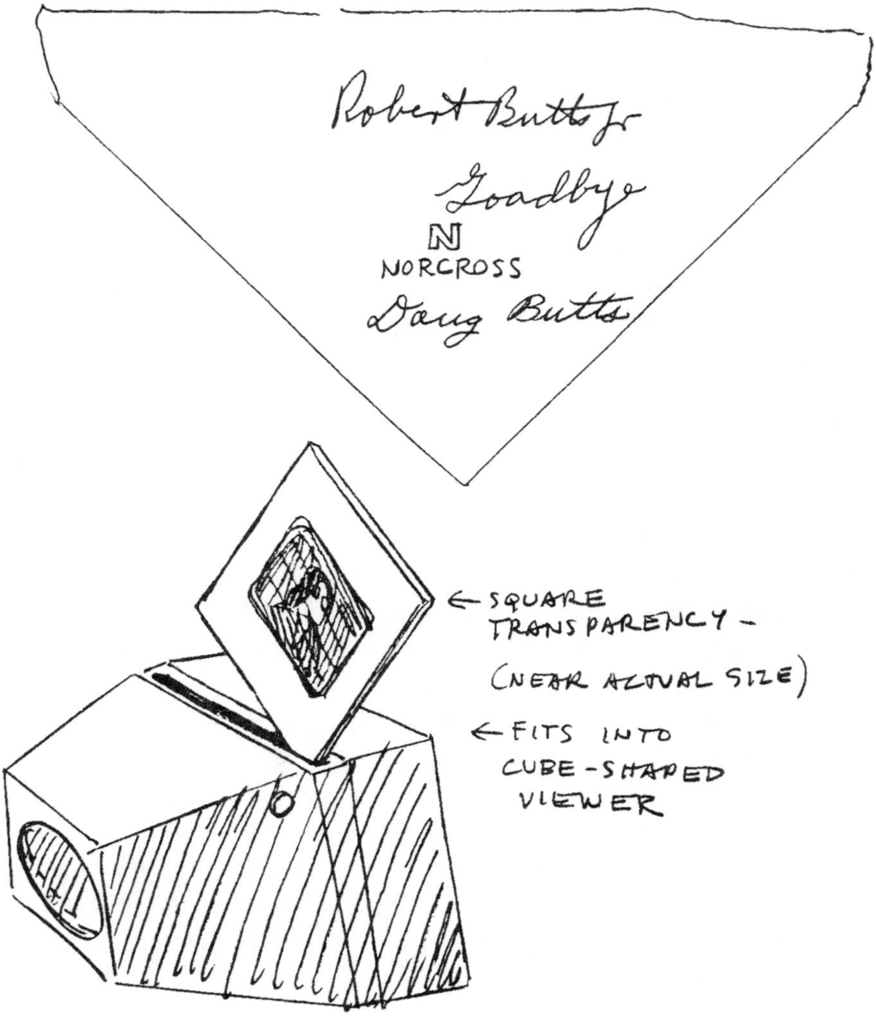

(Tracing of the envelope flap used as the object in the 45th envelope experiment, in the 248th session for April 4, 1966.)

SESSION 248
APRIL 4, 1966 9 PM MONDAY AS SCHEDULED

(The 45th envelope experiment was held during the session. See the tracing on page 72. The object is the flap of a letter that my nephew Douglas Butts and myself wrote on last Sunday, April 3, at my parents' home in Sayre, PA. The tracing is drawn with the same blue pen, my own, that was used to write on the object. The object came into being when Doug, who is 14 years old, was showing me how he writes left-handed. We sat on the couch and used a folded newspaper for a support; this was not steady. I did not intend to use this object for the envelope experiment, but decided to on the spur of the moment after it was made. Jane never saw the object in its finished form before the experiment.

(She had seen the envelope from which the flap was torn however, in a casual way. The envelope enclosed a letter from Doug's recently married sister Linda, who now lives in Brooklyn, NY. Both Jane and I read the letter yesterday; it was written to my parents. I wondered whether Seth would pick up any impressions connected with Linda, but he confined himself to impressions that originated yesterday as far as Jane and I were concerned. The N and Norcross indicated in pencil on the tracing signifies a blind embossed trademark on the envelope flap, but Seth said nothing about this either.

(I sealed the object as usual in the regular double envelopes after enclosing it between two pieces of Bristol.

(After supper this evening young Don Wilbur informed us that he and his wife would not be able to witness the session as scheduled. The Wilburs are discussed in the 246th session. Don left a sealed envelope, prepared to my instructions, with me, but I did not plan to use it for this evening's experiment. Jane knows of the envelope but did not see it. She requested that we not talk about it very much so that she wouldn't focus upon it to any degree.

(After several sessions involving various kinds of personal material we hoped to get back to the theoretical kind. The session was held in our living room as usual. Jane began speaking with her eyes closed and at a rather slow pace. She was not smoking.)

Good evening.

("Good evening, Seth.")

By now it should be obvious to you that you perceive only a small portion of reality; indeed, that your idea of reality is formed and limited by your perceptions.

As you dig deeper into yourself you will find hints of other realities. Yours is not the only system that exists within what you would call the same space as the physical universe. You simply do not perceive these other systems. It is not space or time that divides one system from another. Habits of perception divide them however.

The same atoms and molecules that are perceived in your system as physical objects are perceived in other systems as entirely different realities. Basically the same energy that composes a system projects into other systems, and it is perceived differently. Space, time, size, density, all of these are the results of your own perception.

They have little to do with the nature of basic reality. Distance has nothing to do with space. Realities that you can only perceive in terms of light can, for example, exist as sound, as motion, as color, and can have dimensions with which you are completely unfamiliar. We will end up talking about your quasars, but first we need introductory material.

(In the 246th session I remarked that we'd like Seth to discuss the remarkable quasars, or quasi-stellar radio sources, that have caused so much discussion in astronomical circles lately. They violate the known laws of physics; although at the limits of our observable universe they are much too bright, and their energy is much too fantastic.)

It is natural of course that you interpret projections from other realities into your own, according to the laws and limitations that seem to apply to your own system. You cannot however understand much concerning even the basic structure of your own universe unless you make some attempt, at least in imagination, to project yourselves beyond it.

You cannot now do this physically, but you can do this through the use of the inner senses, trance states, hypnosis experiences, and intelligent use of the intuitions and imaginative powers. The universe is transparent to the inner senses. It is transparent functionally. It exists electromagnetically. All realities within it exist in their own band of intensity.

Past, present, and future, as you know, exist at once in the spacious present. We have been speaking in terms of the personal past, present and future, as it exists for the individual. Let us now consider the spacious present in different terms. What does it mean as applied to the question of the origins of your universe, and those events which you consider historical?

What about the cycles of history? You spoke of these I believe a few days ago. What about the spacious present and your quasars? What about your spacious present and the predictions, for example, of Nostradamus? What about the spacious present and its connection with evolution? All of these questions follow naturally, and should be here answered.

We must therefore apply the principles of which I have spoken outward from the individual to the environment and the historical sequence which he has himself formed. This will involve us in a large task, and yet a necessary one.

Those principles which I gave you as applying to the individual must obviously apply to nations and to peoples. Therefore if the individual can change his own past, then it must follow that a people can change its past, that a nation can change past events, that the future can influence the past historically, and even you see that a death can alter a birth.

Actions, even historic actions, within your system, have their reality you see in other systems also, though they will be perceived in quite a different manner. Remember some of the main points I gave you on probabilities. You see, in some dimension Napoleon conquered Europe completely, and the actions resulting from that probability continue in that dimension.

I suggest a brief break and we shall continue.

(Break at 9:30. Jane was dissociated as usual. Her pace had continued to be broken by pauses, some of them long. Her eyes had begun to open occasionally toward the end of the delivery and she had sipped wine.

(She resumed in a somewhat more active manner at 9:43.)

Now. Psychic energy <u>is</u> the one reality from which all others spring. The outer environment is a reflection of the inner environment.

When it is realized that man actually constructs his own physical universe, and that individual man constructs his own physical image, then you see considerable progress can be made. It goes without saying that the inhabitants of these other probable systems are every much as real as the inhabitants of your own system.

They would consider your own system as a probable universe. They dream as you dream. They utilize atoms and molecules as you do. The systems are divided, but not separated by space or time. They coexist but they cannot meet naturally, as the negative universe coexists with your own but is divided from it.

Now the spacious present obviously contains <u>all</u> of these systems, and these systems are all <u>open</u> systems, for the energy that composes them is the same. They appear to be closed systems, and we shall go more deeply into this particular matter upon another occasion.

You must remember the material I gave you concerning moment points, and the nature of action. All of that material you see applies here. Again, you merely perceive a small portion of any given action, and when you cease to perceive it then it seems to you that the action itself ceases, and so an artificial boundary is erected.

It has not occurred to you, you see, to attempt to look <u>over</u> this boundary, so to speak, because you have taken it for granted that nothing exists on the other side. I am not here speaking necessarily of death, though this is the obvious instance of course. I am speaking of something much more subtle. I am speaking of any small, seemingly insignificant action that you perform during an ordinary day, and here we are coming close.

You perceive only the most initial elements of such an action. It is as if you threw a ball, and could only follow the ball three inches away in space—then the ball would seem to vanish to you. The action would therefore seem completed. You would think it idiotic to image what happened to the ball when you could see it no longer, for habit would work in such a way that the disappearance of the ball would seem natural and normal, and a part of the nature of things.

So, comparing the ball to an action, you perceive but the smallest portion of any given action, even one performed by yourself. It does not occur to you that there is more to perceive. When the ball goes out of sight, so to speak, you could say for our analogy that it goes into the future.

This would be true as an analogy if time were no more than a series of moments, or if the future were a definite but momentarily unperceived reality. When you throw this ball however it does not only go outward in one straight line thusly—

(Jane was speaking rapidly now and her eyes were opening at times. Now she thrust an arm straight out toward me.)

—into this future. Although you see it as doing so, it goes out you see in all directions, thusly—

(Again the gesture; this time Jane threw her arms wide.)

—in all probabilities, in all possible directions.

Not only are you blind beyond a certain arbitrary point, so that the straight line seems cut off and the action completed, but you are blind to all the other directions, you see, that our ball could and does take.

This is difficult to explain to you. As an exercise, occasionally catch yourself in some insignificant action—speaking, touching. If you speak for example be conscious of speaking and hearing yourself speak. Try to think of the words, or to experience them in terms of color. In terms of bulk, of density, of distance. Think of the beginnings of the simple act of which you are normally almost completely unaware, the muscular motions that must be made before one word can be uttered.

Catch yourself in a simple thought and try to experience the beginnings of that action. You will be led into action indeed in a completely new way. Then try to experience this simple action as it affects others, not only emotionally and physically in terms of the changes it elicits from their complicated structures, but also the new actions it requires of them.

You will see what a mysterious, complicated and almost unbelievable ballet results from one simple thought or word from any seemingly uncomplicated action.

You may take your break. But if it seems that we are far afield from the spacious present and quasars, then you are mistaken.

(Break at 10:09. Jane was more dissociated than she had been for her first delivery. Her pace had become much faster. Her eyes opened often toward the end of the delivery for whole sentences at a time. She spoke with many gestures and her voice was a bit stronger.

(It was now time for the 53rd Dr. Instream experiment. As usual Jane's pace now slowed down somewhat. She sat with her hands raised to her closed eyes. Resume at 10:15.)

Now, give us a moment.

Another formal affair. By this I do not refer to a ball, necessarily, but to a formally-scheduled event where formality rather than informality rules. We will give an object shortly.

Perhaps a connection with a charity and this affair. In any case funds from it do not go for profit. The affair is one that is held yearly, I believe—at least in the minds of those who attend there is the memory of previous such affairs, held for the same purpose, and approximately at the same time of the year.

A luncheon for our friend today, of an established kind. Some distant connection here with a museum.

The object seems to be some kind of scarf. A connection with a four and six and with this scarf. It may belong to a woman. It has been on the back seat of a car. It is brown, with tinges of orange or red.

An interlude that was not pleasant at approximately 3 PM this afternoon for our friend, and a letter or package that was difficult to open. This being separate and not connected with the unpleasant episode.

It also seems as if he has recently been in a strange kitchen, speaking with a man. Tables and chairs here of modest wood. Perhaps the man works for Dr. Instream in some capacity. A handyman or janitor.

Do you have an envelope for me, Joseph?

("Yes."

(Jane paused at 10:25 and I handed her the 45th sealed envelope. As usual she took it without opening her eyes, but this evening she held it in her lap without pressing it to her forehead. Instead she sat with one hand raised to her eyes.)

Give us a moment, please. A connection with music. These are impressions.

A connection with squares or cubes that seem to fit one into the other. A printed message. A connection with a child. The color blue. The shape of something tall like a tree; waving lines, or wavering lines.

Yellow. Two. A double exposure. Something that can be seen through. Something outmoded or old-fashioned. Do you have any questions?

("Do you want to say something about the music connection?")

A connection with strong musical interests. The item belongs to, or did belong to, someone with musical interests. An instrument connected here I believe, perhaps indirectly.

("How about the child connection?")

I believe a male.

("How about the double exposure?")

I am not clear here. There seems to be more than one of a kind.

("Do you want to try naming the object?")

A connection with a camera and pictures. I suggest your break.

(Break at 10:35. Jane was dissociated as usual, she said. Her eyes had remained closed through the experimental material. Her pace had been fairly good.

(Before she opened the envelope, Jane told me that while giving the data she had a most definite impression of something connected with photographs and music. As will be seen she was correct on both counts. Jane said she had "two lines of consciousness," and that Seth wanted to lead her very carefully between them. She followed his lead successfully.

(We were easily able to make all the connections except one, which Seth helped us out with after break. See the tracing on page 72, and the notes describing it and its circumstances on page 73. The pencil drawing below the actual envelope object is explanatory only.

("A connection with music." As stated Jane and I visited my parents at their home last Sunday, April 3, and while there met my brother Loren, his wife Betts, and their son Douglas, who is 14. In this envelope experiment Seth again used the actual object as a jumping-off point for some of his data, and this is a case in point. Doug, who helped me author the object, is not musical; however both his parents are professional musicians; both are teachers; Betts teaching music as well as other subjects. Loren does not teach music anymore. For many years he was a pianist in a dance band and taught music at the same time.

("A connection with squares or cubes that seem to fit one into the other." See the pencil drawing on page 72. Both Jane and I thought this a good description of the little plastic viewer and the transparencies my brother brought with him to show us. The transparencies are of Jane and me, taken several weeks ago. They measure exactly square, and the viewer is cube-shaped, the transparencies fitting into it as indicated by my sketch.

("A printed message." The object contains writing. I wrote my own name and

Doug wrote "Goodbye" and his name. The Norcross is printed, in that it is blind embossed. Jane doesn't know whether she intended handwriting or printing in the data. We have had trouble with this category in previous experiments, Jane meaning one thing by writing or printing while I mean something else.

("A connection with a child." Doug is 14 years old.

("The color blue." As stated the writing on the object is in blue ink. The tracing on page 72 is made with the same pen used to produce the writing.

("The shape of something tall like a tree; waving lines, or wavering lines." Jane said the tree data was her way, or Seth's way, of leading up to the data re wavering lines. Doug and I wrote on the object while sitting on a couch. My signature is firm because I had the support of a folded newspaper in my lap. Doug's is unsteady, or wavering, because he held the envelope flat against his leg and tried to write on it with no other support. As stated he was trying to show me how he writes left-handed.

("Yellow." Jane and I didn't make any connections here, but Seth does later.

("Two." Two people wrote on the envelope object.

("A double exposure." Either this is a reference to two, above, or possibly to the fact that my brother brought transparencies with him to show Jane and me. We don't remember Loren referring to any double exposures in a literal sense.

("Something that can be seen through." This would be the viewer shown in the pencil sketch on page 72.

("Something outmoded or old-fashioned." Both Jane and I think this applies to Betts, Doug's mother. Betts took us for a ride Sunday in Sayre. When we drove past a house with a swimming pool Betts remarked that she was too old for such things. Jane and I thought this was unwitting negative suggestion, since Betts at 44 is 3 years younger than I am.

(In all I asked Seth four questions pertaining to the envelope experiment. After answering the first one Jane paused, and I asked the next question without waiting too long. She went along with this technique seemingly without objection. First I asked Seth to elaborate on the music data.

("A connection with strong musical interests. The item belongs to, or did belong to, someone with musical interests. An instrument connected here I believe, perhaps indirectly." Doug's parents, Loren and Betts, have strong musical interests. As far as we know however Doug does not. Nor does his sister Linda, who wrote the letter and enclosed it in the envelope from which the flap used as object was taken. Neither Loren or Betts own any instruments except for a piano, which they both major in. Betts is choir director for her church. Would a piano or organ be the indirect connection? I did not think to ask.

(My second question concerned the child data.

("I believe a male." Doug, coauthor of the object, is male.

(My third question concerned the double exposure.

("I am not clear here. There seems to be more than one of a kind." There are two different signatures on the object.

(For my fourth question I asked Seth if he wanted to try naming the object.

("A connection with a camera and pictures." As stated the object is related to transparencies, in that Doug's father Loren brought his camera and transparencies with him. Jane heard our conversation about pictures and joined in the discussion. She did not know about Doug and me writing on the envelope flap, although she had seen the envelope and flap attached earlier in the day in a casual way.

(Jane now explained at break that Seth didn't want her to say transparencies when I asked her to name the object. While in trance, she said, she had strong thoughts of Loren and Betts and the pictures, although she had no images. She also had no thoughts that she is aware of, of the viewer. When I asked her to explain the object, she explained, the inhibiting idea of the transparencies got in the way. Since Seth didn't want her to say transparencies, a compromise emerges in which a connection with the actual envelope object is given.

(Remember that at the beginning of this data Jane is quoted as saying that she had strong impressions of something connected with both music and photographs. This before she opened the experimental envelope to see the object. Jane knows Loren and Betts well, of course, and the transparencies were of Jane and me. These emotional charges outweighed that contained in the envelope object.

(Jane resumed at an average pace, with her eyes closed, at 10:48.)

We will now end our session. The connections were clear enough to need no discussion.

The yellow however did not come through. This referred to the copper-colored buttons on the boy's jacket, a new suit, I believe.

(True. As soon as Seth explained the data I remembered that Doug explained to Jane and me that he was wearing a new suit. This was when he first arrived. The jacket has copper-colored buttons. Doug hung the coat up carefully after his arrival and we saw it no more that day.)

If you have any questions, or if there is anything in particular you would like to discuss, we will continue. Otherwise we will close the session.

("Why don't you give us a little material on Jane's sinus condition?")

He should religiously give himself positive suggestions before sleeping that the condition will improve. This will be of considerable benefit. It is too late to go into the various reasons for the condition, though we have mentioned some in the past, and these still apply.

Milk aggravates the condition. Presently a peculiar combination of humidity and the dusty heat from your radiators is aggravating also. The nightly suggestions I recommend most heartily. The exercise he read of, done three times daily, would benefit him. We will still devote a session to this sort of thing when you find the time.

("Do you think last Saturday's unscheduled session helped our landlady?")

It did indeed.

(See the 247th session. In it Seth attempted to instruct our landlady, Marian Spaziani, regarding positive suggestion and its application to a benign ovarian tumor.

("Was she surprised that we held the session?")

Subconsciously she wanted a session.

(In the past Marian had always told us the idea of witnessing a session was too scary. Hence our surprise last Saturday, when on a visit to her place she agreed to listen to Seth with no pressure from us.

(After the session was over at 1:30 AM, Marian's husband Jimmy arrived home from work. Marian told him about the session. Jimmy then wondered aloud if Seth could tell him about "anything significant" that was going to happen to him within the next six months. We were drinking coffee by then however and Seth did not come through. Jimmy's question prompted my next query however.

("What did Jimmy mean when he asked whether anything significant was going to happen to him within the next six months?")

Give us a moment here. *(Pause.)* He was thinking of his health, and also of money difficulties of which we have earlier spoken.

(During the 247th session Seth told Marian that Jimmy's health was good. Seth devoted much of the 229th session to what he said were tax and money problems involving Jimmy. As stated at the time, Jane and I have no idea as to the validity of the 229th session. The material was quite detailed; we have yet to hear or see anything to back any of it up. In a recent session Seth said that probabilities might enter in with this data, but that is all we know. Saturday night Jane and I did wonder why Jimmy asked the particular question he did. In the 229th session Seth gave a March 15 date in connection with Jimmy's supposed tax troubles.)

We will close the session. Sometime in the future when you take a vacation from other concerns, we can hold several meetings a week, for perhaps two weeks. Not now, however; when you have the energy, both of you. This would be enjoyable and most beneficial from many standpoints. A crash course, I believe you call it. And now my best wishes to you both.

("Good night, Seth."

(End at 11:00 PM. Jane was dissociated as usual. Her eyes began to open at the near-end of the delivery. She said Seth was warm and emotional at the close, and would have continued had we asked.

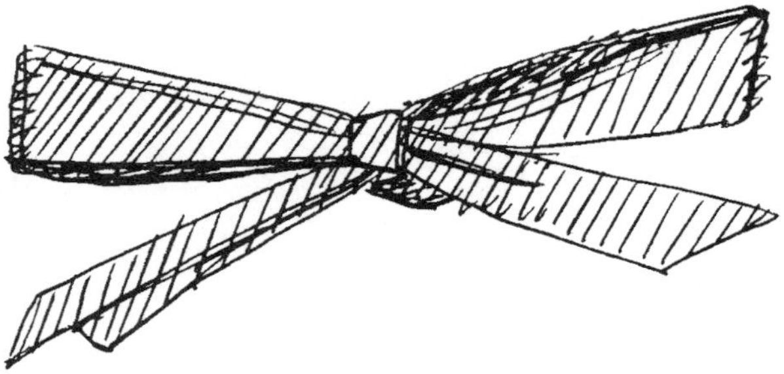

(Tracing of the red satin bow used as the envelope object in the 46th experiment, in the 249th session for April 6,1966.)

SESSION 249
APRIL 6, 1966 9 PM WEDNESDAY AS SCHEDULED

(The 46th envelope experiment was held during the session. See the tracing above. The object was a red satin bow that had been kicking around the studio for some months; at various times I had idly thought of using it for an experiment. I did not think Jane had noticed it particularly, and she confirmed this after the session.

(I remembered very little about the bow, yet subjectively I was sure it had been taken from a greeting card of some kind. I work for a greeting card company, but did not remember seeing other ribbons like it there in particular. I did not recall the card the ribbon came from, nor why I had removed it—if I was the one who had done so. I hoped Seth could fill us in on the details. The bow was in poor condition, and I assumed I had carried it home in a coat pocket sometime last winter.

(Since the object had been thoroughly flattened by some kind of pressure, it was no trick to place it between the usual two pieces of heavy Bristol, then seal it in double envelopes.

(Jane did not feel very well before the session, but when I mentioned calling the session off she insisted on holding it. She began speaking while sitting down and with her eyes closed. Although she was tired her pace was good. She was not smoking.)

Good evening.

("Good evening, Seth.")

Our friend is not at his best this evening, but we shall see what we can do.

I want to stress some points mentioned in our last session, to the effect in particular that you perceive only a small portion of any given action <u>even when</u>

that action has some of its origins within your own physical field.

You perceive portions of such actions consciously, some subconsciously, some with the inner senses, but you do not perceive the whole action. Your perceptions, your physical perceptions, cut a good bit of the portion that you could receive into bits and pieces. Since you do not perceive whole action that occurs within your own system, you do not understand it. So it should not surprise you that you misinterpret projections of other actions from different systems, when they appear as they sometimes do within your own.

When actions from other systems are projected into your own, your own perceptions distort the true nature of the event. To begin with then, you attempt to understand an action that is poorly perceived. You project upon it your own concepts of space and time, and try to interpret the action in their light.

This is certainly the case with the quasars. Until an intuitive insight strikes, the quasars will not be understood.

(Jane's pace was faster now, and her eyes had begun to open as she sipped some wine occasionally. If she was tired she gave no indication. I felt it was going to be one of those sessions where she became really involved with the material.

(Seth began talking about quasars and related background material in the last session. That material in turn resulted from a question I asked, or a comment I made, in the 246th session. Once again, quasars are quasi-stellar radio sources, presumably at the farthest reaches of our observable universe according to our instruments. They contradict our laws of physics, being many times too bright for their size and distance, and emitting much too much energy. See the article on them in Time Magazine *for March 11,1966.)*

Now. They represent energy in a much more pure form than any with which you are acquainted in your system. This does not necessarily mean that such energy as that displayed by the quasars does not exist within your system. We shall discuss that later. But you are not acquainted with the existence of such energy.

Now. Looking from your planet, outward as you think, at the quasars, your scientists believe that they look backward in space, in your terms. This is erroneous. It is true enough within the present framework of your knowledge, and the idea will work in the same way that the cause and effect theory works, which is only up to a certain point.

The idea will seem legitimate, and then suddenly it will fall apart. It will fall apart for a very simple reason, and for a more profound one.

The simple reason, so simple that it appears childlike, is this. If you can look backward from your planetary viewpoint with your physical instruments, and using your own terms and definitions, then from some point you see within the same framework, your scientists <u>should be able</u> to look forward, and they cannot.

That is the simple reason. The profound reason is as simple to say, but more difficult to understand. Using your terms again, and your scientific framework, when you look outward away from your planet, and when you assume that you are looking backward in time, you are simply looking into, or toward, what may be described for analogy's sake, the center, or core, of an infinite sphere; which exists, you see, in your terms as far on the <u>other</u> side of the inner core, and in all directions. You cannot look <u>away</u> from it, for you are not on any outward edge or skin of it, from which to get such a viewpoint.

And <u>time</u> does not exist as a past, present and future in your terms. We will here get rather complicated, I'm afraid.

(Jane was now speaking rapidly and using many gestures. Her eyes were open much of the time and were very dark.)

Even in our discussions we use the terms past, present and future, but I have told you that your future can influence your past, and that the spacious present is the only time reality.

We will <u>say</u> what we have to say, and then clarify for you later as we go along. Now. To look backward into the past, speaking on <u>my</u> terms now and not yours, to look backward into the past entails looking forward into the future, <u>and there is no firm ground</u>, you see; there is no <u>present</u> in a basic manner, no <u>firm ground</u> that is the present, from which to view the future or the past. For they are all one, and you are a <u>part</u> of the spacious present.

I will let you take a break and we shall continue as we are getting across some excellent ideas this evening.

(Break at 9:27. Jane said she was really "out", or that Seth was really "in." She was aware of nothing but the material while speaking, and felt the ideas were good. Her pace had been fast toward the end of the delivery; her eyes had been open much of the time and very dark, and she had spoken with emphasis and many gestures. She now felt much better. She said she wouldn't have been surprised had Seth called off the session in the beginning.

(Jane resumed at a somewhat slower rate. Her eyes were closed but she was smoking. 9:40.)

Let it be understood that for simplicity's sake we have been dealing with analogies that can be understood by you. The fact is you see that we are speaking in terms of simplified dimensions, and of physical properties.

Now the quasars represent pure energy, basically speaking. Your scientists presently have little idea of what this means, for comparatively speaking they conceive of energy in one-dimensional terms. You know what antimatter is. You know what positive matter is. Both of these represent realities that you can understand rather easily.

(For some material on antimatter in particular see the 60-63rd sessions.)

They deal with the manipulation of atoms and molecules. With our quasars we are dealing with something else. We are dealing with energy that has no need of atoms and molecules, and no need of chemical reactions. We are dealing with energy that is instantly transformed into action without matter.

It is <u>electrical</u> energy. Quasars are distributed, so to speak, throughout all realities—throughout all universes, in other words. They do not conform to the camouflage patterns within any system outside of their own. They are not suns, planets, galaxies or universes in those terms.

Their electrical intensity and mass cannot be explained by your physics.

(Jane's eyes had been opening again and her pace was speeding up. Now she put out her cigarette, took a sip of wine, and went into a pause lasting at least a minute.)

Their influence is felt in <u>every</u> universe. Their diffused, or their energy diffused through all systems, <u>powers</u> all systems.

There is no intelligent life within them in your terms. They <u>are</u> composed of endless intelligence. They are not matter, but in your terms they <u>have been</u> matter.

They will not be explained by your science in anything like adequate terms. They represent what you would call an evolution of energy, so far advanced as to be unrecognizable <u>as</u> life to you.

It is <u>their</u> energy that gives energy to your own, and all other universes, and it is their energy that forms the matter of your own physical universe. Yet these quasars represent the power of only a small portion of reality.

The trouble here is that even in our discussions we are to some extent limited by your own concepts, for you do not have words to express what I could say, you see.

I hope to be able to introduce concepts to Ruburt, but intuitively. These will then become also a property of his intellect, and help us put the words together that we need.

The complexity is literally too much for your language. These quasars were not discovered earlier because your astronomers would not see them. That they see them now is a direct result of enlarged concept patterns on their part.

(Jane and I had wondered about this. We had read that some of the quasars were found on old sky photographs.)

What they "see" (in quotes) is of course distorted. What they <u>see</u> has no physical mass however, but only electrical mass and intensity, which is a different thing.

Now, even the home skies about you are filled with other realities, as I have said often. You will perceive the existence of these realities with various instruments in the future, but only their existence. You will not perceive their nature.

I suggest a brief break and we shall continue.

(Break at 10:02. Jane was again very well dissociated, she said. Her eyes were open and very dark for much of the last part of the delivery, her pace fast but broken by pauses, her manner very emphatic. She said that when Seth comes in strong she feels more like him than she does herself. She smoked and sipped at wine.

(It was now time for the 54th Dr. Instream experiment. Jane's pace slowed again, and she sat with a hand raised to her closed eyes. Resume at 10:10.)

Now give us a moment, please, for our Dr. Instream material. We will give the object shortly.

First of all I have the word groan. Now whether this is spelled g-r-o-a-n, or g-r-o-w-n, I do not know. Nor do I know to what it refers.

Other impressions, a mouse. A tiff or argument with a colleague, pertaining to the interpretation of a particular passage in a book, or perhaps in a speech. Having to do with a connection between hypnosis and clairvoyance.

Three one five connected here. Perhaps the passage was on the page number three one five. Perhaps this is the time of the disagreement, or an address number, I do not know.

Would you close the window please, Joseph?

("Yes."

(Jane paused at 10:16, her eyes still closed. Our kitchen window had been open during the evening and traffic noise was audible, as usual. We hadn't been bothered by it particularly before this. I now left my chair to shut it.)

A connection with a young man here also.

Now the object. A cube or square-shaped object like a dice. White, with one black circle on it, or on the portion facing upward.

(Pause.) I am looking at it from far away. Closer, I have the impression of a black and white photograph, with two faces in the foreground, and shadow-shapes in the rear, through which lighter portions show.

Now I have the impression that the shadow-shapes are like a latticework of leaves, with the sky behind them. I do not know if this is literal, but it is the impression I get from the shapes.

Also a date, 1934. A man and a woman in the photograph. The woman wearing a light-colored hat and dress; either this or the dress and hat are in strong sunlight. The hat with flowers that stick up. The man with a white, stiff-looking collar, rather high compared with today's fashion.

Perhaps a connection with the city of London. Also a connection with a ring. And a distant connection with two boys who seem to have been around, or connected with, the two people in some way when the photo was taken.

Do you have an envelope for me?

("Yes."

(Jane paused at 10:22. She took the 46th sealed envelope from me without opening her eyes. She pressed it to her forehead for a few sentences, then lowered it to her lap.)

All right, give us a moment please. These are impressions.

I have the impression of a circular shape, with a smaller square in the center. The square much smaller than the circle.

An agreement reached, or an understanding sought for. A connection with the color red. Five and ten. Something to do with a particular occasion, that is planned.

A note. Dark ink or print. A distant connection with a rose. Something rising, or flowers. A connection with a supper, and with one, nine, four, two.

A distant connection with railroad tracks or parallel lines that certainly resemble them. The number one.

A spring. This last is Ruburt's connection. But three people together, but also referring to a fourth.

A separate small building, or one separate room away from others. And a connection with a gathering. Also with 1963. An address on the object, or two addresses. One paragraph.

Do you have any questions?

("Can you tell us more about the agreement or understanding?")

An agreement or understanding reached having to do with a date set. Ruburt here thinks, you see, of the Easter date with your parents, and the note written at your parents' home. An understanding quite apart from this however.

("How about the five and ten data?")

As something cheap at half the price, that will bring in returns. The connection here being five-and-ten-cent store, or bargain.

I suggest your break, unless you have another question.

("We'll wait, then."

(Break at 10:34. Jane was dissociated as usual. Her eyes remained closed.

(See the tracing of the envelope object on page 82. I felt Seth was on the track with his data, yet because I had so little background concerning it myself the data seemed opaque to me. I found myself feeling the same way about the answers to my questions, so I did not continue to ask them. I also thought the data was mixed up

with the planned visit of my parents to the apartment for Easter Sunday, April 10, and a very short reminder my mother had written in connection with this.

(I used the ribbon as object not only because I wanted to get its background for myself, but because this lack of at least conscious knowledge on my part would simulate the circumstances surrounding an object furnished by someone else.

(Seth helps us out with some data after break. Follows a few points we believe refer to the object itself.

("I have the impression of a circular shape, with a smaller square in the center. The square much smaller than the circle." As stated the ribbon had somehow become much flattened out, but before this the two bows would be circular in shape. As the tracing shows the knot between them is squarish, and quite small.

("A connection with the color red." The object is a red satin ribbon.

("Five and ten." This could apply in that the card would have an excellent chance of being marketed in a five-and-ten store. I say this because most of our merchandise produced at my place of employment is so marketed. I also felt subjectively that the ribbon came from my place of employment, though I cannot prove this at the moment on my own. Seth agrees however.

(We could make other connections but they would require checking out, and extra time. While giving the data Jane had the idea of my mother as being connected with the color red, but did not give voice to this because she believed it was incorrect. We agree.

("The number one. A spring." Jane said the flower data earlier in the material could have given rise to this personal association: She thought of times in her childhood when her grandmother took her on a walk to the park in Saratoga Springs, NY. In the park they often visited a particular sulphur water spring designated as Number One Spring.

(I will add some more notes as Seth deals with some of the data after break. Jane resumed at an average pace at 10:41.)

Now, the numbers referred to a number on the card. I do not know if this was a catalog number, but some identifying number.

(I think both numbers in the data, 1942 and 1963, are year numbers. Jane knows nothing about the filing system at my place of employment, Artistic Greetings. Catalog numbers are not usually year numbers.

(I was still trying to find out from Seth just what card the ribbon had been taken from.

("What card was it?")

The card in the center contained a street. This was the railroad connection, an interpretation of the parallel lines. Trees, a get-well card I believe. The ribbon at the top, and a small bouquet of flowers. The earlier date marked the first appearance of the card.

(The above is a good generalized description of a certain type of card produced by Artistic. Jane has seen cards like this of course. I still had no specific recollection of the kind I wanted.

("Then I did bring this particular card, bearing the ribbon, home from work then?")

In '63 some changes were made or the card was resurrected.

(This process goes on all the time at Artistic, as it does at most such greeting card firms.)

It is now in a file. Some narrow metal rectangular compartment, apart from others of its kind, and there is a connection with the artist here. That is, it has been kept aside because of something having to do with the artist.

(This is possible, although offhand I don't know of any such separate file in my department at Artistic. The file could be in another office however. Perhaps I can check without being obvious about it.

("This is at work?")

The colors, strangely enough, considering the color of the ribbon, were predominately violets and yellows, with some blues.

(Again, this is a good description of a certain type of card produced at Artistic. I dislike them.)

You took the ribbon off during an <u>afternoon</u>, not a morning.

(I work all day Friday at Artistic, the rest of the week mornings only. This has been the routine for the last year and three-quarters or so. Before that I worked full time there. Seth did not specify a Friday afternoon above however, even while stressing an afternoon. If I removed the ribbon on any other afternoon of the week, this would push the time back toward the 1963 given earlier in the material.)

You do not handle the line now, but the card has been kept.

(This too is possible. Due to a reorganization at the first of the year Artistic discontinued several lines of cards and sold the film libraries involved to other publishers.)

A connection with Connecticut. The firm or the artist, I do not know.

(Again, possible. Before the reorganization this year Artistic dealt with many artists and firms in the northeastern states, including New York, Connecticut, Rhode Island and Massachusetts. It still does to some extent. Jane did not know this. Without the card from which the envelope object was taken however, I cannot track down any specific artist or company.)

Your coworker, Curt, handled the card also.

(Seth refers to a young artist I work with. I am not sure just when Curt joined Artistic, except that it was probably after 1963. But not much after. If the card in

question was revamped in 1963 it is possible that Curt might have handled it as one of his first jobs.

("Why did I bring the ribbon home with me, anyhow?")

You did not like the red with the violets.

("I don't even remember doing it.")

You took it off for simplicity's sake, and ended up, I believe, drawing in a ribbon instead.

If you have no more questions we will end the session. Or I will continue on other matters after a break, as you prefer.

("The other day Jane said she's never dreamed of you yourself, although she's dreamed about the sessions. But she's had experiences involving you in her psychological time experiments.")

We will take that up after a break, or at our next session. The choice is yours.

("Later, then.")

My heartiest regards to you both. We have had a good session.

("Good night, Seth."

(End at 10:54. Jane was dissociated as usual. Her eyes had begun to open occasionally toward the end of the session.)

(Tracing of the maple leaf used as the envelope object in the 47th experiment, in the 250th session for April 11,1966.)

SESSION 250
APRIL 11, 1966 9 PM MONDAY AS SCHEDULED

(The 47th envelope experiment was held during the session, as noted by the tracing on page 91. The object was a faded maple leaf that Jane and I had picked up, along with others, on a walk last year, probably in October 1965. I subsequently made a watercolor drawing of this leaf and another. As will be seen the object led to some data that is somewhat difficult to evaluate, but Jane and I believe it legitimate.

(Try as we would neither of us could recall just when we picked up this particular leaf, other than that it was in the early fall. I thought of October, then checked this with the pendulum, which for me is quite reliable. The pendulum agreed with my conscious answer. The location of just where I picked up this particular leaf is important in the data, and this we are sure of. This will be explained. Suffice it to say now that Jane and I will never cease to be surprised at the turns impressions attached to such experimental objects can take.

(The session was held in the front room. Jane began speaking while sitting down and with her eyes closed. Her voice was average and she used many short pauses; between the pauses, oddly enough, her delivery was rather fast.)

Good evening.

("Good evening, Seth.")

It is impossible for you to perceive what these quasars represent. You can only perceive distorted projections of these quasars.

Your interpretation must therefore be made scientifically, according to the laws with which you are familiar within your system. But these laws do not apply outside your system, and they certainly do not apply to your quasars.

What your scientists are perceiving is the form, the camouflage form, which the <u>projections</u> of the quasars take within your system.

It is of course because of your highly distorted ideas of time that you persist in projecting antiquated concepts of past, present and future outward into explorations of your universe. While the quasars appear to be filled with more energy than man can conceive of, still the quasars that are now perceived are but shadows of the reality behind them.

It is only because you are so hypnotized with ideas of beginning and endings that you persist in searching for them in the universe, and you distort data that would otherwise be clear to you. I have told you that the universe expands in a way that has nothing to do with space. But when you try to relate this idea to the universe as you know it, you find yourself up against a brick wall, for what you seem to see out in the universe is indeed space.

We shall take this slowly. Now, energy within any atom expands, but within a space so small that it is almost inconceivable to you. The atom you see does not then grow larger in mass, or expand outward in space, and neither does your universe.

(Jane's pace was better now and her eyes were opening often, for sentences at a time.)

Now. Something else here, that may at first sound unbelievable to you: The quasars are incredibly small, compared to the energy which they emit. The energy itself is so intense that it would seem that their size was considerable, but this is not the case.

They are energy originators.

Their intensity gives them the appearance of mass, but there is no matter involved here, only electrical intensities, so swift that what you have is instantaneous motion and infinite electrical intensities.

It is as if you were somewhere inside an atom, looking toward your own nucleus. When an atom is examined however within your system, you think of it as existing only within your system, for you only perceive with your instruments those aspects of it that are projected within your system.

What you refer to as the nucleus of an atom therefore represents only a small portion of the whole nucleus. Part of the nucleus exists in antimatter. Part of the nucleus exists within other systems with which your scientists simply are not familiar.

They will not be able to perceive these hidden portions of any given atom with the methods they are now using. I have told you in the past that the same atoms are utilized, that is the same given atoms are utilized both in your system and in other systems. In like manner then these giant nuclei, or quasars, are only a part of reality, the part projected within your system.

Atom smashers do not smash atoms. They merely change the atomic parts that appear within your own system. If man ever learned to so manipulate the whole atom, then indeed would there be disasters that have never been imagined.

He can only play with the projections of reality within his own system. He can indeed do much damage, but only to his own camouflage universe. This physical universe is however quite important to him, after all, but he is well isolated within it.

He has constructed matter as an outward manifestation of inner reality. He can to some extent destroy matter, but he cannot destroy the inner reality.

I suggest a break and we shall continue.

(Break at 9:27. Jane was well dissociated once again. She said she has generally been "pretty far out" since the material on the quasars began to come through, a few sessions ago. It is a subject we are very interested in. See page 85, etc.

(Jane said she had an image within when talking about our seeing but part of the atom in our system. She tried tracing out the image on the tabletop with a forefinger, but could get nothing beyond the idea of circles being involved.

(Her pace had been fast between many short pauses, with her eyes open much of the time. She now resumed in the same manner at 9:37.)

The atom is in itself a far more complicated system than you know, and in many aspects your own system is no more than one atom.

When you begin to look further and further into the nature of physical matter, of course you get further and further away from it until at the heart of the matter there is no matter at all, and this is as far as you can go with your instruments; the heart of the atom as you know it.

If you could go <u>further</u> however you would come, in one dimension, to matter again. This would be what you call negative matter. Then going further you would travel away from matter again, until there was no more. And then there would be positive matter again, and so on.

I am speaking of one dimension only, for in other dimensions, and traveling through the same atom, you would come to kinds of matter with which you are not at all familiar, even in theory. For the atom is a structure that deals with the formation of energy into matter, and it runs through, so to speak, all systems that have their basis within any matter system at all.

The invisible barriers of which I have spoken hold you back, so that when your perception fails to yield results then you imagine that there is nothing to perceive. Therefore you imagine that you perceive the <u>whole</u> of an atom, but you only perceive that portion which is projected into your own system.

(Jane now paused for over a minute, sitting quietly with her eyes closed.)

Atoms do not create energy in a basic manner. They make energy <u>usable</u> within your system. Energy appears in your universe through the nucleus of the atom, but the nucleus is not the originator of the energy. It simply seems to be.

The material on mental enclosures, given many sessions ago, will clarify this particular point.

Now, quasars <u>are</u> originators of energy. All energy ultimately returns to them also. They are not on the far limits of your universe. They are projections from another system <u>into</u> your universe. They appear to be where they are not.

Looking out at them, you view the future as much as you view the past, for as you know now, the future and the past are one, and all apparent separation or division is basically an illusion. They exist, in other words, in your own terms, as much in the future as in the past.

We will shortly have something to say here concerning the apparent death of stars, as this will tie in with our quasar material.

Within your system it appears that stars have died, so to speak. They have only left your own system, and you have no method presently to follow the traces of their trails.

They still exist within the same space, using your terms, that they did earlier in your time. But they have changed systems, and you can no longer perceive them. Their reality cannot be picked up by the instruments that you now have, but this does not mean they do not exist within your system. Nor does it mean that they may not reappear within your system.

I suggest a brief break.

(Break at 9:58. Jane said she was again well dissociated. Her pace had been faster between many pauses, some of which were long. Her eyes had been open for paragraphs at a time. She hadn't smoked.

(Jane now made a drawing of what she could recall of the atom image she had attempted at first break. This is the image of circles, representing the whole atom, including the part of it visible to us and the invisible portions. Jane was not satisfied with the drawing because she could not indicate the thickness or depth it should have, she said.)

(She explained her drawing to me, and I have translated it into three colors. The black circle comprises the whole atom as projected through all systems. The blue circles are portions of the whole atom to be seen in various systems. The red circle then is the portion of the whole atom seen in our own system. According to Jane we should think of this drawing as being of many thicknesses.

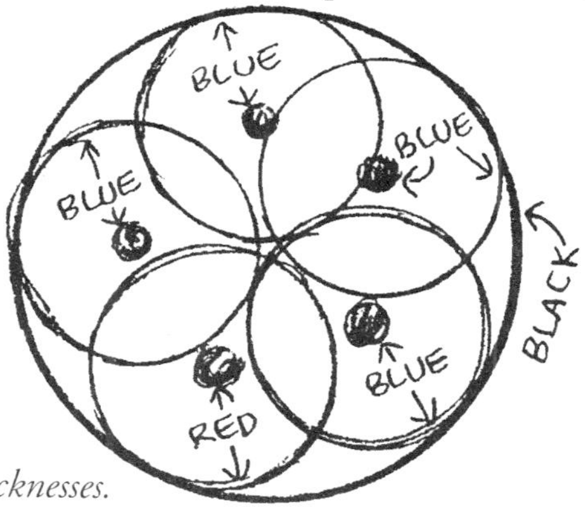

(It was now time for the 55th Dr. Instream experiment. As usual Jane sat with a hand to her closed eyes. She spoke at a somewhat slower pace throughout the data. Resume at 10:10.)

Give us a moment, please. We will give an object shortly. First of all, an impression of an unpleasant occurrence connected with a woman in a blue dress. A separation of a kind that has occurred, and a connection with tall statues.

The object, a shoelace that he holds in his hand.

I pick up a connection with a recent paper that is inadequate. A professional paper or report. Either he is not satisfied with it, or others are not. Having to do with hypnosis. Perhaps the initials F R having a connection with the paper and this data.

Also a connection with a late April event, and a decision that Dr. Instream expects at that time in regard to professional life, I believe. Perhaps connected with the college itself.

Not sufficient faith in the evidence of his own experiments. This is connected to the above. A geographic magazine that has an article on Tibet, on a second shelf in his office. He will know to what this refers.

Do you have an envelope for me, Joseph?

("Yes.")

(Jane paused, and at 10:16 I handed her the envelope for our 47th experiment. She took it from me without opening her eyes, but instead of pressing it to her forehead she held it quietly in her lap with one hand. Once again she held her right hand to her eyes.)

Give us a moment, please. These are impressions.

Connected with the object: The impression of a <u>pile</u>, or pyramid of small things like stones perhaps. The shape of an ice cream cone. A pyramid shape.

(Her eyes still closed, Jane reached out with her right hand and made a large gesture of a triangular or pyramidal shape.)

A connection with a series, and with several unpleasant episodes. A four. Six of a kind. A small round shape in a corner.

A connection with a J <u>V</u>, or perhaps with Vermont, I do not know. Tension, as something evenly balanced. Tension like wires. Connection with a woman sitting down.

Gun. Something to do with a gun, or something triggered, or explosive. With squares that fit one within the other. Nineteen. Red and yellow, strips I believe, and a cardboard backing.

Printed material with a picture. (In parentheses: Ruburt thinks of old-fashioned Shredded Wheat cereal cards, that were gray-blue in color.) Connection with four columns. An m-i-s-s.

Do you have any questions?

("Do you want to say something about the unpleasant episodes?")

There seems to be a series of them.

("What individuals are involved with them?")

Unpleasant episodes remind Ruburt of your parents. *(Jane smiled.)* In connection with the episodes, four, four in the afternoon or four people, two male and two female. A distant connection here with a death in the family involved.

("How about the tension?")

As in trying to go two ways at once. A pulling in two directions, with a balance of tension resulting. Some connection with a child here, and the color purple.

("A male or female child?")

Female.

("Can you give me the child's initials?")

Of the child?

("Yes.")

We will say then a small child. A connection with a small child.

("Do you want to try naming the object?")

It is something from a gathering. Bordered in white, I believe. Darker in the center, or at least outside of the white portions. And something that seems to go inward here.

I suggest your break.

(Break at 10:31. Jane was again more dissociated than usual, she said. Her eyes had remained closed throughout all the experimental material.

(I had been able to ask Seth six questions concerning the envelope data—the most so far, I believe.

(See the tracing of the object on page 91, and the notes on page 92. At first the data meant little, but Seth's answer to the second question furnished the key that made it intelligible to us. It would have been quite opaque to an outsider. This is a case where Seth used the object as a springboard to delve into data that is connected to it through location mainly. My thought was that the bulk of the material he gives had more appeal emotionally for him than the object itself, and he confirmed this after break. Still, the turn the data took was unexpected.

(The connection between the envelope object and the death-in-the-family reference is, simply, that the object was picked off the sidewalk beside the home of my Aunt Mabel, and that Aunt Mabel, Jane and I attended the funeral of the family member. The connection is more complicated than this, but to avoid confusion I will explain this portion mentioned above first.

(My Aunt Mabel lives around the corner and two blocks down the street from us. When Jane and I went for our leaf-gathering walk in October of 1965, we picked up the maple leaves in our collection beside Aunt Mabel's home; this is the section of the street where the maple trees grow, and one of these leaves made up tonight's object.

(Aunt Mabel and I seldom see each other. Jane has met her just three times during the eleven years we have been married. The third time was at the funeral of my Aunt Ella on August 8,1965, in Wellsburg, NY. Thus the most recent time that Jane had a chance to speak at length to Aunt Mabel involved the funeral of a member of the Butts family. In addition Seth dealt at length with Aunt Ella in the 176th session of August 9,1965, the day after her funeral. Note that the object was secured two months after Aunt Ella's funeral. We have noticed this curious time jump before in the envelope experiments, backwards as it were. Jane possessed strong emotional memories regarding the funeral, and clairvoyant knowledge of the envelope object in

some form; evidently Seth responded to, or deliberately chose, what he perceived as the stronger intensities pertaining to Aunt Ella's funeral over the object itself.

(It appears that Jane has formed an association that links Aunt Mabel with funerals, as seen above. If this seems tenuous, we think the idea reinforced by the fact that Jane and me and Aunt Mabel also attended another funeral together—that of Aunt Mabel's husband, who died several years ago. This was the first time Jane met Aunt Mabel. Thus Aunt Mabel was involved with funerals and related activities on two out of the three occasions that Jane has spoken with her; these two occasions being the times when Jane could exchange more than greetings with her, also. Jane and I do not think tonight's envelope data contains any references to the death of Aunt Mabel's husband.

(There is a reference to another death in the data however, this time to the passing of Jane's grandmother many years ago. This will be explained later.

(Jane said that while giving the data this evening she thought of Aunt Ella by name, but did not give voice to this.

(It will be more convenient to go through the data by topic. First then follows the connections with Aunt Ella's funeral through Aunt Mabel, with brief descriptions.

("A connection with a series, and with several unpleasant episodes." This refers to a series of telephone calls Jane found herself involved in when Aunt Ella died unexpectedly. The calls, most of them long distance, involved my parents and my brother and his family, and concerned topics like transportation, expenses, times, etc. I was at work during this period and couldn't help. Jane found this quite unpleasant.

("A four." We believe Aunt Ella's funeral services were held at four PM on August 8,1965.

("Tension, as something evenly balanced. Tension like wires... As in trying to go two ways at once. A pulling in two directions, with a balance of tension resulting." Jane is subjectively sure these impressions refer to the telephone calls she was involved in, and the conflicting desires of the family members. Everybody had their own ideas, and the conflict had to be resolved on rather short notice. Things were of course finally straightened out.

("Gun. Something to do with a gun, or something triggered, or explosive." More references to the situation outlined above. Note that most of this data has meaning for Jane in a strong way because of the emotional content, and that I am relatively unaffected. As stated, the connection between the envelope object and Aunt Mabel and her home had to be made before this data fell into place. I did not understand much of it on my own.

("Unpleasant episodes remind Ruburt of your parents. In connection with the episodes, four, four in the afternoon or four people, two male and two female. A distant connection here with a death in the family involved." The death in the family

reference here could mean only Aunt Ella, which led us to Aunt Mabel and her home, near where we obtained the envelope object. Without going into detail here we can say that four refers both to the time of the funeral services, and an idea involving Jane and me and my parents, in connection with the funeral, that wasn't carried out.

(Now here is the data referring to the death of Jane's grandmother: "Printed material with a picture. In parentheses: Ruburt thinks of old-fashioned Shredded Wheat cards, that were gray-blue in color." Jane was six years old when her grandmother was killed by an automobile while going to a neighborhood store to buy Shredded Wheat. The connection here is a strong emotional one for Jane. Jane remembers clearly that on the day of her grandmother's death she did not like what she had for supper. As children do, she cried and made a fuss. To placate her, her grandmother gave in to Jane's demands for Shredded Wheat, and left the house.

(There follows a group of impressions related to a child. I asked Seth several questions about these. My brother Loren, his wife and his son Doug attended Aunt Ella's funeral. Loren and his wife have a daughter, Linda, who could not attend because she was away at school.

("Nineteen." Linda is nineteen, or was in August 1965. The reasons for assigning the single word to Linda will be seen later.

("An m-i-s-s." At the time this was given it left me in the dark. Jane was quite definite about it however, even spelling it out. In view of the following data we do not think it was meant to apply to Linda.

("Some connections with a child here, and the color purple." We made no connections with the color purple. This child reference is linked by Seth to the tension, and hence to Aunt Ella's funeral.

("Female." Seth gave the sex of the child in answer to my question, thus eliminating Loren's son Doug, who was 13 at the time. Nor do we regard Linda as a child.

("We will say then a small child. A connection with a small child." Seth gave this answer to my request for the female child's initials; Linda is thus eliminated definitely. More important, Jane said that when I asked questions concerning the child, she wanted to say Linda but that Seth wouldn't let her. Backing off from the idea of Linda because she felt it was wrong, Jane compromised with the small child data.

(We did get a line finally on who the small child might be, but not until the next day, Tuesday April 12, when I had a chance to ask some questions. This will be given in its proper place after Seth resumes at 10:50.

(Seth gave a few impressions connected with the object, the maple leaf, itself, at the beginning of the data, and at the end when I asked him to name it.

("Connected with the object: The impression of a <u>pile</u>, or pyramid of small things like stones perhaps. The shape of an ice cream cone. A pyramid shape." As noted, Jane coupled this data with a large gesture of a triangular or pyramidal shape.

See the tracing of the object on page 91. The maple leaf is roughly of a pyramid shape.

("Red and yellow, strips I believe, and a cardboard backing." I used two of the maple leaves Jane and I gathered on our October 1965 walk as subjects for a watercolor painting. The envelope object is one of them. Both of the leaves were fall colors—red and yellow, with some green. There may be other connections here but we did not ask Seth. I don't see the strips reference, or the cardboard backing.

("It is something from a gathering. Bordered in white, I believe. Darker in the center, or at least outside of the white portions. And something that seems to go inward here." This is Seth's data in response to my request that he name the object. The object is something from a gathering—a gathering of leaves. Bordered in white can be a reference to the rough white watercolor paper on which I did the painting. I painted only the two leaves and their cast shadows, and left the rest of the paper white. Thus the leaves are darker in the center of the painting, outside of the white portions.

("And something that seems to go inward here." is interesting to me, a good description of how the two leaves curled at the edges during the several days it took me to make the very detailed drawing. The curling took place as they dried out; they had been damp from being outside. This curl cannot be seen in the tracing on page 91 to any degree. In order to get the object inside the first of the two envelopes I had to flatten it out. This pressure caused the leaf to crack in many places; it is by now very brittle. After the experiment I had to tape it to a sheet of paper in order to preserve it for the notebook in which we keep our envelope objects.

(There are a few other impressions that we made no connection for, nor did we ask Seth about the m-i-s-s data. Jane resumed at a leisurely pace at 10:50.)

Now. Joseph is correct, the impressions were mainly emotional ones, connected with the object.

There is nothing to be gained particularly in my explaining each impression.

("Will you tell us who the female child was?")

It is not strongly connected. The child belonged to the owner of the funeral parlor.

(Aunt Ella was buried in Wellsburg, NY, a small town near Elmira. Jane and I do not consciously remember the name of the funeral director, and at the time of the services did not see any children about. Ann Diebler, whom I work with, lives in Wellsburg; she has witnessed a few unscheduled sessions. The day after this session was held she confirmed that the funeral director has two young adopted daughters, one 10 years old, the other 12. They are in fact sisters. Jane and I cannot say whether or not we ever heard, or knew, that the funeral director had daughters, adopted or otherwise. We saw him just the once.)

We shall be doing some intensive study shortly. The spring season should be a most productive one for us. Now, you may as you prefer dispense with the coming Wednesday and following Monday sessions entirely, as a brief vacation before our spring semester.

(Jane's eyes were open and very dark; she smiled.

("We'll see.")

Or you may hold short sessions, as you wish.

("We'll talk it over.")

I shall then wish you both a fond good evening. You see, there are times when it would not be beneficial for us to miss sessions, and there are other times when this is quite legitimate. Atmospheric conditions enter into these calculations on my part.

My heartiest good wishes.

("Good night, Seth."

(End at 10:56. Jane was dissociated as usual.)

SESSION 251
APRIL 15, 1966 APPROXIMATELY 10 PM
FRIDAY UNSCHEDULED

(As suggested by Seth in the last regular session for April 11, Monday, Jane decided to skip Wednesday's session for April 13, and possibly the following Monday's for April 18. She felt a rather light sense of strain from the weekly routine, she said, and thought the change would be revitalizing. We thought it would be possible also to recoup on the Instream objects.

(An unplanned session was held on Friday evening however, and will be briefly summarized for the record. No notes were made during the session by me, although some of the witnesses made a few. The session had some unusual aspects.

(The witnesses were Ann Diebler, Marilyn and Don Wilbur, and the Gallaghers. The same group witnessed an unscheduled session described in the notes for the 214th session of December 6,1965. See Volume 5.

(The session came about after Jane had played portions of the tape of the 170th session for the group. This is the tape containing the strong voice effects and was recorded for Dr. Instream. It was made with the Gallaghers as witnesses. The other three witnesses are young people and had no idea that such physical performances were possible over a period of hours. Playing the tape was an attempt to answer some of their questions, and in this Jane and I were following Seth's advice of the 246th session. During that session Seth suggested Jane and I do all we can to inform others who are interested in matters psychic. See Session 170 in Volume 5.

(More voice effects were demonstrated now. The session was not actually a long

one, and ended in Jane's physical illness. Seth came through after some of the stronger voice effects on the tape had been played. The stage had been set through conversation and the use of the tape, and I thought Seth made his appearance with the subconscious permission of Jane and me. No one had asked to hear a session.

(As it happened many people who live in the house were away for various reasons, so Seth was well aware that neighbors wouldn't be a hindrance to voice effects—at least as much as usual. One person was still home upstairs however, as I reminded Jane; the reminder had little effect.

(Seth reiterated some of the earlier material he has given us, concerning proofs, apparitions, etc. Once again he went into the reasons why it was possible for Bill Macdonnel to see Seth's apparition during the 68th session for July 6,1964. See that session. The gist of tonight's material on this subject was that Bill allowed his intuitions enough freedom so that he was able to see the apparition for over an hour and to make several drawings of it; by the same token Jane and I were unable to see the apparition because we tried to intellectualize it. Later in the 68th session however I did see, along with Bill, a very striking change in Jane's physical features. We believe this was another form of apparition. See Volume 2.

(As he stated in the 68th and 170th sessions, Seth said that should he materialize in full view in the middle of the room it would not be considered as evidence by those who did not wish to believe it possible; they would ascribe it to mass hallucination, etc. I planned to ask Seth about photographic evidence of such an event, following break, but did not get the chance to.

(Nor according to Seth would the voice effects be accepted as any kind of evidence, until certain measuring instruments were used in a scientifically-controlled experiment. Seth did not get a chance to elaborate on this either.

(Some good voice effects were manifested this evening, although they were not up to those of the 170th session. I would say subjectively that they were probably second best however. Tonight Jane spoke while sitting down, in an informal manner; in the 170th she stood erect with her head thrown back. In the 170th she also spoke for several hours and had time to build up to it; I would estimate she spoke for less than half an hour before break this evening, and but a very few minutes after resuming.

(Ann Diebler asked Seth to give some information on a friend who lives in Norfolk, Virginia. Seth complied very briefly after break.

(Friday afternoon Jane had not been feeling particularly well, but did not tell me. Perhaps this is related to her getting sick after the session tonight; we plan to ask Seth. In fact, the session was cut short by Jane's illness. A long break was taken after the first delivery; Jane's voice was good, her points very emphatic, and her eyes wide open some of the time as she answered questions. She had very little to drink—two small glasses of wine, and felt recovered from her indisposition of the afternoon.

(During the long break I felt that people's attention wandered. Jane later confirmed that she was aware of this, and was upset by it. I am personally not much enthused about such informal sessions, although Seth has said at various times that they can be beneficial in ways that regular sessions are not. But it is not easy to maintain the unflagging attention of a group of people on a weekend night, especially when they gather to eat and drink.

(Everyone present is sympathetic to the Seth experience of course, and as stated I felt Jane and I had given permission for Seth to speak. More often than not after such an experience we wish it hadn't taken place; at the same time we feel that such sessions are another facet of the Seth experience, and as such should take place at least to some extent.

(These experiences always raise the question of control for Jane, but since the sessions began there have been no hints or clues to the fact that she is not in control of them. We do not think any session has been held without permission on both our parts.

(During the long break after the first delivery, Jane had a little more to drink, but nothing out of the ordinary by any means. However when she resumed Seth stated that she had drunk too much and that he did not like to work with Ruburt under such conditions. He would therefore end the session. He gave Ann Diebler a few lines of data concerning her friend in Virginia, which she wrote out. Seth then ended the session. Jane's voice had been quiet after break.

(Shortly after this, while I was in the studio with Marilyn and Ann, I was informed that Jane was being physically sick in the kitchen. I immediately felt that the illness resulted from her conflicts over having the session, and the next day she confirmed this. Peggy Gallagher administered to Jane, and company then left.

(Jane later said that she was sure she hadn't had too much to drink, and that she had become very upset over company behavior while the tape was being played, etc. This was complicated by her self-questioning over the matter of control, and whether we should have nothing but regular sessions. I lean toward the latter view, yet do not want to be too strict; according to Seth spontaneous expression is very important. And of course by and large Jane is interested in regular sessions. She is concerned that unscheduled sessions can be construed as exhibitionism; we think that this plays some part in certain unscheduled sessions. All sessions however have been productive in a variety of ways.

(To date, out of 251 sessions 24 have been unscheduled. Some of these have involved only Jane and me. The rest have involved a small group of interested people, and it is probably fair to say that the question of exhibitionism has arisen in Jane's mind on but three or four occasions. We are very cautious here, actually, hence my earlier statement that after such a session we wonder whether we should have allowed it to take place.)

Artist, Nude Painting Tu

By PEG GALLAGHER

A painting of a nude woman, which has been on display in the window of an E. Water St. gallery, will not be removed—even though the owner says police have ordered him to do so.

William C. Macdonell, owner of the Cameron Studio Gallery at 334 E. Water St., said the only concession he has made is to turn the painting slightly so that it does not face the street.

The oil painting, about 20 by 24 inches, was painted by Macdonell. In washed out shades of gray and orange, it shows a woman sitting reflectively, with a bouquet of flowers in the background.

Macdonell says he was ordered by police on three occasions last week to remove the painting. When he refused, he said, police told him the matter would be turned over to the district attorney.

• • •

Police Chief John J. O'Connor said today he had not ordered the painting removed. And Dist. Atty. Paul H. McCabe said he has received no report on the matter.

However, written reports indicate the police have scrutinized the situation carefully. And it appears that there is some disagreement within police ranks on whether the painting is obscene.

In a written report, at least one officer noted that he considered the painting offensive. And at least one other who went to check it reported that he saw no objection to it.

Chief O'Connor denied that Macdonell had been ordered to remove the painting.

He said he knew of only one investigation, made on Friday, after one anonymous complaint was received. He said he asked an officer to check the painting but did not ask him to remove it.

O'Connor said he was not on duty Saturday or Sunday and did not know whether further action was taken. He plans to check on the matter, he said.

The painting is placed unobtrusively among a collection of brightly colored abstracts, ceramics and metal sculpture.

Macdonell said he put it in the window about a week ago when he changed displays.

He said
to him th
other tha
ing." He
ing he
in art sc.
Macdon
tacted th
First he
at home.
two visits

"I wa
pletely ta
donell. "
scene . .
scene pai
that (the
moralize
Macdor
policem
and tha
the nude

(A partial copy of the article from the Elmira newspaper for April 18,1966, used as the envelope object in the 48th experiment, in the 252nd session for April 20,1966.)

SESSION 252
APRIL 20, 1966 9 PM WEDNESDAY AS SCHEDULED

(The scheduled session for Monday, April 18 was not held, and we enjoyed the change of pace. We hoped Seth would deal with any object Dr. Instream had focused on Monday night, as well as the object for last Wednesday April 13.

(The 48th envelope experiment was held during the session. See the copy of the object on page 104. We had saved the article because it dealt with our friend Bill Macdonnel, who has witnessed several sessions. When Bill visited us early this evening I thought of using the clipping as object.

(I found other copies of the article after the session. The actual copy used in the envelope is as usual on file in our object notebook. On the partial copy attached to page 104 I penned in the row of numbers representing the date after the session. The session was a comparatively short one and Seth did not go into each point in the data. Some of the data is self-explanatory when checked against the article.

(Jane was still not feeling tiptop, but thought she would rather have the session than miss it. It was held in our front room. She began speaking while sitting down and with her eyes closed, in a quiet voice and with short pauses.)

Now, good evening.

("Good evening, Seth.")

I have given you a rest, and this will be as Ruburt correctly supposed a short session.

Give us a moment here, to make some explanations clear.

Ruburt is making certain rather important inner adjustments, that are resulting, or will very shortly result, in a definite expansion of consciousness and ability. To some extent these changes are structural, in that pathways of activity are being formed more completely.

This involves an assimilation on the part of Ruburt's whole personality, that is quite important for his overall development. It is difficult to explain some of this in words, but connections are being formed, actually in terms of psychic structures, so that a much larger amount of inner data will become available to Ruburt on a conscious level.

The pathways are now becoming clear enough so that a change will be effectively apparent. Some of this is the result of the practice gained in psychic manipulation through our sessions themselves.

Generally speaking the same sort of developments are taking place in you also, Joseph, but because of the peculiar and significant balances that exist between Ruburt and myself these developments are perhaps of a somewhat different nature as far as he is concerned.

We are indeed reaching a sort of breakthrough which will be most auspicious. The increase of ability on his part will be a qualitative one and a general one; that is, not one limited to psychic affairs. It is bound to improve his psychic performance however.

It is in the nature of an integration, an integrating reorganization in which insights and knowledge usually hidden in the main from conscious awareness, can now be effectively used and recognized. This integration naturally enough will rather vastly increase the physical performance. However in this period of its initial phases there is bound to be some physical effect as the system stabilizes itself.

Biochemistry is indeed involved, and certain new chemical balances are now being achieved. The result physically has been a slight indisposition which will shortly vanish, and be replaced in fact by a much more efficient health standard as a matter of course.

It is very possible that the sinus condition itself will be very much improved.

Take a brief break and we shall continue, although not for long.

(Break at 9:16. Jane had been dissociated as usual for a first break. Her eyes had remained closed, her pace the same.

(Seth's material above could explain the strange malaise she has been aware of in recent days, and we believe prompted Seth to call for the time off in the first place, in the 250th session.

(Jane's increased abilities could already be revealing themselves. She has been doing very well on her book on dreams recently; this afternoon she remarked that it was going so well that she wondered where the material was coming from. Seth spoke on the integration of our personalities also in the 228th session; the material grew out of his material on the poetry book Jane produced so effortlessly. Our thought is that the dream book material is also appearing in the same way. According to Seth we are just beginning to use our creative abilities.

(Jane resumed in the same quiet manner, her eyes again closed at 9:25.)

I had several points to mention.

The results of this new integration are only now beginning to show in Ruburt's work. They will become more apparent, and the whole Seth book will benefit now also. Ruburt's experience with his friend Marian, was in a strange way also a result of his increased abilities.

He picked up her physical symptoms, you see, sympathetically, and he must learn to guard himself now against such occurrences. This can be done by clearing his mind, and suggesting that all alien impulses or conditions be removed.

As sensitivity increases it will be necessary for him to distinguish among them; that is, to distinguish so that he realizes the differences between his own sensations, and any he may have inadvertently picked up. He will have no difficulty doing this. His abilities have increased, in line with his discipline, so that he will be able to make such distinctions. The first instance simply caught him unawares.

(True. See the summary of the unscheduled 247th session, which was held at the home of our landlady, Marian Spaziani. In the session Seth dealt with the coming operation Marian faces for an ovarian tumor that is benign, and gave Marian ideas for suggestion. Jane visited with Marian one morning early last week, and for the next day or two remarked that she felt quite like Marian's description of her own symptoms. We considered that Jane was reacting to suggestion here, but were rather surprised since Jane knows how to guard against negative suggestion as a rule.

(Jane's eyes had been opening at times. Now they closed, and she sat back to give the data for the 56th Dr. Instream experiment.)

Now give us a moment. These are impressions for Dr. Instream for this evening.

The object, a scribbled pad, small and white. An unusual amount of company. A rendition. Four and three. An encounter that had a disturbing aspect, this involving himself and another man. The man may have had a mustache of the prickly variety, or unusually bushy. Perhaps brown and gray. The disturbing aspect having to do with a book, and the initials A G that have something to do, I believe, with the book.

A distance connection with a voluminous correspondence file, and a particular letter, written in January or February, though not necessarily this year for the letter. There was a misunderstanding connected with the letter.

(Jane paused at 9:34.)

We will hold our regular sessions again beginning Monday. Now I am merely letting you rest for the reasons given earlier.

Ruburt's illness at our unscheduled session was simply caused by a sudden inner panic, brought about because of his realization that the session was more complete than usual.

(Jane took a long pause while delivering the last sentence. See the summary of the unscheduled 251st session. Seth cut the session short, and after the five witnesses had left Jane was physically sick to her stomach three successive times. We both thought it a panic reaction. Later Jane told me she had very little memory of what Seth had said, even in the very strong voice; this is unusual for her.)

He allowed me to come through in a more definite fashion. The channels, so to speak, were wide open because of his increased abilities. He felt a surge of energy however and did not know how to control or direct it.

He has already learned how to do so, and so he is over that hump.

Did you have an envelope for me, Joseph?

("Yes.")

(Jane paused at 9:40, then took the envelope for our 48th experiment from me without opening her eyes. She pressed it against her forehead with both hands.)

Now give us a moment. These are impressions.

A connection with something ripped or torn out. A connection with a schedule, and something not kept.

With something revolving, and with an oval shape that is not a perfect circle. A six and seven. An organized endeavor.

A connection with something distant, with three people in particular. An announcement, as in an announcement of intention.

A reference to several items of a kind. That is *(gesturing)* an announcement made, a reference made, about several items of a kind.

An impression again of an unscheduled event also, or an event not kept. A series of numbers, and an indication of the passage of time. Blue green, written with a pen, or the color of blue ink. A connection with an L initial.

The number impression again, the series of numbers, perhaps with two initials. Here Ruburt is thinking of the address given you by a visitor last evening.

Do you have any questions?

(Jane paused. Since Seth had announced a short session I hadn't anticipated the chance to ask many questions—or even that an experiment would be held. I thought the session might still be cut short though, so I tried my usual last question first.

("Can you say a little more about the object itself?")

Give us a moment... A mishmash, as of tiny crisscrossing wires. A connection with a building that seems to be behind the wires.

(Jane paused again. She still sat with the envelope held to her forehead, her eyes closed. I waited a few moments to see if the end of the session was near.)

If you have no more questions—

("Can you say something about the oval shape?")

More of an egg shape than a circle. White or bluish-white. Small in contrast to a larger shape perhaps. The number 5.

("How about the colors connected with the object?")

I mentioned several colors. The color bronze here.

Now, this is all.

(Break at 9:52. Jane was dissociated as usual. Her eyes had remained closed.

Jane said Seth had surprised her by asking for the envelope. This was definitely Seth's doing, she said, and he asked out of politeness.

(The results of the experiment were good, and note here that they were obtained after a short vacation. When the experiments began any sort of interruption as far as the envelopes were concerned resulted in a letdown in the next few experiments.

(Jane progresses step by step. At the moment she said she feels uneasy when I ask questions pertaining directly to the object, but that she knows this will pass in the light of past experience. In the beginning also she could not name an object for Dr. Instream regardless of questions of accuracy. She does so easily now in most cases. Jane explained that our own experiments call up a chain of personal associations which she must sort out in reciting the data. She is not concerned with this in the Instream material.

(This did mark the end of the session as far as Seth was concerned. Jane and I made the connections that were clear to us. We would have liked Seth's help on a few, but did not ask him to resume. See the copy of the envelope object on page 104.

("A connection with something ripped or torn out." Originally I tore the article out of the paper. Note that signs of this are still visible on the left hand edge. The bottom of the clipping was also rough, and I clipped it evenly with scissors before filing it; this was before I thought of using it as object; Jane of course knew I saved the article because it pertained to Bill Macdonnel. As it happened my clipping the article along the bottom made it fit just right between the usual two pieces of Bristol, and into the double envelopes.

("A connection with a schedule," Bill Macdonnel's gallery referred to in the article is a converted store with an inset door. Thus it has two display windows, one on each side of the door. The so-called disputed painting is in one window. In the window opposite it Bill has a large hand-lettered sign dealing with the hours when his gallery is open to visitors and for painting classes. Bill has been ill recently and has not maintained his advertised schedule, which has resulted in some confusion.

("and something not kept." This can refer to the last sentence above. There can be another interpretation here as will be shown.

("With something revolving, and with an oval shape that is not a perfect circle." In the third column of the envelope object there is a reference to "ceramics and metal sculpture" also in the window with the nude painting that is the subject of the object. Directly in back of the painting is a large circular ceramic sculpture, perhaps a foot in diameter, that is more egg-shaped than a perfect circle. This has a textured, matte surface. Just to the right of this sculpture is another egg-shaped sculpture; this one is of polished silvery metal and is perhaps ten inches across. It stands on a wooden pedestal; the polished reflections in it seem to move as one's viewpoint changes. We

believe this is the oval shape Seth refers to, in light of his answer to my second question.

("A six and seven." Offhand Jane and I made no connections.

("An organized endeavor." Certainly the pressure applied to Bill Macdonnel by three police visits or calls, in an effort to get him to remove the painting from the window. A slightly different interpretation here would be that the police constitute an organization, and that their efforts to have Bill remove the painting constitute an endeavor.

("A connection with something distant," In the sixth column of the envelope object there is a reference to Corning—Painted Post School District, which employs Bill as an art teacher. This is perhaps twenty-five miles away. Bill lives here in Elmira and commutes to work daily. The time he can spend at his gallery in Elmira is thus quite limited—another reason for the schedule of hours posted in one of the windows, as mentioned on page 109.

("with three people in particular." When the police asked Bill to remove the painting from his gallery window, he asked advice from three people in particular. Two of the people are named in the sixth column of the envelope object. These two supported Bill's decision to leave the painting in the window. The third man, Ernfred Anderson, who has a national reputation as a sculptor and teacher at Elmira College, and is a close friend of Bill, Jane and mine, advised Bill to remove the painting. Bill told Jane and me this on his visit earlier this evening, although we had heard this from other friends several days ago.

("An announcement, as in an announcement of intention." The first paragraph of the envelope object contains Bill Macdonnel's intention not to remove the painting from the gallery window even though requested to do so by the police. Bill reiterated his decision on his visit earlier tonight.

("A reference to several items of a kind. That is an announcement made, a reference made, about several items of a kind." Column three contains references to a collection of abstracts [which are paintings], ceramics and metal sculpture. Two of these are plural. Columns five and six of the object contain references to a bookstore and the books on display in the window there. This store is but a few doors down the street—East Water Street.

("An impression again of an unscheduled event also, or an event not kept." Jane is sure this refers to Peggy Gallagher, who wrote the news story used as envelope object. On Friday April 15 Jane and I and the Gallaghers heard about Bill's difficulties. Peggy planned to call Bill Saturday but did not do so. We saw the Gallaghers on Sunday evening and learned that she still hadn't seen Bill Macdonnel. Her story however was printed on Monday, April 18, which means she had to see Bill sometime Monday morning. This was possible because Bill Macdonnel, as a teacher, was still on Easter vacation. See also the "something not kept" reference and interpretation

on page 109.

("A series of numbers, and an indication of the passage of time." When I tore the article from the newspaper I wrote the month, day and year on it, not realizing the date was printed on the reverse side.

("Blue green, written with a pen, or the color of blue ink." I wrote the date at the top of the object with a ballpoint pen containing blue ink—the same pen used to duplicate this series of numbers on the copy of the object included with this session. The reference to green is interesting; my thought being that blue and green are next to each other on the color wheel and perhaps difficult for Seth to distinguish. Both are cool colors.

("A connection with an L initial." Jane and I made no connections here, and would have liked to ask Seth about this.

("The number impression again...initials." As Seth said this block of data pertained to an address Jane and I were given last evening, and is not related to the envelope object. The address also contained a series of numbers.

("A mishmash, as of tiny crisscrossing wires." Seth gave this answer to my question in which I asked him to say more about the object itself. The object consists of small printed type which was folded several times; such an impression of tiny crisscrossings could occur to an entity with the ability to see through the layers of the object, so to speak, or to pick up the impressions resulting from layers. This gets complicated however as will be seen in the next impression. [A later note by Rob: Bill had a small scuplture of criss-crossing wires in a gallery window.]

("A connection with a building that seems to be behind the wires." If Seth can penetrate the folded layers of the object and tell us that printed type is a mishmash, then presumably he could tell us about things on the back of the object also, even when the object is folded.

(There is the top half of a photograph on the back of the object, on the right. The photo is of Hoffman Nurseries, and features a sign. Beyond the sign to the left can be seen part of a station wagon. In back of the automobile can be seen a trestle-like affair, and in back of this indications of a building. It is indistinct in the poor quality photograph, but can be made out. Hoffman Nurseries is a local concern and actually contains many buildings. Portions of three smaller ads on back of the object also refer to local businesses, and would involve buildings.

("More of an egg shape than a circle." Seth gave this in answer to my second question, and continues below. See the data and our interpretation on page 109, with the description of the two near-circular sculptures in the same window of Bill Macdonnel's gallery, with the disputed nude painting. Seth gave the above data when I asked him to clarify his original data on page 108. The smaller of the two sculptures is more egg-shaped than the larger. See the next impression.

("White or bluish-white. Small in contrast to a larger shape perhaps." As stated, the smaller of the two near-circular sculptures, about ten inches across, is of polished silvery metal, highly reflective. This gives it the bluish cast. It also looks whitish, and gray. The quality of light can cause these changes in color. When Jane and I visited the gallery window to check out this data before writing it up, we noted the three colors mentioned above in this particular sculpture—white, blue, gray.

(This metal sculpture, an estimated ten inches across its widest diameter, actually appears quite a bit smaller than the more round or circular ceramic sculpture at a foot across. But there is quite a difference in volume.

("I mentioned several colors. The color bronze here." This was in response to my third and last question, for more data on color connected with the object. Jane subjectively feels the bronze reference above deals with the overall color of Bill's painting, discussed in the envelope object. In the first column Peggy Gallagher calls the painting done "In washed out shades of gray and orange." Jane associates the gray and orange with bronze. I neglected to ask Seth about "The number 5."

(Neither of us had seen Bill's painting at the time the newspaper article was published, or this session held, on Wednesday, April 20. We did see it this morning, April 23. I can say the overall tone of the painting is of an orange gray, [bronze?] with other very muted colors interwoven.)

SESSION 253
APRIL 25, 1966 9 PM MONDAY AS SCHEDULED

(No envelope experiment was held during the session.

(Jane began speaking while sitting down and with her eyes closed. However her eyes opened after a few paragraphs, and remained so for most of the session thereafter. Her pace was average, her voice quiet.)

Now, good evening.

("Good evening, Seth.")

The author whose book on precognition you are reading comes quite close in important respects.

You will note that he has had his own psychic experiences, and has been able to draw knowledge from them and from his own intuitions. He has followed through by using the intellect, but the intuitional data, as always, provides the direct experience upon which the intellect can then work.

*(*The Future Is Now, *by Arthur W. Osborn. University Books, New Hyde Park, NY.)*

All systems of reality are created, or constructed, by those who perceive the

the same manner whether or not you want to perceive a thought that must be made physical, or the image of a consciousness that must be made physical.

You have noticed in our own work that oftentimes information will be perceived by Ruburt in terms of visual images. I do not give Ruburt the information in this manner. The images are formed from my ideas. Usually they are formed by his ideas. I try to direct his image making, but in both instances the same process of image making is involved. You can understand in fact the way in which sense images are organized much more clearly by studying instances where sense images exist without an actual object representing them in the physical universe. This shows that sense impressions are independent, you see, of objects.

You may take your break.

(Break at 9:30. Jane was dissociated as usual. Her voice and pace had been average, her eyes had been open and very dark for paragraphs at a time. She said the time passed very quickly.

(She resumed in the same manner at 9:35.)

Now I have told you time and time again, my friends, that you construct your physical universe and your private environment in line with your inner expectations, for they mirror perfectly the deepest areas of your own inner reality.

This is perhaps the closest I can come in handing you anything that approaches a basic truth. All of our material follows from this, and any other information contained in the material follows and flows out of this primary statement.

I do not speak symbolically, but quite literally.

When you find yourselves therefore noticing more and more the inequalities, the disasters and the shames that come within your sphere of perception, you add to their existence. This may confound what common sense may tell you. However, concentration reinforces the quality which is concentrated upon.

I will not go more deeply into this, for we have mentioned it often, and I address myself now to you both. When you are concentrating upon destructive elements, you lose on two points. You reinforce the destructive qualities by the very act of concentrating upon them, and you rob yourselves of the constructive qualities that you <u>could</u> be concentrating upon, and therefore that you could be reinforcing.

For an example, we will take your friend and her tumor. The tumor was formed by inner concentration. She feared a tumor so strongly that subconsciously she focused her energies in those directions. It existed in her mind long before it was physically constructed.

Had she concentrated upon constructive elements, upon positive and not negative qualities, not only would the tumor itself be nonexistent, but she would have constructed a positive element in its stead. A spiritual growth, for example.

All of these matters, you see, and many more, from the considerations of health and the formation of destructive ulcers and tumors, to the construction of any simple physical object, to the construction of an apparition—all of these are in one way or another connected with inner focus and concentration.

You will in all cases attempt to construct as physical reality your inner conception of what reality is. Your physical environment and conditions are a mirror of your own basic conceptions of reality. If the environment changes it is because your inner conceptions have changed, and no smallest alteration is made within physical reality, that has not first been made within the inner self.

I wanted to mention here a subject that is at least allied. We have not touched upon it often, if at all, and it has to do with something Ruburt wondered about: Mass, or shared, dreams.

Now, your physical universe is obviously composed of shared perceptions, and mass dreams would of course be of the same nature. Mass dreams are indeed a reality. They exist mainly at one particular level, and they have to do with what you may call for now, world pictures.

These help form the reality of human conditions upon your planet at any given time. Those conditions are at least partially the result of such mass dreams.

You may take a break before our Instream material.

(Break at 9:56. Jane was dissociated as usual. Her eyes had been open a good deal of the time. Once again she was surprised by what seemed to be the swift passage of time.

(It was now time for the 57th Dr. Instream experiment. Jane sat with a hand raised to her closed eyes, speaking rather slower than before. Resume at 10:06.)

Now. Give us a moment please.

I do not know to what this refers. There is a round sun or lamp image. Has Dr. Instream been taking some sort of treatment involving a lamp, or staring into a light? Perhaps, since an office or a room is connected here.

Also a connection with two. Perhaps two in the afternoon, or perhaps two treatments or visits to this place. This could refer even to an eye examination, if he had to look at a round bright object.

Another impression, separate from the first, with music—a concert perhaps. A third aisle. A seat to the right of the center.

Now, our object. Small. He fingers it in his pocket. Something like a medal, but not round. Resembling a short squat cross in shape, but more filled in, in the center, and this portion scalloped in some manner, and inscribed. Of dark color. The object is fairly old. A metal color, somewhat of a mixture resembling gray greens, with a silverish colored tinge. A date on it. Connected with the object also an 1874 date, referring to the beginning of a tradition or establishment.

Another impression separate from the rest. Stedgewick, or Sedgewick. Something Dr. Instream has been reading. A connection with a volume, that is bound in a leather-appearing material, but softer. Brown-red in color. The edges of the pages are not white. Perhaps cream colored, and originally tinged with gold.

(Jane paused at 10:20.)

Now, do you have an envelope for me?

("No.")

We will then discuss briefly, very briefly, mass or shared dreams.

There are actually several varieties. For now we will be concerned with mass dreams that have an almost universal nature. That is, dreams that are shared at one time or another by the majority of living persons on your planet.

There are dreams shared by various groups for example also.

This particular kind of dream is concerned with working out certain problems concerning your physical reality, and they are usually not precognitive. They might appear precognitive if you perceived them, because many of the events contained therein will later occur in fact. They are not precognitive however, for in a large measure they bring about, or cause, physical events.

They occur, comparatively speaking, just above that layer which Jung refers to as the collective unconscious. If you could perceive these dreams then you would have a good idea of the main physical events of the future, because you would see them being born.

(Jane now took a pause lasting well over a minute. She sat quietly with her eyes closed. After she resumed her eyes began to open occasionally.)

These are as a rule connected with significant events that affect many countries. They represent in the main deep intents, wishes and purposes. *(Another long pause.)* At times they have immense power to bring about shaking world changes of either beneficial or destructive nature.

(Note the way Jane reversed the order of the two words.)

One individual however is more important than you have ever dreamed, for the intensity and emotion and intent is important here. One man, passionately willing, good or evil, can overbalance, literally, a hundred men. In the dream state too, you see, leaders can be born and make themselves known. The people already know them in these mass dreams, before they are ever known in physical reality.

Now, you may end the session or take a brief break as you prefer.

("I guess we'll end it then.")

My heartiest best wishes to you both. We will continue with this material at our next session, and perhaps I will answer Ruburt's question. He asked why he did not dream of me. *(Jane smiled, eyes open.)* I do not dream of him, either.

("Good night, Seth."

(End at 10:32. Jane was dissociated as usual.)

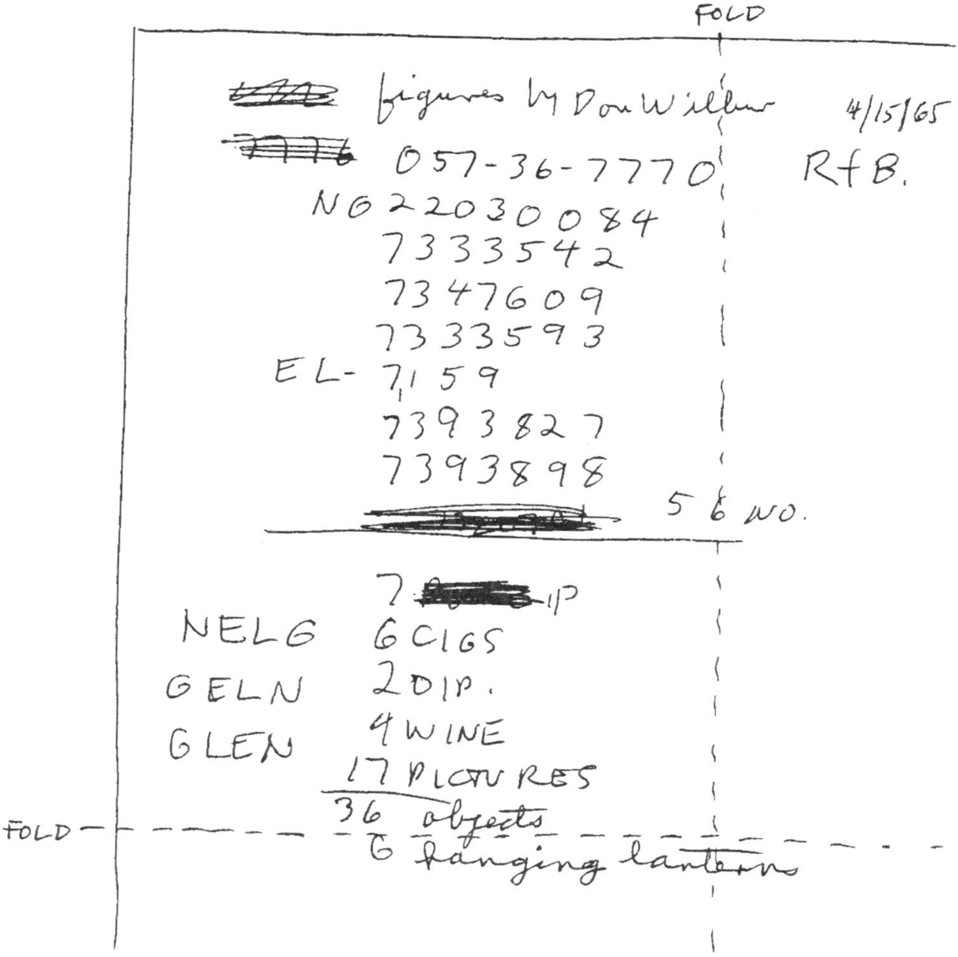

FOLD

[redacted] figures by Don Wilbur 4/15/65

[redacted] 057-36-7770 R+B.

NG22030084

7333542

7347609

7333593

EL-7159

7393827

7393898

[redacted] 56 NO.

7 [redacted] lP

NELG 6 CIGS

GELN 2 DIP.

GLEN 4 WINE

17 PICTURES

36 objects

FOLD

6 hanging lanterns

(Reduced copy of the tracing of the sheet of yellow paper with numbers and words, used as the object in the 49th envelope experiment, in the 254th session for April 27, 1966.)

system. Those who do not construct a system cannot perceive it. Now. There is nothing at all unusual in precognitive experiences. They occur constantly beneath the level of your awareness. However there are certain conditions necessary before precognitions can arise to conscious levels, and there are definite conditions that must exist before what you call apparitions can be perceived.

So-called apparitions, again, are not unusual. They are more or less constant. Many of these apparitions exist in their own system whether or not you perceive them. Some apparitions are constructed by the perceiver and are basically caused by a telepathic communication. But all apparitions are not of this nature. All apparitions however, to appear as or within the physical system, must be constructed by the perceiver in the same manner that all physical objects are constructed.

This does not mean that apparitions are only the result of such construction on the part of the perceiver. The perceiver constructs the pseudomaterial apparition as he constructs the physical image of his contemporaries, but in, or rather and in line with telepathic data that is received by or from the consciousness whose material image is being constructed.

You recall we spoke of primary and secondary physical constructions. These classifications apply regardless of the basic nature of the consciousness that is to be materially formed. An apparition constructed as a result of telepathic data, picked up by the perceiver in message form, will be constructed by him in precisely the same manner that an apparition will be constructed that is a reflection of a survival personality.

The difference is not in construction, for the methods of construction are the same. For example, Mr. A in his bedroom telepathically picks up the thought of his brother many miles distant. Now. If he merely picks up his brother's thought, and the thought is, quote: "I am dying. I wish I could say goodbye to my brother," then the receiver of the message could form the apparition of the dying brother, and then perceive it in his bedroom.

This would be a secondary construction. If however the dying brother made an out-of-body journey before or after death, for a last visit, then the receiver would still have to construct the apparition himself in order to perceive it. But in this case we would have a primary construction.

Nothing is seen directly. You are always forming such constructions, and the methods by which this is accomplished are the same regardless of the nature of the consciousness which is to be perceived in physical terms. In all cases, if the ego consciousness is to be reached, some sense imagery is necessary.

Sense images are built up, you see, in the same manner whether or not you are trying to perceive an apple, a star, or a human being. They are built up in

SESSION 254
APRIL 27, 1966 9 PM WEDNESDAY AS SCHEDULED

(The 49th envelope experiment was held during the session. The object was a sheet of yellow paper upon which our young friend Don Wilbur doodled various numbers and words on the evening of Friday, April 15. I found it while cleaning up after company had left, and decided to use it for an experiment. Jane told me tonight that she didn't remember seeing Don make it. It was produced on the evening of the unscheduled 251st session. Jane ended up physically ill after this session, which saw very strong voice effects. There were five witnesses, excluding myself.

(I dated and initialed the paper when I found it on April 15. Tonight I placed it between the usual two pieces of Bristol and then sealed it in double envelopes. The whole sheet was used and was folded in quarters.

(The session was held in the front room. Jane began speaking while sitting down and with her eyes closed, in a quiet voice and with pauses.)

Good evening.

("Good evening, Seth.")

Now. As you know, all aspects of physical reality first exist within the framework of nonobjective reality.

In certain areas of mass shared dreams, collective mankind deals with the problems of his political and social objective structure. The solutions which he makes within his dream reality are often, however, not the same solutions that he accepts within physical reality.

The dream solutions are held as the ideals, however. Without for example mass dreams, your United Nations would never exist. This type of mass dream is one of several varieties. It is true indeed that all dreams to some extent are shared, for the privacy that you imagine exists within them is, as Ruburt correctly supposed, an illusion.

It is of course necessary at this stage of your development that selectivity be used, and that some standards be drawn that will effectively define apparent limitations and boundaries. The area within these limitations and boundaries you call the self. The self expands as your ability grows, as you learn to retain identity in the midst of diversity.

Practically speaking you see, if you were aware of the constant barrage of telepathic communications that <u>do</u> impinge upon you, it would be most difficult to retain identity. Identity would suffer if it were forced to perceive more impressions than it could effectively handle. Shared dreams are therefore well beneath awareness.

Identity could be called a strong organizing characteristic that perceives impressions in definite ordered form. As identity is strengthened through experience then it automatically expands itself to add further realities which it is now able to manipulate.

I have told you that dream reality is more cohesive than you may have supposed. Such characteristics as shared dreams go a long way to stabilize dream reality. When you dream of others they know it. When they dream of you, you know this. There would be nothing to be gained however in conscious awareness of these conditions.

This is a slight aside. Many people dreamed of Jack Kennedy's death in advance, as you know. On one level this knowledge was available to the man himself. This does not mean that the death had to happen. It was a vivid possibility. It was also one of many solutions to several problems. While it was not the most suitable solution, it was the closest man could come at that particular time in physical reality.

All events are known in advance, but still there is a selectivity that is unknown. Dreams as you know have their own electric reality, their own psychic energy, and their effect upon physical events is extremely strong. The effect is undiluted, so to speak. The emotional intensity of a dream is very seldom recalled in its full strength.

Psychic action is being directed in a way not possible in the ordinary waking condition. Shared dreams present their own historic organization, for the shared memory of your race does not only include physical events, but reaches much further than this.

Dreams you see are also imprinted within the cells electromagnetically. We will take a simple example, those who are not prejudiced against those races who are kept downtrodden. They dream individually and collectively of changing the situation. They act out in their dreams the various ways in which such a changeabout could occur. These dreams actually bring about the resulting change that will then happen in a historic manner. The very energy and direction you see of the dreams themselves will help change the situation.

I suggest your break.

(Break at 9:29. Jane was dissociated as usual. Her eyes began to open during the last ten minutes of the delivery, and her pace speeded up somewhat. She resumed in the same manner at 9:39.)

You see, in the waking state you direct your energy into the manipulation and construction of objects.

In some respects this dissipates the energy, of course. In the dream state you manipulate energy more directly. This is what you are doing of course in self-hypnosis: But, used for therapy, you are still trying to affect or change something physical.

In the existence of what you call the radio stars you have energy that is being manipulated more directly than you can imagine—energy knowing itself, highly individualized. You have self structures so intense that they are able to handle an infinite variety of impressions, share them, use them, and still retain individual identities.

You understand that the radio stars are merely the projection of something else. That is, your scientists with their instruments perceive only the appearance that these structures take when they fall within the physical system. This has nothing to do with the nature of their own reality, for you cannot perceive that in any direct manner.

You cannot for that matter perceive yourselves directly, but only through the sense apparatus which has been adopted by the self. You perceive directly psychological experiences, but you do not perceive these in their undiluted form. You protect yourselves and automatically sift out what is too vivid or intense at any given time.

You do not even perceive sense data with a third of the vividness of which you are capable. This has to do again with the self-protection used. The self does not perceive any impressions, you see, which are so vivid that it could be overwhelmed. As the self learns then it allows greater and more intense impressions.

You may take your break.

("No, I'm all right." I had been sneezing, and Jane paused at 9:49.)

If you are comfortable then we shall continue briefly.

In most instances the full and uninhibited use, even of the outer senses, could sweep an insecure self into fragments. The strength and intensity of any impression cannot be stronger or more intense than the perceiver.

Full and uninhibited use of even the outer senses would lead you to inner reality. Usually only a strong and disciplined self, a well-structured identity, can perceive in this manner, and then only occasionally. Full operation of inner and outer senses, you see, in your present stage of development as a race, would be blinding, as you can see in your reading of drug experiences.

An occurrence only remotely approaching this can be disastrous. Not because it is basically undesirable, for such an experience has the greatest potentials for development of the self. Such experiences can be disastrous simply because the self structure is not yet strong enough to assimilate and contain the intensity of the experience. In many cases dream experiences, as I have mentioned, are much more vivid and intense than waking experience. You do not even remember the majority of these. But the inner self is more flexible, you see, than the ego, and it can therefore contain greater intensities without undue alarm.

We will now take our break.

(Break at 9:59. Jane was dissociated as usual. Her pace had been good, her eyes opening often.

(It was now time for the 58th Dr. Instream experiment. As usual Jane's pace slowed up to some extent, and she sat with a hand raised to her closed eyes. Resume at 10:06.)

Now give us a moment, please.

I do not know to what this refers. I have the impression of a swift, perhaps sudden turn to the left, I believe in an automobile at an intersection. No accident, but another car somehow involved. *(A long pause.)* A school nearby. I believe in the afternoon.

Now for our object. Rectangular, yet it rolls, or can roll. Rather light in weight, as say paper or cardboard, resembling a spool of some kind. But larger than a spool of thread. It is not an esthetic but a functional object. Perhaps it is a roll of paper.

Now, separate impressions. An affair at which ten people were present. Or an affair that was held at ten. Some kind of lists discussed there. Also a specific connection with a kitchen, and with one tall man with a mustache, who has a child, a daughter.

(Pause at 10:15.) Dr. Instream is thinking of a class ring, with an insignia, that is shaped something like a flag but is not a flag, and has a connection with 27, or the year 1927.

Do you have an envelope for me, Joseph?

("Yes."

(Without opening her eyes Jane took the envelope from me for our 49th experiment. Her position, with a hand to her eyes, did not change; she held the envelope in her lap.)

Give us a moment, please. These are impressions.

The word grand. I do not know, a grandparent? We shall see.

Nine. A frame. A connection with two people standing up. Four plus one.

Some connection with gliddiard. Perhaps this symbolizes music. A brief encounter. Six. Connection with a teapot or water kettle. Gold. Several advantages. A looming shape. This can be literal or symbolic, as an unpleasant event could be seen to loom ahead.

Connection with a distant relative. A steeple shape. Small scribbled writing. A window. And perhaps with February of '64.

Do you have any questions?

("What's that about gliddiard?")

Lilliard. *(Jane spelled this word out and I repeated it after her.)*

This was a trio that appeared at the Arnot art gallery.

("Can you say when?")

Ruburt knows that.

("How about the two people standing up? Can you give us some initials?")

Give us a moment. *(Pause.)* We are having some difficulties with this. We will say that the people are yourselves. There seems to be a connection with fire. Something bright, as in a flame color. Also a connection with some <u>old</u> date. Old—something old, or antique. *(Jane gestured impatiently.)*

("Can you elaborate on the teapot data?")

A teapot or a kettle. Ruburt connects this with your mother's house.

("How about colors connected with the object?")

I have the impression again of copper, but this may simply be connected with the kettle impression. Also blue, and white, and one strong darker color. Perhaps a dark green.

I suggest your break.

(Break at 10:28. Jane was dissociated as usual, and her eyes remained closed throughout both experiments.

(As Seth states in closing, the impressions tonight are legitimate, but too far removed for our purposes. Jane and I saw many glimmerings in the material, but needed more specific data; too many meanings could be attached to many of the impressions. The envelope object was made in our presence; because we were present we feel an emotional rapport with the data which would be lacking for an outsider. A couple of examples will illustrate the nature of the data.

("The word grand... a grandparent?" Our young friend Don Wilbur made the envelope object on his usual Friday night visit here with his wife Marilyn. They have a two-year-old son. On Friday nights the parents of either Marilyn or Don take care of the little boy so Marilyn and Don can have a night a week free. Thus the boy has a grandparent(s) for a sitter.

("A frame." The walls of our living room are hung with my paintings and drawings, some of which are framed. On the object Don had idly noted the item, 17 pictures, after counting them.

("Four plus one." The unscheduled 251st session was held on the Friday evening Don Wilbur produced the envelope object, April 15,1965. Present besides Jane and me were five witnesses—the Wilburs, the Gallaghers, and Ann Diebler.

("...gliddiard." "Lilliard." Jane's first attempt at Lilliard was distorted. The Lilliard trio used to play at the art gallery when Jane worked there a couple of years ago. The connection, Jane believes, while far-out, was an attempt to get at Marilyn studying music. Marilyn and Don had visited the gallery last week.

("A teapot or water kettle." Bill Gallagher, who has ulcers, drinks either coffee or tea on his visits, and he was present on April 15. Don also drinks tea or coffee rather often. Our kettle was in use therefore on the evening of April 15.

("Gold." The envelope object was made on a sheet of Jane's yellow typing paper—the kind called second sheets.

("A looming shape... literal or symbolic... as an unpleasant event could be seen to loom ahead." Don Wilbur was faced with such an event on April 15. He was changing jobs, and had to tell his employer that he was quitting. He did not look forward to it because of a variety of circumstances.

("Small scribbled writing", could refer to my own writing, date and initials at the top of the object.

("...a connection with fire. Something bright, as in a flame color." Jane and I are reasonably sure a candle was burned on the coffee table that evening, Friday, April 15. This because we had been discussing Seth's apparent success in regulating the height of a candle flame on various occasions. These are listed in appropriate sessions. Incense is also burned, usually in a joking manner because we bought some we didn't like. Jane, being a smoker, lights matches often. None of these interpretations may apply however.

("Also blue, and white, and one strong darker color. Perhaps a dark green." This is interesting. The doodles on the object were made with a blue pen. We see no connection with white particularly. There is a strong darker color in a couple of spots on the object, where Don blocked out numbers. Since the obliterations are made with blue on a yellow paper, the effect is on the greenish side, and very dark. However, it may be that it was just difficult for Seth to determine between a darker blue and a dark green. Blue and green both being cool colors and side by side on the color wheel.

(Jane resumed at 10:45.)

Now. We shall shortly end our session.

The impressions were legitimate indeed, but far too distant for your purposes. There is no need to take our time and go through them one by one.

We will answer Ruburt's question as our next session.

(As to why Jane hasn't dreamed of Seth himself, although she has dreamed of the sessions, etc. Seth states he doesn't dream of Jane, either.)

I am sorry I did not get to it this evening. My heartiest regards to you both. Unless you have any particular questions I shall close the session.

("I guess not... Good night, Seth."

(End at 10:48. Jane was dissociated as usual.)

(Tracing of the photo of Jane's father Del [for Delmer] and his deceased second wife, used as the envelope object in the 50th experiment, in the 255th session for May 2,1966.)

SESSION 255
MAY 2, 1966 9 PM MONDAY AS SCHEDULED

(The 50th envelope experiment was held during the session. The object was a black and white photo of Jane's father and his deceased second wife, Maxine, taken sometime prior to 1954. Jane hadn't seen the photo in recent months. I placed it between the usual two pieces of Bristol and sealed it in the double envelopes.

(The session was held in our front room. Jane began speaking while sitting down and with her eyes closed. She was smoking however and her eyes soon began to open often. Her pace was average, her voice quiet.

Good evening.

("Good evening, Seth.")

Now. You were earlier speaking of reincarnation, and Ruburt has just finished reading *The Three Faces of Eve.*

We shall tie these two subjects together. The book should make one point plain: Identity, despite all appearances to the contrary, does not reside primarily in the ego. Social identity may possibly there reside, but the basic identity does not.

The four faces of Eve all represented various ego manifestations of one inner identity. The course of the ego is a precarious one, and any number of potential egos exist within any identity. *The Three Faces of Eve* is an excellent title for the book, since the ego may quite legitimately be compared to the face that the identity turns toward objective reality, or the living mask that it dons.

The authors made several excellent points, without however carrying the main point in any actuality. They conceive of the psychological structure as a gestalt, dominated by the ego, formed by various needs and potentialities. When the dominating ego relaxes its control for any reason or becomes weakened, then according to their concept any one of the subsidiary groups may take over.

They do not know however where identity does reside, and consider it the result merely of organized perceptual patterns. Subsidiary potential egos can then seize upon and use the organism's sensual and perceiving apparatus. They do mention, the authors, that this can sometimes be the result of necessity. The next strongest takes over when the captain is down, so to speak, so that the whole can survive.

But identity is much more than this, and basic identity, while using the perceptive abilities, is not that dependent upon them. It is true that the personality is a gestalt, and that every identity has any number of potential egos. It is also true that on occasion one potential ego will take over from another. But this is all highly simplified, for the ego structure is not one thing, but a changing, never constant, actually quite informal grouping of psychological patterns. Each ego uses and interprets the organism's perceiving apparatus in a way that in the overall is characteristic and distinctive.

This characteristic way of interpreting perceived data, and of reacting to it, is not as constant as it appears to be however. The stability and illusion of permanence is highly misleading. The four manifestations of personality all belonged to one identity, and this is perhaps the main point missed. For if the authors say that oftentimes a subordinate or potential ego will take over control when necessary in order to insure the survival of the whole, then this implies a decision that has been made; and who has made it?

The authors ignore this question. The decision has been made on the part of the basic identity. It is not dependent upon any particular ego structure, but it is dependent upon an ego structure for its existence within a physical universe.

It can therefore, without loss of its basic integrity, change egos when such a change becomes necessary. Now. In some cases this may cause inconvenience and considerable psychological difficulties, but when such an instance occurs it is because the ego structure that is being deposed was not carrying out the main aims or goals of the identity which originally gave it that envied position of dominance.

You may take your break, and we shall continue.

(Break at 9:26. Jane said she was well dissociated for a first delivery. Her pace had picked up and her eyes, very dark, had been open much of the time.

(She resumed in the same manner but with a slightly stronger voice at 9:36.)

While identity and consciousness are regarded as the result of primarily physical processes, then the nature of personality will never be understood.

The inner self is always in the process of trying to perfect the nature of that ego which it has adopted. The ego, as you know, is never the same. It bears indeed the stresses that result from daily encounters with physical situations, but it also reaps the rewards that are involved.

The inner self chooses from its available potential personalities the one that it finds most adequate. Sometimes it simply makes an error, for the inner self is not a perfected thing, any more than the ego is. But identity does exist, and the ego is but a pseudoidentity formed for utilitarian reasons, and as such it is of course a part of the basic identity from which it springs.

It has its own possibilities of development and achievement. This should not be forgotten, and all potential egos have, also, their own possibilities. The inner self or identity must express itself through its ego in order to manipulate within physical reality. The inner self is composed of all the potential egos that compose it, but it is more than the sum of these.

Now these potential egos, you see, made up of various potentials and needs and abilities, these pooled resources that belong to the inner identity, did not simply spring into existence. They are the result of psychological experience gained in past lives.

The personality structure does not make sense unless such past experience is taken into consideration. Potentials do not simply appear, they evolve. I have told you that the most minute portion of energy possesses consciousness and has its own identity. This identity of itself is never annihilated. It may form into new gestalts but the identity is retained.

The energy that composes personality therefore consists of an inconceivable number of separate identities. These separate identities form what we call the inner self, which retains its individuality even while the energy that composes it constantly changes. There are continual groupings and regroupings, but basic identities are always retained. The potential egos within any given identity therefore retain their own individuality and self-knowledge, regardless of their relative importance in the order of command.

These potential egos at one time or another will have their chance, as dominant egos, in this existence or in another reincarnation. They represent the overall potentials of the whole identity in respect to physical existence. The identity has in other words latent abilities which it will not use within the physical system, but all of the latent ability ever available lies within the original identity.

I suggest your break.

(Break at 9:57. Jane was again well dissociated. She said the passage of time seemed like ten minutes at the most. Her eyes had been open much of the time.

(It was now time for the 59th Dr. Instream experiment. Jane sat with her right hand raised to her closed eyes, speaking at a somewhat slower rate, with many short pauses. Resume at 10:08.)

Now, give us a moment please for our Instream material.

A sparkle. Something sparkles. A bracelet or watchband. Bulky rather than small, of a linked variety. A square object on it. Either an ornament or a watch, on a man's arm with dark hair on the arm. The shirtsleeve white, rolled partially up. He wears a vest. He is past middle age and he is talking to Dr. Instream. *(Pause at 10:12.)*

He has an ache in his right arm. He gives a list to Dr. Instream. The list is handwritten, on a white paper that is tinged with blue, that is, bluish-white paper. It has to do with a schedule.

Today Dr. Instream looked at an object in a store window. Something like a camera. The number four in connection with this. The man earlier mentioned also brought an object, I believe for Dr. Instream.

A family situation also. This is a separate impression, involving four people, and a get-together. The object for tonight is small and blue and square-shaped, with perhaps an imprint on it. Also perhaps initials. The imprint is something like a shamrock shape, though not precisely.

Do you have an envelope for me?

("Yes."

(At 10:17 Jane took the envelope from me for the 50th experiment. Her eyes remained closed. Her position did not change; since she sat with her left hand still to her eyes, she laid the envelope in her lap with her right hand.)

Give us a moment, please. These are impressions.

Suitable. A connection with something suitable for an occasion.

A grillwork. A separation. A connection with the color yellow, and a loud sound. Something in rows. Something surprising, as when someone says "This is unheard of."

A circular object that is segmented, and perhaps turns. A connection with a destination in the afternoon, and with three.

Stone steps. An invitation. Some kind of connection with a screen, or with a motion picture screen, or camera screen.

The color green. An image, not clearly seen. A child, and seven.

Do you have any questions?

("What did you mean by something suitable?")

Something suitable in terms of desirable for an occasion.

("Is the something suitable related to the something surprising?")

The two are connected.

("Can you say in what way?")

There is a connection between a suitable reaction to be made toward a particular event.

Also the impression of a string or series. A miscellany of shapes in one corner. An implied border. A note.

A connection with October and April.

("Can you give me the year?")

This year.

("Do you want to say something about the shape of the object itself?")

Rectangular.

("How about colors in connection with it?")

Blue and white.

("The child mentioned earlier: Male or female?")

Male.

("Does the number seven refer to the child's age?")

No it does not. I suggest your break.

(Break at 10:28. Jane was dissociated as usual. Her eyes had remained closed throughout both experiments. She had but one image during the envelope data—of white notepaper with blue lines upon it, and she didn't know whether this came from Seth or herself.

(Note that I was able to ask eight questions. This exceeds by several the last high of five in the 254th session.

(As is usually the case when we do not personally know a lot of intimate details connected with the envelope object, Jane and I found ourselves unable to check all of Seth's data. We think of these occasions as being like those where strangers would furnish the object. We could make quite a few connections however, and Seth helps out a little.

(Briefly, the object is a black-and-white photo of Jane's father Del, and his deceased second wife Maxine. Del was about 48 when the picture was taken in the backyard of their home in Santa Monica, California, and Maxine was 38 or 39. Within six months Maxine was dead from cancer. Her death took place in California just at the time I met Jane in Saratoga Springs, NY, in 1954 in January. Jane hadn't seen Maxine for a couple of years and I had never met her.

("Suitable. A connection with something suitable for an occasion." In the photo Maxine is dressed up, including white hat and gloves, and wears a large corsage on the left lapel of her dark-colored suit. The corsage could be something suitable for an occasion. There could also be a play on words here, in that Maxine is wearing one of the old-fashioned square-shouldered two-piece suits in style then: Suitable, suit. Seth elaborates a little in answer to a question.

("A grillwork." In plain view in the photo are picket fences to the right and left of Maxine and Del, plus two large curving trellises bare of flowers or greenery. One of the trellises is in back of the couple. See the tracing on page 124.

("A separation." Jane and I both thought of Maxine's unexpected death while in her late thirties.

("A connection with the color yellow, and a loud sound." We see none and Seth did not elaborate.

("Something in rows." The uprights in the two picket fences.

("Something surprising, as when someone says 'This is unheard of'." Jane said this referred to Maxine's untimely death.

("A circular object that is segmented, and perhaps turns." One of the trellises in the photo is plainly seen on the couples' right. Its construction is segmented, its outside shape made up of curves. In addition the curve of this trellis flows into the curve or arch of the trellis behind Del and Maxine. We think Seth's perception of these curving lines led to the mention of "perhaps turns."

("A connection with a destination in the afternoon, and with three." We do not know.

("Stone steps." Although it does not show in the photo itself, just beyond the photo would be the back steps of the couples' house in Santa Monica. These are either stone or concrete; Jane and I cannot be sure, not having been there for perhaps eight or nine years. At the time the picture was taken there was a small guest house, California style, in back of the main house; here Jane recalls a flagstone walk. This little house was torn down before my first visit to Santa Monica. A flight of four or five steps, stone or concrete, led up to the back porch of the main house.

("An invitation." We do not know.

("Some kind of connection with a screen, or with a motion picture screen, or camera screen." The object was a photograph. These related references could be the

attempts of Seth/Jane to get at the idea of the picture.

("The color green." In the photo Del and Maxine stand surrounded by trees and bushes of various kinds and size, flowers, etc.

("An image, not clearly seen." To the left of Del and Maxine in the photo can be seen the window of a building a lot or two distant. Only part of a window and a wall can be glimpsed through nearby trees. I have indicated the window heavily on the tracing on page 124. The outlines of the building, etc., are hidden.

("A child, and seven." I wasn't sure these two impressions were connected, although Jane gave them together. I tried to clear up the child and number reference later in the questions.

(My first two questions asked for elaboration on "something suitable" and "something surprising." Seth agreed they were connected. Our interpretation connects them through Maxine; something suitable being Maxine's corsage, something surprising being her early death.

(Seth came through with a little more data after the second question:

("Also the impression of a string or series. A miscellany of shapes in one corner." Apparently the picket fence, seen in two places on the photo—to their right and in back of Del and Maxine, and their left foreground. In the photo the tree branches in their left background form an interesting pattern also, with the building mentioned at the top of this page seen behind them; usually when Jane uses the word miscellany to denote irregular shapes the data is too general.

("An implied border." The photo has a white border. It is clearly denoted on the sides and bottom through the contrasting darks of the foliage. It is invisible at the photo's top, the sky merging into the white paper. I have ruled in the border on the tracing on page 124; actually it cannot be seen.

("A note." The object is not a note, and we see no particular connection with a note.

("A connection with October and April." We saw no particular connection. Del's birthday for instance is in December; we do not know the month of Maxine's birthday. My next question asked Seth for the year these months pertained to. When he said "This year." it didn't help us.

("Rectangular." In answer to my next question, concerning the shape of the object. The photo is rectangular.

("Blue and white." Here I asked for colors in connection with the object. Jane said this is when she had the mental image of white notepaper with blue lines on it. She didn't know whether this image came from Seth or herself.

("Male." Seth here gives the sex of the child mentioned on page 128. I had wondered if it was a reference to Jane herself. During break Jane said she believed it referred to a brother of Maxine's. The brother is the same approximate age as Jane,

and lived in upstate New York near Saratoga; hence Jane got to know the members of Maxine's family fairly well even though she seldom saw Maxine herself. Jane said she liked the brother quite well; he is the member of Maxine's family who made an impression on her.

("No it does not." My last question concerned the number seven as possibly referring to the age of the child. With this possibility eliminated Jane and I saw no other connection.

(Jane resumed with her eyes closed at 10:48.)

Now. We shall shortly close our session.

The unheard-of event did refer to a surprising event, of the woman's death. The photograph was taken on the woman's birthday, and the corsage was a surprise.

The boy referred to the only member of the woman's family that made an impression on Ruburt. These are the main points. The woman's suit was dark blue.

My heartiest regards to you both. I will give you some personal reincarnational material very shortly. We simply did not have time for it tonight.

("Good night, Seth."

(End at 10:51.)

Mrs. Berry's Top Interest: People

By PEGGY GALLAGHER

Mrs. Bessie Berry is concerned about people — particularly children.

This is why, after losing an Elmira school board election last year by about 400 votes she decided to make one last try, which won her a seat on the board by a large margin.

"Children and education are my two main concerns," said Mrs. Berry this morning in her office at the County Welfare Department.

The 34-year-old Mrs. Berry is a protective caseworker in the Child Welfare Division of the department, a position she has held for five years.

Her interest in education began when she started working in the Welfare Department.

• • •

"I ran into so many children whose problems seemed to center in education," she said. "So many of them have problems in school and problems at home at the same time."

Mrs. Berry learned of her victory soon after the polls closed at 9 p.m.

"I didn't believe it," said the slim, attractive caseworker. "I had decided against running because it was such a physical strain the last time. But I felt I should lose at least a second time before giving up."

She credits her friends, and the knowledge that she gained in last year's campaign, with her success this time.

"This time I knew what I wanted," she said.

Posters were distributed and a limited mail campaign to about 6,200 homes in the Eastside, Southside and Northside "paid off," she feels. Friends also helped by volunteering to take voters to the polls.

Mrs. Berry plans to spend the time before she assumes office July 1 in learning more about the work of the board.

"I plan on listening and learning and discussing various problems. I feel that I'm capable of intelligently evaluating a situation and I plan on voicing my own opinion," Mrs. Berry said.

• • •

"In accepting the position, I am saying I will represent the whole school district and I mean it. I'm not thinking in just one direction. But I'm going to make sure that everyone is protected and everyone is considered."

Based on personal observation, she has become concerned about "the obvious lack of interest some teachers have for some children."

"I'm not saying that they're not doing their jobs, nor that the schools aren't well run — I know that certain children present problems—but there are some children who just need a little more interest and a little extra help," she said.

Lack of interest on the part of parents is another concern. "If the parents don't care, there is little a teacher can do."

She will be particularly concerned to see that "all of the children being educated have the best teachers in all of the schools."

"There is some feeling that this board is represented by people of the highest level of living . . . the people who have never personally experienced problems. I'm sure they're concerned about them but I wonder if it's their main concern."

• • •

Mrs. Berry is not the first woman on the board. Serving with her will be Mrs. Boyd Spotts.

But she is the first Negro on the board.

"Being a first doesn't faze me at all," she said. "I suppose I was the first in Child Welfare. I don't think of it one way or another."

WEDNESDAY, MAY 4/66

(Reduced copy of the article by Peggy Gallagher, used as the object in the 51st envelope experiment in the 256th session for May 4, 1966.)

SESSION 256
MAY 4, 1966 9 PM WEDNESDAY AS SCHEDULED

(The 51st envelope experiment was held during the session. The object was placed as usual between two pieces of Bristol and sealed in double envelopes. It was a newspaper article by Peggy Gallagher, published in the Elmira Star-Gazette and Advertiser on May 4,1966; today. The photo of Mrs. Bessie Berry was not included in the test envelopes. It appeared on the same page of the newspaper, just above the center column of the object itself, but was attched to another article about Mrs. Berry.

(The session was held in the front room. Jane began speaking while sitting down and with her eyes closed, at a rather slow pace and with pauses, at 9:02 PM.)

Good evening.

("Good evening, Seth.")

We shall continue the discussion begun in our last session.

The overall efficiency of the inner self, or prime identity, is best displayed of course when it adopts an ego that mirrors its own characteristics and intents as closely as possible. There is bound to be a difference however, between the purposes of the inner identity and the ego.

Now, the ego, the dominant ego, does indeed affect the inner identity, and changes it even as it affects and changes the dominant ego. For we are dealing here after all with an interdependent gestalt. The interworkings of the whole gestalt have never been completely understood.

For one thing the self is usually thought of in terms of existence only within one particular time sequence pattern. Its experience however is rooted in the past, as <u>you</u> think of the past. Since there is actually only a spacious present this means that the self is rooted both in the past and in the future, using your terms.

Until it is studied as a multidimensional gestalt, it simply will not be understood.

Reincarnation does not imply a recurring time system, nor does it imply an extension of time as it is normally considered. That is, reincarnation does not imply in a basic manner existence in one life after another, in your time of successive moments.

I admit to you reincarnation does seem to have such implications. This is simply because you insist upon <u>considering</u> reincarnation in the light of time theories that are themselves incorrect. You must instead consider reincarnation in the light of what you know of the spacious present.

Because you are obsessed with the idea of time as past, present and future, you are forced to think of reincarnations as strung out one before the other, and indeed we speak of past lives simply because you are used to the time sequence concept. What you have of course, loosely speaking, is something like the developments narrated in *The Three Faces of Eve.* You have various dominant egos, all part of an inner identity, dominant in various existences. To make the concept understandable to you it is convenient to speak of past and future reincarnations.

In actuality you see, these separate existences occur simultaneously. It is only the ego who makes the time distinction. The various existences are not perceivable by you, or rather they are not perceivable to the ego. In a basic manner, as you know, the past, present and future exist at once in the spacious present.

A hundred and forty-five B.C., a hundred and forty-five A.D., a thousand years in your past and a thousand years in your present—all exist now. Therefore the past existences are present existences. You exist in other words in several guises or reincarnations, at one time within the spacious present. You simply do not recognize that the so-called past exists now as surely as the so-called future exists now.

I suggest your break.

(Break at 9:23. Jane was dissociated as usual. Her pace had picked up considerably and her eyes then began to open fairly often. She was smoking when she resumed in the same manner at 9:31.)

Since all events occur at once, there is little to be gained by saying that a past event causes a present event.

Past experience does not <u>cause</u> present experience. You are forming both past, present and future experience simultaneously. Events appear to you however in sequence, therefore it is difficult to explain many matters to you, because they must be given in bits and pieces.

When it is said that certain characteristics from a past life influence or cause present patterns of behavior, such statements, and I have made some of them, are grossly simplified simply to make certain points clear.

The whole self or identity is aware of the experiences of all the egos, and since one identity forms these egos there is bound to be some similarities between them, and characteristics. The material that I have given you on reincarnation in the past is quite valid, particularly for working purposes, but it is a highly simplified version of what actually occurs.

If you take *The Three Faces of Eve*, in which actually four egos were involved, and imagine each of these egos taking over, so to speak, in completely separate existences, in your past, present and future, then you may come somewhat closer to the true nature of reincarnation.

These four personalities existed however in one physical lifetime. Now to an observer whose time concept was still further segmented, and slowed down in comparison to your own, then theoretically within his time system the four personalities would indeed appear to be four separate existences in fact. In the same manner, you see, several manifestations of one identity appear to you to be stretched out in serial form within a successive time framework.

Obviously however this analogy only carries us so far. You will say, "The four egos belonging to Eve all belonged to one physical body, but in the reincarnational process we are faced with the issue of several bodies, each one discarded and experiencing physical death."

Now, I will tell you the nearly unbelievable. There was not one shared body in the case of the four Eves. There were four separate bodies.

After the first shock this should come as no surprise. As you know, the physical body is itself never the same, and the atoms that compose it appear and disappear constantly while the appearance of permanency is retained. Such a process, and a natural one, took place in the case of Eve.

But as the personalities alternated they took over the organic processes so completely that while the body appeared, generally speaking, to be the same, it was not the same.

It should be remembered here that two personalities were allergic to nylon and two were not. Obviously two personalities made such changes in the physical organism that the allergy was brought on. The organism was physically changed and affected. Even though one personality took over for an hour, still for that hour the physical organism itself was a different one.

It is interesting to note also that these personalities did alternate, and all were in existence at once, so to speak, even though only one was dominant at a given time. In the same way all so-called past personalities are present in your now, but not dominant. Obviously also any future reincarnations are present for those who have other lives still to live in your terms.

There is simply the simultaneous expression of a prime identity or inner self within the physical system. There are as you know other systems.

I suggest your break.

(Break at 9:56. Jane was dissociated as usual. Her pace had become fast, her eyes had opened often and she had sipped wine and smoked.

(During break I wondered aloud if there was much similarity between the various manifestations of the Eve egos, and the relationship between Jane and Seth, particularly when Seth was temporarily dominant.

(It was now time for the 60th Dr. Instream experiment. Jane spoke at only a slightly slower pace as she sat with her right hand to her closed eyes. Resume at 10:04.)

Now give us a moment, please, for our Instream material.

A connection with a death. Whether this is recent, or whether he is thinking of a dead friend I do not know. The death involved the feeling of strangulation. Not that someone was strangled, but the sensations were of strangling.

The number 23 in connection with this. Perhaps the person, a man, died at 23, or 23 years ago, but the number 23 is somehow connected. Also connected with the man is the initial J, though I do not know if this is the man's initial. Perhaps the month of February also here, and cold damp weather. Or a damp climate, perhaps in another country. Maybe England, but someplace cold and foggy.

Now I have the impression of a book, with three lines in the title, the first line being the longest. I also have the impression of a buckle of some kind, and a blotter.

The object for tonight is some kind of ring, or perhaps two rings intertwined. Not the type of ring worn on a finger, but larger. Perhaps the size of very large ring earrings, though the object is not an earring. Two rings are connected in some way. I do not believe that the rings themselves are larger than a pencil—thicker, that is, but the circles inside are large. Nor do I know their purpose. I believe they belong to another object and have been removed.

I believe also that there will be a surprising invitation made to Dr. Instream this week. He will receive an invitation which is unexpected and also surprising.

Do you have an envelope for me?

("Yes."

(Jane paused at 10:14. Without opening her eyes she took the envelope for our 51st experiment from me and pressed it to her forehead.)

Give us a moment please. These are impressions.

Quick. Something quick. A square object, with something like a symbol on it, some markings. A four plus two.

Also a circular object, something transparent. This is Ruburt's connection now: An impression of forgiveness; that is his impression. *(Long pause.)*

A connection with Sep, as in September, or the number designated by that month. A picture of a woman. A connection with an antidote. A red and yellow circular object connected here.

A connection with a shaded street. At least, shapes that appear in this manner. Someone or something tall. Connections with a J and a G, and feet or socks.

Ten. A cross shape, or something canceled, or wiped out or done. It would seem to be of a dark color. This could signify a death connection but I do not know.

Something in the center like a target.

I suggest your break. Unless of course you have questions.

("Can you say something about the picture of a woman?")

Only what I have said. Picture in terms of a photograph connection.

("How about the shape of the object?")

Fairly small. Dark colors and white. Perhaps writing on the back. A distant connection—distant, now, with the year 1947, with the photograph of the woman. There are also others, or at least one more. There seems to be dark fluid colors that give the suggestion of water.

I suggest your break now.

(Break at 9:24. Jane was well dissociated, she said—not aware of outside sounds, etc. Her eyes had remained closed through both experiments and her pace had been good.

(Jane had of course seen the article used as object in this evening's paper. We had discussed it at supper, and also noted that Peggy Gallagher had written it. As stated the photo of Mrs. Berry was not used in the experimental envelope. This photo was included in another article; the photo was centered above the middle column of the object. At the time I prepared the envelopes I thought of including the photo with Peggy's article, but decided against it at the last minute.

(Once again we could not expect to know enough details about the envelope object to make all the connections. We made those we could, but did not ask Seth to clear up any after break. Instead I requested that he say something about the question I had raised during second break.

("Quick. Something quick." Jane associated the word quick here with the fact that Mrs. Berry is the first Negro on the local school board; quick meaning first. In the last paragraph of the object-article Mrs. Berry also talks about being the first Negro to work in child welfare in Elmira.

("A square object, with something like a symbol on it, some markings." Jane said that while giving this data she had a mental image of a box shape. It was multi-dimensional rather than flat, and she could tell there were symbols or markings on it. But we could make no connections.

("A four plus two." In pencil I wrote the day and date in the right-hand margin of the object: Wednesday, May 4,1966. The four can refer to May 4, the four plus two to 6.

("Also a circular object, something transparent." We made no connections.

("...Ruburt's connection now: An impression of forgiveness..." We believe this refers to the recent death of a priest whom Jane knew as a child. Jane received a photograph of him in the mail the other day.

("A connection with sep, as in September, or the number designated by that

month." The number is 9. Near the bottom of the first column in her story Peggy writes that Mrs. Berry learned of her election victory soon after the polls closed at 9 PM. The election was also nine hours long; this is mentioned specifically in the other article about Mrs. Berry, printed just above the article used as object.

("A picture of a woman." As stated a photo of Mrs. Berry was included in the other article about her, printed just above Peggy Gallagher's story. I had considered enclosing the photo in the envelopes with the article but decided not to at the last moment. See the session's opening notes.

(On the back of the object itself can be seen portions of two drawings of women also, in an advertisement. We believe however that Seth referred to the photo rather than the drawings, because of his answer to my first question.

("A connection with an antidote." The idea of antidote or change is expressed in the article through Mrs. Berry's quotes and Peggy's comments; particularly in the last half.

("A connection with a shaded street. At least, shapes that appear in this manner." We saw no connections.

("Someone or something tall." Jane and I haven't met Mrs. Berry and do not know if she is tall. The headline on the envelope object contains the word top. Jane may have associated top with tall, as she did quick with first in the opening impression.

("Connections with a J and a G, and feet or socks." Jane can quality for the J, being a friend of the author of the object. Peggy Gallagher can match the G. Another possibility here is the very large calligraphic G on the back of the object, in the center.

("Ten." We saw no connections. Nor with feet or socks, above.

("A cross shape, or something canceled, or wiped out or done. it would seem to be of a dark color. This could signify a death connection but I do not know." We think this also refers to the death of the priest whom Jane knew in her childhood. The photo of him that Jane received in the mail the other day is actually a halftone reproduction bearing the priest's portrait and a heavy black border all around. It is a black and white photo. On the back are two crosses in black, one fairly large, plus a prayer and a quotation from St. Alphonsus.

(Note that in the Dr. Instream data on page 136 mention is made of a death, and the initial J in connection with this.

("A red and yellow circular object connected here." This data was given after the antidote data listed at the top of this page. Jane and I saw no connections.

("Only what I have said. picture in terms of a photograph connection." Seth answered thus to my first question. I sought elaboration on the picture of a woman data interpreted on page 138. Here Seth connects the picture with photograph. This

eliminates the drawings of two women on back of the envelope object, and we think refers to the photo of Mrs. Berry already described.

("Fairly small. Dark colors and white. Perhaps writing on the back." This came through in answer to my second question, concerning the shape of the object. The data can fit either the envelope object itself, or the picture of the dead priest referred to above under "cross shape," etc. I am inclined to think it refers to the latter. The envelope object was folded three times so that it measured about 4 3/4" x 3". Even with this the photo of the priest measures 3 3/4" x 2 1/2", or still smaller. Neither the object or the priest's picture have writing on the back, but both contain printed type. The problem of semantics here, involving printing, writing and lettering, has arisen before.

("A distant connection—distant, now, with the year 1947, with the photograph of the woman." Not knowing much about Mrs. Berry, we could make no connection here.

("There are also others, or at least one more." At the risk of repetition: There were two articles concerning Mrs. Berry in the paper. One was by Peggy Gallagher and this is the one used as envelope object. Just above Peggy's article the other article was printed. This second one included the photo of Mrs. Berry. The second article also included another photo—this one of a man who was also elected with Mrs. Berry. The two photos ran side by side.

("There seems to be dark fluid colors that give the suggestion of water." Too general. The large calligraphic G on the back of the object is executed in a fluid manner, and this may have given rise to this impression. The object is printed in black, which of course is a dark color. Seth's use of the word color may refer to something other than black.

(Toward the end of this data, Jane said now at break, she arrived at the idea of a relative of hers who lives in New York City being featured in the photograph of a woman data. However she felt this was incorrect; she could feel Seth leading her away from the idea of this relative, and her name, so she did not give voice to it.

(During second break I had wondered if there was much similarity between the various manifestations of the Eve egos, and the relationship between Jane and Seth, when Seth was temporarily dominant. I now asked Jane if Seth might not talk about this, rather than deal with our interpretations of the envelope data. Jane resumed at a good pace, smoking, her eyes opening often, at 10:51.)

Now. I exist simultaneously with the both of you.

This should be obvious, or I would not be speaking with you; obviously therefore I also exist, speaking in your terms, as I am <u>now</u> and as I was. In my terms you see I simply exist in the <u>now</u>.

There is communication between these various aspects of inner identity that are obviously cooperative. As a rule I make no attempt to take over the mechanism that Ruburt operates in any general manner.

He allows me to make some adjustments in it however, and we shall discuss these in detail before too long. Now. One of the egos that was mine, you see, is a part of Ruburt's whole personality, and we use this as a bridgework. I can use it momentarily.

Again, this does not mean that I am a secondary personality. Reincarnation does mean that we are all multiple personalities with an underlying prime identity. I am myself, Ruburt is himself. Or if you prefer, Jane is herself. *(Smile.)*

You forget, you see, that you have also been, and are, part of this identity, Joseph. In your particular cases now you have branched out to form prime identities of your own, though we were originally part of the same.

Now. I am the prime identity that you were part of. And I was myself at one time, so to speak, a part of another prime identity. This development does not always occur, for many reasons. Some fragments of an identity simply do not wish to so develop. In the spacious present you see we are one, yet entirely individual.

Now we may possibly develop into a newer gestalt, for I cannot see all portions—underline all portions—of the spacious present. There are still veils before my eyes. This is a part of the present I do not perceive. If so, it will be one in which identities are completely retained, and there is no question of a dominancy, but of a smooth-working organization.

In the time framework within which you now exist I can help you, but you cannot help me except by allowing me to help you, you see. In the gestalt which could develop we would be in a position of helping each other more equally. Now through you I affect physical reality, and this is indeed one of my purposes.

I affect reality, physical reality, because men's minds are changed according to their ideas, and we shall change these ideas for the better. The ideas, working through men, will affect physical reality for the better. I am here more often than you think. Never, however, in a prying manner.

Now, I am quite willing to continue our session, and so is Ruburt. The hour grows late however, and you had better make a decision on this before I become too involved here.

("Can you speak for another ten minutes or so?")

I can indeed.

The relationship between you and Ruburt was necessary before our sessions could begin. Your own illness, immediately before our sessions, was unfortunately necessary, in that it made you question the nature of your mental reactions toward physical and psychological events.

I helped you then, before you knew me. You were quite literally waiting for Ruburt, and this is why you did not marry earlier. The connections between you, and your development from the same prime identity, made your union an excellent one. There is a constant maintenance of identity, and a search for stability, psychologically speaking. But then identity, sure of itself, seeks to enlarge its experience for it is no longer afraid that experience will swallow it.

Identity always becomes part of that which it perceives, however, and so it constantly forms new gestalts, while accepting as itself a larger variety of experiences. Therefore identity grows, and as I have told you there are no limitations to it. Therefore we are forming new identities, and you have already accepted as part of yourself experiences which previously would have been considered alien, and not accepted.

You change because of any experience. You have, then, changed because of this one. You have become more than you were. I am speaking here to you both. I am not taking you over, so to speak. You are accepting as a part of your whole experience more and more of the reality of what I am. This in no way minimizes me, you see. I make much of my knowledge available to you, but it is still my knowledge, you see. The sharing of it however enlarges my own experience. Now then, I will let you rest. You may take a break or end the session as you prefer.

("Well, it's very interesting but we'll have to end it.")

My heartiest good wishes to you both.

("Good night, Seth."

(End at 11:17. Jane was again well dissociated.)

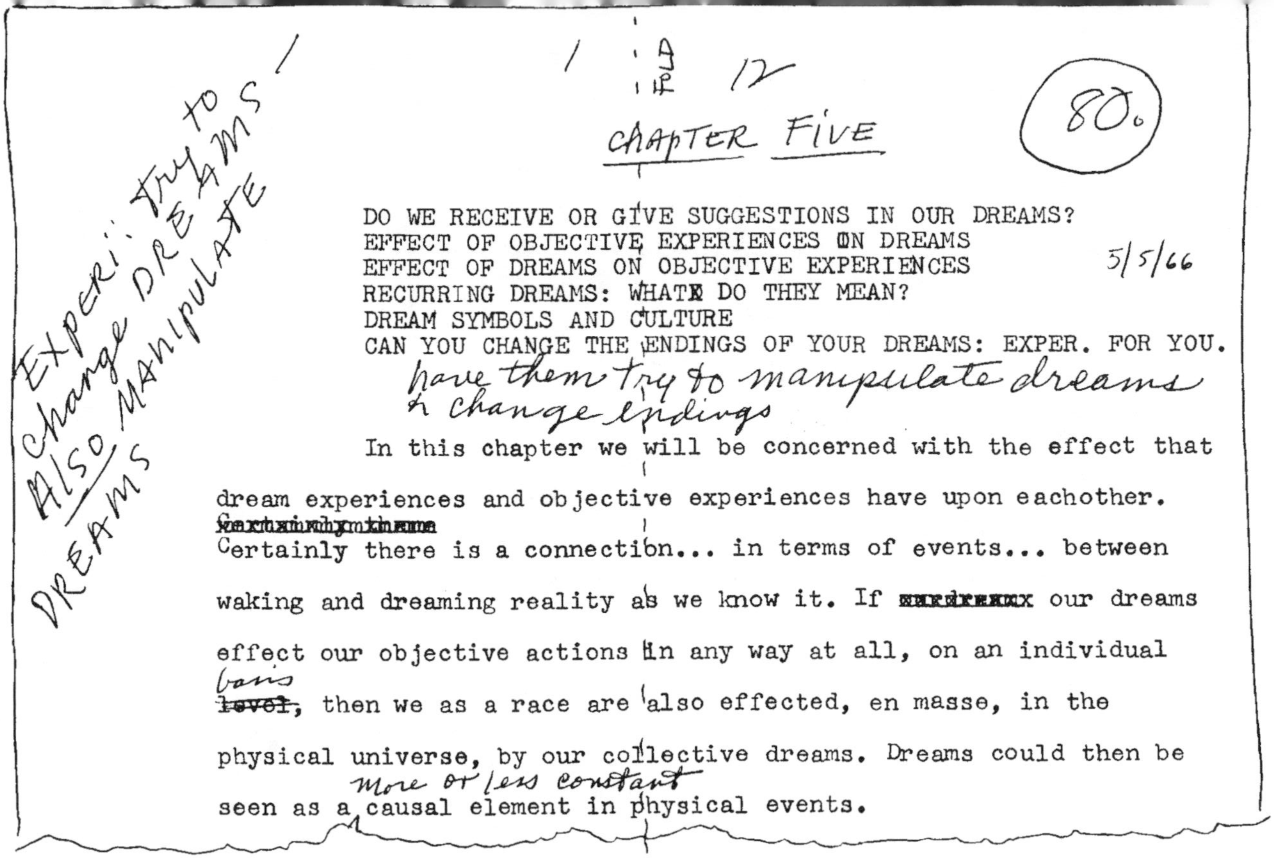

1 FLD 12

CHAPTER FIVE

80.

DO WE RECEIVE OR GIVE SUGGESTIONS IN OUR DREAMS?
EFFECT OF OBJECTIVE EXPERIENCES ON DREAMS
EFFECT OF DREAMS ON OBJECTIVE EXPERIENCES 5/5/66
RECURRING DREAMS: WHAT DO THEY MEAN?
DREAM SYMBOLS AND CULTURE
CAN YOU CHANGE THE ENDINGS OF YOUR DREAMS: EXPER. FOR YOU.
have them try to manipulate dreams & change endings

EXPERI: try to change DREAMS / ALSO MANIPULATE DREAMS

In this chapter we will be concerned with the effect that dream experiences and objective experiences have upon eachother. ~~Certainly there~~ Certainly there is a connection... in terms of events... between waking and dreaming reality as we know it. If ~~xxxxxxxx~~ our dreams effect our objective actions in any way at all, on an individual ~~level~~ basis, then we as a race are also effected, en masse, in the physical universe, by our collective dreams. Dreams could then be seen as a more or less constant causal element in physical events.

(Reduced copy of the manuscript page from Jane's book on dreams, used as the envelope object in the 52nd experiment, in the 257th session for May 9,1966.)

SESSION 257
MAY 9, 1966 9 PM MONDAY AS SCHEDULED

(The 52nd envelope experiment was held. The object was a page of manuscript from Jane's dream book. She had thrown it away on May 5; unknown to her I fished it out of the wastebasket. It is typed on yellow paper and bears her penned notations. The back of it is blank. I used the two pieces of Bristol board and the two envelopes as usual in preparing it for the experiment.

(In the 253rd session Seth told us he didn't dream of us, just as we didn't dream of him, and promised to tell us why soon. Before tonight's session Jane said she hoped he hadn't forgotten to go into the matter.

(The session was held in the front room. Jane spoke while sitting down and with her eyes closed. For much of the time she held a hand to her face, her head down. Her voice was quiet and she paused frequently.)

Good evening.

("Good evening, Seth.")

Now. The basis of all life and of all existence can be loosely termed intuitional. Obviously the intellect is not necessary for life.

All existence is present, as you know. What you term past incarnations take place in the present. You simply invented a continual time system as a vehicle of perception for the ego, and it operates at that level only.

This session will be a relatively informal one, and not as long as our last session.

Now. I do not dream of Ruburt because I do not dream at all, in the same terms that you do. I switch the focus of my attention with conscious intent, so to speak. I take all portions of myself into any particular state of consciousness, and I enter various states of consciousness somewhat in the same manner that you can move from one physical country to another.

I visit you therefore, but I do not dream of you in the way that you might think. Now Ruburt has not, in his imagination, given me a particular physical image, and dreaming at your level involves visual images. So he does not dream of me in that way.

He does contact me however without his conscious knowledge in his dreams on some occasions. We simply speak to each other, but he does not remember what has been said consciously. Of course on other levels he is aware of these communications.

You have also communicated with me in this manner, Joseph, for your edification. You may if you wish suggest that you will remember some of these conversations, and then you may be able to do so, to some degree. *(Long pause, eyes closed.)*

I have a few interesting but minor remarks to make.

Your brother's wife was a baker's daughter, and still has the habit of overindulging in food.

Your mother, realizing too well that her little boys are grown, now you see seeks to maintain her motherhood by asking help from them, since they no longer need it from her. Now, this asking for help represents a need for reassurance that she has indeed been a good parent, and that her sons still hold her in high esteem.

For each time when they come to her aid she says to herself, "If they did not love me they would not help me." At the same time however this help is held up to the father, for it is the mother who asks for the assistance, and the assistance is always in some way held up against the father. This is also a type of revenge, however, for the mother is now in a stronger position, after having been kept in an inferior one for nearly a lifetime.

Your course is a wise one. I foresee some family difficulty in your younger brother's situation. Not in his immediate family but in his wife's family. Perhaps a connection with the new house—its inhabitants, or with those closely connected with it.

You personally, Joseph, are indeed a different person than you were three years ago. Aspects of your personality that you had in a large measure denied, have been allowed to develop.

Now. In regard to the Boston existence, we will try to add a few details. Tonight I am attempting to answer some questions, and give you some reincarnational material in which you are interested. We will do this in our own way. Oftentimes a few sentences of seemingly unrelated material will later be found to be pertinent. On other occasions the unrelated material simply allows me to slyly insert specific information without alarming Ruburt.

(Jane's eyes now opened for the first time. According to Seth both of us lived in Boston before the Civil War, male and female then, as now.)

In connection with Boston, there was a street, I believe called Grant, or there was a building called the Grant Building or residence, which was used in connection with a church. Perhaps as living quarters of the minister.

It is not there now, but perhaps records could prove its existence. You had some difficulty with a left eye. Ruburt is concerned lest this is distorted, because of Miss Callahan's bad eye, but the information is quite legitimate. *(Miss Callahan is an elderly spinster living in our apartment house. See Volume 1.)*

The address itself had two fives in the number. There is a connection with a 1632 date that I do not understand. Perhaps we can clear it up later. *(Long pause.)* A Gaylor family was connected with the church. Rich members I believe, and they were buried nearby. A Sarah and an Oscar.

You may take your break, and we shall continue.

(Break at 9:28. Jane was dissociated as usual. Her pace had been average to begin the session but it had slowed a great deal when she reached the reincarnation data. Her eyes opened just twice, briefly, during the delivery. Most of the time she sat with a hand up to her face.

(She resumed in the same manner at 9:36.)

Write down the word note. It is connected, the word, with Ruburt's name in that existence, and we shall return to it.

Also Grinaldi—

("Grinaldi?" I spelled it out.)

G-r-a-n-o-l-d-y. A connection with St. Ambrose, and the church. *(Long pause.)* Church records kept in a vault in the basement. *(Long pause.)* Later, much later, a track of some kind was built very near by the church property. For a while in later years, the house where you lived had front rooms converted into a barber shop. Perhaps from 1870 to 1890.

Later still, a dress shop, and then a restaurant, as the neighborhood deteriorated. Then, all new buildings. You were portly. The church was near the water, and it was visited on occasion by sailors. *(Many pauses, some of them long. Jane's eyes were closed and she was very restless.)*

Before this it was more elegant, and when it was the ships came in further to the north to dock. As shipping increased the docks moved southward to take in the area near the church.

Give us a moment. *(Long pause. Jane kicked her shoes off.)*

A hill behind the church. Not high, but containing several streets. A lighthouse to the northwest. Several small villages which later became part of Boston, one to the northwest and one to the southwest, separated at this time, approximately 1830, by fields.

There was another town directly west, or an area whose name began with an A, and it was more distant than the other two settlements. You moved here, and then moved back to Boston.

You did not act as a minister in the other location, but worked with lumber. When you returned to Boston you became minister of a church in the same denomination but in a different building. The other, or later location, was a socially better one by contrast, but you did not move in the best circles by any means. The northern area of the city was the most elite.

The word I wanted in connection with Ruburt's name was not note. It was Nostra, N-o-s-t-r-a. This was part of her name: Nostratious was the first name. Elmo—

("Elmo?")

—Elmo was the last name, and there was a professional name that was used also.

I suggest a brief break, and we shall continue.

(Break at 9:58. Jane was dissociated as usual. Her eyes remained closed and her pace was slow. She was aware that she was very restless. Jane said that during one of the longer pauses she felt Seth trying to get at the name Nostratious from the earlier note data. We thought Nostratious Elmo a most peculiar name. In an earlier session Seth told us Jane had been a medium in her Boston life, and that she had misused her abilities. This could account for the mention of a professional name above however. See page 86 in Volume 1.

(It was now time for the 61st Dr. Instream experiment. Jane's pace was once again broken by short pauses as she sat with a hand raised to her closed eyes. Resume at 10:09.)

Now, give us a moment, please, for our Instream material.

A <u>turnabout</u>, or change of plans connected with Dr. Instream. A switching of dates for a definite occasion. This may be connected with a summer event. We will give an object shortly.

A letter concerning a distasteful situation. The letter to or from another man, perhaps in his late fifties, and in another area of the country. Dr. Instream either wrote the letter or received it.

The connection between the two men reaches some decades into the past. Perhaps an initial M or N here. Eyeglasses and some sort of mustache.

The object is like a chain. A slim one of silver color. It is kept in a box that also contains several notes and photographs. Either that, or the box itself is kept next to the notes and photographs. It is worn by a woman.

Right now Dr. Instream has several choices of action available. I mean in this general period of time, not this instant. He is in a period in which he is trying to make decisions of a major nature, concerning the future and his own circumstances.

He has been offered several opportunities or choices. It is not a matter of <u>too few</u> choices, but almost of too many.

Separately now, a connection with the initials P, G, or P, C, and an overdrawn account. Two packages which are not delivered on time. Dr. Instream does not hold the chain which is our object, but watches the woman who wears it.

Do you have an envelope for me?

("Yes."

(Jane paused at 10:18. Without opening her eyes she took the envelope for our

52nd experiment from me. She held it to her forehead briefly then lowered it to her lap; she resumed her earlier position, her head lowered to one hand.)

Give us a moment, please... These are impressions.

A framework, that seems to be wooden, with thin lines like poles. Anemia.

Eight. The connection with anemia leads Ruburt to think of Helga Anderson, or a connection with artists or artwork.

A note. The month of April. An initiation, not completed. The color purple, and perhaps yellow connected here. Connection with an animal. Something disturbed.

The words unholy alliance come to me here. A selection, or something offered from which selections may be made. A star shape. Something round, again, with spokes leading outward, but rather prominent. For us.

A connection with markings and dates, and a connection with a horse perhaps. Some connection here, but distant. Squares. Perhaps a game connection. A small round circle suggesting a postmark. Red or blue.

A connection with a high ledge shape, as one connected with a roof, or lookout from which one can look down and away.

Connection with four people, one of them disheveled, comparatively speaking. Fourteen, and I suggest your break. *(Pause.)*

Unless you have questions.

("Well—")

Also a small screen.

("Can you say something more about an initiation not completed?")

Something not done, but begun. I suggest your break, then.

(Break at 10:29. Jane said she was well dissociated. Her eyes had remained closed through both experiments. I had the feeling that she hadn't wanted me to ask questions, particularly. When I hesitated she called for break.

(Actually this marked the end of the session, but Jane didn't say so until we had gone through the data ourselves. We made our own connections and did not ask Seth to return to help out.

(We were able to make many connections. Also, the same object was used in the next session, the 258th, and it is interesting to see how Seth picks up some of the same points both times. These points of agreement will be noted in the 258th session.

(See the copy of the envelope object on page 142. As stated it is the top half of the first page of chapter five of the book on dreams that Jane is writing. This was the first draft. Jane had thrown it away and I rescued it from the wastebasket in my studio. It is written on yellow paper; the notations were made by a pen with the same color ink as those on the copy. I wrote the date in pencil on the object the day I found it. It was folded once before going into the sealed double envelope. The back side of

the object is blank.

("A framework, that seems to be wooden, with thin lines like poles." We believe this data is reinforced by the "high ledge shape" data given later, and that it refers to my studio, wherein the page of manuscript used as object was written. Jane uses the studio in the mornings while I am working outside. Her desk faces a row of five windows, tall and narrow, and with small panes. The studio is actually a glass-enclosed back porch, second story, converted to year-round use.

(As she sits at her desk Jane looks out and down to the grass of the backyard below. The view is high and quite pretty. To her left is the kitchen roof of the apartment below us, but this is to the side and does not obstruct the view. We believe the framework mentioned by Seth is a reference to the wooden window frames, and that the thin lines like poles refers to the narrow wooden frames holding the glass panes; eight small panes make up each of the five windows.

("Anemia." Seth gets back to this reference in a moment.

("Eight." Eight is one of the page numbers enclosed in the circle in the upper right hand corner of the object, but we don't know if this is what Seth meant.

("The connection with <u>anemia</u> leads Ruburt to think of Helga Anderson, or a connection with artists or artwork." Jane thinks that here Seth was trying to get her to say that an artistic endeavor, meaning the dream book, was involved with the object. Helga Anderson, a good friend, has anemia. She is the wife of Ernfred Anderson, a sculptor who was director of the art gallery where Jane worked part-time for several years. In the chapter five connected with the object, Jane uses a dream of Ernfred's to make a certain point.

("A note." Either Seth saw the folded object as a note in itself, or he refers perhaps to Jane's penned notes on the object.

("The month of April." My penciled date on the object shows I picked it up on May 5,1966. Jane said she wrote the page used as object early in the month of April, and did not throw it away until she had rewritten it a month later. In the next session Seth tells us Jane wrote the object on April 7.

("An initiation, not completed." The object is the first half page from the first draft of chapter five of Jane's dream book, and thus would be something begun or initiated, but not completed. There can be extensions here: Not completed could refer to the whole first draft of chapter five, or to the whole dream book itself. Also, perhaps, initiation could be linked to the suggested experiments for the reader to try, as mentioned in the headings. Jane's idea is that this data refers to the dream book itself being started but not completed.

("The color purple," Jane said this is speculation: She wears a certain purple sweater her mother made for her on days when the studio is chilly in the mornings. She wears no other sweater in the studio; it is, also, too large to wear publicly. But

Jane has no idea whether she wore the sweater on the day she wrote the object.

("and perhaps yellow connected here." The object is written on yellow paper.

("Connection with an animal." Oddly enough, there are several references to animals in the chapter five from Jane's dream book. In the early part of the chapter Jane used the phrase "cart before the horse," and Seth mentions horse a bit later. One of the headings for the chapter is Dream Symbols and Culture. Discussing this subject, Jane mentions that fire helped primitive man "keep the beasts away," etc.

("The words unholy alliance come to me here." The whole of chapter five, from which the object comes, concerns the close relationship between dreaming and waking life. We see the idea of alliance here, but not unholy particularly. Seth might have been spoofing us a bit, or it could be a slight distortion. My notes indicate nothing out of the ordinary in Jane's delivery at the time.

("A selection, or something offered from which selections may be made." The six headings to the chapter five, shown on the object.

("A star shape. Something round, again, with spokes leading outward, but rather prominent." Jane immediately thought of this diagram when she read over Seth's data. It is on the back of page 112 of the first draft of chapter five of the dream book. Jane believes that she quite possibly made the diagram on the same day she typed up page 80, which was used as envelope object. Page 112 was used in the final version of chapter five, fortunately, and so was not thrown away. I had not seen the diagram before. It is one Jane made to help her see clearly certain points involving the whole self, and waking and dreaming states. There was much handwritten copy beneath it. Jane located the diagram immediately after this session. She said it is the only one she made for the dream book; she has the habit of making many notes on her manuscript, but very few diagrams of this kind.

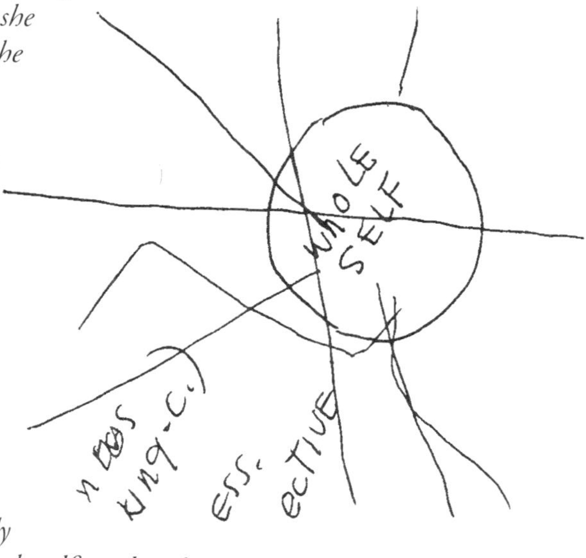

("Something disturbed." This data should have been included after "Connection with an animal." on page 147. We see no connections.

("A connection with markings and dates," Markings can be either the typing itself on the object, or Jane's notes and corrections in pen. I penciled in the date,

May 5,1966, on the object the day I found it and thought of using it for an experiment.

("and a connection with a horse perhaps. Some connection here, but distant." See the interpretation of the "connection with an animal" data on page 149. In the early part of chapter five, from which the envelope object comes, Jane used the phrase "cart before the horse."

("Squares. Perhaps a game connection." Games figure prominently in chapter five of the dream book. To make some of her points in the chapter Jane uses a recurring childhood dream of her own. This dream involved the large playground she visited often in waking life, across the street from her school in Saratoga Springs, NY. There were many kinds of games to be indulged in at the playground in waking life. In addition, in her recurring dream Jane kept recreating a series of games at the playground, in a section where there were none. There is more to the dream, but enough is said here to make the game connection.

("A small round circle suggesting a postmark." In the upper right-hand corner of the object is the page number, enclosed in a circle, and in approximately the position of an envelope postmark.

("Red or blue." I am not sure, but when taking the data from Seth I wondered whether this could be connected to the postmark data. At times it is difficult to tell. I used a period after the word postmark however in the notes, so consider the red and blue separately. Jane made the notes on the object with a dark blue or gray pen that gives the impression of dark blue. She said she felt red or blue refers to the fact that she uses two different pens in correcting manuscript—a red one and a blue one; but we are not sure.

("A connection with a high ledge shape, as one connected with a roof, or lookout from which one can look down and away." See the interpretation of the "framework" data on page 148. As stated, the manuscript page used as object was written by Jane in the studio at the back of the apartment. The studio is a second-floor converted porch with two sides made up of five windows each. Jane sits at her desk facing the row of windows to the west; from there she has an excellent view of the backyard and the street beyond. She "looks down and away" at grass and flowers, etc., and to her left, not obstructing her view, is the porch roof of the apartment on the ground floor.

("Connection with four people, one of them disheveled," I wanted to ask Seth questions about this data but did not get the chance. The object is part of the first page of chapter five of Jane's dream book. In chapter five Jane discusses dreams furnished by four people specifically—Jane, myself, Bill Gallagher and our landlady, Marian Spaziani.

(Jane believes the term "disheveled" refers to herself here. See the recurring childhood playground dream, mentioned in the data dealing with the interpretation

of "a game connection." This dream, over a period of a couple of years during her childhood, had a powerful effect upon Jane; she has talked about it ever since I have known her. In the dream Jane constructed a set of games, involving physical apparatus like swings and jungle gyms, in a section of the playground where in physical life none existed. The morning after one of these dreams Jane would hurry to the playground before going to school, to investigate to see if by chance there were swings, etc., in that particular section of the playground. There were none. She would then have to hurry to school; most often she would arrive late, and breathing hard, and disheveled. She remembers this clearly.

("Fourteen," We speculate: Not seeing any other connections offhand, we count fourteen lines of type on the object, including the chapter headings.

("Also a small screen." It took Jane two days to make the connection here, and when she did it was very vivid. At the end of the session she said she'd had no images while giving the envelope data. Association a couple of days later reminded her that she had indeed had one mental picture—that of a small television screen, and quite clearly. These images can be difficult to recall, particularly on the spur of the moment, and Jane has had other instances where they came to mind some time after the session.

(The TV screen entered the data because Jane used an analogy in the first couple of pages of chapter five of the dream book, involving a TV screen; she mentioned it quite extensively on two pages. The analogy does not show on the half page used as object. It begins on the bottom half of the same page—but not in the first draft of chapter five of the dream book. It is found instead in the second draft; rewriting the chapter, Jane then inserted the television screen analogy to help make some points clear.

(Two days after the session Jane found herself reading over her second draft of chapter five. Coming across the TV analogy made Seth's data about a screen clear to her—particularly when it also reminded her that she'd had a good image of a TV screen while giving the envelope data. Had she not chosen to reread, this block of material would have been missed.

("Something not done, but begun." I asked Seth but one question, asking for elaboration on "An initiation not completed." See the first interpretation of this on page 148. Jane believes the bit of data above refers to the fact that she had begun the dream book, but hasn't finished it yet.)

SESSION 258
MAY 11, 1966 9 PM WEDNESDAY AS SCHEDULED

(The 53rd envelope experiment was held this session. The object was the same

object used for the last session, the 257th. See the copy of it on page 142, and the notes concerning it on pages 143 and 147, as well as our interpretation of Seth's data concerning it; this also begins on page 147.

(This is the first time during the envelope experiments that the same object was used twice in succession. I was curious to see if Seth would repeat any of his impressions given in the 257th session. This he did do, though often approaching the same topic or impression in new language. We think the data from one of the experiments reinforces that of the other.

(Once before, in the first and 18th envelope experiments, an object was used that was similar but not identical by any means. In the first experiment in the 179th session, Seth came through with one accurate impression. In the 18th experiment, held during the 212th session, a few more impressions were obtained; but overall the results were interfered with by other factors in a way that doesn't seem to happen these days. See Session 179 in Volume 4, and Session 212 in Volume 5.

(There follows from her dream notebook Jane's account of one of the dreams she had on Tuesday, May 10,1966: "This whole dream was in images. I saw the universe... or whole reality, an infinity of spirals and stars, in depth somehow. Someone told me? or I just knew... that many of our cherished ideas concerning reality are completely wrong. It was a revelation type dream, except that now I can't remember anymore about it. Perhaps someone else was showing me all this; not sure though."

(The session was held in our front room. Jane began speaking while sitting down and with a hand raised to her closed eyes. She used many pauses, some of them long. Her voice was quiet.)

Good evening.

("Good evening, Seth.")

First, I will discuss Ruburt's dream. It contained several revelations that cannot be put into words.

The information was perceived through the inner senses, and though Ruburt is not consciously aware of the dream's importance the inner self has assimilated the knowledge. He will most likely have several other dreams of this nature within a short period of time.

It is correct to say that the truth can never appear completely undistorted when words are used, for the words themselves almost <u>cloak</u> as much as they reveal. *(A long pause; Jane was very restless.)* The dream, I believe, was a part of a series of three dreams, the other two yet to come. He was also involved in some astral travel. This is not unusual, for the inner self frequently leaves the body when the body sleeps.

All Ruburt could <u>remember</u> of his dream was the knowledge that many of mankind's most cherished conceptions about reality are completely false. He was shown a multidimensional diagram of reality as it exists in terms of the spacious present, and in terms of qualities that represent dimensional points.

In the diagram for example, each star would represent a moment point in another system. It appears as matter within your system, from your viewpoint, and exists as matter within your system. But it exists as something entirely different, you see, within another system. You perceive but the lowest point of its reality, so I will tell you now that the various stars and planets and heavenly bodies that you observe in your universe do indeed exist as such, but only within your system.

All you can perceive of them, you see, is matter, because you automatically transform all data into matter patterns because of the nature of your own perceptions. Since you observe matter, it obviously has a reality. However, these heavenly bodies appear as something entirely different, you see, within other systems.

What you call dimensions represent states in which reality is perceived. You perceive reality in three dimensions, and you have a glimpse of reality in a fourth dimension. There are many dimensions however in all directions. These heavenly bodies represent moment points in other systems. As they are projected into your system however, they are only perceived in terms of matter.

(See the 149-152nd sessions for material on moment points, and sessions 246-250, and 254, for material on quasars.)

Now, I will tell you further that these dimensions merely represent various capacities of consciousness. All these dimensions exist at once, and even within your system, but your consciousness cannot perceive them.

You must interpret them in your own terms. You form the system within which you operate. The heavenly bodies for example are moment points to other systems. They actually exist as such within your system if you could perceive them as such.

It is easier then to say that they appear as matter when they are projected into your system, but this is not precisely correct. Nothing but the various stages of consciousness separates the dimensions, you see, but the separation is quite effective nonetheless.

Now I suggest your break.

We hinted, incidentally, of something along these lines in our sessions on moment points. This material tonight represents the information given to Ruburt in his dream.

(Break at 9:22. Jane was dissociated as usual. Her pace had picked up considerably and her eyes had begun to open often, to the point where she lit a cigarette and sipped wine. She said that if the above material represented what her dream

meant, she had no memory of it consciously. I was about to ask Seth who gave Jane the data in the dream when break came.

(Jane resumed with her eyes closed and at a slower pace at 9:33.)

Other systems exist within the same space occupied by your own, but you cannot perceive them.

The inhabitants of some of these systems can perceive you. All of these inhabitants of various systems cannot perceive you however. Some are more or less within the same level of consciousness, but the perceptual mechanisms are entirely different.

Survival personalities exist in a system that is within the same space as your own. They can perceive you, but you as a rule cannot perceive them. They pass beyond that system however, even as you pass through your system into theirs, and little by little they move away from your system entirely.

The heavenly bodies as moment points conform to certain mathematical principles, though your idea of mathematics is extremely limited. Even using your mathematics, you can still only conceive of reality in certain terms. It is difficult to put this into words. I must reemphasize this. Your mathematics still deals, comparatively speaking, with a very slim area. *(Jane smiled, eyes wide open and very dark.)*

You can conceive of a fourth-dimensional cube, for example, but you cannot conceive of a fourth-dimensional thinking process. You cannot conceive of a fourth-dimensional psychological structure. You cannot think *(smile)* in fourth-dimensional terms. You cannot use fourth-dimensional imagination, you see.

No thought has been given to the personality structure as it exists in a fourth-dimensional reality, or in a fifth-dimensional reality, and yet a fourth or fifth-dimensional personality structure contains the most important hints of all.

Now certainly you recall our material on the inner senses. *(Pause, eyes closed.)* Try for a moment to consider these in terms of a fourth-dimensional personality structure... We are forced now and then to slow up, so that Ruburt can get proper words.

In each dimension the inner self begins to handle further aspects of reality. The primary personality must therefore deal with a much larger number of perceptions, while still maintaining its identity. It manipulates in a larger number of dimensions, until it is able you see to handle many, not just one, of its own egos at any given "time"—and you may put time in quotes—while still maintaining its own inner stability and individuality. It takes on more roles, you see, and the psychological structure becomes more complicated as the inner self becomes sure enough of itself to admit ever more stimuli, while still retaining its own core.

This material is as important as any I have given to you, and we shall be concerned for a while with personality structures as they exist within other dimensions.

You may take your break.

(Break at 9:52. Jane had been dissociated as usual. Her pace had again become good. Her eyes had begun to open frequently and she had spoken with emphasis and many gestures.

(It was time for the 62nd Dr. Instream data. Jane spoke with many short pauses, a hand raised to her closed eyes. Resume at 10:00.)

Now give us a few moments please.

We will start with the word more. I do not know to what it refers. More of something: The name Moore, M-o-o-r-e, or a moor *(gesture)* meaning land. That is our first impression.

Now. A mine, or something deep in the earth. A hole, underground. This may or may not be a reference to death.

A four plus one.

Now, our object seems to be round, like a top: And also, like a top, capable of some motion. Brown and white in color, moving counterclockwise I believe, upon a small standard. It may be some sort of scientific device—I do not know, but it is a mechanical device.

He attended an affair with an upstanding audience, an audience who stood up to applaud at the end of the performance. Some recent connection also—another impression—with a small child.

He has reached a decision now, or very nearly, about the matters mentioned in our last session. There seems to be some connection with the Midwest here, or at least further west than his present location. Perhaps someone further west had to do with his decision.

A package delivered to him this week, with some connection with the initials M A or A M. I do not know to what the initials refer, perhaps merely that the package was delivered in the morning, or perhaps the sender.

Two students in his office today, for disciplinarian reasons. A G here.

Now, do you have an envelope for me?

("Yes."

(Jane paused at 10:08. Without opening her eyes she took the envelope for our 53rd experiment from me, then pressed it to her forehead with both hands. She began speaking in a quiet voice and with many pauses.)

Give us a moment, please. These are impressions.

A connection with a trial, or something tried. I do not know if this is trial in terms of judgment, or in terms of an attempt, you see.

A fold. Four. Seven. A connection with mass, or a word that sounds like mas-todon.

Shapes that are stacked. Something like jungle gyms in a playground.

A border. Perhaps in black. Some lines of printed or written material. An M, and a connection with flowers. Movement and weight.

Heat, or red. A date. 40. A groan, or something grown. An L.

Do you have any questions?

("How about colors connected with the object?")

White. Brown. Dark lettering.

("Can you give the content of the lettering?")

The content?

("The subject matter of the lettering. Something about what it says.")

Some connection with an invitation, or an attempt, perhaps to communicate. *(Jane gestured with the envelope, which by now she had lowered from her forehead.)* Give us time... Mention of building, or implied mention... *(Pause, but I didn't wait long enough.)*

("Can you say something more about mas-todon?")

...written to or from a woman. *(Pause.)* No, I cannot.

("Do you want to try naming the object?")

It is not empty on either side. Rectangular with a border.

("How about the four and seven you mentioned?")

I suggest your break.

(Break at 10:20. Jane said she was well dissociated during the experiments. Her eyes had remained closed through both experiments. She was very surprised to learn that the same object had been used for the envelopes in the last two sessions.

(See the copy of the envelope object on page 142 of the 257th session. Again, it is the top half of the first page of chapter five of the book Jane is writing on dreams. It is the first draft, and was thrown away by Jane and saved by me, unknown to her. I dated it May 5,1966 in pencil. It was typed on yellow paper, corrected by Jane with a dark pen. I folded it once putting it into the double envelope.

(The idea in using the same object a second time in succession was to see whether Seth would come up with the same, or similar, impressions, both times. Seth does deal with some of the same impressions in both experiments, using different language each time, and this will be indicated where we think it occurred.

(We started out tonight by making our own connections, and Seth helps us on a couple before ending the session.

("A connection with a trial, or something tried. I do not know if this is trial in terms of judgment, or in terms of an attempt, you see." We think this refers to

attempt. Chapter five of the dream book contains suggested experiments for the reader to try, involving waking and dreaming states and their interchange, etc. On the object itself, the word try is used twice in Jane's notes, having to do with the reader's attempt to manipulate dreams. The chapter from which the object came contains many other such references also.

(Since these "try" or trial references are included on the object itself, we see a similarity in the above impressions and the "markings and dates" data Seth gives in the 257th session. See the notes on page 149.

("A fold." The object was folded once for insertion into the double envelopes. See the fold indicated in the copy on page 142.

("Four. Seven." Jane remembered writing the object early in April, and thought it quite possible these two numbers referred to April 7 as the specific day she did so. Seth confirms this after break.

(This would tie in with two impressions Seth gave last session: "The month of April," and "A connection with markings and dates."

("A connection with mass, or a word that sounds like mas-todon." Since mass was mentioned first, we think this refers to "en masse", near the bottom of the object. There are also references to animals in chapter five; Jane discusses these under the chapter heading "Dream Symbols and Culture" on the object, and mentions that fire helped primitive man keep the beasts away. We thought the primitive reference might have conjured up mas-todon, and that this in turn would support Seth's "Connection with an animal" data in the 257th session. After break Seth tells us we are right about mass, wrong about "todon."

("Shapes that are stacked. Something like Jungle Gyms in a playground." Jungle Gyms in playgrounds, made of tubular metal formed into various sizes of cube and square, give the impression of being stacked cube on cube. Games and playgrounds figure prominently in chapter five of Jane's dream book; the envelope object is the first page from chapter five. Jane's childhood playground in Saratoga Springs, NY, is described in chapter five, as well as a vivid recurring dream which had this playground for a setting. In both waking life and the recurring dream, games such as Jungle Gyms played a leading role.

(This data is amply reinforced in the 257th session by two impressions: "Squares. Perhaps a game connection." page 147, and "Connection with four people, one of them disheveled," page 147. The notes interpreting these two impressions will explain both Jane's playground dream, and the playground itself, in more detail.

("A border. Perhaps in black." My own idea is that this refers to the recent death of a priest Jane knew in her teens. A couple of weeks ago she received notice of his death, with a photo of him edged in heavy black. There is a connection between the priest, Father Ryan, and Jane's playground dreams, and the playground itself in

Saratoga Springs. The playground is directly across the street from the Catholic school Jane attended. The school was actually housed in a complex of buildings that contained also a church and the headquarters and living area of the particular priestly order serving Saratoga and environs.

(Father Ryan lived there. Jane met him toward the end of the long period during which she had her recurring playground dreams. However she never told Father Ryan of the dreams—nor anyone else except her mother. Jane said it is interesting to remember that from the classroom in which she had many long talks with Father Ryan, she could look across the street at the very section of the playground which served as the setting for her recurring dream.

(A note here: On page 148, see our interpretation of Seth's impression, "Anemia," and Jane's connecting this with our friend Helga Anderson. Writing of Father Ryan now reminds us that he died of leukemia—also a blood disorder as anemia is. Note that Seth merely said that anemia reminded Jane of Helga Anderson; Helga is not given as Seth's impression. Perhaps the anemia impression is a distortion of leukemia. However, we think Jane's Helga impressions and the interpretations leading to the envelope object and the dream book in general, to be legitimate.

("Some lines of printed or written material." Father Ryan's mourning photo contained printed type on the back. The envelope object contains both typewritten and handwritten material.

(In the latter case, the above impression would be linked with the following impressions given in the 257th session: "A note." "A selection..." "A connection with markings and dates," "and perhaps yellow connected here." etc.

("An M", We can make M connections but do not know if we are correct. One could be Marian Spaziani; Jane uses a dream of Marian's in chapter five. In this case see the "Connection with four people..." data on page 147. The word manipulate is found twice in Jane's handwriting on the object itself; but there are also three other words on the object that begin with this letter: Mean, en masse, and more.

("and a connection with flowers." One of the chapter headings on the envelope object is Dream Symbols and Culture. Under this Jane discusses how we react to the symbolic meaning of objects. For an analogy here she uses flowers—Easter and lilies, for example. The analogy takes up several typewritten lines, and mentions several kinds of flowers.

("Movement and weight." Jane feels subjectively that this refers to the four specific dreams, furnished by four specific people, that she discusses in chapter five of her dream book. These are represented on the object itself by the chapter heading, "Recurring Dreams..?" among others. Movement is especially prominent in the dreams discussed, and in three out of the four can be violent or strong: Flying,

swinging, running as fast as one can. The fourth dream concerns driving at an average rate of speed. Both movement and weight, bodily weight for instance, enter in chapter five when Jane discusses physical matter and how its attributes change according to individual perception.

(In the previous session, the 257th, the four dreams and their originators are discussed under the impression on page 150, "Connection with four people..." "Perhaps a game connection." Page 150 also.

("Heat, or red." Again, one of the chapter headings on the envelope object is Dream Symbols and Culture. Under this subject Jane discusses the symbolic and cultural meaning of fire for primitive man.

(This echoes the "Connection with an animal." data interpreted on page 149 of the last session. Note that Seth picked up data connected with this particular chapter heading several times.

("A date." The object contains my penciled date, May 5,1966, representing the day I found it after Jane had discarded it. On May 5, I decided to use it in an envelope experiment.

(If the date impression above refers to the object itself, this recalls the "markings and dates," data on page 149 of the last session. Possibly also "The month of April." on page 148.

(Sometimes it is difficult to tell; perhaps date, above, could be said to refer to the next impression.

("40." Jane said this refers to the year 1940. It was during this year that her recurring playground dream was strong and vivid. She was 11 years old. At this time she had yet to meet Father Ryan.

("A groan, or something grown." Jane said this refers to the fact that the original version of chapter five, from which the envelope object was taken, grew to be two chapters, five and six, in the final version in her dream book.

("An L". We saw no connection.

("White. Brown." Seth gave this in answer to my first question, concerning colors connected with the object. Jane said this refers to an experience from her own childhood, which is discussed, again, under the Dream Symbols and Culture heading on the envelope object, in chapter five. Her experience involved a pair of her mother's brown and white spectator shoes, and was connected with her mother's illness. It made such an impression on Jane that even now she does not wear shoes bearing this particular color combination.

("Dark lettering." This too came through in answer to the first question. The object itself does bear dark lettering—both the typing and Jane's penned notes and corrections.

(This echoes Seth's data in the last session under "markings and dates," page

149, and "small round circle," page 150, etc.

("The content? Some connection with an invitation, or an attempt, perhaps to communicate." These impressions resulted from my second and third questions, concerning the content of the lettering on the envelope object. Chapter five of the dream book of course contains many invitations to the reader to try various experiments listed, to communicate back and forth between the waking and dreaming states, etc. Invitations and attempts to communicate are also mentioned on the object itself.

(This could recall the impression of "A note." on page 148 of the last session, plus several others from the last session. This invitation...communication data also picks up the first impression given in tonight's session, interpreted on page 155: "A connection with a trial..."

("Give us time... Mention of building, or implied mention." This too came through in answer to the second and third questions, concerning the content of the lettering on the envelope object. Jane believes it refers to her recurring playground dream, and the fact that her school was directly across the street from the site of her dream. See the notes under "A border. Perhaps in black." on page 157, describing the physical relation between the school, the priests' home quarters, and the playground. The relation with building here is a little unusual. Although the building was directly across the street from the playground there was no access between the two. A high fence surrounded the block-size playground, with the two entrances on an opposite side and end from the school; hence a child to reach the school from the playground had to travel at least one full block, and possibly two.

("Written to or from a woman." This too came through in answer to the second and third questions, concerning the content of the lettering on the object itself. Jane of course wrote the page of manuscript used as object.

(This would be dealt with in the last session under such impressions as "A note." on page 148, "Yellow," page 149, "A selection," page 149, "markings and dates," page 149, and others.

("No, I cannot." This in answer to my request as to whether Seth could say any more about the mas-todon impression, interpreted on page 3016.

("It is not empty on either side. Rectangular with a border." Here I asked Seth to try naming the object. I believe the answer refers to the photo of the deceased Father Ryan. See the notes following "A border..." on page 157.

(The envelope object was folded once. It bore typing and writing on one side only. Perhaps the folding, giving the impression of a layer of markings on more than one side, was confusing to Seth. He has sorted out such impressions before however. To me at least the border on Father Ryan's photo is more of a border than the implied border on the object itself.

("I suggest your break." Seth came through thusly when I asked him about the

"Four. Seven." impression interpreted on page 157. Jane and I believed it meant the date, April 7, on which Jane wrote the page of manuscript used as object. Seth agrees after break.

(This recalls "The month of April." and "markings and dates," impressions given last session, as well as others.

(Seth gave 24 impressions about the envelope object in the 257th session. He gave 21 impressions concerning the same object in the 258th session. In the notes for the 258th session I note 11 impressions that could refer to the impressions given in the 257th session. This is not a strict total by any means; it could be more or less. There can be as many interpretations of this material as there are individuals, and nowhere did Seth say that the same object was being used in both experiments.

(Personally I believe it quite likely that Seth was perceiving impressions related to the object in some manner, or concerning the object itself, in both sessions. There are a total of 45 impressions from both sessions, and it seems that many of them were relevant to the object in some way.

(Jane resumed at 10:43.)

We will now close our session. My heartiest wishes to you both.

The mas-todon was a distortion of two impressions. We picked up the word mass, and also a connection with an animal, which was your cat. In trying to vocalize the impressions however, we made the obvious and rather amusing error.

If you have no questions then we will end the session.

("Were we correct in most of our interpretations of the data?")

You were indeed. The first version of the chapter was written on April 7.

("Good night, Seth."

(End at 10:40.)

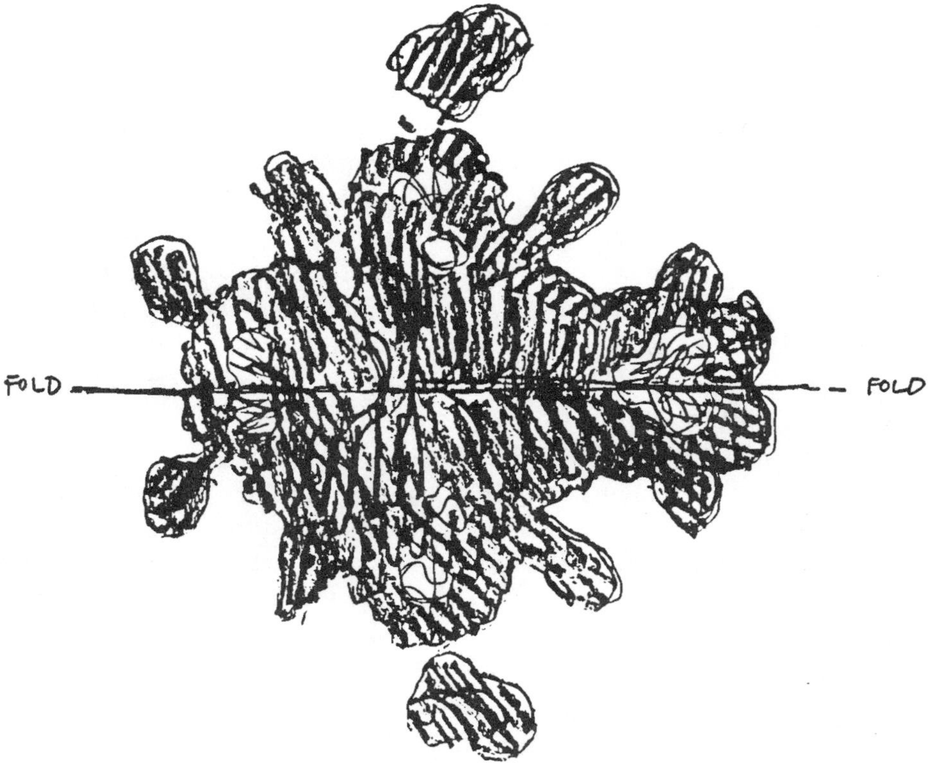

(Reduced copy of the tracing of the paint pattern used as the object in the 54th envelope experiment, in the 259th session for May 16,1966.)

SESSION 259
MAY 16, 1966 9 PM MONDAY AS SCHEDULED

(The 54th envelope experiment was held tonight. The object was a homemade pattern made on light-colored paper, with hand-ground gray brown earth color for pigment and polymer medium for binder. It was folded once as indicated in the making. The effect is like an inkblot, except that the quality and texture of the paint is much superior as far as charm goes; this particular hand-ground pigment, which I make myself by heating a certain Italian earth color, has a texture like fine cement

or roughened stone. Since it is a heavy-bodied pigment, it was built up in spots on the object as much as $^1/_{32}$ of an inch thick. The whole pattern was made up of lines and white spots which do not show very well in my tracing. I placed the object, folded once, between the usual two pieces of Bristol and sealed it in the double envelopes.

(Jane of course had never seen this object, or any others like it, because I have never made them before. I made two of them on May 10, 1966; I dated one of them and used the other in the envelope. The pigment color is quite dark, but not black. The stonelike or rough surface and the dark color enter into the experimental results.

(The session was held in the front room. Jane began speaking while sitting down and with her eyes closed, and in a quiet voice. In the beginning she used some long pauses.)

Good evening.

("Good evening, Seth.")

We shall have more to say, concerning for this evening, fourth-dimensional personality structures.

You exist in many dimensions, although the ego is not aware of such existence. The ego can be taught however. What it cannot experience directly it can still understand to some degree if it is given the proper information. There is no reason for Ruburt to be surprised at Mr. Fox's thesis on dreams and out-of-body experiences.

*(*Astral Projection*, by Oliver Fox.)*

Our own material has hinted in these directions very strongly. Ruburt is quite familiar with such excursions, though egotistically he is only slightly aware of a few of them. There is no need to get too complicated, so we shall deal only with fourth and fifth-dimensional personality structures for now.

You do exist therefore in both of these dimensions. The ego cannot participate directly in such experience. There is a compliance on the part of the ego, however, that allows it to step aside so that it does not block inner awareness of other-dimensional existence. It is difficult, but not impossible, for the ego to correlate the information gained. Dreams involve as you know several dimensions. The dream state itself is a very loose term, for there are several layers of consciousness within it, and there is no limit to the states of consciousness that can be achieved, ideally speaking.

Practically speaking however there are usually only three. Your own fourth-dimensional personality structure obviously operates constantly. One of the main purposes and goals of the whole self is to become aware of all such existences, and to correlate them into an identity structure.

The Fox experiments are quite valid, with some changes that you will make, I imagine. At one level of the dreaming state it is possible for you to recognize and align yourself with that portion of yourself that is aware of itself within fourth-dimensional reality. You have both occasionally learned to take our waking consciousness into the dream state, and here Fox is correct, for you must start at this point.

You begin to manipulate the dream state, or rather you begin to manipulate yourself within dream reality, which is something different. It is an entirely new environment. In ordinary dreaming, without the awareness of usual waking consciousness, perception of dream reality is limited and instinctive. All in all you get along quite well. You are like a child in objective reality. When you learn to take waking awareness into the dream condition, you are reaching adolescence, so to speak.

When you reach adulthood, following our analogy, then you will learn to be successful in manipulating dream reality as you now manipulate objective reality. For if you create your dreams, you also create your objective environment. The dream reality is as real and actual as physical reality, but it can be changed you see by you, as physical reality can be changed.

It is training for fifth-dimensional existence, and you will be working with an odd kind of time, to you. You will be forming new gestalts of experience, using past, present and future as a painter chooses his colors, combining them into various paintings.

You are at the early stages of this development, but it will come. These realities within the dream universe may be created by you, but they are as actual as the piece of cake that you eat, or the poison that you may swallow. As your common sense protects you in the physical universe, so you must use discretion as you progress into the manipulation of dream objects.

I suggest your break.

(Break at 9:25. Jane was "out" as usual, she said. Her pace had picked up considerably. Her eyes had begun to open, and she had lit a cigarette and sipped wine. She resumed in this more emphatic manner at 9:32.)

Now there are points of difference indeed in fourth-dimensional reality for you, as there are points of reference in objective reality.

We have already explained the ways in which agreement is reached within physical reality, as to the dimensions of objects. In somewhat the same manner agreements are reached in fourth-dimensional reality.

For example, Mr. Fox's dream meetings were quite valid. This is what happens in such a case. Those who agree on such a meeting within dream reality must have certain abilities developed. They must be capable of taking waking consciousness into the dream state. They must be able to manipulate within it. Each of them therefore constructs, you see, the dream location at which they have agreed to meet, a point not thought of by Ruburt's Mr. Fox.

When you are considering dream reality, it is easier for you to understand that you construct the reality therein. You find it more difficult to understand the same thing about physical reality.

As a result however, you are somewhat less apt to accept dream reality as actual, and I must tell you that it is, particularly since you are considering certain experiments along these lines. You are in control as long as you realize that you are in control.

Now. There are indeed portions of dream reality that you yourself may not have constructed, but that are constructed by others. You recall that in physical reality you can only perceive your own constructions, as a rule. Now, my dear friends, this does not apply to dream reality.

This is indeed an important point.

Form of any kind, and there is form within dream reality, form is first of all a potential form, existing within psychic energy. The potential form therefore exists long before it's physical materialization, as far as your physical perceptions are concerned.

Physically therefore the house that you will live in within five years may not exist, in your terms, now. It may not have been built yet, therefore physically you do not perceive it. Such a house however does have form, and does exist within the spacious present.

Now. In certain levels of dream reality forms that you do not as yet perceive as physical, do exist. They can be seen and perceived. In certain dreams you do perceive them. Within dream reality you can come in contact with many other kinds of reality with which you do not ordinarily have to deal.

A year ago this information would not necessarily be practical for you. With the experiments you have in mind it becomes highly practical. Your abilities are developed enough so that these experiments should be successful, with some additional training that can only be achieved through experience. Some hints from me will help, but I would like to give you some idea, you see, of what to expect.

When you are only operating within physical reality, you have a fairly simple set of rules to serve you. Within dream reality you are much freer. The ego is not present. The waking consciousness, dear friends, is not the ego. The ego is merely a small portion of waking consciousness. The ego is the portion of waking consciousness that deals with physical manipulation.

Waking consciousness is taken into the dream state, but the ego is not. The ego would immediately falter, and cause immediate failure and catastrophe. What you will meet in your experiments are varieties of conditions, and until you have learned the control it may be difficult to distinguish between them. Some you can manipulate, some you cannot.

Some dream locations will be of your own construction. Others will be of constructions quite strange to you. They will belong to other dimensions entirely, and you may blunder into them. You are in a basic manner, you see, outside of your own system when you attempt to bring your waking consciousness into the dream state.

You are in the process of evolving another form of consciousness, that is individually. This will be new to you to some large extent. In the past any such experiences have been accidental on your parts. I have been involved in some instances with Ruburt on such occasions.

Now I was not <u>dreaming</u> of him, and he was not <u>dreaming</u> of me. I was simply leading him rather gently into new dimensions. When he is ready to embark he will do so. He cannot push himself in this direction, for the whole self sets ups safeguards. You are both however nearly ready.

Now I do not like the term astral bodies, simply because of the sometimes weird connotations connected with the phrase. There is a kind of idea, or mental body, a counterpart in many ways, but not always, to the physical body, which is the structure the self <u>takes</u> in what you may call for now fourth dimension.

Certain dream experiences are valid out-of-the-body experiences, in that you do indeed travel in this mental vehicle. It does have a form, somewhere between matter and nonmatter.

In physical existence usually you simply do not perceive it. There is a psychic structure also that has a form. This is the self as it appears within what you may call for now fifth-dimensional reality, but it does not exist at all in terms of matter. On occasion you travel in this form.

There is more I want to say here. However you had better take your break for our Instream material.

(Break at 9:59. Jane said she was well dissociated. Seth was giving her the material so fast that she had trouble keeping up with it; her delivery had been so fast I had barely managed to keep up with it, in turn. Her eyes had opened often; her voice had been good, her manner emphatic, with few pauses.

(It was now time for the 63rd Dr. Instream experiment. Jane's pace now slowed as she sat with a hand to her closed eyes. Resume at 10:05.)

Now, give us a moment please for our Instream material. We will give an object shortly.

I have the impression of a name, I believe Severn, S-e-v-e-r-n. I do not know to what it refers. There seems to be a hill here also. Perhaps a person named Severn lives on a hill.

Now, the object is some sort of a chain. Widely woven, rather than one with small spaces in it. The object is reminiscent of paper chains made by children, with wide loops, and of many pastel colors.

The object does not belong to Dr. Instream, but was borrowed, and has a strong connection with a woman. Still, it seems to be mechanical, rather than for example a jewelry chain. It has a mechanical use, and perhaps a connection with two boxes, rather small in themselves, which are raised and lowered or moved, by the chain.

There are two round objects connected with it also, perhaps ball bearings, made in Japan. The object may also be connected with the initials B, S, or S, B, though I do not believe these represent a person's initials.

Also a date, 1937. Other impressions, not connected with the object: A misuse. Dr. Instream believes that something is being misused. A connection here with a framework of associations having to do with psychology. And a misfit.

A distant connection with two children, girls, I believe relatives. If they are not twins then they look very much alike, or they are two of a kind in some way.

Do you have an envelope for me?

("Yes.")

(Jane paused at 10:16 without opening her eyes. She took the envelope for our 54th experiment, pressed it to her forehead for a moment and then lowered it to her lap. Her left hand remained raised to her face.)

Give us a moment, please. These are impressions.

Dark printed matter. A square object, perhaps a small square shape at the top center of the object, balanced by another shape at the bottom center.

A film connection, black and white. A decoration, or something memorized, as four score and seven years ago... That is, a phrase known to many, and rather cliché.

The square shapes again, now, as in small patterns.

Connection with an image of Ruburt. Black and white again rather than color. A connection with the early 1960s.

A forthright statement, numbers, perhaps a room number. This leads Ruburt to think of Oswego and your stay there. A connection with a federation of some sort. A connection with a man, not yourself, perhaps with your landlord.

Do you have any questions?

("Do you think the object is a photograph?")

The question is not a good one. *(Jane smiled.*

("Then can you say something more about the decoration?")

No more than I have said. If the object is not a photograph, it is closely connected. I have the <u>impression</u> of a black and white photograph.

Give us a moment, please...

With a block or blocks, as rocks or steps of stone. *(Jane gestured, her eyes still closed.)* Also a connection with a building that is not seen from the front but from the side, perhaps from a verandah.

Something overturned. The feeling of a fluid dark color, broken by white shapes that appear like blocks. Perhaps some connection with a pond or pool shape. The object marked in the middle of the back, in pen or pencil.

Perhaps J B and a date. I do not get the feeling that the object has to do with the <u>immediate</u> present, in that it was not a part of your experience, directly.

I suggest your break.

(Break at 10:29. Jane was dissociated as usual. Her eyes had remained closed through both experiments. She said that Seth had felt like giving many impressions.

(As soon as she opened the double envelopes, Jane said the object looked like a <u>man</u> to her, with either horizontal edge uppermost, and that she thought this impression had given rise to the photograph data. See the tracing on page 162, and the description of the object on page 163. This marked the end of the session for all practical purposes as far as Seth was concerned. Jane and I made the connections we could and did not ask Seth to elaborate.

("Dark printed matter." As stated, the pigment used on the object is quite dark, a burnt gray brown, but it is not black. Jane's impression of it, I noted, was that it was darker to her than to me. I don't know whether Seth uses printed here to mean an ink applied to paper or newsprint, or just some other substance applied to a surface as in the case of the object.

("A square object, perhaps a small square shape at the top center of the object, balanced by another shape at the bottom center." Throughout the data Seth keeps attempting to refine this shape or block image, with some success. Although none of the shapes on the original object are square, they do give the impression of being balanced one upon another. Any object produced like the envelope object will give a feeling of balance, no matter what the design, as long as both halves are printed or impressed in full. On the original many small white interstices show that are not visible on the quick tracing. It seems Seth had a correct impression.

("A film connection, black and white." As stated Jane at once thought of a man when she saw the object, and this she thinks led to the film connection. It comes up again, as does the black and white data. To Jane the color of the pigment on the object is quite dark.

("A decoration," The object is a decoration.

("or something memorized, as four score and seven years ago... That is, a phrase known to many, and rather cliché." We don't know where this impression came from,

and are quite puzzled by it.

("The square shapes again, now, as in small patterns." Seth's refinement here is to the point. The original object contains a multitude of fine patterns made by the rough paint when I pressed the folder paper together. It is very charming; the patterns are almost like the veins in a leaf. Flecks of white scattered throughout also.

("Connection with an image of Ruburt. Black and white again rather than color. A connection with the early 1960s." Again, Jane thinks the dark pigment on the object gave rise to this data, with the date perhaps referring to the year a picture of herself was taken.

("A forthright statement, numbers, perhaps a room number. This leads Ruburt to think of Oswego and your stay there. A connection with a federation of some sort." Again, this data puzzles us. The object has no connection with Oswego, NY. Jane has used federation, and words like before re large buildings such as post offices, etc., so it seems that here federation refers to the college at Oswego, where Dr. Instream teaches.

("A connection with a man, not yourself, perhaps with your landlord." The paint blot on the object reminded Jane of a man, which could give rise to the man data here. However I am connected with the object since I made it.

("The question is not a good one." Just for kicks, I asked Seth if he thought the object was a photograph. This because of the numerous photo and man references in the data. At this time, of course, before Jane had seen the object, I had no idea that it would remind her strongly of a man, and hence possibly give rise to the photo data.

("No more than I have said. <u>If</u> the object is not a photograph, it is closely connected. I have the <u>impression</u> of a black and white photograph." Presumably because of the reasons cited above. My second question asked for elaboration on the decoration data, and resulted in some more information.

("Give us a moment, please... With a block or blocks, as rocks or steps of stone." This block or rock or stone data could be connected to the data in the paragraph just above this one; although Seth took a long pause in between. At any rate it seems that the texture, the rough stonelike feel and appearance of the pigment on the object, could have given rise to the rock or stone impressions which in turn could conjure up the step data and so lead to the idea of a photo.

("Also a connection with a building that is not seen from the front but from the side, perhaps from a verandah." This building data could thus have resulted from the steps mentioned above. If Seth is talking about a photo here, Jane and I do not know offhand what one it could be. We have photos of buildings in our album, of course, but no specific building or location comes to mind.

("Something overturned." The irregular shape of the pigment on the object; a similarity here between it and some liquid spilled.

("The feeling of a fluid dark color, broken by white shapes that appear like

blocks." The wet pigment used to make the object was a fluid dark color, of course. Seth now uses the block data to refer to the whites scattered through the object on the original. Some of the whites are of a block shape, roughly, but more often simply irregular just as the pigment is.

("Perhaps some connection with a pond or pool shape." Again, this applies to the irregular shape of the pigment on the object, and is close, and in the same vein as the "something overturned," and "the feeling of a fluid dark color" data. We regard these three impressions as good.

(I neglected to deal with Seth's next impression, "The object marked in the middle of the back, in pen or pencil."

("Perhaps J B and a date." Jane, or Seth, getting at the idea of photograph again. As stated earlier, I made two similar objects with the same pigment on May 10,1966. I dated and initialed the one not used in the envelope experiment; this gives an RB and a date, but I doubt if this is what Seth is getting at here.

("I do not get the feeling that the object has to do with the <u>immediate</u> present, in that it was not a part of your experience, directly." Just the opposite. The object was part of my experience, in the immediate past. Jane had never seen the object or any like it, since I had never made any before; perhaps this data came out because she herself was thus not involved with the object in any way.

(Jane resumed at 10:45.)

We will now end our session. My heartiest wishes to you both.

("Good night, Seth."

(End at 10:46.)

(Front) *(Back)*

(Tracings of the matchbook cover used as the object in the 55th envelope experiment, in the 260th session for May 18,1966.)

SESSION 260
MAY 18, 1966 9 PM WEDNESDAY AS SCHEDULED

(The 55th envelope experiment was held during the session. Notes pertaining to the object will be found along with Seth's data given during the experiment.

(Jane was especially logy before the session, and remarked that she didn't feel much like having one. She decided to go ahead, however. I felt somewhat tired also. It was a warm and rainy night, which didn't make us feel any more active.

(Jane began speaking while sitting down and with her eyes closed. Her pace was slow and she used many pauses, some of them long. A few of these will be indicated.)

Good evening.

("Good evening, Seth.")

Now, we will have a short session.

There are a few points however that I wanted to make this evening. First of all, any effective large-scale space travel will be mental travel.

(Seth first mentioned this in the early sessions, shortly after January 1964.)

I use the term space travel loosely. In some conditions such expeditions will be powered by pooled mental or psychic resources. You may journey within your own solar system using physical vehicles, but you will not make any effective breakthrough beyond your solar system unless psychic and mental resources are developed.

Of course mental or psychic journeys into other dimensions and systems are possible, and when I speak of dimensions here I am not referring to space systems. Mentally you can cut through space, physically you cannot. In some of your dream states you do travel through other dimensions and other systems. The extent of these dream travels is determined by your own ability.

Some of you are rather rigidly held within your own system even in your dreams, and though you exist within other dimensions such individuals are not aware of them. *(Long pause.)*

Now. Mankind did at one time have what you may call a heavier body than at present. *(Long pause, over one minute.)* This particular body type has not vanished entirely by any means. The mental body, sometimes called the astral body, is the next one that you will inhabit. You inhabit it <u>now</u>, of course. *(Long pause.)*

Training and disciplined experimentation in the manipulation of this body will be of great benefit, for you will be facing some of the conditions that you will have to face when the physical body is discarded. *(Long pause.)*

You will be gaining considerable experience of a vital kind. *(Long pause.)* You will learn to maintain stability and identity in the midst of a bewildering number of strange and previously unknown situations. With time you and Ruburt would do well indeed to set up experiments in which you try to contact each other while you are in the dream state. *(Long pause.)*

Perhaps I shall contact you both some night under those circumstances. Once more, remember in your dream experiments that you will be able to perceive not only your own constructions, but upon some occasions the constructions of others.

As you progress the sense of identity will be strengthened to meet, you see, the new challenges. As I mentioned earlier, in your cases the personality has set up certain safeguards so you will be in no danger. When such safeguards are not erected however, there is some danger. *(Long pause.)*

Ruburt's own experience, in maintaining his own identity independently, while also allowing me to speak through him, will be to his benefit. It is, you see, quite possible for an individual in his dream travels to visit other planetary systems, of the past, present or future. Such visits are usually spontaneous and fragmentary.

It is best that they remain so. Take advantage of them when they happen within the dream state, but at this time do not attempt any such endeavor from the trance state. There are too many difficulties involved.

Now I suggest your break.

(Break at 9:26. Jane was "out" as usual. Her pace had remained very slow. Many of the pauses during the delivery lasted for over a minute. Her eyes began to open finally, and she smoked a cigarette and sipped iced tea. She said she thought the session would be short.

(Jane now began to give the Instream material for the 64th experiment after break. As usual she sat with a hand to her closed eyes. Her pace actually speeded up a bit comparatively. Resume at 9:34.)

We are going to have a brief session.

I will give you our Instream material now. Give us a moment, please. Incidentally we are having a short session to give Ruburt a rest, and also to give you a rest, Joseph.

Now, for our object. One or two small white objects, perhaps dice. If not there is a close resemblance in size, shape and color. The numbers 7 and 3, perhaps facing upward. The objects may be connected with a small chain, in the manner of cuff links. A Q. I do not know to what this refers. Also four pieces of paper.

Now, general impressions. A soreness in the throat, or a discomfort there on the part of Dr. Instream. A meeting with a stranger, a man, in his office, and some connection with Detroit. A group of four guests in particular, men I believe, to his apartment. This is separate from the earlier mention of the stranger. The initials S P A in connection with the group.

Now, do you have an envelope for me?

("Yes."

(At 9:23 Jane took the envelope for our 55th experiment from me without opening her eyes. She pressed it to her forehead briefly, then lowered it to her lap but kept the other hand to her eyes.)

Give us a moment, please. These are impressions.

A connection with a spade. Four. Connection with a meeting. The impression here of something underground. I do not know whether to interpret this as a burial or not.

Writing. Five, perhaps five lines. A card. Plants or flowers. 1963, or at least a 19 and a 6 3. A path in a particular direction to be taken. Four people standing up. Implication of an error.

A large round circular shape, perhaps inside of a rectangular one, and crisscross lines in the shape of a cross. The impression of movement, and some impression of a machine, perhaps an airplane.

Do you have any questions?

("How about colors on the object?")

Give us a moment. Red and green. A black or dark color against a light background. Also a <u>dim</u> yellow.

("Can you say something more about the four people standing up?")

Two men and two women.

("Can you give us any initials?")

Perhaps a J and a G. I suggest your break, unless you have any particular questions of course.

("Do you want to try to name the object?")

A note. I suggest your break.

(Break at 9:58. Jane was well dissociated, she said. She wasn't aware of the traffic noise for instance, even though the windows were open. Her eyes remained closed through both experiments.

(See the tracing of the envelope object on page 171. I found it in a drawer of my desk about an hour before the session and decided to use it for the object on the spur of the moment. I opened up the match folder and removed the matches, then sealed it in the usual double envelope. I knew Jane hadn't seen it for at least a couple of years, and after the session she confirmed that it had been longer than that.

(I picked up the matchbook in a restaurant, Mother Goldsmith's in Saratoga Springs, NY. Jane has been familiar with the place since childhood, and on our infrequent visits to Saratoga we always stop in. I dated this particular matchbook on the inside when obtaining it—August 1963, which was before these sessions began in December 1963. The book is printed in black on a <u>dim</u> yellow—as Seth calls it—cardboard stock. All the copy on it, except for Nate Goldsmith's name beneath the caricature of him, is in this dim yellow against the black background.

(It wasn't until Jane and I began to study the envelope data that we realized it referred to more than one visit to Saratoga on our part. This immediately complicated things. Interpretations became elusive indeed, and part of our knowledge that

two visits to Saratoga were involved was subjective only. Had we realized this by the end of the session we would have called Seth back to help out. As it was we didn't appreciate what had happened until the time came to write these notes. Another complication is that while we cannot pin down all the data, we feel that most of it is quite legitimate.

(I will indicate below where we believe the two Saratoga visits are referred to in the envelope data. The first visit was in August 1963, the second was in the summer of 1964. On both occasions Jane and I were on our way to York Beach, Maine, on vacation; both visits to York Beach played a part in these sessions, and exact dates can be found in appropriate sessions. See Session 9 in Volume 1.

(The connection between the envelope object and our two visits to Mother Goldsmith's is strong enough, in that Jane and I ate there both years. We saw the same hostess both times also—a girl Jane went to school with in Saratoga. We did not see Nate Goldsmith or his wife on the first visit, and the reasons we did not see either of them on our second visit are given in our data interpretations.

("A connection with a spade." On our second visit, in 1964, Jane and I were told that Nate Goldsmith had died. We do not know just when he died, but believe it was after our first visit. Jane did not know the Goldsmiths intimately, merely to speak to. Also on the 1964 visit we were told the restaurant had been, or was being, sold.

(The spade impression here is apparently elaborated upon by Seth an impression or two later, in connection with underground data. There can be a connection with the black color of the suit of spades in a deck of playing cards, and the black of the object.

("Four. Connection with a meeting." This too took place on the 1964 visit. Jane feels subjectively sure that here the meeting between us and her father, Del, and his third wife, is referred to. The meeting was arranged by mail beforehand. Jane and I planned to meet Del and his wife, who were already camping at Saratoga Lake, there, and spend a few days with them before going on to Maine. This we did.

("The impression here of something underground. I do not know whether to interpret this as a burial or not." Possibly the death of Nate Goldsmith; we learned about this on our second visit. Jane, or Seth, has used the underground idea several times now in connection with death.

("Writing. Five, perhaps five lines." Once again, we do not know just what Seth means by writing—type like this, printing, handwritten script or lettering, etc. The front cover of the object contains five lines of large type against the black background. The object was presented flat or opened up in the envelope, so also visible at a glance would be more than five lines—eight to be exact exclusive of the name on the caricature. I hand lettered inside the cover also. The phone number on the top

fold of the object contains a five, but we don't know whether this means anything.

("A card." The object is manufactured of the usual cardboard stock used for matchbooks. There could be other connections.

("Plants or flowers." We don't know.

("1963, or at least at 19 and a 6 3." See the tracing of the object on page 171. Inside the front cover I penned the date, August 1963.

("A path in a particular direction to be taken." Jane feels this applies to the address of the restaurant on the object.

("Four people standing up." Four people were involved on our second visit to Saratoga, of course, but we don't know what the standing reference involves.

("Implication of an error." This is a good connection, involving both our visits to Saratoga. It is personal and so is not given in detail here, but can be explained by us at any time.

("A large round circular shape, perhaps inside of a rectangular one", can refer to the caricature of Nate Goldsmith on the back of the object. The drawing is made up of rounded lines and shapes, is rounded in overall shape, and fits into the black rectangular frame. We don't particularly know why Seth uses large here, unless he means that the drawing could not be much larger and still fit into the rectangular shape.

("and crisscross lines in the shape of a cross." Jane said this data goes with the earlier underground and spade data, and is a symbolic reference to the death of Nate Goldsmith. Seth has used the cross idea before in indicating things ended, etc.

("The impression of movement, and some impression of a machine, perhaps an airplane." Jane said this refers to our automobile trips to Saratoga, the object being obtained on the first of these in 1963.

("Give us a moment. Red and green. A black or dark color against a light background. Also a dim yellow." My first question concerned colors on the object. We don't know what the red and green refers to, since these are not present on the object. The object is however printed in black, against a light background. Seth's description of a dim yellow is a most apt description of the color of the cardboard stock used for the object.

(Possibly the yellow data also grew out of the gold in Nate Goldsmith's name, which appears on the back of the object, as well as Mother Goldsmith's name appearing on the front.

("Two men and two women." I asked Seth to elaborate on the four people standing up data. Two men and two women were involved in the meeting referred to earlier: Jane's father Del and myself, and Jane and Del's wife. This on our second visit.

("Perhaps a J and a G." I asked Seth for initials of the people at the meeting.

The J can refer to Jane, but not the G. The initial G of course shows up on the object itself, twice, in Nate Goldsmith and Mother Goldsmith's.

("A note." I asked Seth to name the object. Perhaps the good amount of writing on the object, front and back, plus mine on the inside, gave rise to this data.

(Jane resumed at 10:10.)

Now we will close our session. My best wishes to you both. I am quite prepared to go on for some time. However you can stand the change, and so we shall close early. I shall look in on you now and then, however.

("Good night, Seth."

(End at 10:11. Jane was "out" as usual. She said Seth felt affectionate at the end of the session. She held the session tonight not only because she didn't want to miss it, but because under similar circumstances in the past the results have been good. She had confidence that if she really shouldn't have a session Seth would either call it off entirely or make it very short.)

(261st Session, May 23, 1966. Tracing of the pencil drawing of Jane, used as the object in the 56th experiment.)

SESSION 261
MAY 23, 1966 9 PM MONDAY

(The 56th envelope experiment was held during the session. The object was a pencil drawing I made of Jane this afternoon, without her knowledge. I looked down on her as she sunned herself, my viewpoint being the back row of the studio windows on the second story. The sketch took but a few minutes because she moved so frequently, and I was much amused at her restlessness; this mirth plays a part in the experimental results. The drawing is on porous paper with a slight yellowish cast. I placed it between the usual two pieces of Bristol, then sealed it in double envelopes.

(Before the session Jane said she had no idea of what Seth would talk about. She began speaking while sitting down and with her eyes closed. She had left a cigarette burning however, and her eyes soon began to open. Her voice was quiet, her pace quite slow.)

Good evening.

("Good evening, Seth."

(One minute pause.) There are several points I would like to make. For all practical purposes, you will find yourself in some sort of body form in your out-of-body experiences.

These body forms however are necessary camouflages, for you cannot yet think of identity without some kind of physical body. Therefore you project yourself in a body form. It varies according to your own abilities, and without it you would feel lost indeed. The form itself is not important, but the form can tell you something about the dimension in which you are having experience.

The dream body is the one with which you are most familiar. It has been called the astral body. It strikes you as being physical, though you can do things with it that you cannot do with your physical body. You can levitate with it, for example. As a rule you do <u>not</u> go through walls with this body. This is the body that you use for ordinary dreams. Levitation is possible with it, but on a very limited basis.

When you enter a different dimension the abilities of the body form change, and for all intents and purposes it is a different body form, which we will call a mind form. It still seems physical in shape, but you can walk through physical matter with it, and you can truly levitate with it within your solar system, but you cannot go beyond in this mind form.

You can travel anywhere within your solar system however with it. In the first form it is possible to perceive the past, present and future on a limited basis. In the second form this perception is on a larger scale, the scope of consciousness being further opened. Now this is the form that you will use if you meet appointments with others within the dream state.

The third form we may call the true projection form. In it, it is possible to travel beyond your solar system, and to perceive the past, present and future of other systems as well as your own.

The form that you use does not dictate the various abilities. You don the particular form in line with your abilities. You do the best you can, in other words. *(Smile.)* It is possible to begin an experience in one form, and change to another, or to go from the first to the third. On such occasions you must therefore, you see, pass through in reverse direction. The forms do merely represent various stages of consciousness.

At physical death, after the last reincarnation, then the normal body form is the dream body, and excursions are made from this point, you see. It is possible to suddenly switch from the third form to the dream body, but at a considerable jolt to the consciousness, as a rule. Transition is simply too sudden.

Now I realize that Ruburt is not too happy with me for bringing up this next point. Intellectually he is highly critical of it. On another level however he knows very well that it is legitimate. There are indeed others who can help you in such experiences, and who often do while you are in the dream state, whether or not you know it. They can be of great assistance as guides.

I suggest your first break.

(Break at 9:25. Jane was out as usual. Her pace was a little better as the session progressed, although her eyes remained closed for most of it.

(Jane confirmed that she did not like the "spiritual guide" connotation. Seth's material upon resumption stems from the fact that Jane, housecleaning lately, had switched our bed from a north-south axis to east-west. Resume at 9:31, eyes open, smiling broadly.)

Now my dear friends, you will find all projections much easier if your head is to the north.

Ruburt will not be happy with this. Projection is certainly possible in any case. However at your period of development it would be simpler to have everything working for you that you can. It is up to you to make decisions. Perhaps the other comforts that the room affords you with the bed in another position, is worth it to you for a while. This in no way changes the fact that projections are more easily executed with the head to the north.

One small interesting point here. Ruburt's projection upon first looking over the Fox book was quite legitimate.

(Astral Projection, *by Oliver Fox. After reading part of this book very recently, Jane achieved her first deliberate projection.)*

However the window *(smile, eyes open)* you see, was a quite valid fabrication of his own. The projection was a projection. The window through which he ascended was a symbol necessary to him. The actual physical window was behind his head, you see, so he felt impelled to have a window in front of him, in order to get out of the physical house.

I found this amusing. The symbol was a highly valuable one however, obviously. You will both improve with practice. Because of your ideas, you see, you experience more difficulty in getting out of the physical house. *(Smile.)* Ruburt's window image, had the experience continued, would have effectively done this for him. He did not have the confidence to imagine himself, you see, passing through the physical walls.

Instead he has to form the imaginary image of a window, which is in itself some feat, and then project himself through this. It is quite all right. I merely wanted to point out what he did. When you project from the dream body, you see, consciously you are already outside, as a rule. You have already made the initial change away from physical focus.

The mass of valid projections are indeed made from the dreaming body. When the excursion is over the return to the dream body is made with no strain, you see, for the ego is little concerned. In most such instances however the knowledge is then not available to the waking self at all.

Now. Some of Fox's suggestions are excellent. They will allow you to take the waking consciousness along with you. As your abilities develop and as you become more accustomed to the experience, the waking consciousness will recall more and more, and not become frightened. When it becomes frightened you see it forces the whole experience to end. If it were not taken along the same experience might have continued, and greater benefits been achieved for the whole self.

But the training here is vastly important, and a manipulation of consciousness in this way has definite advantages. It will take some work on your part, but you will indeed by able, perhaps with some use of suggestion, to realize, when in the dream state, those occasions when you are projecting.

Then you can prolong the experience, and recognize it as a valid out-of-body excursion. The mobility of consciousness will automatically allow you greater freedom in using your inner perceptions in waking life also. For this is a motion of consciousness, a motion that has little to do with the motion of the physical body.

However there is a chemical energy used in all such out-of-body experiences. The chemical reaction results in an electromagnetic connection between the consciousness and the physical body, and without it there would be no return to the physical body, in your terms. Of course it is mental energy that

<u>makes</u> the chemical energy possible, however. This freedom of consciousness is not dependent upon physical existence, you see.

During your present life however the connection must be maintained. I will give you a break before our Instream material. I do want to mention however that all consciousness within your system has the same sort of freedom within certain degrees.

I suggest your break.

(Break at 9:53. Jane was pretty well dissociated. Traffic noise from the open windows hadn't bothered her. Her pace had been much faster. Her eyes had opened often and she had smiled often.

(It was now time for the 65th Dr. Instream experiment. As usual Jane's pace slowed somewhat, and she sat with a hand raised to her closed eyes. Jane hesitated for a moment, saying that Seth was waiting for "just the right time" to contact Dr. Instream. Resume at 10:04.)

Now, give us a moment for our Instream material.

My first impression is of <u>blocks</u>, and a turnstile. Has he visited someplace with this kind of entrance, for example, or does he have a photograph of such a place...

A <u>fine</u>. Perhaps money must be put into the turnstile to make it move. A connection with a large building on the other side here, and a sign. The letter D connected with the sign. Down, or <u>downs</u>, I do not know. Perhaps stairs leading down.

The object he has chosen has a strong connection with a <u>place</u>. *(Jane began to rub her eyes strongly.)* The object is not utilitarian, that is, you cannot do anything <u>with</u> it, but it represents something else.

It may be a photograph of the earlier mentioned impressions, you see, if not a photograph *(Jane's eyes now opened, wide and very dark. This is the first time they have done so during such an experiment.)* A picture of some kind—an image of another man, rather than the thing itself.

The impression of a fence or border here, shown in the picture. *(Eyes open and closed.)* It is of an <u>old</u>, rather than a new place, I believe, connected with a stone building. *(Eyes open again; with gestures.)* Perhaps the building is in some way on exhibition, or one must pay to enter it. Again, this is a picture of some sort, and not the building itself.

The building *(eyes open)* has a <u>resemblance</u> to an English-type mansion, or large building of this sort, set in fine grounds. The turnstile may simply be symbolic—you may have to <u>pay</u> to enter the building. Perhaps on some sort of tour.

(Eyes now closed for rest of data.) Numbers five, six. A postcard. Also some connection with a French location.

Now other impressions. A meeting of four people in the afternoon. They seem to have white hair or blonde hair. None of them is a dark-haired person. *(Long pause.)* There is another man standing up. They are around a round table, in a fairly large room that seems to be empty except for themselves. One man has a watch on a chain.

Do you have an envelope for me?

("Yes."

(Jane paused at 10:17. Her eyes were still closed. She took the envelope for our 56th experiment from me without opening them. She pressed the envelope to her forehead with one hand while keeping the other to her face.)

Give us a moment, please. These are impressions.

Mirth. Yet also a connection with an unpleasant event. A rectangular card, with printed matter. Some larger lettering, and then some small.

The color red. An impression of many people. Connection with a tall man. The letter L. Perhaps the number 17. A twist.

A pattern of wavy lines, or <u>wavering</u> lines. *(Gesture.)*

Missed, an occasion missed earlier. The <u>impression</u> now of looking down, from a high position... That is connected with rocks. Or of looking down *(gesture)* from a high position into a hole.

A thin border on the object, and horizontal lettering. Reaching in the center out toward the margins. A card, such as the kind sent out by <u>organizations</u> for invitations.

Do you have any questions? *(Jane lowered the envelope to her lap, her eyes still closed.*

("Can you give me some initials connected to the object?")

Give us a moment... *(Pause)* B and L and G.

("How about those wavering lines?")

The sort of lines for example that a map would have to indicate small roads, or the lines like cracks in a dry ground.

("What's that about mirth?")

I am not sure here. It seems a connection with a party. But also a connection with something unpleasant, so I am not sure.

("What does the horizontal lettering say?")

I think there is a red color, and rather large lettering, perhaps four or five lines. Come... An invitation to do something, or go somewhere, or to <u>join</u>. Perhaps 24, referring to a day of the month. Five or 6 for the month perhaps.

("Do you want to name the object?")

I have done as much to name it as I can. I suggest your break.

(Break at 10:29. Jane was far out, she said. She wasn't conscious of anything

but the experiment, and her eyes remained closed through all of it. She had a few images during the experiment and these will be mentioned in place in the data.

(Seth answers a few questions after break. In the meantime Jane and I made our own connections. See the tracing on page 178, and the notes on page 179.

("Mirth." As stated earlier, I felt pronounced amusement while making the drawing used as the object. Jane moved almost constantly while posing unwittingly, and I had to work very rapidly while at the same time being careful she didn't look up at the studio windows on the second floor and see what I was doing.

(Seth mentions another possible connection with mirth in answer to my third question. But his answer to that question also makes us believe the interpretation above is the correct one.

("Yet also a connection with an unpleasant event." Jane said the unpleasant event was the fact that earlier two neighborhood children had been quite noisy and active running about our yard; she had wanted to go sun herself after lunch, but put off the expedition until the children had gone, by 3:00 PM. She wanted to go over the manuscript for her dream book, without interruptions. Also, the same two children had been romping through Jane's freshly spaded garden out back, which did not cheer her up. The garden site is about 25 feet from where Jane sat while I sketched her.

(Jane's dream book manuscript does not show in the sketch; at the moment I made the sketch the manuscript was invisible beyond her right side. Another book does show, as well as a glass of ice tea, a book of matches and a cigarette.

("A rectangular card, with printed matter." The object is on a rectangular piece of heavy, porous-type paper, similar to card stock. Jane said she had an image of the correct size and proportion of the object, and that Seth was trying to get this data across to her. She had no image of a drawing, or herself.

(The card bears my writing, but strictly speaking this is not printed matter; which need not refer to writing at all.

("Some larger lettering, and then some small." Jane feels this is a distortion of my writing or lettering on the object. I would say lettering is a closer description than printed matter, being more specific.

("The color red." Jane wore plaid shorts of a predominantly red color. Also, she sits on a Mexican serape, one of two given to us by her father several years ago. This serape bears alternating bands, each one perhaps four inches wide, of white, red and blue.

("An impression of many people." Here Jane said she had the impression of a party, but decided to drop this line of association. This came from the mirth reference, she thought, and she was not sure the chain of association was correct. Sometimes it is left up to her as to what train of thought to follow. Again, Seth

expresses uncertainty about the party-mirth connection in answer to my third question.

("Connection with a tall man." Jane's father Del, who is 6' 2", gave us the serape Jane was sitting on when I sketched her this afternoon.

("The letter L." We don't know. L as in lawn, or as in Del...

("Perhaps the number 17." We don't know.

("A twist." We don't know. Jane was moving almost constantly as I sketched her, and her motions included many bodily twists and turns. This may apply, when considered with the next data.

("A pattern of wavy lines, or of wavering lines." The drawing used as object contains many lines, few of them straight. Jane said that in particular this data referred to the serape upon which she sat, and the tasseled edge or fringe beneath her lower legs. The drawing is organized into a pattern.

("Missed, an occasion missed earlier." See the interpretation of an unpleasant event on page 184. The "missed" here refers to Jane putting off her sunbathing until the neighborhood children had gone. She went outside around 3:00 PM, when I made the sketch. Originally she had wanted to go out after lunch, but waited.

("The impression now of looking down, from a high position..." This is an excellent description of my position in the second-story studio, looking quite straight down as I sketched Jane on the lawn. She was perhaps twelve feet below me. Jane had an image in connection with this data, which is explained below. At the time I made the drawing I wondered if Jane would sense the fact even though she didn't see me. Jane paused noticeably before she continued.

("That is connected with rocks." Although Jane had the serape spread on grass, she sat within perhaps five feet of the flagstone patio which is directly underneath the studio. These stones, or rocks are not cemented down, merely loosely fit in place, and are always being kicked astray. They are of all sizes, from a few inches to a foot or more across.

(This rock data and related data is a case where Jane decided to pursue her original impression of being up high. Often, she said, it is left up to her as to whether to so develop an impression. Sometimes she doesn't know what to do. This time she followed up to some degree because she also had an image, of someone standing on high, looking down from some kind of rocky perch. She believes this image was distorted to some degree.

("Or of looking down from a high position into a hole." This too resulted, Jane said, from her pursuing the above line of association.

("A thin border on the object", The border might be called thin on the bottom and left edge of the object, since the drawing runs out almost to the edge here. There is plenty of room however on the top and right sides.

("and horizontal lettering." My writing on the object follows the horizontal or

long dimension of the object. There is a possibility this could also refer to the organization data, to be discussed shortly. Or—could this refer to the book Jane had with her, or the manuscript of her dream book, also with her?

("Reaching in the center out toward the margins." In the drawing Jane's left arm and both legs reach out toward the bottom and left edges of the object.

("A card, such as the kind sent out by organizations for invitations." Jane had an image here, of a rectangular card of the kind that used to be sent out by an art gallery where she worked up until a year of so ago. This image card was the same size and proportion, she said, as the rectangular paper the envelope object is drawn on; she believes Seth gave her this data to reinforce that idea.

(Jane did not have this image when she gave the "rectangular card" data interpreted on page 184.

("Give us a moment... B and L and G." My first question asked for initials connected to the object. Jane said that when giving this data she knew the initials referred to different things, not just one. So we speculated that B referred to Butts, L to lawn, and G to glass. Seth confirms this after break. Note that I didn't indicate lawn, actually, in the sketch, although Jane's cast shadow falls partly on the lawn.

("The sort of lines for example that a map would have to indicate small roads, or the lines like cracks in a dry ground." My second question asked for more on the wavering lines impression discussed on page 185. See the copy of the object on page 178. The drawing is composed of thin pencil lines in part at least, and these could in the abstract represent small roads on a map, or lines like cracks in dry ground.

(Jane didn't have much to say about the map simile, but thought the ground crack idea pertinent. While sitting in the sun, smoking the one cigarette she had with her—it is shown in the sketch, which means she smoked it after I finished the drawing—she looked for a bare spot of ground against which to put the smoke out. In doing so she realized that the ground was quite dry, and that we needed more rain.

("I am not sure here. It seems a connection with a party. But also a connection with something unpleasant, so I am not sure." My third question concerned the mirth data, discussed on page 184. At that time Seth didn't come up with a party connection with mirth, although he mentioned party later on. He did connect mirth to something unpleasant, however, and we believe this to be the correct connection. Here above, he is also unsure about the party connection, the something unpleasant data interfering.

(Jane now said that her personal association of mirth hooked it up to party ideas, so my question may have called this to her mind. Jane pointed out that the glass and cigarette in the sketch might also be called party props, however.

("I think there is a red color, and rather large lettering, perhaps four or five lines." My fourth question asked for the content of the horizontal lettering mentioned

by Seth. Seth named both horizontal lettering and red before in the data. As stated on page 184 Jane wore shorts of a predominantly red plaid in the sketch, and the serape she sat on contained broad bands of red.

(We don't particularly know why Seth called my writing on the object large. It does consist of five lines. Once again, Jane paused noticeably before continuing.

("Come... An invitation to do something, or go somewhere, or to join." Jane believes this data grew out of the gallery card data interpreted under organizations on page 186. There is another connection; Jane mentioned it tentatively but we had no way to be sure. Seth confirms it after break however.

("Perhaps 24, referring to a day of the month." The envelope object bears the date on which I made the sketch—May 23,1966. Seth is one day off.

("Five or 6 for the month perhaps." The drawing was made during the fifth month, May.

("I have done as much to name it as I can." Here I asked Seth if he wanted to name the object.

(After the experiment, and after we had interpreted the data, Jane recalled one impression she had which she had not mentioned. The impression was "Star shape." Looking at the drawing, Jane felt it applied to the radiating lines on the crown of the straw hat she wore as I sketched her. We think this legitimate for Jane uses such calligraphy in her paintings.

(Jane resumed at 10:59.)

We will indeed close our session, and in our next session I will continue with this evening's discussion.

Now, I could often carry our sessions longer. I have been keeping them short for your convenience. Not so much because of the time used in the session, Joseph, but because of your labors in recording them.

The G and the L did refer to the glass and the lawn.

("Did Jane know I was making the drawing of her?")

No. The invitation however did have some application, though there was some distortion. When you talked to Ruburt there was an implied invitation on his part, for he would have liked you to have gone down.

(When I first saw Jane on the lawn below the studio windows, I leaned out to joke with her briefly. I thought of joining her myself, but did not mention it because I did not want to lose painting time. Nor did Jane openly ask me to join her.)

We will now close our session. One remark: It will do Ruburt good to work vigorously about the house, and that is all.

("Good night, Seth."

(End at 11:02.)

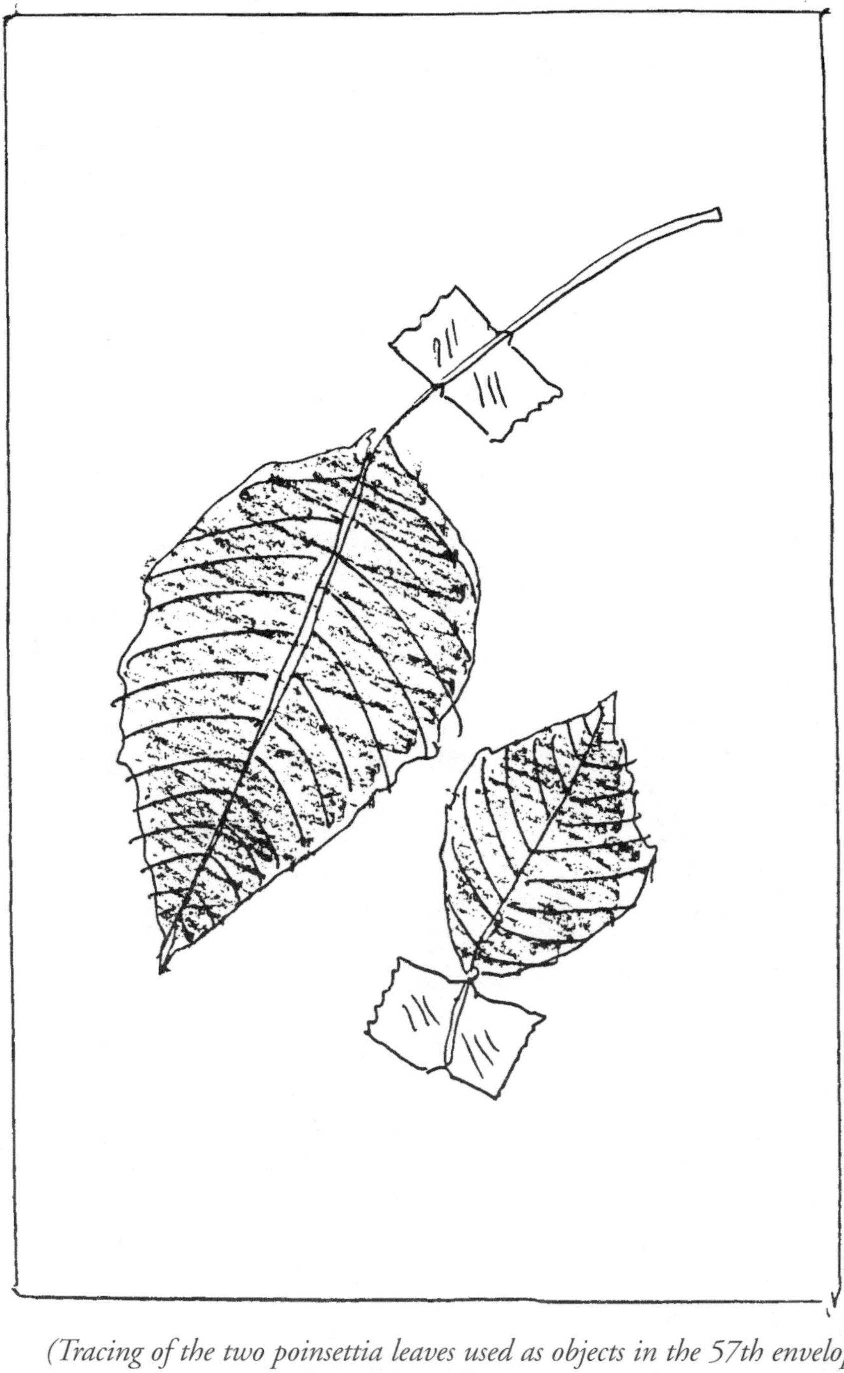

(Tracing of the two poinsettia leaves used as objects in the 57th envelope experiment, in the 262nd session for May 25,1966.)

(Back)

SESSION 262
MAY 25, 1966 9 PM WEDNESDAY

(The objects for the 57th envelope experiment were two leaves taken from our poinsettia plant. The plant is an old one, and one of our favorites. We see it every day of course but I was sure Jane wasn't aware of these two specific leaves separately. The plant also has an interesting history, which will be brought out later. I taped the leaves to one of the two pieces of Bristol used in these experiments, sandwiched it against the other piece, then sealed the two in the usual double envelopes. Note that the word "top" is penciled on the back of the Bristol; this was done by me after the experiment, but before Jane saw the objects, as will be shown later.

(Jane had been housecleaning, and to air the place out all the windows were open, still, at session time. Thus Jane began speaking in a voice quite a bit stronger than usual, evidently to counter the constant street noise. Her eyes soon began to open; she began speaking with a smoking cigarette in her hand. Her pace was fair.)

Good evening.

("Good evening, Seth.")

We will continue our previous discussion.

I want to give you some idea of the conditions that you may expect to meet in any successful projections, so that you will be prepared to some extent. For simplicity's sake we shall call the body forms of which we spoke in our last session, forms one, two and three.

Now, form number one will spring out of an ordinary dream state. In spontaneous projections you may become conscious in form number one, legitimately project, <u>return</u> to the ordinary dream state, and project again several times. You can expect therefore that these projections will be difficult to interpret, though you may find the experience intact in the <u>middle</u> of the record of any given dream.

The excursions with form number one will be of your own system, and largely connected to the earth, although past, present and future may be involved. You may, for example, visit New York in the year 2,000. This is at least <u>possible</u>, you see, using form number one.

The projections here are fairly short in duration, though exceptionally clear. You may encounter phantoms from your own subconscious however, and they will seem exceedingly real. If you realize that you are projecting you may simply <u>order</u> any unpleasant subconscious phantoms to disappear, and they will do so.

They will do so in the same way that a <u>nightmare</u> will disappear if you realize that it is a product of your own subconscious. If you treat it as a reality however, then you must deal with it as such, until you realize its origin, or return to the ordinary dream state.

(Long pause.) In form two, you will not as a rule encounter any subconscious phantoms, and usually you make the change to form two from the state in which form one is used. The ordinary dream elements will not be as frequent, nor will they intrude as much into the experience itself.

A longer duration of projection is possible. The vividness is extraordinary. You will begin here to perceive very clearly constructions that are not your own, where earlier these were but dimly glimpsed. A certain period of orientation will be necessary, simply because these other constructions may be bewildering. Some will exist in your future. Some may have existed in your past, and some were thought of but never physically materialized.

But the reality of all of these constructions will be equally vivid, you see, for they are indeed equally real. I will give you one very simple example. Suppose you find yourself in a room with certain people, and you recognize later upon awakening that this room and these people both belong to a particular sequence in a novel. You think then, "This was no projection, simply a dream."

It may however be a valid projection. The room and the people exist, but they do not exist in the manner which you endorse as reality. They exist in another dimension, but as a rule you cannot perceive it. In this case, you see, since the book has already been written you could say that the scene was a past event, at least of the imagination, at the time the author conceived of it.

Obviously, physical reality only happens to be the portion of reality you recognize. The paintings that you will paint exist now. It is possible for you to project yourself into one of your own future landscapes. This would not be an imaginative projection. This is what I am trying to tell you.

You had better take your break.

(Break at 9:28. Jane was dissociated as usual. Her eyes had opened often, and she had smoked and sipped iced tea. Her pace had been average.

(A question had occurred to me as Seth spoke and I voiced it now: Were any of the results of our experimental data, involving either Dr. Instream or our own envelopes, the result of unsuspected projections on Jane's part? Seth refers to the question later in the session.

(Jane resumed in the same manner at 9:35.)

You may find yourself in the midst of a battle that was once planned in some general's mind, a battle that never materialized in physical reality.

In such a case incidentally, you were not a part of the battle, and you cannot be harmed. However you might be attracted enough to project yourself spontaneously into the body of one of the soldiers, in which case you could experience pain, until your own fear pulled you back. It will be a matter of learning control under such conditions. *(Long pause, eyes opening often.)*

There are various situations which you must learn to handle, attractions and repulsions which could pull you willy-nilly in any direction. Experience is the only way for you to learn how to handle these.

What is required is a steady maintenance of identity, under conditions which will be new as far as your conscious awareness is concerned. In the cases about which we have been speaking, I cannot emphasize too strongly that actual projection into other dimensions occurs. Many such instances are often considered mad dreams, because there is no way to check against physical events. The events never happened in physical terms.

(Very restless, rubbing eyes heavily.) Now listen carefully for a moment. It is possible in form two to project to a future event *(eyes now open wide and steady, very dark)* in which you will be involved, and by an act that you make in the projection, alter the course that this future will take. *(Smile.)*

Such an action would therefore appear to happen twice—once in your present, and once in your future, you see. But in the future *(smile)* you would be the one whose course is altered by this traveling self from the past.

(Eyes continually open. Delivery very emphatic, with many gestures.)

Let us take an example. You sleep. While asleep you project yourself into the year 1972. There you see yourself considering various courses of action. For a moment you are aware of a sense of duality as you look at this older self. You say you should do this or that, give a definite decision, you see. This may happen in several ways. We will go into this sort of thing more deeply in another session.

(Eyes open.) In any case this future self of yours heeds what you say. Now, in the actual future you are the self who one way or another, you see, hears the voice of his past self. *(Jane leans forward, knocking on the tabletop for emphasis, eyes wide.)* Perhaps in a dream, or perhaps in a projection, made into the past.

Before our break I will leave you with a few questions. *(Smile, lighting cigarette.)* Was there something your future self had forgotten? Did the future self request information, and did this request cause the present self, you see, to make an actual and legitimate projection into the future?

You may now take your break. I do intend to answer your question, incidentally, when we get to it.

(Break at 9:57. Jane was well dissociated. Her pace had been average but her manner very emphatic. She had smiled often and used many gestures. Her eyes had been open for paragraphs at a time. She had been aware of nothing but the material, she said.

(It was now time for the 66th Dr. Instream experiment. Jane sat with a hand raised to her closed eyes. Resume at 10:04.)

Give us a moment, please, for our Instream material.

A slide rule. I have the impression of a classroom, large with many windows on one side of the room... *(Long pause.)* Facing west, the windows facing west.

Perhaps two windows also on the south side; though I am not sure these are windows on the south side, but window shapes in any case. The others are windows. There is no building immediately outside of them, but grass and street or a courtyard.

I believe that Dr. Instream was here just before twilight this evening. At one time with five particular people, talking to them. At an earlier time there were more people in the room, a small crowd. I believe that hypnosis was under discussion. The slide rule may have been used somehow in a demonstration.

Something on a desk. A small circle of glass on a flat base. Perhaps a paperweight, I do not know. The speaker handled it often. It is of palm size, that is, the palm easily fits over the glass circle portion.

The object seems to be a <u>bead</u>, or something resembling a bead. Much smaller than the other object, and round. It may be of metal.

Now do you have an envelope for me?

("Yes."

(At 10:13 Jane took the envelope for our 57th experiment from me without opening her eyes. She held it to her forehead with its long axis horizontal, as she almost always does. This position is rather important to the results of the experiment, as will be shown. Jane remembers holding the envelope in this fashion, and I watched her do so.)

Give us a moment, please.

Again, I have the impression of something round—more oval, perhaps. Fairly large in the center of a square or rectangular object.

Also something in the center of the oval. *(Jane now lowered the envelope to her lap with her left hand, sitting however with her other hand still to her closed eyes.)* Two horizontal lines, rather widely separated from each other.

A small starlike shape, perhaps in the lower right hand corner, holding the object this way. *(Jane gestured with the envelope which she now held so that the short dimensions were horizontal to the floor. I noted this position and watched her closely to see if she changed the envelope's position as the experiment continued.)*

A connection with 1961.

Yellow and red. A tall tree, exceptionally tall, I believe. Ruburt here thinks of his mother Marie. We will simply mention it.

A connection with the month of February. An initiation. Something on the back or inside of the object. Did the object once open up?

The impression of continued writing. A connection with a note, I believe, or a card that opened, with writing or copy on an inside page. Orange. The orange seems to be connected with black also. Or dark color. Perhaps like dark lettering.

The impression of a water connection. With something beginning with an M, and something beginning with a G, and with four objects.

Do you have any questions?

("Can you say something more about those two horizontal lines?")

I have the impression of two dark horizontal lines, one rather toward the top and one rather toward the bottom. *(Jane again gestured with the envelope. She held it in the same position as noted before, the small dimensions parallel to the floor. She hadn't changed its position by idly turning it, for example.)* Both inside, but just an oval shape. Holding the object this way. *(The same gesture again.)* Now I suggest your break. Unless you have any more questions.

("Well then, try naming the object.")

(Pause.) I have the impression, holding the object this way, *(again the same gesture)* of a rectangular object, a card that is connected with a picture, and strongly connected with something that opened, as a letter could open to another page.

Also a dim connection with the word master. Master list, I do not know. I suggest your break.

(Break at 10:25. Jane said she was really "out." Way-out, she said, not aware of anything but the data and the connection to or with her mother, Marie. Her eyes had remained closed through both experiments, her pace had been good.

(Jane always sits quietly for a few moments after leaving trance until she is fully oriented. This gave me enough time to once again see that she held the envelope in the same position relative to the floor. I called her attention to this, then marked the outer envelope "top". Next I marked the inside envelope the same way, then the two pieces of Bristol the same way as Jane watched. The two leaves were sandwiched between the Bristols. Note the top marking in pencil on the back of the object, as indicated on the tracing on page 189.

(Jane had one image which will be mentioned in place. We were able to make quite a few connections, and Seth helped us with one after break. The session was over now however for most practical purposes. Since the object did not originate with us, we were not able to make some connections which we supposed were probably valid. The history of the poinsettia plant which furnished the leaves used as objects will unfold to some extent as we interpret the data.

("Again, I have the impression of something round—more oval, perhaps. Fairly large in the center of a square or rectangular object." As noted Jane held the envelope to her forehead with the long axis parallel to the floor. No matter which long edge was uppermost this places the large poinsettia leaf in the center of the card as far as the short edges are concerned. Even so the large leaf would be off center, either above or below, as far as the long edges are concerned. I hoped Seth would mention two objects, but he did not.

(Seth goes from round to oval, which is more specific as far as the leaf is concerned, and from square to rectangular, which is more specific as far as the rectangular shape of the piece of Bristol to which I had taped both objects is concerned. The bigger of the two leaves is fairly large as far as the overall size of the piece of Bristol is concerned.

("Also something in the center of the oval." Evidently Seth here picks up the fishbone pattern formed by veins and stems in one or both of the objects, as the next data develops.

("Two horizontal lines, rather widely separated from each other." Since Jane had held the envelope to her forehead in the position above indicated, it can be seen that the "spines" of the two leaves, taped to the Bristol, would be roughly horizontal to the floor and thus to her vision. Provided Seth gives this data in our terms in such cases. We wondered if by horizontal Seth, or Jane, could possibly mean parallel, since the leaves are quite parallel to each other on the Bristol.

(Seth's use of the word separated here is the closest he came to indicating two objects.

("A small starlike shape, perhaps in the lower right hand corner, holding the object this way." By now Jane had lowered the envelope to her lap while giving the data, and held it with a short edge up as explained. See my indication of this by use of the word top on the back of the tracing on page 189. I determined this as explained low on page 193. With the object held in this position, it can be seen that the smaller of the two poinsettia leaves would be in the lower right hand corner or the lower left hand corner, depending on whether the piece of Bristol to which the leaves were taped had the leaves facing toward Jane or away from her.

(Seth uses the word perhaps here, so he may not have been sure, or Jane may have been a bit unsure. He does mention right hand corner. We believe the starlike shape a good reference to the internal pattern of the leaf. This kind of radiating line pattern is one which Jane uses in her paintings, and in past experiments has been interpreted as "sun shape," "star shape," etc.

("A connection with 1961." The plant from which the two leaves were taken was once the property of our neighbor here in the apartment house, Miss Callahan, an elderly retired teacher. Jane first saw it in Miss Callahan's apartment at Christmas

of 1964, when Miss Callahan received it as a Christmas present.

(Jane immediately realized a poinsettia connection with 1961, however. In 1961, shortly after we had moved to Elmira, a friend with whom Jane worked at an art gallery gave her two poinsettia plants that we had for several years. This is easily remembered because the two 1961 plants are the only other poinsettias we have ever owned. We have for instance never bought a poinsettia plant for ourselves, or as a gift, etc.; the two 1961 plants and the plant which furnished the objects for tonight constitute the only three poinsettias we have been involved with. The 1961 plants were outright gifts. The third plant I found on the back porch of the apartment house last winter, where it had been discarded by Miss Callahan. More on this later.

("Yellow and red." The plant I acquired secondhand via Miss Callahan is the only poinsettia we have. The two 1961 plants died a couple of years ago. Oddly enough, none of our three plants have ever bloomed for us. Their blooms are red leaved, of course, with brilliant yellow centers; I have painted poinsettias many times on my job, for greeting card designs. Interestingly enough, Jane used to see our present plant in bloom in Miss Callahan's apartment, before Miss Callahan disposed of it.

("A tall tree, exceptionally tall, I believe." The plant we now have, which furnished the leaves used as objects, is, we have been told, quite old and tall for a poinsettia. Many people have remarked about this. The plant stands perhaps three feet tall; this may have given rise to Seth's tall data here. The stems have acquired a woody, brown texture. In addition, the day I removed the leaves used as objects from the plant, it stood on our bathroom windowsill. This is quite high; the plant on the sill gave the illusion of reaching almost to the ceiling.

("Ruburt here thinks of his mother, Marie. We will simply mention it." We don't know the source of this data. A childhood association of Jane's, involving poinsettias?

("A connection with the month of February." We don't know. At first Jane and I thought this might refer to the month I found the discarded poinsettia on the back porch last winter. It was a bitterly cold day and the plant had begun to wilt when I found it at noontime. However, upon reflection we realized we had the plant with us last Christmas.

("An initiation." We don't know.

("Something on the back or inside of the object. Did the object once open <u>up</u>? The impression of continued writing. A connection with a note, I believe, or a card that opened, with writing or copy on an inside page. Orange. The orange seems to be connected with black also. Or <u>dark</u> color. Perhaps like dark lettering." These impressions came together, and we can offer no connections. Seth seems to be quite insistent upon the subject of writing or a note, so they may be valid. As stated, Jane saw the

plant which furnished tonight's objects, as a Christmas present in Miss Callahan's apartment at Christmas of 1964. Jane considers it possible that here Seth is getting at the idea of a folded note or card being attached to the plant when Miss Callahan received it as a gift. However Jane can recall no such note or card upon seeing it in 1964. Nor can we check with Miss Callahan, who has suffered a considerable loss of memory as a result of a series of strokes since 1964.

("The impression of a water connection." There can be at least two. As stated, today the plant which furnished the leaves used as objects sat on our bathroom windowsill. Due to the architecture of our bathroom this puts it within a foot or so of our sink. Also, since it had been quite a hot day, Jane watered the plant again at supper time—something she usually doesn't do at that time of day.

("With something beginning with an M, and something beginning with a G," We didn't know, although we speculated that the initials were a distortion of Miss Callahan, or of Merry Christmas, both these ideas being related to the source of the poinsettia plant which furnished the leaves as objects. Seth helps us out on this after break.

("and with four objects." We saw no connections.

(My first question asked Seth for more data about the two horizontal lines. See page 194. "I have the impression of two dark horizontal lines, one rather toward the top and one rather toward the bottom." [Jane gestures.] It will be remembered that when Seth gave this data the first time, Jane held the envelope to her forehead with its long dimensions horizontal to the floor. As explained, this meant the spines of the two leaves were also roughly horizontal to the floor and her insight. Seth elaborates a bit here now, although Jane now sat holding the envelope in her lap, and with its short dimensions parallel to the floor.

(When the envelope is held in the horizontal position, the spine of one of the leaves is above the other, or one toward the top and the other toward the bottom. They are not dark, however. In poinsettia leaves at least, the central spine is a lighter green color than the rest of the leaf.

(More data follows from the first question: "Both <u>inside</u>, but just an oval shape. Holding the object this way." [Jane gestured again, the envelope in the same position, short end up.] From this we infer that Seth refers to the spines of the leaves, and not their stems; yet mention is made only of an oval shape, singular.

(I now asked Seth to name the object: "I have the impression, holding the object this way" [gesture in the same fashion as above], "of a rectangular object, a card that is connected with a picture", resulted in Jane having a mental image here. She saw, she said, the rectangular shape of the Bristol to which I had taped the two leaves. She also had an image of something darker in the center of the rectangle, and interpreted this as a picture instead of "something real." Upon seeing the object, Jane

realized the dark areas of the leaves matched the dark areas she had seen mentally, yet the image hadn't been sharp enough to see as leaves; it came through in a generalized picture interpretation instead.

(Seth added more as a result of the second question: "and strongly connected with something that opened, as a letter could open to another page." We believe this data to be separate from that in the paragraph just above. Once again Seth brings in the writing connection, previously described on page 196. We can offer no interpretations here, either.

("Also a dim connection with the word, master. Master list, I do not know." Nor do we.

(Jane resumed briefly at 10:47.)

We will close our session.

There was a visual distortion. We should have had M C, rather than M G.

(Which leaves us just about where we were—Miss Callahan, Merry Christmas...?)

My heartiest regards. I would speak with you longer, but my friend Ruburt has said good night to me, and as always I respect his wishes.

("Good night, Seth."

(End at 10:48. Jane said Seth felt fine and could have continued indefinitely.)

SESSION 263
MAY 29, 1966 APPROXIMATELY 11:25 PM UNSCHEDULED

(A very short unscheduled session was held Sunday evening, May 29, after company had left. The session did not particularly grow out of the evening's conversation; perhaps more so from a short discussion Jane and I held when we were alone at last.

(The first part of the session is summarized, the notes being made immediately, at 11:28. The balance of the session is verbatim as indicated. Jane first came through as Seth while sitting at ease on the couch. We had been wondering aloud if the bulk of the material would ever be published verbatim. Seth came through to say quite definitely that the material would be published verbatim—not all of it, literally, but certain large areas of it. He did not give a date or year, etc., and I did not ask.

(Seth told us the Seth book which is now at Jane's publisher would be published, and that her dream book would also. Jane sent the dream book to another publisher last week. After a pause Seth said the verbatim material would be published

also, but gave no hint of a date.

(Seth then went on to say that the bridge personality would be dispensed with eventually, because it would no longer be needed. See sessions 141-143.

(After receiving the above material I moved over to a table to make notes on it. Jane sat opposite me, her eyes closed part of the time, and resumed as Seth at 11:28.)

You will do very well financially in the next few years—so well in fact that you, Joseph, will feel yourself compelled to sell your paintings in order to hold your own. An absurd compulsion, I might add. *(Smile, eyes closed.)*

There will be new developments in our sessions, and new experiments with others, as a result of Ruburt's first book.

Simply note this: 5 and 7 and Tennessee, the 5 and 7 the numbers of letters in a name. Now, and S and a G, and there will be physical signs for dear Ruburt, when the time comes for physical signs.

I will not keep you.

("That's all right.")

A 4 and a 6, with a block between, the block having to do with a period of time. Once again, I am with you more often than you suppose, and I shall be with you this evening when you dream.

("Are we going to dream of you?")

You may not dream of me, but I will be in your dreams, you see. My heartiest wishes to you both. The street in Boston had to do with the word bleak.

("Bleak? B-l-e-a-k?"

(Jane nodded, her eyes closed.

(End at 11:34. Jane said she was very well dissociated. Her eyes had been open about half the time. The mention of Boston occurred we supposed because a little earlier we had spoken of the Boston reincarnational material Seth had given us in the 257th session.)

SESSION 264
JUNE 1, 1966 9 PM MONDAY

(The session due Monday, May 30, was not held due to my own indisposition. Tonight I asked Jane if Seth would discuss the Instream object that ordinarily would have been named Monday.

(Jane knew that no envelope experiment was planned for the session.

(The following dream and experience is taken from Jane's notebook; it concerns her results obtained after she deliberately lay down from 8 to 9:30 AM, Monday, June 1, to attempt projection. She wrote out the account immediately upon arising:

(I am not sure of some of these events as far as sequence goes, and also believe I forgot some of the experience itself. I believe I also fell into inconsequential dreaming or sleep after the last event.

(I see plants I have planted long ago; flourishing and beautiful, and can be used for decorating or repotted. I think that here I had a false awakening and told Rob about the beautiful plants. I also thought they were symbolic of the work put into my books. It is possible that this was preceded by a levitation dream.

(The false awakening: I tell Rob about the plants, and perhaps make a note to record the dream. "Then I realize this is a false awakening, and that I should be able to project. I am sitting in the bathroom when I realize this. I try to levitate or project. I hold my legs out and my feet feel strange: There is an odd sensation, a shifting of some kind. Then I really project. There is an experience of seeing many mirrors, through which I travel. The mirrors are not solid. Feeling of motion, and the mirror scenes also move."

(I was in a landscape with two women. We were leaders of some kind. Running over the hills, I leap from ground to a high ledge. I am not satisfied with the leap, so move "backward through the air" to my original spot, and do the whole thing over. Then I have another false awakening in which I tell Rob about the dream and levitation.

(Then I'm in a house of our friends Lydia and Atlee; many kids and animals. "I talk to Rob. He is in one room and I am in a hallway. Suddenly I see two Robs: Rob's double is in another room, that I can also see from my viewpoint. I keep talking to Rob and tell him to stay where he is. Then I check, moving closer to the other room. Sure enough I can see both Robs clearly. They both talk, so I tell Rob to come into the hall so he can see what I see. He does, and both Robs see each other. Others, hearing us, see both Robs also."

(Then Lizzie Roohan calls out to me from next door and I go over to see her. She is younger than I remember her; perhaps in her fifties. There is a fabulous cultivated garden nearby, perhaps several of them. Also perhaps some difficulty about neighbors who wouldn't keep up their own land.

(Jane's notes concerning the dream: The actual separation from physical body is the most vivid experience of the whole sequence—if separation is what it was. This is the first time I definitely realized I had a false awakening, then consciously tried to project from it. I certainly seemed to do so.

(The following dream and experience is from my notebook for the night of Tuesday, May 31:

(In full vivid color. One of the most unusual dreams I have ever had. There are probably gaps in my recall of it.

(I stood on a narrow ledge at night, on a cliff side, with several men I knew

well in the dream but not in waking life. There was a fire burning in a circle of stone at our feet, and we all held long poles like broom handles. I dropped a lighted match into a littered ashtray, which flamed up; when I tried to put the fire out I found I couldn't.

(Then I was watching the fire spread in the stone fireplace. Once again trying to put it out, I poked it with my stick. Instead I knocked chunks of ground out of the bottom of the circle, and could look through space at other cliffs and trails far below. At the same time the others with me cautioned me to stop poking. I realized now that the end of our ledge was held up now by only a thin column of stone, but didn't feel alarmed at this. The stone column seemed to be aglow, or hot.

(Then I was on a vacation trip in the tropics. I believe the same group was with me. I had a pair of binoculars to watch others on the trails. There was a woman here in the dream but her role is beyond my accurate recall.

(Now one of my close friends—I cannot recall his name, if I ever knew it—was due to ski down one of the trails. I was very concerned for his safety. The man, in a green uniform, sailed down a trail and into the air. At this time I seemed to be in a bed, suspended first over the trails, and then in a room.

(My friend was now either a miniature *man, or very far away; actually I am quite sure he was miniature size. I saw him coming in for a landing, tiny and green and apparently out of control. He swooped down beside my bed, skidded along the top of a covered radiator, crashed into a wall and fell down onto another radiator top at a lower level. The landing was very rough and I cried out in dismay as my friend bounced and skidded around. I believe he was about four inches tall, and I saw his skis twisted over each other as he fell.*

(I was so concerned for my friend's safety and welfare that I scooped him up in my hands, and held him between them like a child holds a trapped fly. I then felt my tiny friend, who by now seemed to be even smaller, buzzing and banging against my palms, trying to get out.

(Now I was in a shack in the tropics, again at night, with the rest of the group. I still held my green friend inside my cupped hands. I felt him buzzing, very vividly, still trying to escape. We stood before a crude wooden table we were going to use as an operating table. I was going to operate, or somehow bring my friend back to full size. I saw no instruments. The shack was lit by glowing kerosene lanterns, or some kind of such yellow light. I think it was quite dirty.

(Then I saw that someone had left the shack's door open, and that everything, the walls, the ceiling, the open door, etc., was covered with hordes of insects of various kinds and colors, all crawling and flying about. This made me very angry, for as I felt my friend buzzing inside my hands, I wondered how I would know him from any other insect once I released him in order to help him.

(Jane began speaking in a rather quiet voice and with quite a few pauses. Her eyes were closed to begin, but she was smoking and they soon began to open frequently.)

Good evening.

("Good evening, Seth.")

First, some general comments. You are both learning rather quickly. Ruburt's projection from the dream state, through a false awakening, was indeed legitimate. He gave himself no suggestion beforehand, yet the overall suggestions that he has given himself stood him in good stead.

The mirror however is the mirror in your bedroom. He projected through this physical matter without realizing that he did so.

Now your own dream, Joseph, also involved projection, but with less intent behind it, and some less control, though very little control occurred in either case. You will learn control as you go along.

On Ruburt's part we had a definite manipulation of consciousness that was directed to some extent. You projected once into the past, and I was one of your friends. This episode was the less distorted. One episode involved a small future projection, and was intermixed with ordinary dream elements. This involved the operating episode.

The miniature episode is extremely interesting, and rather complicated to explain. *(Pause.)* Give us a moment here. *(Pause, eyes closed.)*

First of all, the episode involved a transitory period, to bring you to the operation situation. The means chosen by you originally was somewhat different. You intended to project yourself into one of the small insects in the room, you see, but you were unable to do so.

The original fear for your friend was a sympathetic fear of a patient, who was to be operated on. The particular patient had chills, hence your interpretation of the skiing episode, and snow.

There was a definite projection, however, to the psychic healer's shack. I was involved here also, rather good-naturedly, hoping to help you.

We will skip a bit around here. The plants in Ruburt's dream did represent the books upon which he has worked and is working. The projection was quite legitimate. The Lydia episode contained many ordinary dream elements. You were indeed present, *(smile)* with Ruburt in some of his travels, but you have forgotten.

Ruburt saw two of you. He saw your form number two as described earlier, in which you were also traveling, you see. *(See the 262nd session.)* The other was Ruburt's dream form of you, created by himself in the dream state. When you appeared in form two he was conscious enough, you see, to recognize your arrival, and then to point out to you the dream image which he had already created. And you were able to see it because of your own state.

Now when Ruburt dreams that he has discussed a dream with you, in most cases he has indeed done so. You have both conversed quite naturally in forms number two. With enough training, these conversations can be recorded in both of your dreams. The amount of work necessary is literally astounding, but I tell you that you can both do this; and you can make general, through your work, a knowledge of the true potential of the dream state.

You have both advanced, particularly you see because you do not have the ego to contend with as an adversary. The quest has become a part of your egotistical concern. Therefore it will work for you. *(Long pause. Eyes open, then closed. Smoking.)*

Now. The small friend is rather difficult to explain in your experience. The color green is also amusing. You were the friend, you see—

("I wondered about that.")

—wanting to project as a green insect. The idea was too alien, and you split your consciousness so that you watched the small man in green.

We will take a break, and continue.

(Break at 9:27. Jane was dissociated as usual, her eyes opening often, her pace fair.

(I had my dream on the evening of Tuesday, May 31, then wrote out my account of it the next morning before going to work. This is not the full account reproduced in this session but a summary containing the main points of the dream.

(On Wednesday, at about noon, Jane bought the July issue of Fate Magazine. *It contains a long article about a Philippine psychic surgeon who is being brought to this country next fall, when he is to operate on patients with surgeons and others as witnesses. The article goes into detail about the scientists who have watched the psychic surgeon operate at his home in the Philippines, and about the surgeon's home and "operating room," which is but a shack containing a crude wooden-slatted table. Although the surgeon's surroundings are not sanitary, no case of infection has been traced to him.*

(I noticed the similarity between the last part of my dream, wherein I was to operate without instruments in a tropical shack, amid surroundings not clean and containing insects, etc., and the description of the psychic surgeon's quarters, and that his shack was situated in the tropics. I explained it to Jane at break and hoped Seth would comment as to any clairvoyant elements in the dream.

(On Tuesday, before the dream, I remember thinking casually about Fate Magazine, *and that perhaps a new issue was out. The thought was quite brief and without emphasis. I do not know when the magazine comes out, although I suppose it is on the first of the month or thereabouts. I did not mention my thought to Jane.*

I was alone when I had it; I was therefore a little surprised to see that she had bought the magazine the next day, Wednesday, but the surprise was not connected with my recalling my dream. Until I read over my notes Wednesday evening I had forgotten the dream.

(Jane resumed at 9:32.)

This will be a short session.

Now. You did clairvoyantly see the article in *Fate Magazine.*

Your various complaints this week were connected with Ruburt's painting and housecleaning. The housecleaning connection I believe you understand.

("Yes." Through the pendulum.)

The painting connection is not difficult. You felt guilty because you have not offered to help paint your parents' home, inside or outside, although your mother has dropped frequent and heavy hints. Both of these feelings were activated because of Ruburt's activities. *(Pause.)*

The canker sores should clear up and give you no difficulty. *(Jane lit a cigarette, her eyes open and very dark.)* They are connected here also. You believe them to be the result of infection caused by uncleanliness, you see. *(Smile.)* Do you understand this connection?

("Yes.")

The whole episode however, once it happened, was very well handled by you. *(Pause.)* Give us a moment.

(Jane paused again at 9:37. Her eyes were closed, and they remained closed even though she smoked while giving the Dr. Instream material. Her head was down and she sat with a hand raised to it. This is the 67th Dr. Instream experiment.)

Now for Dr. Instream. Monday. The object was composed of four squares. Either it was transparent, appeared so, or was connected with something transparent. There may have been a small series of numbers in each of the four squares—several numbers, perhaps. *(This material for Monday, May 30.)*

The object itself had something to do with a box, or box shape, that was a container. Several bright colors, and some dull.

(Pause at 9:39. This is the 68th Dr. Instream experiment.) Tonight's object is shaped like an arrow or sword, but smaller, and seems to be either dull, or sharp on one side and dull on the other, of a dull gold color, and with a rounded top.

Now, not connected with the object, I have the impression of gray view, and perhaps the initials J P, or B. I believe P is correct. The number three, referring to a day or a month in connection with the initials, and something a score of times.

A separate impression now... 1886, in connection with a book he may be reading. *(Pause.)*

Now I will close the session, or after a break you may continue as you see fit.

("We'll take the break then.")

(Break at 9:44. Jane was out as usual; her eyes had been closed as indicated.

(Seth's material on page 204 agreed with what I had learned myself by using the pendulum, both today and earlier in the week. I hadn't told Jane what results or answers I obtained through the pendulum.

(Jane resumed at 9:57.)

It is important for your training and development that consciousness be brought into the dream state.

Projection is a normal occurrence under dream conditions. However for the further development of consciousness and of identity, the so-called waking I can be of great benefit.

You will learn to manipulate and control various levels of awareness, and the habit will carry over into other aspects of reality. With continued development you will be able to keep appointments and pass information in the dream state, and have your records to prove it.

The trick is to achieve the proper balance. As Ruburt discovered, you can try too hard to take waking consciousness into the dream state, so that you simply cannot sleep as easily. Trial and error will show you the proper balance, and each successful attempt gives you added experience and control.

Later your experiences themselves, within a dream, will tip you off as to which form you are using, so that you will know what is possible under these particular conditions.

If you want to record any given experience in its clearest form, then you should train yourself to wake up immediately afterward. Otherwise later ordinary dreams will be remembered falsely as being part of the projection experience.

Now I will end the session, so you can have some small relief in typing. I will see, again, this evening, if we cannot all meet in your experiences. We shall see if you remember.

We will keep the appointment whether or not you remember. Now, I am prepared to speak; however I thought you could do with a short rest.

("I guess so.")

My heartiest regards to you both.

("Good night, Seth."

(End at 10:07. Jane was out as usual, she said. Her eyes had opened fairly often, her pace had been average, and she had smoked.

(It is Friday evening as I type this; our dream records since Wednesday give no indication that either Jane or I remembered meeting each other, or Seth, or whether all of us met together.)

(Front)

(Back)

(Tracings of the Polaroid color photograph used as the object in the 58th envelope experiment, in the 265th session for June 6, 1966.)

SESSION 265
JUNE 6, 1966 9 PM MONDAY

(The 58th envelope experiment was held this evening. The object was a faded color Polaroid photograph. The picture was taken by Don Wilbur on April 4, 1966, as noted on the back. Don and his wife Marilyn were due to witness the 248th session on April 4, but last-minute developments prevented them doing so. Don left the sealed envelope he had prepared for the session with me, however; I kept it until the Wilburs were able to witness a session. The photo is of a decorative garden cat, bearing a shining glass glaze, and was made by Marilyn.

(I did not know the contents of the envelope, nor of course did Jane. She had seen Don hand me the envelope on April 4, but since none of us had ever mentioned it since then I was hoping she had forgotten about it. After the session tonight Jane confirmed she had forgotten that I had the envelope. Even when the Wilburs arrived for the session tonight, Jane did not remember it.

(By coincidence Don had sealed the object in an envelope of the same size as those I use for the experiments. He did not use double envelopes, but had achieved the same effect by first wrapping the object in opaque white paper rather loosely; this also obliterated any hard edges that might have given sensory clues. Seth however discounts any possible data obtained through fingering, etc.

(Ann Diebler also witnessed the session, for a total of three witnesses. The three have heard Seth speak before on a few informal occasions; this was their first regular session. All have read some of the material.

(It was a hot, muggy night, and windows were open. The night seemed especially noisy, and Jane began speaking from the first in a heavier voice. Her eyes were closed, her pace good from the start.)

Good evening—

("Good evening, Seth.")

—and of course welcome to our friends.

We shall mainly be concerned this evening with the material which we have been discussing. There were some questions however that you had in mind, and I shall endeavor to answer them.

I am particularly concerned, you see, with this matter of projection, simply because your own abilities will rather swiftly lead you along in that direction. Therefore whatever information I can give you will be of great practical benefit. I do not want either of you traveling about unless you know what you are doing.

Specifically I wanted to mention the matter of subconscious fabrications. Now. Initially particularly, you <u>will</u> meet with these; you must remember that you are wandering in completely different dimensions, and the rules with which you are familiar simply do not apply there.

Joseph, I leave it up to you to slow me down when necessary.

("It's okay so far." Jane was speaking quite rapidly.)

You are familiar, all of you, with subconscious fabrications as they exist in the nightmare condition. Now on occasion when you are projecting from a dream point, you will meet such subconscious images. Your ordinary standards of reality mean absolutely nothing when you leave the physical system, therefore you will encounter, simultaneously perhaps, images that are subconsciously formed; quite valid images that belong in another dimension; constructions created by others within another system; and for any control at all, you must learn how to distinguish one from the other.

(Smile, eyes closed.) You see, even I can tell that our guests are not subconscious fabrications, and I would be pleased indeed if they granted me the same privilege. You will have control, you see, over your own subconscious images if you recognize them as your own constructions.

Without such recognition however an encounter could be unpleasant. You have little control, and I am speaking here now all evening, of projections and their circumstances—you will have little control over the constructions of others. If, for example, during projection travel you encounter a disturbing image, you must first will it to disappear. If it is a subconscious fabrication it will vanish, but if you do not will it to vanish it will remain, and then you must deal with it as a reality.

In somewhat the same manner, a nightmare will run its course and lead you into terror unless you realize that the nightmare is self-created. In which instance it will disappear.

I cannot emphasize too strongly however the fact that the ordinary standards by which you judge reality will not here apply. And Joseph, you must learn the new rules. Our small friend in the corner *(Jane pointed to Ann Diebler)* must learn the new rules. Now. Every image that you meet, and every experience, will be varied within its own framework. And do not forget that the experiences which you encounter will have an effect upon your own personality, as vivid or more vivid than the effect of any waking experience.

We have explored the various forms in which you may travel. I have also told you that the form in which you find yourself can be a tip-off to you. If your levitation experience seems to carry you outside of your solar system, then you know that you are using the third form, and that your abilities for the time are almost limitless, comparatively speaking. Any image that you see in any case must be accepted. Now. Physically speaking it does no good to call such images hallucinations, for they are no more hallucinations than the chair in which my friend Ruburt now sits.

(Eyes open, smiling, very emphatic with gestures.) Ruburt told one of your friends to respect physical reality. Whether or not the automobile is a sensory hallucination, it can kill you, he said. And I tell you, whether or not these images are hallucinations, they can be dangerous, and you must respect the reality in which they exist.

(To me:) Is your hand tired?

("No.")

Then, I want to be sure that you realize that some of these constructions that you will encounter will belong to another system. They will not be your own constructions. You are safe as long as you do not meddle. You may explore, and freely, and that is all.

We are going to take a very simple example here, an imaginary projection, and explain the steps as they will happen, more or less.

(A loud knock came on the hall door, but Jane continued.)

First however, before we begin this I will let you take your first break.

(Break at 9:22. The knocking came again, loudly. I did not notice, being busy writing, but Don Wilbur said the first knock really jolted Jane out of her trance, or at least the deeper stages of it, even though she continued speaking. Later Jane told me she had been very well dissociated. Her pace was fast, her eyes opened often, and she had used many gestures and much emphasis.

(Jane later said the interruption had been a shock to her. She was surprised, since interruptions have not bothered her the last few months.

(Our visitors did not know of the sessions. If they had noticed the rather strong Seth voice through the door—it was quite audible, we were sure—they gave no sign. The visitors left at 10:04. We had used the intervening time as a break, and Jane resumed in the same active manner at 10:05.)

Now. We will say that you are attempting a projection from a light trance state. Much of what you have read in your Mr. Fox's book is quite legitimate.

*(*Astral Projection*, by Oliver Fox. University Books.)*

Some of the effects however, of which he speaks, are the result of his own psychological makeup. You can avoid the unpleasant sensations that he has described if you realize this.

(We had discussed this at supper time. Jane had noticed a close similarity in some of the effects described by Oliver Fox, and those she had experienced on her own while doing psychological time, as long as two years ago.)

Otherwise, you see, you will expect them, and they will happen for that reason. The method that he gave is quite sufficient as far as the initial stages are concerned. However there is much more involved, in what he calls the pineal doorway projection.

These are my instructions. You may consider this your first lesson. We will go by easy stages, for we do not want you betwixt and between. You may induce a medium trance in whatever way you choose. On occasion this will be spontaneous, as you know. For best results in the beginning it is good to make a projection attempt when you already feel physically drowsy, but pleasantly so. When you have induced the trance state, then begin to examine your own subjective feelings until you find recognition of the inner self.

This involves a recognition of yourself as distinct from the fleshy fibers in which you reside. Then begin to imagine this inner self rising upward. You should experience even at this point an internal sense of motion. This motion may be from side to side, as you gently shake yourself loose, so to speak.

It may be a rushing upward. Whichever motion you experience there will be a moment where you feel yourself, your identity and consciousness, definitely withdrawing from the physical organism. Before you attempt the projection, however, the suggestion should be given that the physical organism will be well protected and comfortable. Now when you feel the consciousness withdrawing, there are two things you may do. I suggest the first step I shall give you in preference to the second.

The first step is this. Forget the physical body, or what you are to do with it. Will yourself out in a quick motion. There is no need to experience the voice hallucinations mentioned by the author, Fox. If the projection is a success you will instantly lose contact consciously with the physical body. You simply will not be in it.

Now your consciousness will not be in it, but it is hardly lifeless. Its maintenance is being controlled by the consciousness of the individual cells and organs of which we have spoken. I will give you alternate methods of projecting, but I will be concerned now with what you can expect the few moments after you have left the physical body.

Now, I am going to give you a short break to rid ourselves of the pussies. *(Our cats were noisily playing at Jane's feet.)* Then we will briefly give the Instream material, and perhaps briefly also whatever envelope material you may have for me. Following this we shall return to the material which we have been discussing, for you shall be in need of it shortly.

(Break at 10:22. Jane was out as usual, she said, and the cats hadn't particularly bothered her. We put them in the studio. Jane's pace had been good, her voice fairly strong, her eyes open often. It had not been a quiet session. Besides the interruption there had been noisy neighbors downstairs, heavy traffic, etc.

(Jane's voice was still good when she resumed at a slower pace, her eyes closed, while giving the 69th Dr. Instream material. 10:31.)

Give us a moment please for our Instream material.

These are impressions. The object twirls. There are four objects that seem to be connected, four vertical wooden polelike objects, with one horizontal bar approximately in the middle. That is, one bar on the other side.

There is a metal rod that connects these two horizontal bars. *(Pause.)* The top portion of the vertical objects moves. The objects stand on a small wooden platform with wheels. We have an object that seems to be something like a child's toy.

The initials S G seem to be connected to it. *(Pause.)* And a child, male, approximately two years old.

There are five events that Dr. Instream will attend specifically, and for which he is planning. Two of these will take place in a different city. The day for one is July 14. *(Pause.)*

Do you have an envelope for me?

("Yes.")

(Jane paused at 10:35. Without opening her eyes she took Don Wilbur's envelope and pressed it to her forehead for a moment before lowering it to her lap. This was our 58th envelope experiment.)

Give us a moment please. *(Pause, head down.)* These are impressions.

Four, plus one or two. Connection with a meeting. Colors green and yellow. The impression of stairs or steps. *(Pause.)* Something ascending in this fashion, you see.

(Her eyes still closed, Jane gestured largely with her hand and arm. She indicated a slope or angle upwards of perhaps 30 degrees, perhaps less; in a straight line, and quite definitely.)

Connection with high round objects. Also perhaps with a July date, and with square objects, in design fashion.

Some distant connection with a mission. I do not know to what this refers *(Jane shook her head)* and with objects in a row, or a series, perhaps of numbers.

M and G, F and O. Something to do with tomorrow. That is, tomorrow as far as the object is concerned, or to do with the future, this being indicated on the object.

The impression of the four again, and graduating, as something graduates in size perhaps.

Do you have any questions?

("Just how are the yellow and green connected to the object?")

Perhaps yellow in the center of a slightly rectangular shape, outlined in green. A visual connection, with square or rectangular objects in the center of a larger area, with modern connotations as a design might have. Perhaps connected with spindly lines or strings.

("What does the M and G refer to?")

They are not together, but separate. They are not initials.

("Are they on the object itself?")

They refer to objects on the object, or strongly connected with it.

("How about F and O?")

(Pause.) The F may refer to a person. The O, I believe, is simply a shape, that is, a circle shape.

If you have no more questions, then you may take a break and we shall continue briefly.

("Okay.")

A distant connection here incidentally with a birthday and the number seven.

(Break at 10:45. Jane had been dissociated as usual, and her eyes had remained closed, through both experiments.

(Seth had a few comments on the envelope data after break, but the Wilburs and Jane and I had by then made the connections with the object. See the tracing on page 206, and the notes on page 207.

("Four, plus one or two." On the back of the object Marilyn Wilbur had written April 4, 1966, as well as the name she had given her ceramic sculpture. This date is the day Don took the picture and gave it to us. April is the fourth month; the number four also shows; and the number 1 in 1966. A 2 also shows in the serial number on the right back edge of the object. We don't know whether Seth might have referred to this, and since I didn't know what the object was either I couldn't ask questions to help clear it up.

("Connection with a meeting." As stated, Don took the picture for specific use as an envelope object in the 248th session, due April 4,1966. The projected meeting would thus involve four people; the Wilburs could not attend at the last moment, but Don delivered the object personally on April 4, so there was an actual meeting of three.

("Colors green and yellow." Don took the picture of the ceramic cat as it sat on a brick wall cutting across grass as indicated in the tracing on page 206. This particular roll of Polaroid color film had been exposed to heat; Don took the chance that it would still give legible pictures. As it was the color print used as object has a dull, overall brownish cast, yet the local colors are still visible, to a reduced degree.

(The grass immediately in back of the cat is light yellow brown in color, shading off to a darker greenish brown around the edges of the photo. See the tracing.

("The impression of stairs or steps. Something ascending in this fashion, you see." Here Jane gestured positively that something rose on the object at perhaps a 30-degree angle, perhaps less. This is my estimate. There are no steps shown on the object, but the brick walk is in perspective, and rises perhaps at a 20-degree angle from left to right. The separate bricks in the walk, which are not cemented together incidentally, could perhaps have led to the use of stairs or steps.

(Jane regretted having one impression while giving the above data that she did not give voice to. Once again, it is often left up to her as to whether to speak an impression aloud, pursue it, or choose to ignore it. She did not pursue this one. It was the word "stone."

(Jane's gesture, incidentally, was a smoothly rising one, as the brick walk smoothly rises on the object. She did not indicate the angular construction of stairs, for instance.

("Connection with high round objects." As can be noted on the tracing, Marilyn's ceramic cat is composed of round or circular components. The cat's head rises especially high in the modern fashion.

("Also perhaps with a July date," The date on back of the object is April 4, 1966. As soon as Jane saw this she said that she was subjectively sure she had interpreted the four date as July fourth instead of April.

("and with square objects, in design fashion." The bricks in the photo are rectangular, not square. As stated they are not cemented in place but set together irregularly; the pattern they make is a nicely designed one. The walk is in front of the trailer the Wilburs inhabit in a nearby small town.

("Some distant connection with a mission. I do not know to what this refers" Here Jane shook her head in giving the data. We speculate that mission here refers to Don's trip to our apartment last April 4, from his out-of-town residence, to tell us that he and his wife could not attend the 248th session after all; on this visit he gave us the object used this evening.

("and with objects in a row, or a series, perhaps of numbers." The date on the object can be thought of as a series of numbers; we think however that here Seth refers to the six-digit serial number on the back of the object, along the right-hand edge: M507832.

("M and G", raises once again the question of what meaning to assign to initials. The M can refer to Marilyn, who made the ceramic cat. Marilyn said the G did not refer to any person with that initial that she knew of, in connection with the object. However, she thought it might refer to the fact that the ceramic cat has a certain type of high-gloss glaze fired on; this glaze being made of glass.

(Seth helps out here a little in answer to my second question.

("F and O". We hesitated to give meanings here, and received some help from

Seth in answer to my fourth question.

("Something to do with tomorrow. That is, tomorrow as far as the object is concerned, or to do with the future, this being indicated on the object." When the Wilburs discovered they couldn't attend the 248th session as witnesses on April 4,1966, the day the photo used as object tonight was taken, I saved the object for future use when they could be witnesses, as explained. In this sense perhaps it can be said the object had a meaning assigned to it concerning the future. But there is nothing on the object itself to indicate this.

("The impression of the four again", refers we believe to the first impression, interpreted on page 212, and involves the April 4, 1966 date on back of the object.

("and graduating, as something graduates in size perhaps." Since the brick walk in the photo was photographed in perspective, there is a graduation in the size of the bricks. They are largest in the lower left hand corner of the object, tapering up to the right border.

(Since I didn't know what the object was all my questions were asked in the dark, so to speak. My first one asked just how the yellow and green were connected to the object. "Perhaps yellow in the center of a slightly rectangular shape, outlined in green." The object is rectangular, but more than slightly so. The above data is a good description of the yellowish brown grass in back of the cat's head, as explained under the yellow and green data on page 212; and of the way the yellow grass merges into the darker green brown grass around the edges of the photo. See the tracing on page 206.

(Seth continues in answer to the first question: "A visual connection, with square or rectangular objects in the center of a larger area", refers to the rectangular bricks marching up across the center of the object. "with modern connotations as a design might have." refers to the very modern, rounded or circular design of Marilyn's ceramic cat. "Perhaps connected with spindly lines or strings." refers to the abstract pattern created, in line form, by the narrow crevices and shadows around the individual bricks, all these lines being interconnected.

(All in all, we consider Seth's answer to the first question to be very good.

(My second question asked for more data on the M and G: "They are not together, but separate. They are not initials." We of course had this answer before giving our own interpretations of the M and G data on page 213. We had assigned the M to Marilyn's name, thus using an initial, and the G to the glass glaze on the cat. Seth agrees with this interpretation after break, so there is some contradiction here.

("They refer to objects on the object, or strongly connected with it." The third question sought to pin the M and G data down further. Thus the G for glass glaze refers to the cat shown on the object, the M to Marilyn who made the cat. We wouldn't be sure of this however without Seth's confirmation after break.

("The F may refer to a person." The fourth question asked about the F and O

data. Marilyn and Jane thought the F referred to f as in feline, or the f sound in the name Lucifer, the name which Marilyn gave to her ceramic creation. "The O, I believe, is simply a shape, that is, a circle shape." The ceramic cat is composed of forms circular in shape. See the tracing on page 206.

("A distant connection here incidentally with a birthday, and the number seven." Seth added this bit of information at the last, just before break. There is a number 7 in the upper left hand corner of the object, on the back. Marilyn said however that she felt this data could refer to the fact that her father's birthday is on March 7, and that the camera which Don took the photo used as object belongs to her father. Seth agreed with her after break.

(Jane resumed at 11:15.)

Now. Once your consciousness is outside of the physical body, then you are dealing with a different kind of reality indeed. This is experience every bit as real as any other.

You may or may not have the sensation of traveling through the doors or windows. This is dependent upon the particular kind of projection involved. The molecular structure of the projecting self is of a different nature. There is no change in the physical nature of the door, for example. The molecular structure of the traveling self changes.

There is no danger of not returning to the physical body, generally speaking. If in your projection you seem to be flying past treetops, then you are indeed doing so. The physical body is obviously not doing so.

Now you can meet and speak with some others on these excursions. It is possible, with much training, to arrange such meetings; for any kind of scientific proof of course this would be a necessary preliminary. You must learn to react to new conditions quickly.

Now I have told you that you may legitimately visit not only the past, present and future as it existed, or will exist in physical terms; but you may also visit realities which never existed in physical terms. In our earliest sessions I emphasized that the intensity regulated the duration of an experience. Now, many events that were only imagined and never took place, physically speaking, many such events still exist. They are simply not a part of your definition of reality. You may therefore visit a museum which was planned in the 16th century, but never built. Such a museum has a reality as real, you see, as the house in which you live. Ordinarily you only perceive physical reality. In projections you may visit other realities such as these also—which you may be tempted to call imaginary, but they are not.

A study of any up-to-date scientific thesis on the nature of sensual perception in general will show you that sense data exists independent of the perceiver, yet not necessarily in physical terms.

Such information, incidentally, is basic if the last points are to make any sense to you at all. At any time in a projection you may will yourself to return, and you shall.

Now I have been speaking of projection from a trance state. You may of course project from a dream, and not realize that you have done so. Upon awakening you may then be frightened to find the physical body in what amounts to a trance state, while the mind is wide awake. As I believe Ruburt told our small friend, such has been the case on rather frequent occasions with her. *(Jane, her eyes open, pointed at Ann Diebler.)*

Projection from a dream state is something else again, therefore, and when it is executed successfully then you have a fine example of the self as it changes the focus of its own awareness. Here the critical consciousness is quite apparent, while the body sleeps. Projections occur quite naturally under these conditions. For the development of the whole self however, and for the perfection of such experiences, it is beneficial that such projections be carried out by the conscious wish of the projector. You learn therefore to manipulate your own consciousness in different realities than the ones with which you are usually concerned.

There are strange benefits that can result. Some cases are on record where individuals are suddenly propelled out of the path of danger. This involves instantaneous projection. The fear and panic that could make the body vulnerable is not present, and the body escapes danger precisely because consciousness is not there to cause panic reactions.

More generally however, and quite simply, such projections allow you to practice in dealing with realities that you will meet when you no longer operate within the physical system. The conditions then will not frighten you, for you will be familiar with them.

Now I am prepared, my dear Joseph, to carry on the session as long as you wish. You have inconveniences of time and so forth.

("Well I'm afraid it's getting late. How were our interpretations of the envelope data?")

We will then continue with this at our next session. For if you are to have instructions in projection, then I prefer that I give them to you.

The birthday impression was correct.

The M and the other impressions as you have recorded them. Some of the data was distantly connected, and nothing is to be gained now by taking the time to explain it. The idea of envelopes brought by guests is a good one however, and I do approve.

My heartiest wishes to you all, and we shall now close our session, unfortunately.

("As always; good night, Seth.")

(End at 11:37. Jane was dissociated as usual. Her pace had been rather fast, her voice good, her eyes open often. She said Seth could have continued indefinitely.)

(Front) *(Back)*

(Tracings of the rifle tag used as object in the 59th envelope experiment, in the 266th session for June 9,1966.)

SESSION 266
JUNE 9, 1966 9 PM THURSDAY

(This session was due yesterday but was not held. John Bradley, our friend from Williamsport, PA, who had witnessed a group of sessions, visited us yesterday evening. Jane, John and I then journeyed to the home of the Gallaghers, where the session was to be held. When unexpected company arrived at the Gallaghers shortly before 9 PM however, Jane and I put the session off until tonight.

(The 59th envelope experiment used as object a tag that had been attached to a rifle we had bought in October 1962. Jane hadn't seen the tag since. See the tracing on page 217. The tag is printed on typical card-weight stock in two colors, red and black as indicated. The face of the tag is gold coated, the string red. The object was sealed in the usual double envelopes, between the usual two pieces of Bristol. The results of the experiment were quite unusual, and Seth goes into the mechanisms involved.

(A very heavy rain and hailstorm developed at 8:30 this evening. It appeared to be over by 9 PM but actually was not. Our windows were open, and Jane began speaking in a voice heavier than usual, as in the last session. Her pace was average, her eyes closed to begin.)

Good evening.

("Good evening, Seth.")

Now. You wanted some data that would serve to explain the results of your first experimental seance.

(See the 11th session, for January 1,1964, in Volume 1.)

In order to understand my answer it is necessary that our material on the construction of physical matter be understood. We shall also be considering the nature of sense perceptions very shortly, and this data will also help to answer your question.

(We need answers concerning the rather spectacular results obtained in the 11th session because Jane is writing a chapter on this seance for the Seth book. We had always thought we'd get the answers when we took the time for them.)

In reference to the second pair, or set of fingers, for example, these were not so-called spirit hands. We were manipulating energy, and forming it into pseudomatter. These were secondary constructions, if you remember the distinction between primary and secondary constructions given earlier.

("Yes." See Sessions 208-11 in Volume 5.)

Now. Bear with me, for some new background material is necessary here. All physical matter exists first as an idea or mental image. The idea of mental image has its own reality, and is charged with energy, and this energy can never be withdrawn. You only accept data when it appears within the physical camouflage system. As you know this severely limits your conception of the real.

We are making some simplified statements here to make the idea clear. Data, valid data, which is not materialized as physical form, at any given time still exists as potential physical form. Some such data will be materialized in your future, as for example plans existing only in the mind will later be carried out and utilized within physical form.

Some such data will never be utilized. Some such data will be utilized time and time again. Now you see the energy does not reside within any given physical object, but in the idea form that is within it. Physical objects do not exist as such in a basic manner. You can only perceive large areas of reality data however by transforming it into terms that can be picked up by the physical senses.

As you know, you create or construct all physical matter. What you see are your own constructions. This does not mean however that there is not something within or behind what you perceive. All thoughts are composed of energy, and from our discussions you realize that there are electrical intensities within whose range all reality exists.

Every thought therefore has this kind of reality, which is the only reality, basically speaking. *(Long pause.)* Sense data itself has a reality independent of any given object. This sense data has its own intensity. If you can tune into that intensity, so to speak, you will automatically translate it into physical data, and you will perceive a physical object.

If you tune into that intensity imperfectly, you will have a pseudophysical object, that is in one or more respects different from a normal object. It may be obvious for example to some of your physical senses, and not to others. It may be only partially materialized.

In such cases however definite atoms and molecules are utilized. Now. In our seance we were, again, manipulating energy and forming objects from it—objects that you could perceive with your physical senses. The whole matter, if you will forgive my pun *(smile)* on matter is highly intriguing, and we shall have several sessions at least, dealing with the reality of sense data, and the unreality, comparatively speaking, of matter itself.

The whole discussion will be leading us to an investigation of the similarities and differences between such data as dream objects, hallucinated objects, and physical objects.

Now you may take your break.

(Break at 9:26. Jane was dissociated as usual. Her slow initial pace had picked up, her eyes had begun to open frequently, and she had sipped iced tea and smoked a cigarette.

(She resumed in an even more active manner at 9:35.)

There is no basic difference you see between a hallucinated object and a so-called physical object, except for the number of persons who perceive them.

Now. In the experimental seance, due to the circumstances and lack of training on Ruburt's part, we redistributed some energy. Ruburt, during the seance, weighed somewhat less than his usual weight. Very little actually. With his help certain portions of energy were used to construct pseudoimages.

Again, these images are as real as <u>any</u> physical matter is. *(Long pause.)* Now once energy is formed into <u>any</u> kind of a pattern, the identity of the pattern is maintained. If it will help you, think in terms of a memory image. Except you see that in many cases the object may never have <u>existed</u> in physical reality.

What you perceive with your physical senses is of course real. It is one of the forms that reality takes. But if you insist upon believing that <u>only</u> physical data is real, then you see you will never learn what is within it.

Reality changes its form in order to become known to itself. It constructs varieties of consciousness with varying kinds of sense apparatus, or perceiving apparatus. Each consciousness then perceives reality in a different fashion. Yet all fashions you see are legitimate, as far as physical sense apparatus is concerned. But the mental or psychic energy <u>behind</u> all this is the one <u>basic</u> reality.

(Jane's pace was now fast and energetic, and she used many gestures. Her eyes were very dark, and open wide for paragraphs at a time. She was smoking again.)

Now you can translate inner data into the terms of the outer senses, but always some distortion is absolutely necessary, for the very method of perception you see colors that which is perceived.

The objects that you will see and the places that you will visit, in dream or out-of-body experiences, are basically as real as any physical object or location, because neither are <u>basically</u> real. Nor of course are they <u>un</u>real. As soon as you begin to translate an idea you are distorting it. The inner senses you see do not distort the data, but when you attempt to make such data available to the ego, then distortion to some extent must enter in.

The images seen during the seance were quite as real as anything else in the room. They could have been photographed, <u>if</u> any one of the three of you had held the camera. *(Broad smile, eyes dark. Seth refers to three here because Bill Macdonnel was a witness to the session.)*

I spoke briefly of the form that appeared in the mirror. Now <u>that</u> appearance was something else again, and was somewhat in the nature of the experience <u>you</u> had much later. *(See the 219th session.)* You see you <u>pick up</u> the idea even with that form, then you attempt to translate that data into physical terms. The attempt is bound to bring distortions, but without the distortions you could not consciously perceive the data. The distortions in all cases form your physical camouflage patterns.

You may take a brief break before our Instream material.

(Break at 9:57. Jane was dissociated as usual. Her energetic delivery lasted until break. It had been fast and emphatic.

(It was time for the 70th Dr. Instream experiment. Actually this material was a makeup for last evening. Jane's pace slowed, and she sat with her hands raised to her closed eyes. Resume at 10:04.)

Now give us a moment for our Instream material. These are impressions. *(Pause.)*

White flakes, resembling snowflakes. I have the visual impression of a round glass globe, one of the old-fashioned variety. When you turn it upside down snowflakes fill the globe.

The object is something like this, but that is not it precisely. I believe it is larger, and sits on a table with a white cloth. Dr. Instream recently received a package of books, I believe. There is some question as to whether or not he will be at the same university next year. Uncertainty on his part, and some speculation.

A connection with mucilage, perhaps there is a jar of it close to him, or he has been working on something requiring glue. Some kind of a framework of light wood, that is, lightweight wood.

Do you have an envelope for me?

("Yes." Jane paused at 10:12, then took the envelope for our 59th experiment from me without opening her eyes. She held it to her forehead briefly, lowered it to her lap, then raised it to her forehead again.)

Give us a moment, please. *(Pause.)* I have the impression of something that begins with an M. Perhaps we can return to this later. It seems to be connected with a word that sounds like much or munch.

The impression of an empty area, perhaps with a border.

The impression of two people. One bending down or over, perhaps a woman, and another smaller person, facing each other. One slightly taller, or tall in any case.

Now these may be objects, or representations, rather than persons, but I have the impression of two persons, and the impression that they are both women. In any case these two objects seem to be together, toward the lower center of the object perhaps, holding the object this way.

(Her eyes closed, Jane gestured with the envelope, which she was holding with its long dimension parallel to the floor.)

A four and seven, perhaps, though I am not sure, connected with the upper left-hand corner, holding the object this way. *(The same gesture repeated.)*

A connection with an initial expense. The impression on the object, on the lower bottom, of very small rectangles or squares, *(pause)* one after another—bright, but outlined in darker color, as perhaps a transparency of some kind.

The impression of dark color, as in a negative. The numbers five six...

(It had begun to rain a while ago. Now the storm resumed in full fury, the worst rain and hailstorm here in 16 years according to later reports. There is a large patio roof outside our living room windows, and this is covered with aluminum roofing. The sound of rain upon it is usually very pleasant. Now however the hail created a drumfire so loud that I could barely hear Jane, although she sat but three feet away. I almost called a halt, but since she seemed prone to continue I did also. The racket was disconcerting and I had to ask her to repeat some of the data.)

J, and/or perhaps June. A connection with an establishment, and the numbers 1471. *(Jane paused and lowered the envelope to her lap.)* Do you have any questions?

("Who are the two people?")

I have the impression of a woman and a shorter woman or child, perhaps. The impression has to do with shapes. They seem to be bending down or over.

("What colors are connected with the object?")

The impression I mentioned of dark, and perhaps purple. Also a brownish tone. Perhaps a blue dress. Or the object that I pick up as a woman is a blue one.

("Can you give us more details on that initial expense?")

A cost and that is all on that.

("Do you want to name the object?")

I have the impression that it is a picture or transparency of some sort, or strongly connected. That is if the object is not a picture or transparency it seems to be strongly connected with one.

The impression again of the rectangular or square shapes in a series at the bottom, across the bottom *(gesture)*, surrounded by darker areas. Also the number 9.

If you have no more questions you may take your break.

("Okay." I could have asked more questions, but the rain and hail made so much noise I could hardly hear Jane.

(Break at 10:27. Jane was out as usual. Her eyes had remained closed through both experiments. Her pace had been fair. Surprisingly enough, her voice hadn't increased in volume to rise above the noise of the storm. Jane now said the storm hadn't bothered her, so this fact may account for it. She evidently heard me without trouble.

(See the tracing of the object on page 217, and the notes concerning it on page 218. As usual at break Jane and I went over the data to make what connections we could with the object. Without Seth's help, in some detail after break, we were greatly puzzled by the data. That is, we could speculate on the reasons for what seemed to be many distortions, but had little idea of the causes. Since we could pick out a few items in the data that seemed to apply to the object, we took it that Seth had correctly tuned in on the object itself, and that Jane's translation of the data had been distorted most of the time. For this reason, immediately below will be listed only those parts of the data we think apply. The rest is cleared up by Seth after break. Actually we found the experiment most interesting, and unique in the series so far.

(Clues were available however. As soon as she opened the double envelope and saw the front of the object, Jane announced that the picture thereon was of a moose. Actually it is a black line drawing, in some detail, of an eagle. We pursued this impasse for some little time. Jane insisted the drawing represented a moose; she interpreted the spread of the eagle's wings as stylized antlers. My tracing is quickly done on page 217, and shows little detail, but the drawing on the actual object is very well and finely done, including individual feathers on the wings, etc. I could see little relationship between an eagle and a moose here except in the most abstract sense. It was easy for us to agree that Jane saw a moose instead of an eagle because she wanted to. Intellectually she agreed that the drawing was of an eagle, but said that she saw a moose.

(As I began typing these notes on Saturday June 11, two days later, I showed Jane the envelope object again. Her opinion on the drawing had not changed; she still regarded the drawing as that of a moose, with the eagle's wings representing stylized antlers. As for the rest of the drawing other than the wings or antlers, she said she couldn't see anything in it "in particular" that represented an eagle.

(As soon as she saw the object and identified the eagle as a moose, Jane said the M and "munch" data, given first, applied to the moose idea.

(Below are a few points that apply to the object itself. Seth concurs that a few such items did come through the general distortions.

("The impression of an empty area, perhaps with a border." There is such a comparatively large empty rectangular area at the bottom of the object on the back: a boxed-in area for a price to be inserted. No price showed on the object however.

("The impression of two people. One bending down or over... Now these may be objects, or representations, rather than persons, but I have the impression of two persons... In any case these two objects seem to be together, toward the lower center of the object perhaps, holding the object this way." These are excerpts from succeeding impressions as a group, and are given here because Jane thinks the bending over idea here derived from the way the wings of the eagle bend in and down toward each

other; they are together, or close, at the base, and in the center of the object.

(Jane held the envelope with the long dimension horizontal, but we do not know the position of the object inside them at that time. It is possible the tag was simply upside down. Perhaps this gave rise to Seth's mention of lower center.

("A connection with an initial expense." Our buying the rifle represented an initial expense for us in October 1962. We owned no previous weapons, ammunition, cleaning equipment, etc.

("The impression on the object, on the lower bottom, of very small rectangles or squares..." On the back of the object is the phrase "Side-opening loading-port for easy rapid-load." As soon as she read this Jane said this was the source of the above data, well distorted. But Jane was subjectively sure.

("A connection with an establishment," We regard this as general, although of course the store where we bought the rifle is an establishment, one of a chain in the northeast.

("...impression of a woman and a <u>shorter</u> woman... The impression has to do with shapes. They seem to be bending down or over." This in answer to my first question, concerning the two people. Jane said, again, that she believed the bending over idea expressed here stemmed from the bending of the eagle wings.

("A cost, and that is all on that." The third question sought more detail on the initial expense data. As stated the rifle was an initial expense, and did cost us.

("I have the impression that it is a picture or transparency of some sort, or strongly connected...." My fourth question asked Seth to name the object. There is a picture on the object. According to Seth after break his data was legitimate as given to Jane, but was distorted by her.

("Also the number 9." In the upper left-hand corner on the back of the object, in very small type, is the number: Part 999-30.

(Jane resumed, smiling, her eyes opening often, at 11 PM. The storm had once again died down.)

Now. Here we have a case of fine subconscious distortion, beautifully executed.

Ruburt does not approve of guns. The quite legitimate visual data was quickly and frantically transformed. You saw this happen in a different way—after the envelope was opened, when Ruburt insisted on seeing the moose instead of the eagle.

(While Jane was giving the envelope data I detected nothing out of the ordinary in her delivery. She sat with her eyes closed, speaking quite calmly and easily as she usually does. The storm outside was the only one I was aware of.)

It is quite amazing that any legitimate data got through, and little did. There was a complete subconscious refusal to interpret the data, and a complete reversal in this case. For instead of the gun, which to Ruburt signifies destruction, purposeful destruction, you have the distortion of the eagle shape on the gun label, into a woman and child image, signifying of course creativity in this case.

Some small effort was made to keep the original visual data but even this was sacrificed for the same subconscious purpose when it became necessary.

The gun was purchased during a national crisis, and was therefore connected with fears in any case.

The blue was a reference to the typewriter, which was purchased at the same establishment, when Ruburt eagerly tried to substitute one test item for another, you see.

(We had thought of this, since this typewriter was bought at about the same time, from the same store.)

The words "Side-opening" were neutral to Ruburt. However he interpreted them literally you see in terms of the small transparent rectangles or squares. *(See page 224.)*

His data was legitimate from me, but it was deliberately distorted on the part of the subconscious.

The cost did refer to the cost of the gun. The black and the negative ideas were his own ideas connected with a gun in general.

I insisted on using phrases meant to put him back on the right track, by saying that the woman shapes were shapes, but I could not get this through clearly enough. Our friend will not see what he does not want to see.

If you have no questions we will end the session.

("I guess not then. But it's been very interesting.")

I have never seen a better example of stubborn subconscious distortion. *(Smile, eyes wide and dark.)* My best wishes to you both; even to Ruburt.

("Good night, Seth."

(End at 11:11. Jane was out as usual. Her pace had been fast, her eyes open often.

(At the end of the session she was still convinced the eagle looked like a moose, although she agreed it was actually an eagle because I said it was. Jane mentioned showing the object to others to get their opinion.

(As stated, she still felt this way two days later. She again suggested, today, June 11, that we show the object to others.)

(Copy of the drawing of a begonia plant, used as the object in the 60th envelope experiment, in the 267th session for June 13,1966.)

SESSION 267
JUNE 13, 1966 9 PM MONDAY

(The 60th envelope experiment used as object a quick black line drawing, on porous white paper, that I made of a giant begonia plant at the office. The plant sits on a taboret beside my drawing table. It has grown beautifully from a tiny slip that I took to the office approximately last March. Jane has not seen the plant, hardly ever visiting the office.

(Nor had she ever seen the drawing used as object, nor did she even know it existed. We have the plant here in the apartment from which the slip came however, and its history will be given in the envelope data. I placed the object between the usual double Bristol and sealed it all up in the usual double envelopes.

(Part of tonight's session is omitted, where indicated, because of its personal content.

(Jane's eyes were closed when she began speaking but they opened almost at once. For most of the session they remained open, usually quite wide, always darker than usual. Most of the time she stared directly at me, using many gestures, speaking with many smiles and in a voice often somewhat heavier than usual because of our open windows.

(As soon as Jane dispensed with the Ouija board when these sessions got under way three years ago, she took to pacing the floor endlessly while giving a session. Her eyes of course were open constantly; this state of affairs lasted for well over a year. When Jane began speaking for Seth while sitting down her eyes closed; she evidently is just now ending this phase, or at least modifying it.)

Good evening.

("Good evening, Seth.")

Now. We will shortly become involved in the discussions begun in our previous session.

(Smile.) First of all however, a small note to our friend Ruburt. From me, dear Joseph, but on your behalf. Now. I would suggest that afternoons Joseph not be disturbed for any but the most unusual matters. It would be best indeed if Ruburt imagined that you were working out of the house, and he should be able to do this.

Your privacy during these hours is very important to you. He knows this of course, but forgets it. You may <u>if</u> your prefer close your bedroom door you see, neatly dividing your apartment in half during working hours. I do not know why you have not thought of this yourself, or in any case why you have not put it into practice.

There has been a seasonal excitement in the air that will soon now diminish to a more normal tone. I hope you appreciate my note on your behalf—

("Yes.")

—since Ruburt usually makes a serious effort to follow my suggestions.

The bird episode, you see, bothered him deeply. He made an effort not to call on you, but emotionally you see he felt that the whole world should stop to help his bird. *(One of our cats nearly killed a young robin today, and Jane is trying to nurse it back to health.)* The episode however was one of a series of interruptions of your private hours, and I do seriously recommend that you be allowed your work period without disturbance.

A healthy overall emotional climate now fills this apartment house, however. If you both learn to keep interruptions under control, you can make the best use of this emotional vitality. For it is, for all its exuberance, a balancing factor.

Now. As I said earlier, sense data does have a reality, but this reality does not reside in an object. The object represents your interpretation of the basic reality. The energy belongs to the idea. In other words, the prime energy within physical reality resides precisely in those intangibles which do not, because of their nature, appear within physical frameworks. They give life and reality to the physical framework.

(Pause, and gesture, eyes closed.) There is not something "out there," you see, which exists independently. There is something within that exists independently, and whose reality you perceive in a highly distorted fashion, through the use of the outer senses.

The inner senses can and do perceive this reality in an undistorted fashion. Your brain is itself a camouflage pattern. It can only translate and perceive what seems to be the evidence of the physical senses. It cannot step outside of itself. *(Smile.)* It is that which it attempts to investigate.

It is as much camouflage as the glass on the table, *(pointing)* and its knowledge must come through the physical system. Now. The mind is uncamouflaged. It perceives the uncamouflaged reality of sense data, or its sees the energy that exists. It sees the energy independently of the physical object, you see.

You can intellectually understand what I am telling you, but the brain *(shaking head)* cannot experience reality directly. This experience must come from the mind, through use of the inner senses. I want it understood that camouflage physical reality is indeed a reality, even while it is a distortion of something else.

The material that I have given you on the nature of matter should make it clear that every atom and molecule has its own condensed, coded consciousness, and that no gestalt or formation of any kind can occur without the cooperation and comprehension of the consciousnesses involved.

The idea shape itself is not one unitary thing, for example. The idea shape of this chair is not an absolute unitary, disembodied, or unspirited concept. *(Very energetic delivery, eyes wide. Jane pounded on the arm of her rocker.)* The idea shape of this chair is a composite, a gestalt, formed on the part of each atom and molecule that composes it.

We will have more to say. However I suggest a brief break.

(Break at 9:26. Jane was dissociated as usual, she said. She also said that since her eyes were still open at the end of the delivery, she closed them in order to come out of the trance.

(Jane resumed in the same active manner at 9:42, and spoke until 10:04. This material is omitted here. This brings us to the 71st Dr. Instream data. Jane now resumed once again at a somewhat slower pace, sitting with a hand raised to her closed eyes. Resume at 10:20.)

A short note: It is because I realize you have a time shortage that our sessions have been fairly brief of late.

Now, a moment for our Instream material. *(Pause.)* These are impressions. *(Jane's voice became somewhat stronger.)* A scramble. He has been rushed, in a period of high activity.

The object is a chain, or connected with a chain. It is of dull silver color, of necklace length perhaps. Two other objects are connected with it. Two other objects have been on the chain at various times. One, a fairly oval object, of an inserted brown background, and a raised cream-colored area.

The other object connected with the chain was heavier, of a square shape, and connected with a male.

Now for some other impressions, not connected necessarily with the object. The letters N, P, G, A. I do not know to what these refer. A small cross, connected with Dr. Instream's past. The date 1873, connected with Dr. Instream's parents, or parent.

A connection now with a move of some kind.

Do you have an envelope for me?

("Yes."

(Jane paused at 10:29, and took the envelope for our 60th experiment from me without opening her eyes. She pressed it to her forehead with one hand.)

Give me a moment, please. *(Pause.)* These are impressions.

Four. Lettering, I believe handwriting. Seven and three. Oval and brown. A date on the object. A connection with March, perhaps 4 or 24. Six three. Lineage.

Connection with a fabric. Twelve of a kind connected here. A salary or payment connection. Five in a circle. The impression of splendid, something splendid.

A distant connection with monolithic. A group of men. A score. Connection with a meeting at seven, or by seven. A card written on both sides. Your initials, Joseph.

Connection with another woman. That is, beside Ruburt. February or March, and a grand view.

Do you have questions? *(Jane changed hands on the envelope, but continued to hold it to her forehead.)*

("What's that about lineage?")

I am not sure. I am thinking in terms of family connections. However, the word may have to do instead with, for example, type on a card.

("Do you want to give me some colors on the object?")

Brown and oval. Now, I have the impression that the object is roughly divided into four areas, in this manner, you see, with fairly dark lines. *(Her eyes closed, Jane made a vigorous and large crossing motion with an arm, thus:*

In making this sign, she stressed the horizontal attributes of it, and repeated it.

("Yes.")

The four areas could be different in color, and fairly bright—perhaps also a pale blue. I do not know if this is a symbolic impression or not. *(I would like to add that while making the above cross sign, Jane held the envelope with its long dimension also horizontal. This has a bearing on the data, we believe.*

("Who is the other woman beside Ruburt?")

I believe an older woman.

("Initials?"

(Pause.) You had better wait on this. *(Pause.)* The older woman data leads Ruburt to make personal associations which could be distortive. *(Pause.)*

We will try here with the initial A, or G.

("That word monolithic is interesting.")

This is in connection with a drawing or design. And mono, also meaning one.

("How about that five in a circle?")

The impression is visual. The circle outlined in yellow, I believe, and I see visually a red five inside. *(Jane gestured.*

("Do you want to name the object?")

(Pause.) I have come as close as I can this evening.

("Okay.")

A connection with a framework of some kind. Perhaps wooden, and I suggest your break.

(Break at 10:40. Jane said she was well dissociated during both experiments. Her eyes had remained closed throughout. She recalled having one image, and this was associated with the cross sign she had made.

(See the tracing of the object on page 226, and the notes on page 227. Seth returns after break, briefly, but doesn't add anything to our own connections with the envelope data.

("Four." We don't know.

("Lettering, I believe handwriting." My signature and the date are written on the object.)

("Seven and three." We don't know.

("Oval and brown." The little sketch used as object shows but the top few leaves of the giant begonia. These show as oval. The interesting thing here is that the larger leaves of the plant at the office are now beginning to show definite brownish tones. As stated Jane has never seen the plant at the office in its fine growth—merely a slip from a parent plant here in the apartment. Since this house plant also is developing a brown cast, Jane could know this easily enough once she, or Seth, picked up the idea that the envelope object represented a begonia.

("A date on the object." Yes.

("A connection with March, perhaps 4 or 24." Jane and I have thought back, and conclude that it is very possible I took the slip to the office during March. The plant is perhaps a foot tall now. We are sure I didn't take it any earlier than March, so feel Seth is quite possibly correct here, without being able to demonstrate it. Neither of us have any idea of what day, 4, 24, etc., I took the begonia slip to the office.

("Six three." Jane pronounced this data as six, three, not 63. We don't know what it means however. Six shows twice on the object, and we speculate that March is the third month of the year.

("Lineage." We think this a good reference to the fact that my begonia at the office, which modeled for the object, is a descendant of the plant here at home. This parent plant, given to Jane by our neighbor on the same floor of our apartment house, Miss Callahan, also has other descendants growing very well.

(In addition, Jane has asked me at various times to bring home a slip from this office plant, so that she can start another pot; she has been quite impressed with my descriptions of how well the office plant has been doing.

("Connection with a fabric." This puzzled us for a moment at break. Jane

then remembered that the parent begonia here at the house had its pot, until recently, wrapped in an orange-colored burlap type of fabric. As a matter of fact, she had cleaned the last shreds of this fabric from the pot holding the parent plant today; these shreds had been stuck, unnoticed, on the bottom of the pot.

(We do not know if the pot holding the office begonia had ever, also, been wrapped in fabric. It is a possibility, since the pot as well as the plant came from the apartment, and one of Jane's pet activities is decorating the plant containers with various materials and in various ways.

("Twelve of a kind connected here." We don't know. We speculated, again, that the double six in the date on the object can add up to twelve.

("A salary or payment connection." As I sit at my drawing board at the office, perhaps a foot or eighteen inches from the begonia plant which served as a model for the envelope object, I am given my paycheck each Friday afternoon.

("Five in a circle." My sixth question concerns this data, and our interpretation is given there.

("The impression of splendid, something splendid." It is no stretching of the truth to say that the office begonia plant is quite a splendid one.

("A distant connection with monolithic." Our dictionary says monolith, while referring to one of a kind, also can mean one of large size. The object is a drawing of what is called a giant tubular begonia.

("A group of men." We believe this to be a valid interpretation: My drawing board at the office, with the begonia beside it, happens to be the first in line of several. Just beyond my board is a very large table that is used to spread out very large printed sheets before they are cut up into individual cards, etc. This table is perhaps three feet away. Around it are clustered groups of men every day, going over the current job on the press. Foremen, printers, directors, artists, etc.

("A score." We don't know.

("Connection with a meeting at seven, or by seven." We don't know. Perhaps another reference to the group of men idea?

("A card written on both sides." The drawing used as object is done on a porous paper that is somewhat thicker than most papers, yet is not actually card stock. I used a black felt marking pen to make the drawing; this is indelible, and the ink soaked through the porous paper until the drawing is quite easily visible on the reverse side. This cannot be seen on the tracing on page 226.

("Your initials, Joseph." I signed and dated the object, using the first initial and last name.

("Connection with another woman. That is, beside Ruburt." As stated, the office begonia plant grew from a slip taken from a plant here in the apartment. This parent plant was given to Jane by our neighbor on the same floor, Miss Callahan, a

retired school teacher in her late 70s.

("February or March," See the second impression on page 230. As said there, we think it quite likely that I took the plant slip to the office last March.

("and a grand view." We are not sure. We offer this: Miss Callahan has a nice view from her apartment windows. She spends much of her day sitting at a window admiring the view, and never fails to mention it when Jane visits her. However she doesn't use the phrase "a grand view." Jane says Miss Callahan favors the adjective "lovely" instead.

("I am not sure. I am thinking in terms of family connections. However the word may have to do <u>instead</u> with, for example, type on a card." My first question, concerning the lineage data: See page 230. Seth didn't elaborate very much. There is no type on the object. Can family connections be applied to the descendants of a parent plant?

(The second question asked for colors on the object: "Brown and oval." This is a repeat of the data given on page 230, which can refer to the office begonia. Jane now continued before I could ask another question:

("Now, I have the impression that the object is <u>roughly</u> divided into four areas, in this manner, you see, with fairly dark lines." See the notes with this data on page 230. Jane, while holding the envelope, and the object inside it, horizontally, made a vigorous crossing and vertical motion with an arm. See the tracing on page 226. The drawing shows that the leaves of the plant are climbing up a wooden stick. With the object held horizontally, the stick is also horizontal and divides the drawing in half easily enough; the horizontal attribute of her gesture was stressed by Jane. The fairly dark lines on the object are obvious.

(There is a less clear vertical division to be seen on the object while in the horizontal position, although the brush marks in the upper left corner help to mark off a portion. This would give perhaps three quarters on the object definite enough, and possibly this gave rise to Seth's statement about rough division into four areas. Jane continues:

("The four areas could be different in color, and fairly bright—perhaps also a pale blue. I do <u>not</u> know if this is a symbolic impression or not." The object itself is in black and white only. We offer a pale blue connection however that we have been aware of for several years. Miss Callahan, who gave Jane the parent begonia which led to the making of the envelope object, is inordinately fond of blue. We do not know if Seth would call this a symbolic connection. Miss Callahan's apartment is largely blue. Her living room has pale blue painted walls, including a floor to ceiling painted blue bookcase. Her divan is covered with solid blue, as is a matching overstuffed chair. The other chair is of a blue printed pattern. The rug is a darkish violet and gray, close to a blue, etc.

("I believe an older woman." The third question sought to find out who the other woman was beside Jane. See the woman data on page 230. We think this answer reinforces our interpretations of the woman data, and the symbolic blue data just noted. Miss Callahan of course being considerably older than Jane—about 78, we believe. Again, Miss Callahan gave Jane the parent begonia which furnished eventually the office begonia; a drawing of the office begonia was used as the envelope object for tonight.

(My fourth question asked for the initials of this older woman. The question made Jane hesitate: "You had better wait on this. The <u>older</u> woman data leads Ruburt to make personal associations which could be distortive." (Pause.) "We will <u>try</u> here with the initial A, or G." Jane said the question brought her mother to her mind; Seth however did not want to give her mother's name, which is Marie Roberts, or those initials; and Jane did not do so. But A or G as far as we know do not apply to Miss Callahan either, whose first name is Florence.

(I now made a comment: "That word monolithic is interesting." Seth replied: "This is in connection with a drawing or design. And mono, also meaning one." The envelope object is a drawing. See also the interpretation of monolithic on page 232.

(The next question was: "How about that five in a circle?" "The impression is visual. The circle outlined in yellow, I believe, and I see visually a red five inside." This puzzled us, and we think it contains some sort of distortion as far as the red five is concerned. Part of this data may be valid. As a joke one of my coworkers at the office hung a homemade chain from the top of the wooden stick which supports the begonia. The stick is visible in the drawing used as object. I did not of course show the chain in the drawing.

(Checking the day after this experiment, I found that the chain contains five large links, each perhaps two inches in diameter. The chain is made of gold coated stock, that is card stock that is gold on one side. The gold side of the stock is on the outside of the links so that they sparkle when sunlight strikes them. Seth's mention of a visual impression, and the yellow and circle data, reminded me of the chain. We cannot determine the meaning of the red five data however.

(We do not know whether the chain interpretation is correct. It would be very interesting, if so, since Jane has never seen the chain, nor as stated even the plant itself since I took it to the office. Nor did she know the paper chain existed; she is quite sure I did not tell her of this, and I have no memory of doing so.

("I have come as close as I can this evening." This when I asked Seth to name the object. Jane then added:

("A connection with a framework of some kind. Perhaps wooden", can refer to the wooden stick which shows in the drawing used as object. The stick supports the begonia plant, and is a framework in this sense.

(Jane resumed at 11:07.)

Now. I will keep you but briefly, though I could speak for some time.

In our early test experiences Ruburt would not have been able to let test data come through this clearly, on an evening when you had indulged in a conversation such as you did tonight.

("I wondered about that.")

Since our time is limited, I have emphasized our material, with our experimental data.

We will now then close the session, as I would not now add more to your work load. My heartiest wishes to you both, and to Ruburt, who thinks an eagle is a moose.

("He still does." See the drawing of the envelope object used in the last session, on page 217. Today Jane told me the eagle still looked like a moose to her.)

This is to be expected. One note: The significance of course of the bird who could not fly, and Ruburt's background, and the subsequent doctoring attempts on his part. My best wishes.

("Good night, Seth. Thank you."

(End at 11:15. Jane's eyes opened often. She was out as usual.)

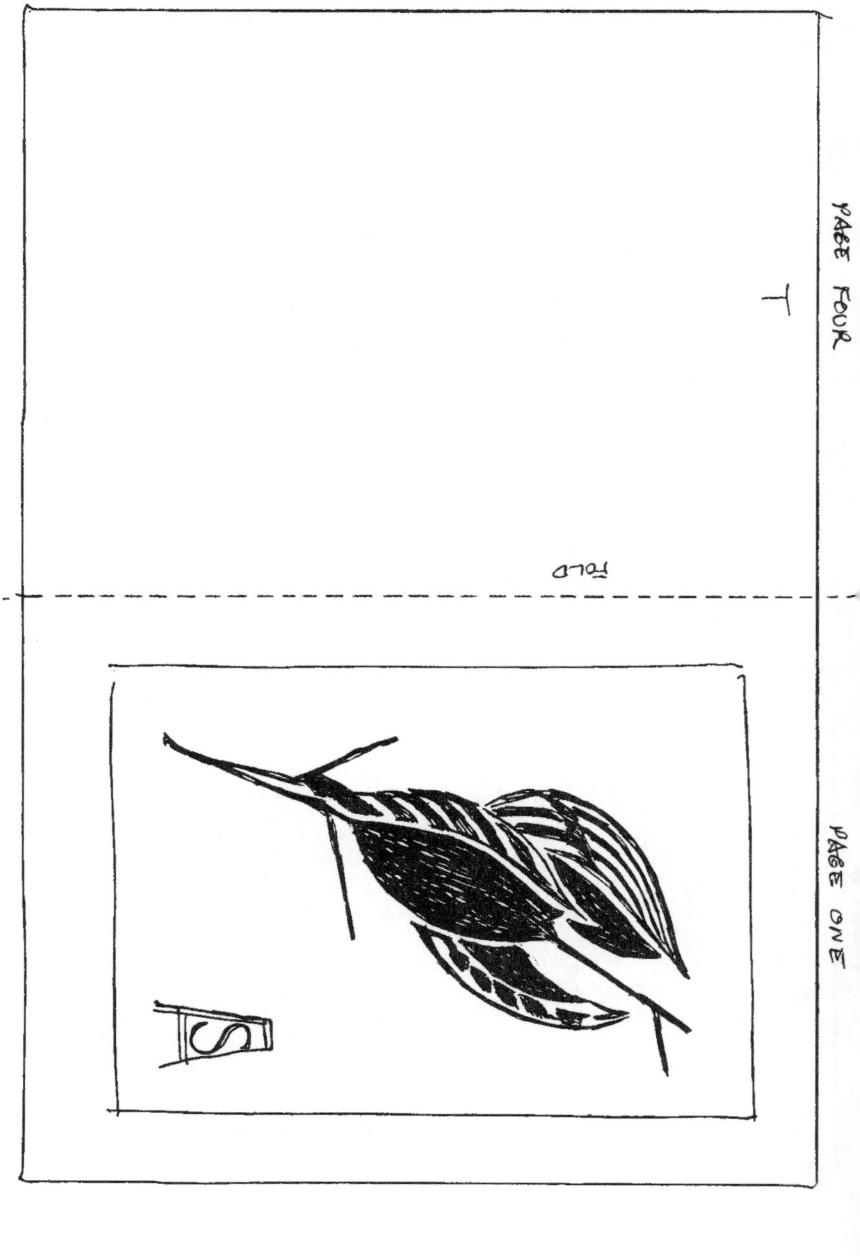

(Reduced copy of pages 1 and 4 of the announcement used as object in the 61st envelope experiment, in the 268th session for June 15,1966.)

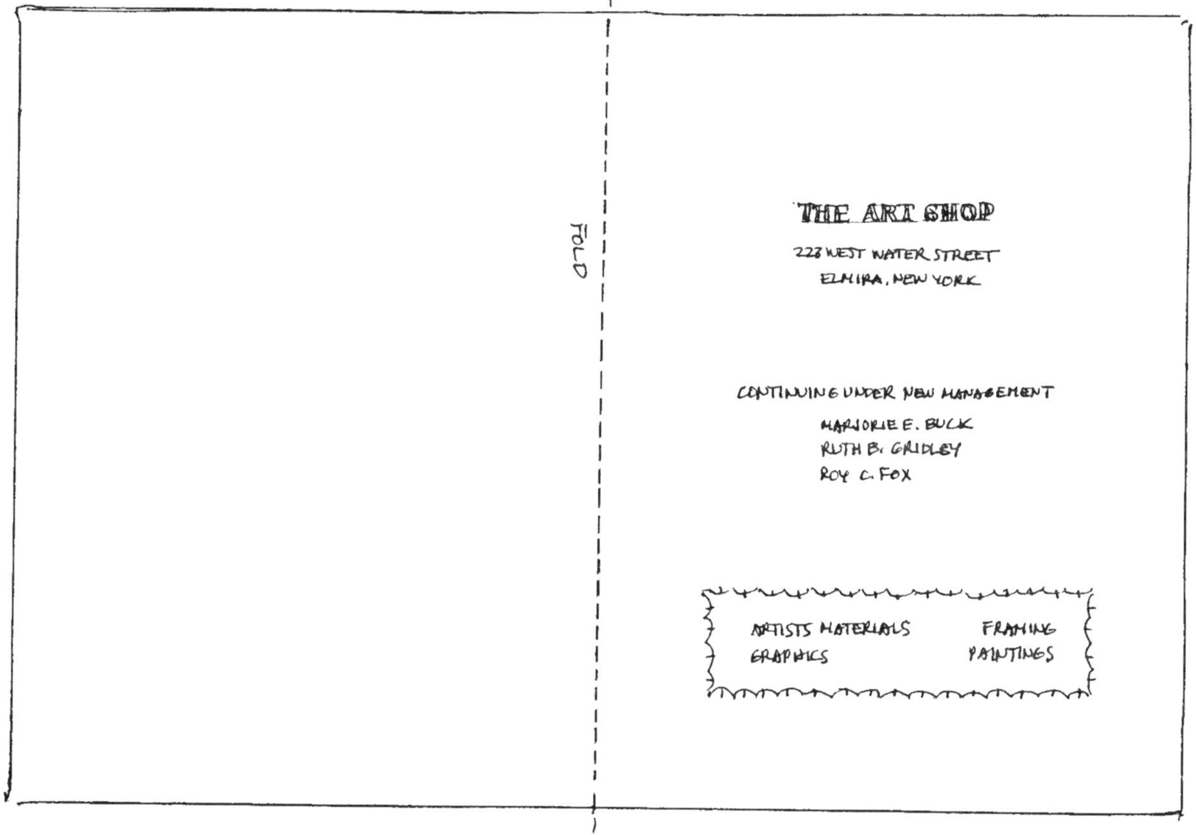

(Reduced copy of pages 2 and 3 of the announcement used as object in the 61st envelope experiment, in the 268th session for June 15,1966.)

SESSION 268
JUNE 15, 1966 9 PM WEDNESDAY

(The 61st envelope object is an announcement Jane and I received in the mail a few days ago. This contrasts with the object in the last session, which Jane had never seen and did not know existed. Tonight's object is printed in black on lightweight card stock, which is an off-white color. The object was prepared for the experiment in the usual manner, using the two pieces of Bristol and the double envelopes.

(Marilyn and Don Wilbur witnessed the session.

(Once again Jane began speaking in a heavier voice, since our windows were open because of the warm evening. Her eyes remained closed for the entire first delivery. Her pace was good.)

Good evening.

("Good evening, Seth.")

My welcome as always to our guests.

My condolences to Ruburt, in his attempt to win out over natural forces, and to upset those balances which are so necessary. We shall have more to say about this bird episode. There are connections here that we shall use in another discussion.

(See the last session. Jane had been trying to keep alive a young robin that had been caught by one of our cats last Monday. This morning we found the bird had died during the night. It had been kept outside, in a safe place, and fed, etc. Last night at perhaps 10 PM, as we sat in the living room, Jane suddenly announced: "The bird is dead." But we did not go to check.)

Now. You recall certainly the material dealing with the inner senses. Experiments and experiences using psychological time, and <u>all</u> projection events, deal rather directly with the use of these inner senses.

Such experiences as projection will therefore involve you in extremely vivid movement and sensation. You may to some extent, and you should, use your critical faculties when you are projecting. However you cannot emphasize these too strongly or you will terminate the experience.

Training will allow you to maintain the proper balance. Usually you do not use all of the inner senses in any given projection experience. Now, for this reason you see certain projections will seem entirely different than others.

You remember that I listed briefly the three forms that you use during your projections. Now I will also say that in the first form you usually use certain inner senses; in the second form you use more of these, you see, and in the third form you make an attempt to use all of them, though very rarely is this successful.

You should find it interesting, when you note waking or dream projections, to notice the overall form of perception that you seem to be using. You will automatically shield yourself in a large measure from stimuli that is too strong for your own rate of development. This balancing attempt may lead to an unevenness of experience during any given projection.

As you know however, it is almost impossible for you to be aware of the full perceptions possible, for the ego would never stand for it. Oftentimes, even in simple dreams, you feel concepts, you understand a particular piece of information, without a word having been spoken.

(Jane's voice was by now somewhat heavier and stronger.)

As you know, this is characteristic of one of our inner senses. In some projection experiences you will also know, or experience a concept, and at first you see you may not understand what is happening. You usually think out an idea. There are some experiences that involve what we shall call pseudoprojections.

In these you experience as actual the innermost reality of a given concept. Now this may, or may not, be a valid projection. There are ways to discover whether the projection is a pseudo one or a valid one. For one simple example, Ruburt experienced a valid projection begun from the dream state, some time ago.

Now this was valid. However it is also very similar to an experience in which the individual feels himself inside of a concept.

I leave it to you, Joseph, to slow me down when you wish.

("It's okay.")

Ruburt was in the third form, and he did indeed project beyond your solar system. This was still a projection within the physical universe however. He was given information which he did not recall consciously. When you experience clearly *(smile)*, when you explore the inside of a concept, you act it out. You form a temporary but very vivid image production.

If the experience of Ruburt's had merely been this, it still would have been pertinent, for when you understand a concept in such a manner, you never forget it. The knowledge becomes part of your physical cells, and of your own electromagnetic structure.

I want to make this clearer however. Suppose that you suddenly understand the concept of oneness with the universe, and that this particular inner sense of feeling concepts is to be used. You would then construct, as you construct dream images, a multitudinous variety of shapes and forms meant to represent the complicated varieties of life. You would then have the experience of entering into each of these lives. You would not think what it was like to be a bird, you would momentarily be a bird. This does involve a projection of sorts, and yet it still must be called a pseudoprojection.

A valid projection you see would involve the actual projection of one of your forms, so that it actually did enter these various other forms.

Now you may take a break, and we shall continue.

(Break at 9:23. Jane was dissociated as usual, she said. Her eyes remained closed. Her voice had become somewhat stronger, her pace good.

(She resumed in the same energetic manner, although her eyes began to open after a paragraph or two. 9:37.)

You see, some experiences will be simple attempts to use the inner senses more fully. You are at a point where you can utilize these to a much larger extent. Some such experiences will appear to be projections, and as we go along I will tell you how to distinguish between them.

You will be able to look back and see your physical body upon the bed on some occasions, and in other cases you will not be able to do this. The form that you see will allow you to have some idea of your abilities in any given projection. You may begin a projection in one form, and then project from <u>it</u> to another form.

Do you understand?

("Yes." Jane stared at me, her eyes now open steadily. Her voice was again stronger.)

In the first form, you can look back, and see your body. If you project from this form into another in order to intensify your experience, then from this second form you will <u>not</u> see your body upon the bed.

You will be <u>aware</u> however of your body, and you will experience some duality. In the <u>third</u> form you will no longer be aware that your body is on the bed, and you will not see it.

In the third form your experiences will be more vivid. They will involve you perhaps in other systems beside your own, and you will have little contact with your physical form. For this reason projection in the third form is the most difficult to maintain. The possibilities are truly fascinating, but there are dangers that do not exist when the other two forms are used.

Your consciousness is far divorced from the physical organism, and it would be dangerous to stay <u>away</u> for any extended period of physical time. It would for example be quite possible to return to the physical body from this form, <u>and not recognize it as your own</u>. We would not want you to have such an experience. There is confusion and disorientation that <u>can</u> occur, using this third form. You need have no worries however, since as a rule your excursions will be along the lines of your own development.

Using this third form, there would be a tendency for you not to recognize your own physical situation. It would be difficult to carry the memories of the present ego personality with you. This third form is the vehicle of the inner self. The disorientation that it feels is the disorientation, you see, that it will feel when the physical body is deserted, or at the point of death.

The disorientation is only temporary, and when the form is severed from the physical body, then all the memories and identity within the electromagnetic system become part of the inner self, of course.

But this is not an instantaneous process, and in any projection attempt there is no need whatsoever for this to be carried any further. This form is used however for purposes of instruction. It is used now and then to acquaint the whole personality with those circumstances that shall at one time affect it.

There are occasions, though they are rare, when the disorientation period is completely passed, and connection with the body is therefore nearly broken. We shall not however deal with this situation. Most of your projections will be in the first and second forms.

Usually you will project from the physical body into the first form, and then perhaps into the second form. Occasionally this will happen and you will not know it, despite all your attempts to ascertain your circumstances. There are indeed however ways and signs that tell you when you switch from one form to the other, and we shall indeed see that you know these. You should both—this is Joseph and Ruburt now—you should both have several examples of projections within the first and second forms in the following months, if your development continues at its present rate.

I want to mention the difference also in experience and sensation, between a projection that begins in the dream state, and one that begins in a trance state, and also to discuss what Ruburt calls <u>awake-seeming</u> dreams, for there are several points here that you do not know, and they are fairly important.

I suggest a break now for our Instream material.

(Break at 9:59. Jane was out as usual. Her pace had been good, her voice fairly strong, her eyes open for most of the delivery.

(Jane now sat leaning forward, with both hands raised to her closed eyes as she began giving the 72nd Instream data. Resume at 10:10.)

Give us a moment please for our Instream material.

A page, perhaps from a book. Having to do with, or mentioning, a scourge of some kind. Perhaps a time of plague. Now this could be fiction, or a historic account *(pause)*, but mention of a disease.

There is a connection with the past also, perhaps past treatment of the disease, or perhaps this is a historic connotation.

The numbers 175 and 377, I believe. These could be page numbers, I do not know. Or there could be a connection also with the 13th and 17th centuries. A connection also with fire mentioned. Livestock and rats.

A small, very white object also. It seems to be a cube with the side to the right lighter somehow than the other sides. The object may lay on the page of a book.

Other impressions not connected with the object—a letter from a cousin, received by Dr. Instream. Also the initials J C. *(Pause.)*

Do you have an envelope for me?

("Yes."

(At 10:16 I handed Jane the envelope for our 61st experiment. Her eyes still closed, she pressed it to her forehead, its long dimension parallel to the floor.)

Give us a moment please. These are impressions.

Ten. Something twisted. Something repeated, perhaps, though I am not certain, five times. Connection with a framework that is broken, or cut off.

This is difficult to put into words... The impression of something going forward, as of a path, you see, that is wide, and then narrows into the distance. *(Her eyes closed, Jane made a gesture with both arms that the Wilburs and I interpreted like this:*

(Jane's hands came together at arm's length.)

That may need some interpretation, but that is the impression.

(After the gesture Jane switched the envelope to a vertical position as she put it back against her forehead. From now on I watched carefully to see that she held the envelope in the same position until the end of the delivery, so that I could mark the top dimension thus,

should it be necessary to our interpretation of the data, and the Wilburs verified that the position of the object itself was thus determined by marking in succession both envelopes as they were opened at break, the two pieces of Bristol, and finally the object itself.)

A border. A top. Connection with an invitation. A house. Four vertical lines, and a present, or gift.

Do you have any questions?

("Can you say something more about going forward?")

The impression is difficult to bring into clear focus. *(Pause.)* It may be symbolic. A movement, for example in a forward direction, or something that leads into the future.

This way *(Jane gestured with the vertical envelope without changing its basic position)*, the impression of a long line, approximately down the center, or a thin dark object, and a small object in the lower right-hand corner.

Perhaps a connection with a June date, and some designations on the other side of the object—perhaps in the upper left-hand corner. *(Still holding the envelope in the vertical position and in her right hand, Jane lowered it enough so that she could touch the envelope's upper left corner with her left hand.)*

Some writing. *(Pause.)* Now, I believe handwriting. And perhaps with an older man. That is, perhaps a connection with an older man.

("What was that about top?")

A designation of some sort. Perhaps initials or date, in the upper left-hand corner, on the <u>other</u> side of the object. *(Jane again touched the object in the upper left-hand corner as she held it vertically. I wasn't sure this information came through as a result of the question, feeling instead that the question had somehow interrupted her.*

("How about colors?"

(Again I seemed to interrupt. Seth now went into something new as far as the envelope data is concerned. The Wilburs and I agreed later that Seth evidently decided to insert the following material just on his own, and because the time, and Jane's trance state, seemed right to him. There is also a general idea connection with what follows and the envelope object.)

Now, we will try something here. I am up above, looking down at a room in which four people sit at a table. They are members of a family. Of your family, Joseph.

I believe your brother Loren is one present. *(Pause.)* The number 17, a date in July which will be significant to him, or his close family—not necessarily to <u>him</u>, you see. *(Pause.)*

(Now Seth went back to the envelope data as usual.)

A rectangular object, with white background. Also gray. A connection with a future event.

I suggest your break.

(Break at 10:31. Jane was dissociated very well, she said—really out. She thought Seth had done this deliberately to compensate for the traffic noise coming through our open windows, and because the witnesses had, in the beginning of the data, unwittingly distracted her by moving papers, coughing, etc.

(As noted on page 242, I asked Jane to hold the envelope in the same position as she came out of trance. Since she leaves the trance state easily and quickly, she heard me and complied. The envelopes and Bristols were then marked as noted, and finally

the object itself. This shows as T at the top of page 4, in the copy on page 236. See also the notes on page 242.

(The Wilburs, Jane and I made the envelope connections. Seth confirmed our interpretation of a couple of them after break.

("Ten." The object is a notice Jane and I received in the mail recently, stating that a local artists supply store was continuing in business under new management. Tonight's session was held on June 15. I had thrown away the envelope the object arrived in, but both of us remembered receiving the object last Friday, on June 10. Seth confirms this later.

("Something twisted." The printed drawing on page one of the object is made up of a complicated pattern of curving lines, which Seth could have interpreted as twisted. The same impression could result from the fancy box at the bottom of page 3.

("Something repeated, perhaps, though I am not certain, five times." Seth wasn't positive here. We believe he was getting at the construction of the drawing on page 1 of the object. The three sections of milkweed pod shown are made up groups of lines; each group contains about the same number and arrangement of lines, whether one would consider them black or white. One could find arrangements of five lines in each of these groups, but could also count more or less, depending on approach. We believe the idea of repetition here to be valid.

("Connection with a framework that is broken, or cut off." In the lower right hand corner of page 1 of the object is a monogram consisting of the letters A and S, for Art Shop. The right leg of the A is cut shorter than the left leg. When Jane saw the monogram she said the A represented a framework to her, like an A-frame house, and that the right leg was shorter.

(The word "framing" appears at the bottom of page 3, and is itself enclosed in a fancy frame, but evidently Seth wasn't referring to this.

("This is difficult to put into words... The impression of something going forward, as of a path, you see, that is wide, and then narrows into the distance." Jane made her gesture, as described on page 242. "That may need some interpretation, but that is the impression." I sought more information on this impression by the first question. At the time of the above data Jane held the envelope horizontally. There can be a literal interpretation: The drawing of the milkweed on page one of the object is V-shaped in the abstract sense—wide at one end, narrowing to a point, as did Jane's gesture. Also the A in the Art Shop monogram narrows somewhat but doesn't come to a point. There can also be a symbolic interpretation, and Seth raises this possibility in answer to the first question.

(Jane now switched the envelope to a vertical position, and as explained on page 242 I marked the object T for top, as shown in the copy on page 236. See page 4 of the object.

("A border." Page one of the object contains a blind embossed border. This shows as a pen line on the copy on page 236; actually the border has no color in it. Perhaps, also, the box at the bottom of page 3 of the object could be called a border.

("A top." We don't know, unless Seth perhaps referred to the fact that the object was made up of a folded sheet; perhaps as Jane held the envelope page 1 of the object facing her.

("Connection with an invitation." Since the object is a notice that the Art Shop is continuing in business, it is an invitation to continue trading there. Also Jane and I have been personally invited by the three new proprietors, whom we know, to continue doing business with the Art Shop. Additional note by Rob: Later, shop is moved to a house.

("A house." As stated in connection with the "framework" data on page 244, the A in the Art Shop monogram on page one of the object meant framework, or A-frame house, to Jane.

("Four vertical lines," While giving this data Jane held the object vertically, as indicated by T on page 4. The data is too general to be sure; the drawing on page 1 would have some upright lines in it while the object is held vertically, but nothing exactly vertical.

("and a present, or gift." Besides selling painting supplies, the Art Shop sells a variety of gifts—ceramics, books, frames, paintings, prints, sculpture, postcards, etc.

(The first question asked Seth to comment further on the "going forward" data on page 242: "The impression is difficult to bring into clear focus. It may be symbolic. A movement, for example in a forward direction, or something that leads into the future." A literal interpretation was given on page 242. Here, the symbolic interpretation can be the fact that page 3 of the object states that the Art Shop is "Continuing under new management."

(Jane continued, gesturing with the object held vertically: "This way, the impression of a long line, approximately down the center, or a thin dark object", refers we think to the stem of the milkweed drawing on page 1 of the object, running from top to bottom. The rest of this data follows:

("and a small object in the lower right-hand corner." With the object held as marked by T on page 4, the A-S monogram for the Art Shop is seen to be in the lower right-hand corner of page 1. This is speaking intrinsically. We don't know for instance whether Jane held the envelope with page one of the object toward her face, or with page 4 toward her face; nor do we know whether this matters, or if it influenced Seth's data.

("Perhaps a connection with a June date", See the "ten" data on page 244. Jane and I were able to determine that we received the envelope object in the mail on June 10. Seth confirmed.

("and some designations on the other side of the object, perhaps in the upper left-hand corner." Holding the envelope vertically in her right hand, Jane pinched the upper left corner of the envelope with her left hand. See page 243. There is printed matter on pages 1 and 3 of the object; folded, this puts one printed page behind the other, which could give rise to Seth's use of "other side." The Art Shop address at the top of page 3 however is neither to the right or left, but centered. We don't know if the upper left-hand corner data derived from Jane holding the object with page one facing away from her, for instance.

("Some writing. Now, I believe handwriting." There is no handwriting on the object, only type. In the past Jane, or Seth, has intermixed terms for printed copy, calling it printing, writing, type, etc.

("And perhaps with an older man. That is, perhaps a connection with an older man." Roy Fox, whose name appears on page three of the envelope object, is in his early 60s.

(The next question asked Seth for more data on the top impression. We don't know whether the following data is in answer to the question: "A designation of some sort. Perhaps initials or date, in the upper left-hand corner, on the other side of the object." Jane again indicated the upper left corner of the envelope, as she still held it vertically. This appears to be a repeat of the left corner data given on page 243, and as stated there, there is nothing in particular in a corner with the object held as marked on page 236.

(The third question asked for colors connected with the object. Seth gets around to answering the question, but first inserts the material concerning my brother Loren: "Now, we will try something here. I am up above, looking down at a room in which four people sit at a table. They are members of a family. Of your family, Joseph."

("I believe your brother Loren is one present. The number 17, a date in July which will be significant to him, or his close family—not necessarily to <u>him</u>, you see." We did not ask for this data; it came through spontaneously. We saw one reason why Seth could have chosen to insert it here in the envelope data, and Seth confirms our speculation later. Our idea was that Seth sought to use the idea of a relative connection with the object. Ruth Gridley, listed on page 3 of the object as one of the Art Shop's new management, is my first cousin; Loren of course is my brother. But we still think the Loren data is separate in the main from the envelope data.

(Now Seth answered the question: "A rectangular object, with white background. Also gray." The object is rectangular. It has a white background. There is no gray on the object, but as soon as she saw the fine print on page 3, Jane said this to her meant the impression of gray.

("A connection with a future event." Future events are implied by the object through the copy on page 3: "Continuing under new management."

(Jane resumed at 11:12, speaking very jovially, her eyes open.)

We will now close our session, out of my due passionate regard for you. I am as always quite willing and able to carry on for some time.

It is beneficial for us to have these particular witnesses, and it is good experience for you. I understand quite well the necessary limitations that we have to work with. You have the opportunity to ask me any particular questions you have in mind, Joseph, or we may end the session as you may prefer.

("Was our interpretation of the ten data correct?")

Ten did refer to the date, the tenth of June.

("Jane wants to know why her bird died.")

It is not too late this evening for me to set him straight on his birds and bees. *(Seth was very active, smiling, vociferous.)* It is however too late, I fear, for you.

("Well then, how did our cat get out of the house?"

(Recently we acquired a second cat, a stray. It had the habit of coming and going at all hours. Last night Jane let it in at about 1 AM, after hearing it scratching at the backdoor. In order to do this she had to fully dress before walking down the long hall outside our apartment. Jane fed the cat and locked our apartment door as usual before returning to bed. I know she was up at this time because she woke me getting back into bed, and told me the second cat had come home. I also heard this cat and our first cat, Willy, playing in the living room.

(When we got up this morning cat number two was nowhere to be found. The hall door was locked. When I went to work this morning Jane went out to the garage with me. After I left, she found cat number two in the yard. Question: How did the cat get there? We decided to ask Seth tonight.

(Broad smile, eyes wide open.) I should never be the one to tell you this, for my friend Ruburt will be after me with a broom next.

("Why?")

Someone in this household walked in their sleep, and opened the door. The cat is not good at projection. Our friend Ruburt does not remember his nocturnal walk. Since we are with friends, I will tell you that he remembered his womanly modesty even in his sleep, and he once more donned the clothes that he donned earlier, you see, when he let the cat in.

The dear little pussies annoyed him. He was too lazy, you see, to rise from bed. He wanted to sleep. He had his cake and ate it too.

(I fell back to sleep at once after seeing Jane return to bed at 1 AM. Jane said she remembered that the two cats were very noisy as they played together in the dark apartment, and that she remembered wishing they would stop. But she had no memory of getting up a second time, dressing, etc., to put cat number two out again.)

Now, I am—you may or may not take notes now, Joseph—you see, rather present with you this evening...

(Seth was in an excellent and humorous mood, and spoke for a while longer. I stopped taking verbatim notes at 11:20. Seth spoke to the Wilburs and me about the implications behind the death of the young robin, among other things, and verified that the Loren data in the envelope experiment was also intended to use the relative idea to tie it to the envelope object and my cousin Ruth.

(Seth called it a night, presumably, at 11:30, but then returned, still in a fine and smiling mood. He said Jane would not like the sleepwalking idea, which Jane confirmed later. He also told Marilyn Wilbur that he saw her, through Jane's eyes, as an individual—a question Marilyn had raised earlier in the evening. In the past on various occasions Seth has said he usually sees witnesses, and myself, as a composite electromagnetic image that embodies our past, present and future, as well as these attributes in whatever other lives we might have had. He has explained that this is easier, usually, than focusing so sharply on the one physical and psychic personality in our temporal now.

(The Wilburs left us. Jane and I thought the session over, but Seth returned briefly again at about 11:45, to comment in a hearty manner that during the physical lives Jane, Seth and I lived together in Denmark, during the 1600s, I did him out of considerable money. Bits and pieces of our reincarnational material crop up throughout the sessions.

(Seth returned once more at 11:54, this time again in answer to our speculations concerning the second cat and Jane's sleepwalking episode. Here is the rest of the story involving the second cat: After I left for work and Jane had taken the cat into the house, she discovered to her sorrow that the cat had somehow gotten its lower jaw caught in a new collar we had put on it the day before, and that evidently the cat's lower jaw had been forced open in this strained position for some hours. Jane had to use scissors to cut the collar off. The cat promptly fell into a stuporous sleep, that lasted all day.

(We were wondering how long the animal had been forced to struggle with its jaws open in this manner when Seth came through. Jane spoke with her eyes open while standing quietly by a table. Seth told us that Jane, in her sleep, put the cat back out at 3 AM. The cat got its lower jaw caught in the collar "shortly after," and remained so caught until we found it shortly after 7:30 AM.

(Thus Seth returned three times in all. Jane had been well dissociated each time.)

IMPRESSIONS ATTACHED TO SESSION 268
FRIDAY, JUNE 17, 1966

(The following are the impressions Jane received at 10:22 while holding Don Wilbur's watch:)

1) 1943.

2) April date.

3) tall man with grey hair...sort of prickly.

4) a connection with someone else beside Don with the watch.

** correct—the watch was a gift from his wife.*

5) small stupid incident immediately before or after the purchase.

** correct—It was a Christmas gift and he had bought the same item, a watch for his wife. They both knew what the other had bought and decided to open them Xmas eve because they knew.*

6) graduation—no.

7) another package involved.

** correct—The smaller watch package was slipped inside of a larger package.*

8) also, some connection with something misplaced or stolen—I don't think it's the watch that was misplaced or stolen.

9) color yellow.

10) 4 people together.

11) creed—I don't think that's the word.

** perhaps in connection with Christmas.*

12) old man in a wheelchair—not connected with the watch.

** Don knew a woman who was crippled with arthritis who spent a lot of time in a wheelchair. She was a small woman... Jane's impression was of a small person.*

13) initials S.G.—that seems as if that would apply to the Gallaghers...ha, ha.

14) something about the 6TH grade—another watch perhaps.

** The 6th grade was significant in the mind of Don although it is not likely he received another watch then. He has owned several other watches in his life though.*

(Additional note by Rob regarding 12: Jane also had an impression of dark hair in connection with the arthritis data. This was correct according to the Wilburs on Friday night, June 17, but now I do not recall just how. RFB - 6/20.)

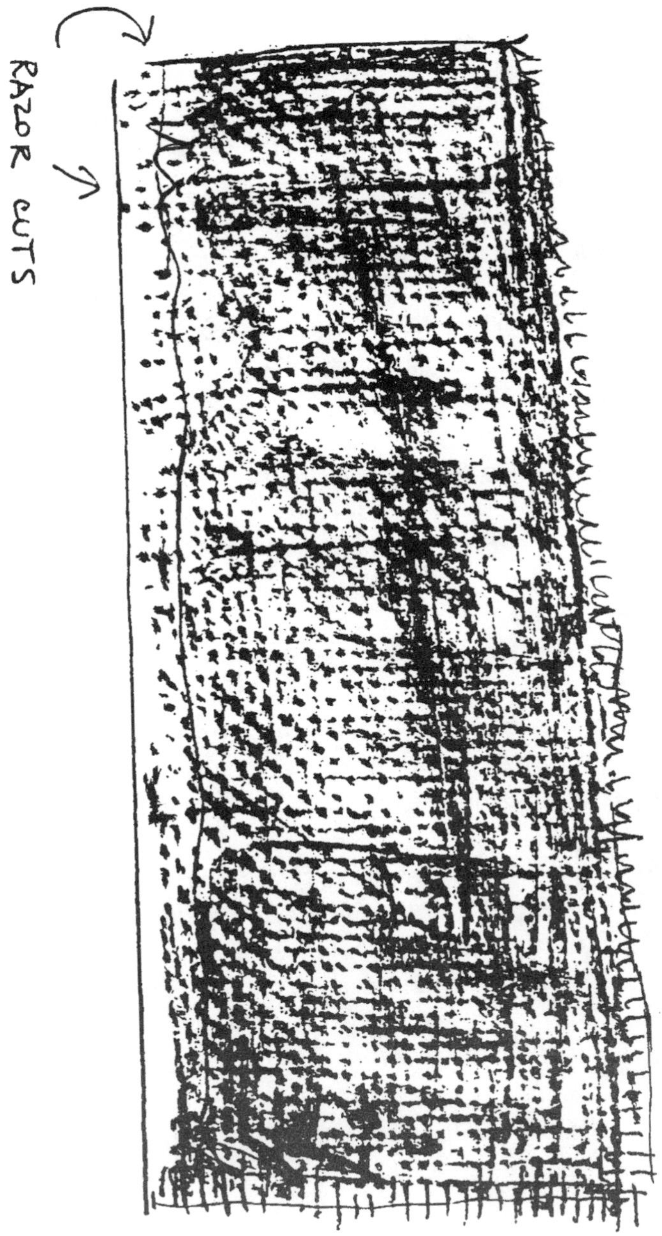

(Rubbing from the piece of burlap used as the object in the 62nd envelope experiment, in the 269th session for June 20, 1966.)

SESSION 269
JUNE 20, 1966 9 PM MONDAY

(The envelope object for the 62nd experiment was a piece of cream-colored burlap; it shows up dark on page 250 because of the method of reproducing it. Jane was with me last Saturday, June 18, when I bought the burlap to use for some experimental canvases for painting.

(I glued a square of the burlap to a wood panel with a very white acrylic gesso that is used to prime artists' canvas, then used a razor blade to trim off the excess around the edges after drying. Hence the razor cuts on the object as indicated. Also along the bottom edge of the object a coating of the white gesso was to be seen, residue from the panel itself. Jane had seen me experimenting with the panel also, of course.

(The envelope results contained a few valid points. The results were well below par however. Jane was very tired before the session, although she said she felt fine when I questioned her. Had I realized how tired she was the session would not have been held; both of us have been extremely busy lately and cramped for time. Jane said she did not let me know she was tired, because under such circumstances sometimes excellent material has come through.

(Jane was smoking when the session began, and her eyes were open from the beginning. Her pace was average and she smiled broadly.)

Good evening.

("Good evening, Seth.")

I hereby *(smile)* offer you sincere congratulations upon your birthday.

("Thank you." I'm 47. Jane is 38.)

Ruburt was so concerned that your coworkers did not hold a party for you, so I made certain that I duly congratulate you. *(Pause.)* Ruburt sent out messages. Your guests today were hardly uninvited—at least subconsciously.

He wanted them to wish you a happy birthday. None of this operated on a conscious level. Consciously he wanted to be alone. His anger at your coworkers <u>generated</u> the energies that found immediate outlet, pulling people here. Then of course it came to nothing, because he would not disturb you. All in all, an amusing demonstration. *(Pause.)*

(Jane and I had been quite puzzled at the visitors of this afternoon and supper time. All friends, they arrived this way: A group of two, a single, a group of three, for a total of six. They stayed long enough so that Jane got no work done during the afternoon, or very little. In addition one of them was a coworker of mine, and told Jane the office had forgotten today was my birthday; when they remembered, they planned a party for <u>tomorrow</u>.)

Now. There were some notes I wanted to give you concerning dreams in which you feel certain that you are awake. When these dreams are unusually vivid, then the ego is aware of participating. The ego is not using its critical faculties however as a general rule.

As you realize, you can use the critical faculties. But you see when you do so you realize that you are not in your normal waking condition. In awake-seeming dreams you are indeed awake, within of course a different psychological framework. Indeed, within a different framework of reality.

You are operating at a rather high level of awareness, and you are using inner senses. These enable you to perceive an added depth or dimension, and this is responsible for the increased sense of vividness, and also for the sense of exhilaration that sometimes occurs within this particular sort of dream.

The next step of course is to allow the ego to use its critical faculties also within the dream state. You are then able to realize that while you are indeed awake, as you seem, you are awake within a different condition.

When this occurs you will be able to use your normal abilities in addition to other abilities used while in the dream state itself. You will be certain of your identity. You will realize that your physical self is sleeping, or in a dream state, and that the inner self is fully awake. Now this represents a definite increase in the scope of consciousness, and a considerable expansion over the usual limitations set by you upon the self.

Only then can you fully begin to manipulate the conditions that exist, and communicate the knowledge that you receive to your own ego. For the time, you see, the ego becomes a direct participator in such experiences—at least to some degree.

Almost all of your dream experiences do involve projection of one kind or another. These experiences vary in intensity, type, and even duration as any other experiences vary. It takes a good deal of training and competence to operate with any real effectiveness within these situations.

All in all the intellect plays some part, but the intuitional qualities are the most important. There are chemical changes that occur with the physical body when projections occur. There are also electromagnetic variations. These vary according to the form in which the projection occurs.

The projected form does make some impression upon your physical system. In other words, it is possible for it to be detected. It is a kind of pseudo-image, materialistically speaking, but it has definite electromagnetic reality, and chemical properties.

Now. Animals have indeed sensed such apparitions. There is hardly any magic involved. They react to the chemical properties of the apparition, and build up the image from it—from them, the properties.

These chemical properties however are more diffuse in an apparition than in a physical form. The chemical composition of a storm perhaps will give you an idea of what I mean. They are indeed small disturbances, you see—they form small disturbances within your physical system.

As a rule they are not solid in the same way that clouds are not solid, and yet they have shape, and to a certain extent boundaries, and of course movement. They definitely have a reality, you see, though you cannot usually perceive it with the physical senses.

Perhaps this diffused quality is the most important difference between such an apparition and a physical form. There is an atomic structure. In some ways however the structure is less complete than a physical form. There is always a minute difference in the physical body's normal weight when the individual is projecting. The excess chemicals built up during the waking condition are used to help form the projecting images. There is a slight loss of electromagnetic potency and chemical potency when the individual is projecting.

You may take your break, and I shall continue.

(Break at 9:30. Jane had been dissociated as usual. She knew her eyes had been open most of the time. Her voice had not been as strong as usual lately however. She remarked casually that she felt somewhat tired. Her delivery had been quite active and emphatic though.

(Jane resumed in the same manner at 9:46.)

There is much to be considered here. Identity is not dependent upon physical existence.

Electromagnetic reality belongs to the inner self. It is not a property that belongs to physical matter, although it does appear in physical terms. *(Pause.)* The second and third projection forms have electromagnetic realities. *(Pause.)* We are going slow here to get this material through clearly.

The chemical properties of the body are the result of certain electromagnetic changes. Chemicals are therefore byproducts of electromagnetic realities. The electromagnetic properties, again, belong to the psychic, not the physical structure.

In physical existence a certain portion of the inner self's electromagnetic properties are used by the physical structure of the body. Subtle changes occur in the body when the inner self projects. This projection is not dependent upon physical life—that is, the survival of the human personality also is then not dependent upon physical survival, nor need it be supported by physical life. The electromagnetic properties simply revert to their original source with the inner self, and are no longer utilized in the construction of a corporeal image.

All consciousness exists first and primarily in electromagnetic terms, although consciousness may project itself into many various forms. It is never completely imprisoned within those forms however. You see, I have somewhat explained this to you. *(Smile.)* As physical beings your perception, your physical perception, is slowed down to a necessary but very extensive degree.

The span of a whole man's lifetime is no more than a moment point. The ego is the portion of you equipped to explore and experience this moment point in depth. *(Smile.)* Value fulfillment demands this slowing down of perception. This is most difficult to explain. Consider using psychological time. You have experiences within a few physical moments of physical time, experiences that are entirely <u>independent</u> of your time structure.

You are exploring the inner contents of a moment, delving into its experience. Now this is what the ego does you see within a lifetime, only to a greater degree. In projections, and in your dreams, your perceptions to some extent enable you to leap out of the ego's time limitations. The physical body is indeed the ego's vehicle. You do not need it, you see, for projections.

(Smile, pause.) We have just covered some rather important material, and we shall discuss it more thoroughly. You may take a brief break before our Instream data.

(Break at 10:04. Jane had been out as usual, her delivery very intent, her eyes open often.)

(While giving the 73rd Dr. Instream material she spoke with a hand raised to her closed eyes. Resume at 10:12.)

Give us a moment, please. *(Pause.)*

The numbers 4 2. Perhaps in connection with someone's birthday. A male, relative of Dr. Instream.

Now. Ruburt knows of the hypnosis symposium, having seen a clipping. We will give some impressions concerning that symposium.

One quite unpleasant event, involving a man with an <u>M</u> initial. *(Pause.)* Perhaps in connection with another man with an <u>E</u> initial. The M may stand for Milton, or a close-sounding name. This will be in the form of an argument, I believe, before several persons, though it could occur before many persons. *(Pause.)*

An element about the symposium with which Dr. Instream disagrees strongly, very strongly. Some particular plans made perhaps despite his original wishes.

The object for tonight, some kind of buckle, of metal or metallic color, scratched. *(Pause.)* Also a design or initials *(pause)* scratched deeply into the object. *(Long pause.)*

Four six, or 1 9 4 6, connected with the object. It is now, or was connected to, something that looks like an elasticized belt. *(Pause.)*

Do you have an envelope for me?

Yes. *(Without opening her eyes Jane took the double envelope for the 62nd experiment from me, and held it to her forehead in a horizontal position.)*

Give us a moment please. These are impressions.

It seems to be somehow connected with turbulence of some sort. The impression that the object has a border, a line border. That it is rectangular in shape. *(Pause.)*

Smidgeon—I do not know to what this refers. Also a distant 1947 connection. The impression of a card that somehow connects two houses. The visual impression is of an object or representation on two balancing sides of the object, as for example here and here, you see...

(Still holding the envelope horizontally with one hand, Jane indicated each end of the envelope with her other hand.)

A florid complexion. Six. A cluster of shapes, rounded. Holding the object this way, lettering of some sort in here. *(Now holding the envelope vertically, Jane ran a finger along the bottom edge of the envelope.)* Perhaps on two sides of the object.

The color green, yellow. Pointed flower or star shapes. Again, a connection with a disturbance, with a knife. This is the pointed impression. I do not know if the knife is literal. Sharp, something sharp.

Ruburt thinks of a newspaper article, about a murder. A formal affair of a conventional social nature. An inadequacy. Something canceled or expired. The color white and four lines, perhaps with white between them.

Do you have any questions? Red and white squares connected here.

(I had the choice of trying to guide Seth back to the object through questions, or of trying again with new data. It had soon become clear that the impressions were off, although at this time I didn't know why. Seth's accuracy had picked up toward the end of the data, however. Jane sat waiting.

("Do you want to try another set of impressions?")

Very well, give us a moment please. *(Pause.)* Well then, we shall see.

A circular object, like a target. Red color, surrounded by white. Perhaps by a white square. Also the color black. *(Pause.)* Perhaps a connection with something not asked for, or not wanted or required. *(Pause.)*

Still, there seems to be a newspaper connection. Printing or black ink, I do not know. J. B. A box or container, perhaps that once had flowers.

I suggest your break.

(Break at 10:26. Jane had been dissociated as usual. When she came out of trance now her eyes were bleary, and it was obvious that she was not at her best. She

said that she knew the first data was off when I asked if she wanted to try again.

(Strangely enough, she had two good images while giving the inaccurate data, she said—one image for each set of data. The first concerned a card shape, rectangular, with balancing designs on each end of it while held horizontally. See page 255. The second image was of the target shape also mentioned on page 255.

(We will interpret the data we feel applies. Jane, incidentally, said she never used the word smidgeon that she knew of. See the rubbing of the envelope object on page 250, and the notes on the next page.

(From the first data, page 255: "Pointed flower or star shapes. Again, a connection with a disturbance, with a knife. This is the pointed impression. I do not know if the knife is literal. Sharp, something sharp... Ruburt thinks of a newspaper article, about a murder." Seth also mentioned a connection with turbulence at the start of the data. There can be a direct connection with the envelope object, and a newspaper connection; it seems that both are somewhat distorted, and that one perhaps influenced the other.

(As indicated on page 251, the object was cut off the edge of the wood panel with a razor blade; the blade had to be sharp to slice cleanly through cloth, and such cuts were made on two sides of the object.

(As always when doing such work, I spread newspapers on my drawing table. Jane saw me doing this, and knew I was experimenting gluing the burlap to panels to make painting surfaces. I made this particular panel from which the envelope object came on Saturday afternoon, June 18.

(The newspaper connection also developed because on the front page of today's paper for June 20th, was the story of a local woman being murdered with a knife. So although I used newspapers while developing the envelope object, I couldn't have used the particular newspaper which carried the murder story, since this news developed two days later. Jane and I had talked about the stabbing at supper this evening however, and evidently the knife connection here and with the object caused the distortions.

(At the end of Seth's second try at the envelope data, he once again came up with the newspaper connection: "Still, there seems to be a newspaper connection. Printing or black ink, I do not know." The black ink connection is interesting to me. As I worked with the materials on the newspapers, I wondered whether it was such a good idea, fearing that perhaps the acrylic glue I was using might dissolve the black printing ink enough to cause it to dirty the white burlap I was handling. There was no real trouble although I did get a few faint smudges on the burlap; I removed them without trouble. I do not know if Seth referred to this, or merely black ink being connected with newspapers.

(Jane resumed with her eyes closed and at a slow rate at 10:49.)

We will close our session.

Ruburt was simply exhausted, and that is all.

The object did not have sufficient emotional connections to offset his exhaustion. The yellow piece of burlap might have done this.

(We bought two colors of burlap while shopping Saturday, the white I used to experiment with, and a piece of light yellow that I gave to Jane. Jane had become involved with the yellow material, trying it out as a curtain, slipcover, tablecloth, etc., and she made plans to buy some more. She had become quite enthusiastic over the idea.)

The newspaper connection was correct, as you thought, and the sharpness. His own associations operated, though he did not realize it. It is to be expected at times, and is quite natural.

Now, my heartiest wishes to you both.

("Good night, Seth.")

(End at 10:52. Jane was now very tired, and finally admitted it.)

SESSION 270
JUNE 22, 1966 9 PM WEDNESDAY

(No envelope experiment was held.

(Jane was smoking as the session began and her eyes soon began to open. Her voice remained quiet; there were many people in the yard outside our windows but it was too warm to close ourselves in.)

Good evening, dear friends.

("Good evening, Seth.")

My dear Joseph, there are indeed balances that operate. You need not fear that subconsciously you are going to invite hordes into your home, nor that Ruburt will subconsciously do so.

There is also something you forget. You are your subconscious self, and oftentimes what makes no sense to the ego makes good sense to the overall personality. Still, there are psychological balances that always operate when the overall personality gestalt is operating effectively, as it is in both of your cases.

The overall needs of the personality are always taken into consideration by what I have called in the past the inner ego. Now this portion of the self is indeed self-conscious in the highest meaning of the term—aware of the subconscious portion of the personality, aware of the primary conscious framework that you call your ego, and constantly directs the overall activities. This portion is aware of the complicated workings of the nervous system and all bodily functions. It is the overseer. It knows when to allow subconscious needs and wishes their fulfillment. It knows when to put fulfillment off for a time. It is this part of the personality that is in charge of overall stability.

Now. This inner ego can also operate within the dream state, and in certain awake-seeming dreams it is the portion that realizes that the personality is not in its normal waking condition. It is this portion of the self that is with you in the most excellent projections. The inner ego is the part of the personality that contains the highest aspirations and capabilities. It has been called by psychologists the subliminal self.

When in such dreams your perceptions seem exceedingly clear, you can be certain that the inner ego is operating. Now all portions of the personality, of the present personality, belong to this inner ego. It functions constantly, and yet it is always in a state of becoming. It is more than what you are at any given moment in your time. It contains, and is, the psychological blueprint containing the full potential of the present personality within any given incarnation.

It is the director of all the subsidiary psychological subpersonalities that form the acting-present primary personality. It gives and takes. It prevents unconstructed aspects from gaining control, unless of course there are strong reasons why such control is necessary in the long run.

It dabbles in both your future and your past, speaking now in your terms. As you create a painting, and the painting is still an aspect of yourself, so it creates the whole personality, which is an aspect of itself. It operates in both the waking and the dream state. It often forms the content of each. It is more knowledgeable than any one aspect of the personality. It is more knowledgeable than all other aspects of the personality, for it forms them together into a cohesive whole.

It is therefore the director of all activities, both in the waking and dream condition. It is the inner ego from whom you receive your inspiration, and it is the inner ego which gives consent to our meetings.

You may take a break, and we shall continue.

(Break at 9:22. Jane was well dissociated, her manner very active, eyes open often, smoking, etc. Resume at 9:31.)

I told you from the beginning that the inner ego is aware of data that is received through the inner senses as well as data from the outer senses.

It is the prime identity of the whole present personality. In many cases it is the I of your dreams. It is definitely the I of your creative activity. It is the I, you see, which survives physical existence, and the physical, physically-oriented ego is only a part of it.

If only the physically-oriented ego survived, very little indeed would survive at all. The physically-oriented ego is hardly aware of your experiences in their entirety. The physically-oriented ego, if it alone survived, would contain only your conscious memories. Even now, in physical existence, you operate on a much deeper and more complicated level than this. Events and experiences which are forgotten, or which escaped the physically-oriented ego, still affect your activities in this life, and if they did not your physical existence would be brief indeed. *(Jane pounded the tabletop for emphasis, eyes wide and dark.)* Any survival that was based upon the survival of the physically-oriented ego alone would be as shallow as a paper cutout. These things escape you. You take it for granted that the physically-oriented ego represents your own psychological identity, you see, and this is an illusion. It contains a portion of your psychological feeling of identity, but only that.

Feelings and sensations and memories that it knows nothing of have built up your psychological identity, and given you a sense of continuity. Of these this ego knows but little. Intimacy with your self and with your own identity, that is intimate knowledge of your own identity, resides in all portions of the self, and is not dependent upon a survival based upon the survival of the physically-oriented ego. This would represent a sham of a survival indeed.

There is a basic difference you see between a survival personality, and the personality as you know it. The individual in physical life shows his surface face, so to speak, outward. Inner psychological realities are hidden beneath the physically-oriented ego simply because it cannot afford to deal with them. Its one main purpose is simply to allow the personality to operate effectively within its physical environment.

The surviving personality has a different psychological balance. The outer ego no longer shows its outside face, so to speak, *(again Jane struck the tabletop)* but takes its place with the other aspects of the personality. You might say that it becomes the subconscious, although I am speaking now simply to get the idea across, and this is not precisely the case.

It is true however to say that the memories of the physically-oriented ego take their place with memories that were once subconscious. I am speaking now of the psychological makeup of the survival personality. The memories remain in physical existence. There is no real distinction between psychological reality and physical reality. The physically-oriented ego manufactures this distinction of necessity.

The survival personality does not need to do this. To him all realities are psychological realities, a thought as real as a chair—in fact, much more real. Therefore, communications between survival personalities and physically-oriented personalities are bound to suffer difficulties, and these difficulties are the result of the change of psychological frameworks.

We are going to have a brief session this evening, and after a break we shall have the Instream material.

Now, Ruburt's book on the nonphysical self will sell, and shortly. Put down the initials G S here, and let it go for now.

(Break at 9:46. Jane was way-out, her delivery fast and emphatic, yet quiet.

(While giving the 74th Instream data she spoke at an average pace, with a hand raised to her closed eyes. Resume at 10:00.)

Give us a moment please, for our Instream material.

The object seems to be a scroll of some kind—something rolled up, as you roll up paper. Perhaps it contains a list. It is colored however, perhaps with a metallic color, *(pause)* of silver color.

A turnabout for Dr. Instream. He has changed a decision, from one decision to an opposite one. *(Pause.)* I believe that he should have kept to his original course.

A roll of string. He has been tying things together. Some difficulty with his throat, or his wife's throat, on the left side. *(Long pause.)*

A master lunch today. That is, a lunch which is a meeting of several people at least. The scroll object can be used vertically or horizontally. *(Pause.)*

Now, do you have an envelope for me, Joseph?

No. *(Jane paused at 10:09. She knew before the session began that there would be no envelope.)*

I will usually ask to show my willingness. We will then close our session, unless of course for any reason you request that we continue. You may as well be thankful for the time when it is offered.

("Well, can you say a few words about Jane's nightmare?"

(Referring to a very vivid nightmare Jane had last night; she has complete notes on it.)

Give us a moment, please. *(Pause, hand to closed eyes.)* We shall insert the material during one of next week's sessions, as Ruburt is blocking me. *(Pause.)* Is there anything else?

("Is Catherine a male or female cat?"

(We named our second cat thinking it a female, but now have strong reason to believe we made a mistake. Male or female, the cat is now called Catherine, and answers to it. Jane laughed briefly, eyes closed.)

Surely you can find out the answer to this question for yourself.

("Oh."

(Long pause.) I am simply giving you a moment in case you think of any more important questions.

("Well, I guess not.")

My heartiest wishes to you both. And reread this evening's session several times, for you will discover that it answers several unspoken questions.

("Okay. Good night, Seth."

(End at 10:14. Jane was dissociated as usual. Seth didn't say so but she received from him the definite feeling that Catherine is a male. Jane was concerned about blocking the nightmare data, wondering if it was perhaps clairvoyant. Seth returned briefly at 10:15.)

There was no personal danger to either of you, as far as Ruburt's dream is concerned, and that is all for now.

("Thank you."

(Besides involving Jane and me, the nightmare also involved members of both our families. Jane was now surprised to learn it had been necessary for me to shake her out of the nightmare last night; she had thought she came out of it spontaneously.)

SESSION 271
JUNE 27, 1966 9 PM MONDAY

(Jane was indisposed. When I asked her if she wanted to have a session she said she would try, and let Seth make the decision as to whether she continued. Her eyes began to open soon after she began speaking in a quiet voice at 9:01.)

Good evening.

("Good evening, Seth.")

A brief note. Ruburt should continue with his exercises, as they are unusually beneficial for him. I suggest this in fact very strongly. They allow him to step aside in a regular and disciplined fashion, from the worrisome aspects of his ego.

Their psychic benefits quite outweigh their physical benefits for him in particular. At such times as now, the ego imprisons him, and he does not allow himself inner freedom. The exercises give a daily relief, and creative refreshment. They will also be indirectly a help in our sessions.

This will be a brief session, incidentally, for rather obvious reasons. However the difficulty is quite temporary.

Now, give us a moment, please, and we shall give our Instream material now. *(Pause at 9:07, before the 75th Dr. Instream material.)* These are impressions.

A stone object, with an edge. Fairly sharp edge, I believe. *(Pause.)* The object is rectangular, and for stone fairly uniform. *(Eyes open briefly.)* It is gray in color. A metal object sits on it, perhaps in miniature. I have the impression that the object <u>on</u> the stone represents a man on a horse.

The whole object may itself be in miniature. I am not sure of the miniature connection however. The object seems to have a purpose or function connected with a desk. *(Pause.)*

It would seem too small for a paperweight. Perhaps there is a connection with a rubber stamp. *(Pause.)*

A tie-up of sorts this evening, in which Dr. Instream was involved. *(Pause.)*

We will have a full session Wednesday.

If Ruburt will begin his exercises again he will notice an immediate improvement. In any case you are quite welcome to an evening off, and I therefore give you my heartiest wishes.

Good night, Seth.

(End at 9:15. Jane was dissociated as usual. This was the second time recently that her eyes had opened while she gave experimental material; perhaps this will become more usual.)

SESSION 272
JUNE 29, 1966 9 PM WEDNESDAY

(Jane now felt much better. She had received a proof of the dust jacket for her ESP book today, and both of us liked it very much. Her eyes began to open almost as soon as the session began, and she was smoking. Her pace was good.)

Good evening.

(Good evening, Seth.)

Now, I am glad to see that our friend Ruburt is again spry, good-natured, and himself again.

The book jacket is indeed one to be proud of, and the book will be a book to be proud of. There is a small matter I would like to clear up. There was no subconscious distortion on Ruburt's part, when I told you that the nonphysical self book would sell. I am speaking of this instance only.

I knew that the book would be returned shortly, and this is the reason that I gave you this reassurance. In some other instances concerning the same kind of matters, some distortions did occur. These were not basically distorted passages, only partially so. I believe two poetry books will sell. One is the psychological book. Now, this is undistorted, and if this does not materialize, than <u>I</u> am wrong, not Ruburt, for once. <u>Or</u> probabilities enter in. Obviously Ruburt must send the books out, for example.

Later in the session I will slip in a few remarks, if possible, concerning the

ESP book.

I would like to devote a little time this evening to a matter that concerns Ruburt rather deeply. You may or may not include this in your official records, as you prefer.

This has to do with the attack made on Ruburt by your domestic cat. Several issues are involved: Ruburt's own mood at the time, for one thing. Now. The cat senses both of your moods immediately. It is psychically very close to you both. Being a house cat, it is closed in with you. As a rule you both radiate strong constructive energy. For a short period of time, Ruburt turned his creative energy, as he knows, I believe, inward rather than outward, knotted it up, misdirected it, did not focus it properly, and turned it into destructive energy.

Now all energy you see is creative energy, and constructive. When it is not properly used it backs up so to speak, and explodes or erupts in what seems to be a destructive manner. This is what happened, to some degree.

Now. Ruburt would not turn any destructive energy loose upon you, my dear friend, for he loves you too deeply. He is too mature now to turn such destructive energy inward in a strong manner, against his own organism. He would not willfully turn such energy loose even upon an animal.

Usually his aggressive feelings are automatically sublimated into his work. He grapples with ideas and with words. The destructive energy however found no outlet. It therefore took the point of least resistance, and he quite subconsciously of course projected it upon his pet. It was not that he actually focused the energy purposely upon the cat, merely that the cat's spongelike psychic nature received it full force.

At the same time the animal was denied the usual constructive psychic atmosphere in which it usually is allowed to operate. The situation in the bedroom was not important in itself. The cat was nervous, bewildered and somewhat frightened however to begin with. The situation was simply the point at which the cat, in self-defense, threw back the destructive energy which it had received, and I must say in fury and full measure, and in the only way it knew.

Now, the other smaller episodes involving Ruburt and the cat alone have always occurred during the same process, only when lesser emotional crises were involved. You were quite right in saying that Ruburt fears violence. This is one of the keynotes of his personality, and rather obviously this has to do with his early life and his mother.

There is much more here. However he began his creative life very early as an outlet, you see, for aggressive and violent feelings. As an infant and a young child he had a strong temper, which terrified him, and he indulged in childish tantrums. Children know much more than they are given credit for.

Is your hand tired?

("No.")

The child even then realized that violence and aggression was somehow connected with his mother's illness. He also, that is Ruburt also, felt the violence that is a part of his father's personality. Suddenly the tantrums ceased. He held them back in pure terror of the consequences, for suddenly the violent-tempered mother was immobile. He feared the same fate. The father had completely disappeared. To the child the father simply vanished from the face of the earth, an equally fearful fate.

The child took all this as the punishment for violence. The mother now could no longer be violent in act. Not only that, but she was helpless to resist violence. This made the child hold back the most natural of aggressive feelings. In most cases the child can slap the parent. It may be slapped back, but it knows the slap will not really kill the parent. It is pretend.

In this case the child did not dare slap the parent, for even the slightest move upon the mother's bed, the slightest most unintentional motion, made the mother cry out in pain. Not only unintentional violence then of the simplest kind, had to be avoided, but the unintentional motion and the thoughtless childish move. This was aggravated because when the mother became frightened she pleaded with the child to sleep with her.

Again, the quick nervous turning of the child upon the bed bought instant cries of anger and of abuse. We are getting this material through very well, and it is important. However I will give you a break for the sake of your faithful hand.

(Break at 9:32. Jane was as well dissociated, she said, as she has ever been: "He had me so that I was more him than me... Now, how did he do that?" She could have been talking about a stranger, she continued, yet knew what she was saying and that she talked about herself.

(She resumed in the same very active manner, her eyes open about all of the time, at 9:42.)

Now. It has always been extremely difficult for him to defend himself physically. As a child he simply would not do so, and to make matters worse the mother taunted him for being a coward.

That he finally defended himself against her, defended himself against her emotionally and psychically, is all the more astounding. The main reason that he does not see her is not because he fears her, but because he fears the violence in himself that he has never dared direct toward her.

He projects it so that it seems to originate in the mother. At the same time the mother experiences unrecognized feelings of violence against the daughter, that <u>she</u> has never been able to express in <u>physical</u> terms.

She did express this violence, and again with fury, through verbal attacks to which Ruburt was extremely sensitive. But Ruburt did not even dare to express his violence <u>verbally</u>, because of the parent-child relationship. Added to this was the fact that the child loved the parent much more strongly, you see, than the parent ever loved the child.

Now symbolically <u>any</u> attack upon Ruburt becomes an attack by the parent, against which the child in Ruburt dares not retaliate. Flight becomes the only answer, the only sure solution, as flight from the parent was the only solution, for the parent could not run after.

The cat therefore was allowed to chase our friend through the apartment. Beside the rather ordinary humiliation, there was the deep bewilderment, you see, for this was the first time, symbolically, that the parent could pursue physically. If it were not for these early connections Ruburt would not have been so panic-stricken.

I am trying to explain this rather thoroughly, for once he realizes these connections he will not need to fear this quite human and natural aggressiveness. It only turns into violence, and into a fear of violence, when it is so meticulously denied.

With the particular cat episode, we have something else. The mother had an absolute terror of cats, and considered them the personification of evil. She used the cat symbol as the symbol for her own mother-in-law. She was extremely unbalanced, the mother, emotionally, and considered her husband's mother, who was a foolishly naive, good-natured and innocent thing, as a personification of evil.

Ruburt knew this well. He has since grown to like all animals but at the moment of the attack, you see, the cat instantly became this personification of evil to him, and again his primary concern was to flee. There was never an instant in the whole affair when he thought of striking back.

He does not see his mother because he imagines subconsciously that he is protecting her from his own violence against her, lest after all these years it might erupt. Now this is ridiculous. This restrained violence has been excellently used for creative purposes.

It is only when a break occurs, you see, when the creative energy blocks up, that such difficulties arise. For these reasons it pains him deeply to write, even to an editor, words that are not docile.

When he was not docile as a child there was vicious instant retaliation of a most complicated nature. There was ordinary <u>retaliation</u>, in that he was punished through word attacks, and through such corporal punishment as the invalid could give. But, and here Joseph we come to the real heart of the matter, the mother retaliated in the main not by a direct attack upon the child, but by causing the child to believe that its misbehavior could be, and very nearly was, going to result in the death of the mother. As any child does, the child at times wished for the parent's death, and here we see the mother acting out her own death in order to punish the child.

This could happen as a result of the smallest transgression, if the mother was in a particularly unstable condition. When the death was not acted out in drama form—this you are familiar with, we shall not go into it here—then instead the mother pretended to have an attack of one kind or another, and she told the child that the child was directly responsible.

The child therefore until its teens dared not be anything but docile. The personality was a strong one however, and the rebellion found no outlet except for creativity. Now the present personality suffers pangs of remorse over the slightest imagined wrong it may do to another.

When this builds up and enough small legitimate injustices are borne, docilely, then we have an explosion of a sorts. Everyone else you see has a right to gripe, he feels subconsciously, but he cannot. He is terrified to do so. When he manages to do so he is jubilant out of all proportion. His swearing you see allows him leeway.

Now I suggest your break.

(Break at 10:10. Jane was again very well dissociated. She said she could feel herself begin to protest when Seth got to the part concerning her mother's pretending of death, but Seth led her over the rough spots well.

(Jane resumed in the same manner again at 10:19.)

Now. We will give our Instream material this evening. However while the conditions are right I will continue. There are some issues that should be made clear. *(Smile.)*

Now you become, Joseph, the voice calling Ruburt a coward, you see. I am speaking of course from the viewpoint of Ruburt's subconscious.

<u>You</u> grew up in an environment, my dear friend, in which violence and aggressiveness became one, were expressed in some degree by both parents. But this expression was denied to the children, and you longed to retaliate. Your father's <u>aggressiveness</u>, normal male aggressiveness, was blocked up, and directed against your mother. You longed to express your natural violence, you normal aggressiveness, and you also feared to do so, and dwelled mainly in your own world.

As a <u>rule</u> you do not express these feelings in the <u>area</u> where they would normally be expressed, and you also use them as a basis for creative work. As such they are valuable. You are twice angry at Ruburt's lack of aggressiveness in the business world, therefore.

All of this needs to be said, you see. You are both learning at a rather amazing rate. In the past you turned some repressed violence inward against yourself. Ruburt's selling jobs were very practical for a time, for they allowed him to release aggressive feelings. You become angry when you think, rightly, that Ruburt is too docile in his dealings, but this is because you are angry at your own lack of power as a child to retaliate against the atmosphere of violence that you sensed in the child's home.

You are also angry at Ruburt's docility because it reminds you of your father's lack of aggression in his business dealings. When all this is out in the open as it is now, you will find that both of you can deal much more effectively with the outside business world, and you will not be hampered as you both have been.

Now give us a moment please for our Instream material.

(Pause at 10:30. Jane sat with both hands raised to her closed eyes. This is the 76th Dr. Instream experiment.)

For our object, a mirror, or something that reflects, as a very shiny surface. *(Pause.)* Connected with dark leather, as a belt. This could be a shiny buckle.

An error, discovered only recently, perhaps this week, involving a list of names.

The buckle, or belt, or similar object, is a gift I believe to Dr. Instream. A connection with it and a May, late May, date.

Close by him now a small box with a miscellany of objects. *(Pause at 10:35.)* Perhaps the box of walnut, or there is a walnut connection here.

Four plus one equals five. This has to do with an added, or unexpected guest. Four were expected, and five arrived.

Do you have an envelope for me?

("No, I guess not.")

We will then take a break, or you may end the session as you prefer.

("We'll take the break."

(Break at 10:36. Jane was again way-out—she had been all evening, she said. Presumably to let the emotionally charged material come through easily. Not all of it was new to us.

(Jane resumed, her eyes again open most of the time, at 10:45.)

We will shortly end our session.

If you read this material carefully it can benefit you more than either of you now realize. You are indeed both improving. However since the conditions were right this evening, this was the time to give you this material.

I should not need to tell you, Joseph, that a rebuff or reproof by you is intensely felt by Ruburt. This does not mean of course that you should not speak your mind, merely that the fact should be taken into consideration.

With what you both know now you should work out an excellent balance, you see, in your business dealings, in the same way that you have worked out an excellent balance in your creative and personal lives.

Now these emotional confessions of Ruburt's annoy you considerably. They are not necessary. However your annoyance can be tempered with somewhat more understanding, and <u>this</u> in itself will tend to minimize their occurrence. When he indulges in this sort of thing he is feeling rebellious, you see, and this is a result of the built-up aggressive feelings of which I have been speaking.

Subconsciously he feels that you are saying shut up, and this angers, humiliates and bewilders him. He struggles against such disclosures to begin with. Instead you see methods can be used to direct the emotions in other channels. You can get him to talk about other matters by asking for example about what he has written for the day. The subject chosen by you must be one in which he is immensely interested however. He will understand that you are merely trying to redirect him, and will not feel that you are restraining his freedom to say what he wants to say. He will understand what you are doing, but that is all right. He knows the emotional situation with your mother, and will not object.

Now I will leave you both, and I hope you will see that I have done you both a service, for this is my intention. The storm with Ruburt has passed, and you have both learned much because of it. It is a minor storm indeed, compared to what would have occurred some years earlier. He does not move furniture as erratically as he did, and is learning despite this to use his energies constructively.

The garden work is a help. It would be for <u>you</u>, had you the time. There are unfortunate connections with your father however, that might at <u>first</u> mitigate against your enjoyment, though old experience with the land would soon come back to you.

(Reincarnation here. I believe Seth refers to my previous existence as a landowner and farmer in Denmark in the 1600s.)

I repeat: Ruburt should make a daily habit of his exercises. If you have any questions I will answer them. Otherwise we shall close our session.

("You were going to say something about the ESP book." Jane recently received word from her publisher that the book would be off the press later in July.)

You will both be pleased with the book itself, and with its response. *(Eyes wide open and very dark.)* <u>Now</u>. This is not a distortion: The book will quite literally change your circumstances for the better, and lead into areas with which you are not now acquainted.

There will be foreign sales, not counting the Canada printing. There will be pocketbooks. All of this is not in a snap *(Jane snapped her fingers)* but it is not in any distant future, either.

The sales will be more than you expect. The book will mark the beginning of a change in your living conditions, and financial outlook. You will become involved with four people in particular who will help you. *(Long pause, eyes closed.)*

Now. I am doing this for you: I have the impression of a six in regard to the nonphysical self book. Now this is not six years. I do not know however whether it is six weeks you see, or six months. I cannot cut it that fine, for various reasons.

My book will of course sell. *(Long pause. Here Seth refers to the book Jane is doing on the material itself.)*

There is a man who wears a hat in his office who will be connected with one of these books. It is a characteristic of his. He is perhaps 46, but he is definitely between 46 and 56. *(Pause.)* There is a G connected with him.

I have done the best I could *(smile)* for you, and were it not for the hour and your hand and the time involved for your records, I would speak to you longer. I... You may or may not take notes... I am with you rather strongly this evening, and I wish you both well. Regards from your dear old uncle Seth. *(Smile.)*

Ruburt denied the cat its usual psychic reinforcement also, you see. Incidentally, working with the earth will almost always restore him.

("Good night, Seth.")

(End at 11:12. Jane said she was very well dissociated—if possible, even more so after the Instream material. Her eyes had been open almost all the session, her manner very active, her pace quite good at times.)

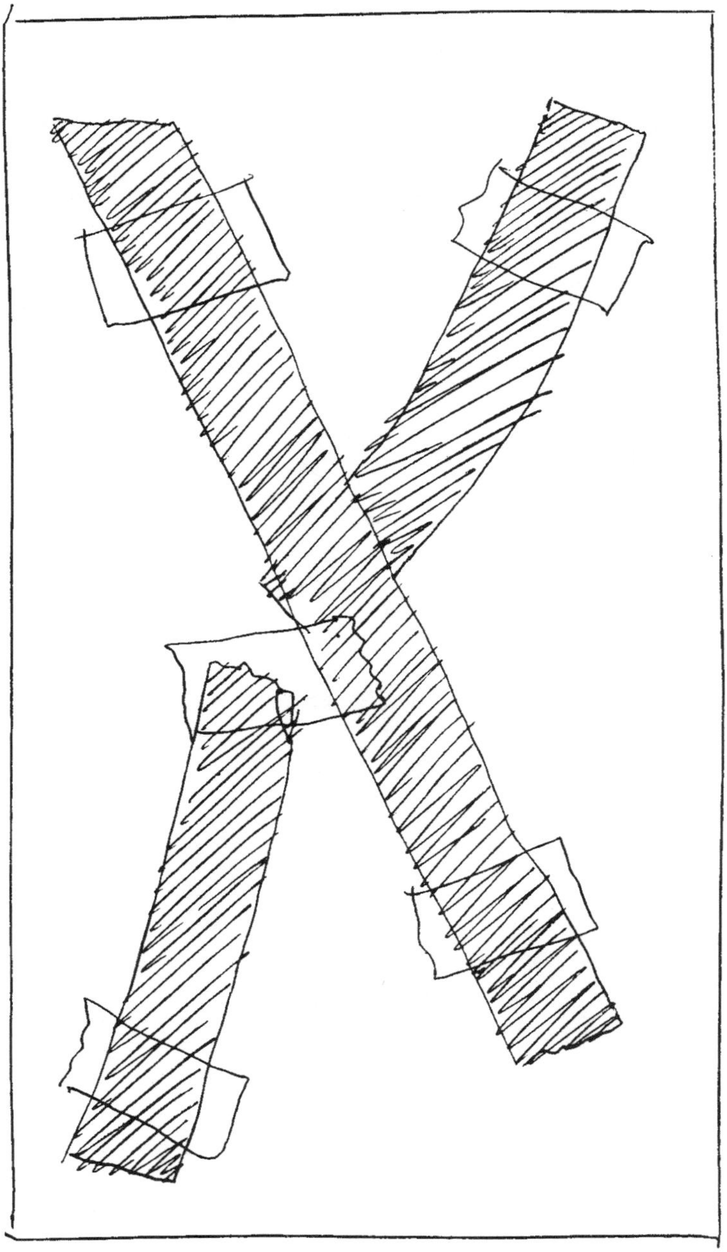

(Tracing of the ribbon used as object in the 63rd envelope experiment, in the 273rd session for July 18, 1966.)

SESSION 273
JULY 18, 1966 9 PM MONDAY

(The 63rd envelope experiment was held during the session. The object was two sections of a red ribbon taped to a piece of heavy Bristol board. I found the ribbon in the bed of our cat on about June 20. I knew nothing of its history consciously, and hoped Jane and Seth could help out. As it developed Jane was somewhat hard-pressed to identify the ribbon, did so eventually, and with Seth's verification. We regard such objects, where we know little of the history, as being like objects furnished by others.

(On July 10,1966, I wrote Dr. Instream canceling our series of experiments with him, because we hadn't heard from him since January 1966.

(This was our first session since June 29,1966. Jane said she had no idea of what Seth would talk about. She began as usual at 9 PM, her eyes closed, sitting down, in a good voice and with pauses.)

Good evening.

("Good evening, Seth.")

My welcome after your vacation.

We will return to our material dealing with projection shortly. First however it is necessary that the nature of identity itself be studied more carefully. The nature of identity is strongly dependent upon the innate ability to draw upon, utilize and direct psychic energy.

There are as I have told you no limitations to the self. It grows by growing, and by constant use of its abilities. It can be said that all consciousnesses and all identities are but one. This in no way negates the existence of any given identity however. All identities are more dependent upon each other, and yet more independent, than you imagine.

Various aspects of the personality exist whether or not you are aware of their existence. When you do become aware of their existence, your awareness in no way negates their independence. You simply expand psychically. Portions of the self live a more or less independent existence, both while the dominant personality sleeps and is awake.

When and if the dominant personality becomes aware of this situation, it automatically expands. It consciously contains experience that was previously subconscious. Now. The inner ego is quite familiar with the existence of the physically-oriented ego, but the physically-oriented ego is not usually familiar with its inner counterpart.

When through training the ego becomes more aware of this inner self, the whole personality benefits. The whole self as it exists at any given time can be glimpsed through studying the actions of the physically-oriented ego, as seen in physical manipulation, and in studying the activities of the inner ego as seen in dream experiences. Obviously some training is necessary before this can be achieved.

Later you may be able to follow this inner self even while the physical ego operates in its normal manner, but this is much more difficult if overall personality balance is to be maintained. It should be fairly obvious that identity hardly resides exclusively within the physically-oriented ego. In one sense, identity is always a becoming, and it can never be a static, finished thing. For it knows itself through change, and that which is finished cannot change.

You see I would like you eventually to progress to a point where you can manipulate almost as freely within nonphysical reality as you do within physical reality. And of course be <u>conscious</u> or aware of the experience.

Your own personalities will set the pace, for they are well-balanced ones. All of this demands spontaneity and control. This is the motion of consciousness. It is unfortunate that identity is considered generally as a rather static and permanent acknowledgment, for it is not.

Our material on the nature of action will be helpful here. The ego, the physically-oriented ego, is a convenient figurehead. It represents only an imperfect glimpse of a given momentary appearance—the portion of the self that happens in any given instant to show itself.

You do not know the self as it is within <u>physical</u> existence, and until you do you cannot hope to know what survives physical death, or what part of you is awake while the ego sleeps. When I refer to the ego I do so for simplicity's sake, since the term has meaning to you. There are obviously portions of the self that never operate <u>directly</u> within physical reality.

Consider this analogy: The self as a moving circle, such as a Ferris wheel. A tree in front of the wheel will represent physical reality. The whole self, or the whole wheel, is composed of many selves in various positions, as the many people who sit on the Ferris wheel. As the wheel turns you call the person or the self who faces the tree the ego, simply because this is the portion that faces physical reality, represented by our tree. But the self who faces the tree one moment is not the self that faces it the next moment, and the operator of the wheel is never in evidence, you see.

I suggest your first break.

(Break at 9:30. Jane was dissociated as usual. Midway through the delivery her eyes began to open often. She resumed in the same manner at 9:40.)

I do not mean to imply a mechanical connection however with our analogy.

The driver of our wheel in this case never appears in the seat that faces physical reality. He is in a strange position, in that he is an overall self, composed in part of the sum of these other selves, and yet more than the sum.

The selves who ride the wheel therefore also provide some of the power that runs the wheel. It is only because you stress similarities rather than differences that you do not realize that the self that you call the ego is but the appearance, in one particular perspective, of many quite different aspects of the personality.

Perhaps if you imagine a spotlight directed on the seat in front of the tree, you will see this more clearly. You cannot see the other selves on the wheel, you only see the one spot that is lit, and the light is that of physical perception. There are different lights, however. If others watched and saw only that portion of the self that was clear in <u>their</u> perspective, then they would imagine that they saw the primary self also.

The inner ego is the self who drives the wheel with purpose; at the same time there are many other wheels and many spokes... Our moment point analogy will also help you here. The sleeping self will of course be considered the primary self from the standpoint of its own reality. I cannot emphasize too strongly the fact that all of these portions are self-conscious. They may not be conscious of the other selves however. The inner senses connect all the selves, and the movements of consciousness are far more complicated than that of a Ferris wheel.

You are receiving instructions, you see, now in physical reality. You are also receiving instructions in <u>other</u> realities. You are not aware of these consciously. Certain portions of your personalities are learning, within their own perspective, to venture into physical reality, as you are learning to venture into nonphysical reality.

Certain portions that deal rather directly with the manipulation of psychic energy are being instructed also. All of this is more complicated than it would seem, and yet extremely simple when the basic principles are understood.

The psychology of personality cannot be grasped unless reincarnation is taken into consideration, but even then this only represents energy operating within one system. The personality operates simultaneously within many systems. Projection represents practical application. Such experience allows you to unite various aspects of the self, and to bring the whole self into sharper focus. As a rule projection in some areas can only be achieved by those who are living their last <u>earthly</u> cycle.

I suggest your break.

(Break at 10:00. Jane was again out as usual. Her eyes had been open most of

the time. Her manner had been active, she had smoked, sipped wine, etc. Resume at 10:08.)

It is true that the whole personality, or whole self, does not directly manifest itself within physical reality.

However, the personality as it is manifested can never be understood if it is taken alone. There are sufficient hints and signs that do appear, to give evidence of these other portions of the self. Now there is one important point in particular in all this that should be emphasized, and I will repeat it: Certain portions of the self do not manifest themselves directly within physical reality. They do not operate directly within physical reality, and the word directly is significant.

They do not on their own perceive physical objects as such. We will refer to this later, for it will help you understand the ways in which so-called extrasensory perceptions are utilized, both on a conscious and a subconscious basis.

Now, do you have an envelope for me, Joseph?

("Yes." At 10:14 Jane took the sealed double envelope from me for our 63rd experiment, without opening her eyes. She pressed it to her forehead in a horizontal position. Before tonight's session we agreed to hold envelope experiments on Mondays only.)

Give us a moment, please. These are impressions.

Sometimes, incidentally, when we work toward a specific image, we must work using associations of Ruburt's that I try to direct to the proper direction. *(Pause.)*

Parallelogram, or something parallel, rather emphatically so. Like roads with white markings, and with fairly large areas between, and with darkness around or outside also.

Connection with a nurse, or nursing. A small cube, perhaps gold color, that is the cube perhaps is gold colored.

Scripts. Four. Objects perhaps—that is, four objects perhaps indicated.

A distant connection with the country. The word seisograph comes to mind. Or marks like earthquake marks on a graph. *(Eyes still closed, envelope still to forehead. Pace good.)*

Printing I believe at the lower center, outside of a margin, or implied margin. Very small, the printing very small, perhaps d e l. Part of the word delivered, I do not know. Perhaps a connection with some item delivered. *(Envelope lowered to lap.)* And with music, or marks that suggest notes. A note, you see.

This was to lead us to the word note. An assembly connected here. 7 3 0; perhaps 4, 4 1 0. *(Each number pronounced separately.)*

Something to do with a dying out or fading away, as a score.

Do you have any questions? *(Pause at 10:25.*

("Well, you didn't say anything about color particularly.")

The early image was of emphatic contrast, of darks and whites.

("Can you say something more about the country connection?")

This came from the parallel line connection. As of roads, mentioned earlier.

("What's that about a nurse?")

I am afraid that is all I can give you on that impression.

I suggest your break.

(Break at 10:28. Jane out as usual. Her eyes had remained closed, her pace good. She said she had images within only when Seth "said so". She was not unduly nervous at the idea of an experiment after our vacation.

(See the tracing on page 270 and the notes on page 271. As stated I picked the red ribbon used as object from the bed of our cat on about June 20, with little idea of its history. It developed that Jane had to think hard in order to tentatively link the object with a hand-knit sweater she had received from her mother as a birthday present. Jane's birthday is May 8, but she received the package sometime after this; we located a letter from Jane's mother dated May 10, in which she discusses mailing the sweater to Jane soon. [This session was held on July 18.]

(Seth confirms after break that the object was linked to the sweater package. We made our connections during break, of course, and felt them strengthened by Seth's information. More history will be given as we interpret the data.

("<u>Parallelogram</u>, or something parallel, rather emphatically so. Like roads with white markings, and with fairly large areas between, and with darkness around or outside also." It is interesting to note that Jane said after the session that she doesn't know what a parallelogram looks like. The ribbon arrangement on the Bristol of course is an X shape rather than parallel; both shapes are geometrical. The dictionary assigns this shape to a parallelogram,

and this to parallax:

(Nor did Jane know the diagram for parallax. We believe she was on the right track in spite of her semantic difficulty, however, with the roads data and the white markings, areas between, etc. Jane's personal idea was that Seth used parallelogram to lead up to the rest of the data here. In this respect see page 274, where Seth mentions Jane's associations.

(Jane located the inside box in which the sweater was packed, and remembered

this box being inside another. The ribbon from which the object was taken was around the outside box, she felt; she also remembered a note with the sweater, but we could not locate it. We did find her mother's letter of May 10th however.

("Connection with a nurse, or nursing." Jane's mother is a bedridden arthritic in a nursing home at Middle Grove, NY. A nurse friend at the hospital there runs her errands for her, etc., and mailed the sweater to Jane shortly after May 10,1966. Jane's mother mentions the name of the nurse, Fran, specifically in the letter of May 10.

("A small cube, perhaps gold color, that is the cube perhaps is gold colored." We could make no connection here although Seth helps out after break.

("Scripts." Seth, after break, reinforces Jane's idea that a note was enclosed with the sweater, but we cannot find the note and so can't demonstrate this.

("Four. Objects perhaps—that is, four objects perhaps indicated." No connections. The ribbon itself is in three pieces, for instance, and is tacked to the Bristol by five pieces of tape, etc.

("A distant connection with the country." We believe this data and the parallelogram data are related, since the latter developed into the mention of roads. The nursing home or hospital in which Jane's mother is cared for is also actually in the country, outside the small town of Middle Grove,NY. The ribbon which served as envelope object of course helped wrap a package coming from Jane's mother. Seth confirms the data relationship also.

("The word seisograph comes to mind. Or marks like earthquake marks on a graph. Printing I believe at the lower center, outside of a margin, or implied margin. Very small, the printing very small, perhaps D E L. Part of the word delivered, I do not know. Perhaps a connection with some item delivered." Again, see Seth's comments on page 274, concerning his use of Jane's associations. We think the above block of data is a good example of his attempts to have Jane talk about the delivery of a package to our door. Seth and Jane here seem to permit the use of such association in a much freer manner than in the past.

(Note the mispronunciation of seismograph also. There is of course no printing on the object, the printing idea being symbolic only in this case.

(We think the above data also leads into the next: "And with music, or marks that suggest notes. A note, you see." Again the use of free association... "This was to lead us to the word note." As stated, Jane remembers a note being enclosed with the sweater sent to her by her mother. We could not find the note however. Jane believes the note was actually written on the back of a birthday card. We located the letter of May 10 from Jane's mother, concerning the mailing of the sweater to Jane, but do not believe the above data refers to that letter exclusively, although there is evidently some connection.

("An assembly connected here. 730; perhaps 4410." We see no connections for these numbers. The zip code number for instance for Middle Grove is 12850.

("Something to do with a dying out or fading away, as a score." There is a possible connection with this data and the letter to Jane from her mother on May 10,1966. This letter too is written on a card. The front of the card contains a picture of three cherubs singing. One of them plays an accordion, the other two hold sheets of music on which the scores are clearly visible. Note the mention of music also in the data on pages 274 and 276. Besides telling Jane about the sweater, Jane's mother wrote in the May 10 letter of the death of a family friend, Father Ryan, and enclosed a news clipping account of the funeral, which was to be held shortly. Father Ryan died of leukemia and his death was expected; it could correspond to "dying out" or "fading away".

(Had we not found the May 10 letter we wouldn't have thought of the connections immediately above; even as it is I would hesitate to claim them without further data from Seth. Jane thinks they are legitimate.

(I asked Seth three questions, asking for elaboration on color, the country connection and the nurse, or nursing. His answers merely reaffirmed the original data. See page 275.

(Jane resumed in a quiet manner at 10:52.)

We are endeavoring to keep the sessions within a convenient time schedule.

The package however did refer to the sweater. The box was wrapped in a layer of brown paper tied with a red ribbon; the whole then inserted into another box, a commercial box from a store, in which a nightgown had once been placed.

There was a note. The small cube referred to a small golden square of sachet, which was originally in the box but not sent to Ruburt.

We will end the session, and I look forward to our next. For your own edification, it is best that you have more information regarding any test object, to make your work easier and facilitate your checking procedures.

("Good night, Seth."

(End at 10:57. Jane was dissociated as usual, her eyes closed.)

SESSION 274
JULY 20, 1966 9 PM WEDNESDAY

(No envelope experiment was held during the session.

(As the session began Jane's voice was at once loud and quite a bit deeper than usual. This wasn't her really strong voice by any means, yet it echoed from the living

room walls; this effect I believe was accentuated because we had taken the rug up from the floor for the summer. But the voice was a good one, the best in many sessions. The windows were open and it easily rose above traffic sounds, etc.

(Jane's pace was average, her eyes closed. She was also smoking, and her eyes, exceptionally dark, began to open after a few paragraphs. The session is quite unusual in two respects, as will be seen.)

Now, good evening.

("Good evening, Seth.")

Before we speak any further about projections, the structure of the self must be more thoroughly discussed.

Its composition is not easy to explain in your terms. At your end there are strong chemical and electromagnetic connections that you do not understand. These in large measure help form the physically oriented ego, or at least form its characteristic manner.

Without these chemical and electromagnetic connections, *(voice louder)* the ego as such would not exist. The ego is largely dependent upon the physical mechanisms that compose the corporal image. It has its beginnings with corporal birth. While we speak of <u>the</u> ego, this part of the self is hardly permanent or constant, but ever-changing. However the intellect is also a portion, or an attribute, of the ego.

Obviously the ego is a part of the whole self. Directly its experiences must be physically oriented, and yet with training it can also learn to appreciate realities that are not physical. It must not be pushed, but with the proper attitudes it can and must participate to some extent in all psychic experiences, if the overall stability is to be maintained.

Now where the ego operates you will always find chemical repercussions; to some extent or another then the physical body will be involved. Deeper or less familiar portions of the self exist without a chemical manifestation. These usually take electromagnetic forms to some degree however.

Now certain chemical changes must come about in the physical organism before projection can occur. Were it not for these you would still be imprisoned within the corporeal image. You know that dreaming has definite chemical bases, that chemicals built up during periods of waking existence are released through dreams. Not only are they released but they form a propelling action that allows energy to flow in the opposite direction. As chemical reactions allow the body to utilize energy and form physical materializations, so the excess built up then becomes a propelling force, allowing action to flow in what <u>you</u> would term subjective directions.

Now this same chemical reaction must also occur, only more strongly, before a legitimate projection of the self from the physical organism can occur. This is one of the main reasons why such projections happen rarely. Usually, and without training, the chemical excess is used in the dreaming process. In periods of exuberant energy and well-being a more than normal amount of excess accumulates. This can trigger a projection.

Also in periods of momentary indisposition however, the dreaming process may be blocked and the chemical excess accumulated. Again, a good time to try projections.

These chemical excesses are a natural byproduct of consciousness that is bound up in physical materialization. The more intense the characteristic experience of reality, the greater the chemical excess that is built up. Consciousness itself, when physically oriented, burns up chemicals. The more intense the individual the hotter the fire, so to speak, and the greater the chemical excesses that must be released.

Released they must be, or the organism would not survive. Periods of intense activity may also then generate this additional chemical propellant. Now. Although this necessary chemical fuel is generated through intense activity of a mental or psychic nature, it is released, making projections possible in alternating periods of quietude and rest.

Is your hand tired?

("No.")

(It was 9:29. Jane did not take a break. Her delivery was by now very animated and her eyes had begun opening often. The voice was just as strong as before, showing no signs of fatigue. Occasionally Jane sipped some wine and smoked a cigarette.)

There must be a disciplined focus of this propellant therefore, if projection is to be achieved. Now. Periods of heightened sexual activity of a strong and deep nature will help. However, periods of no sexual activity will also help. On the one hand the chemical excess is built up as a result of overintensity. On the other hand, and in the latter case, it is built up because psychic and sexual release has not been granted. Eggs and asparagus are helpful.

I am obviously not suggesting a whole diet composed of eggs and asparagus. These plus fish oils are beneficial however, but not when taken with acid foods. Periods of especially intense psychic and mental activity can help you achieve projections. Periods of very little, unusually sparse, mental and psychic periods are often apt to result in projections—also however for the same reasons given concerning sexual activity.

Now I am speaking not only of legitimate projections, but of projections vivid enough to be recalled and recorded. Projections in other words in which the ego can take at least some small part. Spontaneous projections of which you are not aware occur frequently.

I suggest a more thorough examination of your dreams here, for many of them contain such spontaneous projections. They are most apt to occur in the early hours, between 3 and 5 A.M. The body temperature drops at such times. Five in the afternoon is also beneficial from this standpoint. The drinking of pure water also facilitates projection, although for obvious reasons the bladder must be empty.

The north-south position is extremely important in this context, and indeed a necessity for any efficient dream records. The reasoning parts of the brain can work most efficiently along with the intuitive portions of the self when the physical organism is in that position.

Joseph, if your hand is tired we shall break.

("Okay.")

(Jane stopped speaking at 9:42 but did not come out of trance. This is the first such instance in the sessions. Her manner had been very active, her eyes open often, her voice strong. Now she sat without moving perceptibly, her eyes closed, for two minutes. I got up and moved around, then sat down again.

("I'm ready now." At 9:44.)

The whole organism operates more effectively, generally speaking, in such a position, but more than this, the whole self operates more as a single unit. The intellectual processes are to some extent diminished in other positions. This has to do as I have said with electromagnetic properties.

In other positions it is the ego and intellect that suffer most, and since our purpose is to enlighten them as much as possible, this is not to our advantage.

Energy is most easily utilized in this position, for one thing, and this cuts unnecessary restrictions to a minimum. There is a vast difference between ordinary dreams and projections, whether or not the projections occur from the dream threshold. Dreams are constructed and sent upon their way. As you know, they maintain an independence within their own dimension.

Projections involve many more aspects of the whole self, and are a mark that the personality is progressing in important ways. The inner senses are allowed their greatest freedom in projection states, and the whole self retains experience that it would not otherwise. When this knowledge becomes part of the usual waking consciousness, that is when you realize what you have done, then you have taken a gigantic step forward.

An almost automatic determination must be set up however if projections with conscious awareness are to be anything but rare oddities. With you both the problem is somewhat different than it might be with others. These chemical excesses are used up for one thing in your own creative work. You do this now automatically.

It goes without saying that your work will gain immeasurably through the extended experience of projections. The yoga exercises allow you, when they are faithfully executed, to draw an abundance, indeed a superabundance, of energy. This energy results also in chemical excesses that can be utilized in projections without drawing away energy for your work.

The expectation and the knowledge that you are part of all energy will allow you to realize that all the energy you require will be given, since you are part of it. Only your own attitude, only any man's attitude, limits the amount of energy at his command.

I find myself trying to instruct you both again in the true nature of practicality.

Is your hand tired?

("No." 10:10.)

Your attitudes toward what is possible determines what is possible for you in very definite terms. Your attitudes create possibilities and impossibilities. Your attitude toward money creates your bank account. I am not speaking of your personally, alone. These laws apply to all. What you expect you create, and that is the beginning and end of it, whether you are speaking of psychic matters or physical matters.

Until you learn this you learn little, and until you learn this you do not know what it means to be practical. If you did not think projection was possible for you, you would never achieve a projection. You create your reality, and no one else can create it for you.

Now. There are definite chemical changes during projections. There are also electromagnetic changes that can be perceived with instruments. Certain electrical fields will also make themselves known under these conditions. The fields have always existed but they will only become apparent to physical instruments when they are being crossed. In other words, at the very act of projection.

The mirror in your bedroom is an excellent aid, incidentally. Certain temperature variations are also helpful. A cool body temperature for example, and the outside temperature, or rather the room temperature, between 73.8 and 75.9 or .10. High humidity is poor.

The color of a room is important. Your room, the bedroom, is a good color for this purpose. Cool colors are best. Too-warm colors are detrimental, being too closely allied with earthly aspects. For various reasons in your particular climate, May, October, February, March, are best. August can be beneficial according to the weather. Also September, April at times. Too-warm weather is detrimental.

Now this has to do with the electrical currents about the skin, and sweat on the body. Also with saline composition of the body at various times of the year.

When you want a break, please say so.

("All right, we'll take one now."

(At 10:15 Jane stopped speaking once again, ad sat very quietly, as before. Her voice had been strong and clear throughout, varying little in strength through the session. Since she was still in trance I thought it voluntary, and that she must feel in excellent form this evening. Her eyes were now closed.)

Walk about if you prefer.

(I did, stretching. In an aside as I paced about, and as Seth, Jane assured me there was no rush to get back to notes, etc. But I was ready to resume at 10:18, and the strong voice once again boomed out.)

These projections take a strong propelling force, for you are literally traveling from one dimension or reality to another. And yet you will retain awareness. All of this evening I have been speaking of projections in which awareness is retained, and not of more frequent projections which are usually forgotten.

The psychic energy necessary is considerable. It is twice as considerable when you attempt to manipulate in these seemingly alien conditions. Yet you must do so, and safely return.

We shall discuss various kinds of projections in detail, for you will become acquainted with them. Unless the structure of personality, or of the self, is clearly understood, projection itself will not seem possible. A self that is conceived of as a physical composition only would never be able to project, nor survive physical death.

Through the years a history of personal projections will serve to prove to you the nonphysical aspect of the self. You may even meet me *(smile, eyes open wide)* in some future projection. My meetings with you here involve to some extent projections on my part and on Ruburt's part. As yet he is not consciously aware of these projections. When I am here, he is often somewhere else. Part of him remains to keep check on me, and unfortunately this is the part that could be, but is not as yet, aware of his other surroundings.

You often project when you are painting, and you do not know it.

Now I will give you both a break.

(Break at 10:29. Jane now came out of her trance for the first time since 9 PM. As far as we know this is by far the longest trance she has undergone. Nor was her emergence from it easy; she seemed to grope her way out of it slowly, eyes blinking with effort many times before they finally opened clearly.

(She was, she said, "way-out," very well dissociated indeed. She had little recollection of her surroundings while speaking, and was quite surprised to learn her eyes had been wide open much of the time. She recalled a couple of cigarettes and a sip or two of wine, but these actions were "removed" from her.

(She knew, she said, at once that the voice was strong and loud. From the moment the session began she was "within the voice," as though wrapped in a cocoon. The voice swept her along as it has on a few occasions in the past. Nor did she know she would be kept in trance during breaks to rest my writing hand. She thought Seth did this to keep the session short, yet get lots of material through. She felt a sense of strangeness at break time because she didn't leave trance, but was not worried, nor did she try to get out of trance. Jane said she now felt quite tired.

(The moment the session began Jane felt a great sense of confidence that she knew wasn't hers—a sense that things were going to go extremely well. Throughout, her voice has been loud and strong, with an echoing quality engendered by our walls and the rugless floor.

(Although tired, Jane resumed at 10:40.)

We will continue this discussion at our next session.

Circumstances were good this evening, and I decided to take advantage of them. If you did not have to rise so early in the morning I would continue. However we do have all the time in the world, indeed.

My heartiest wishes to you both. You should find this evening's material helpful and instructive. As always I regret leaving you, but more than usually this evening, since I came through so well.

I intend to outline the steps involved in the various kinds of projections for you. And now good evening.

("Good night, Seth.")

One small point, however. You project also while you are in the waking state, but you do not realize this. Training can help you however, though this involves more work, and you will not reach that stage of realization for some time.

(End at 10:45. Jane was again just as well dissociated as before, although this time her eyes remained closed. Seth, she said, could have continued all night, without strain, but he did not push her to do so. She just knew he could.

(Jane said that some part of her that receives concepts from Seth, eventually decides that she has had enough, and then stops getting new concepts. Jane puts the last concept into words, and the session then ends.

(Jane now felt very tired, whereas usually she doesn't after a session.)

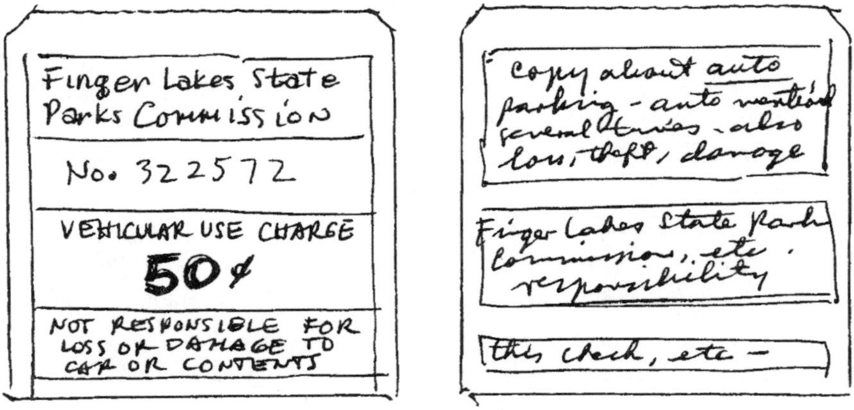

(Front and back tracings of the parking ticket used as the object in the 64th envelope experiment, in the 275th session for July 25,1966.)

SESSION 275
JULY 25, 1966 9 PM MONDAY

(The envelope object for the 64th envelope experiment was a parking ticket obtained at Robert Treman State Park, near Ithaca, NY, on July 12,1966, on our recent vacation. It is printed in black on card stock, with the serial number in a light blue ink. I enclosed it between two pieces of Bristol, then inserted this into the usual double envelopes. Ithaca is 30-some miles northest of Elmira.

(We visited the park three times during that week, but I kept the date for the ticket straight by attaching a penciled slip to it. As it happens some of the envelope data arises out of our two subsequent visits. The first visit was on Tuesday, July 12, the second on Thursday, July 14, and the third on Saturday, July 16.

(The back of the object contains fine print concerning automobile parking regulations, damage or loss, responsibility, etc.

(Jane said before the session that she had no idea of what Seth would talk about. Her eyes were open from the beginning of the session, she was smoking, and her voice was average with pauses.)

Good evening.

("Good evening, Seth.")

Now. Using energy generates energy.

The more creative energy you generate, the more you are able to generate. You do not use up energy in biological terms, and to think so is an error.

To refrain from using energy is to have less of it. The use of energy is the basis for personality and the intensity of experience. There is no such thing as hoarding energy. The creative individual has more vivid dream experiences and more vivid waking experiences than other individuals. Creativity should not be considered as the property of those who work in the arts however, for it is not theirs exclusively.

Creativity is an emotional and psychic characteristic. It can be used in various ways. The dreams of the highly creative exist multidimensionally. Projections rarely occur except to creative individuals. Now I am taking considerable time to deal with projections because on a spontaneous basis they occur more or less constantly.

Conscious projections—I should clear this: Projections that are conscious ones—usually occur only to highly creative individuals. Spontaneous projections however do occur constantly to every consciousness. You do not dwell within your physical universe as completely as you imagine, and as I have told you, you exist as long out of it as you do within it.

This does not mean that you do not exist however in the apparent interval. Our discussion concerning the nature of matter is important here, for I explained the pulsations that occur in atoms. Your perception of time causes many difficulties when you try to examine reality as it exists independent of matter. The limitations of verbal communications make some explanations difficult. *(See Volumes 1 and 2, for example.)*

You understand the concept of the spacious present. It appears to you of course that this room and everything within it is more or less in constant existence, between the limitations of its creation or manufacture, and death or material decay. Within the time structure of your perception, this chair for example has been in constant existence since you purchased it.

I have told you that pulsations occur as energy enters into an atom and then departs from it. There is an interval in which the chair simply does not exist, but you do not perceive it. A mechanism something like an afterimage allows you to see matter as continuous.

Now the length of this interval would seem unbelievably brief from some perspectives or systems, and centuries long, you see, if viewed from different systems. You yourselves do not perceive it at all. Consciously you do not perceive the intervals *(smile, eyes wide open)* during which you yourselves simply do not exist as material organisms.

We have, again, almost a mental afterimage that gives you the illusion that one moment leads smoothly to the next. You do exist during these intervals, but you do not exist in any physical terms. It is not a matter—if you will excuse my pun—it is not a matter of the consciousness escaping from the body. It is a matter concerning the fact that no physical body exists from which to escape.

The consciousness exists however. The consciousness as it reasserts itself within physical reality has no memory of the interval in which it did not physically exist. The inner self however retains all memory. Dreams allow consciousness to disentangle itself from physical reality. For various reasons the intervals here, you see, are to some extent recalled.

A large variety of dreams are the memories of this nonphysical existence that constantly occurs, though in waking life you are seldom aware of them. This cycle that psychologists have recently discovered, having to do with the various dream levels, corresponds to the ebb and tide of consciousness as it appears within and disappears from physical reality. It creates physical reality, as you know.

You may take your first break.

(Break at 9:27. Jane had been dissociated as usual. Her eyes had been open often, pace and voice average. She resumed in the same manner at 9:35.)

There is an ebb and tide. Your consciousness is not fully focused within physical reality, even during those intervals when you exist within it. The focus varies considerably, and in certain rhythm.

The amount of focus and the intensity varies according to the individual, but consciousness is never entirely focused within physical reality. Now when conscious projections occur you are taking advantage of these intervals between materializations. You may call these nonintervals, actually.

Your idea of time does not exist within such intervals. You do not even take it with you. Now these nonintervals are indeed openings into other realities, and you can theoretically explore them. They exist as actually as physical reality. You are doing the same thing when you realize you are dreaming, and decide to explore, say, a distant landscape that appears within the dream.

You may say that these noninterval experiences are subjective, but no more are they subjective than your physical life is. Theoretically you could explore these endlessly. Practically you cannot. Now in your physical life as you know it, you are indeed exploring such a noninterval. Do you see?

("Yes.")

For this is a noninterval to the inner self. This material is extremely important. One portion of you leaves the inner self to explore in depth a particular noninterval. To the inner self no time passes. You experience of course physical time. This noninterval however creates its own interval points that you also explore, in your dreams and waking projections that escape your ordinary consciousness.

In exploring these nonintervals however *(smile)* you also create that which you explore, for none of this exists without creative consciousness. This evening's material, read along with the discussions concerning the nature of action, will give you a more comprehensive idea of what I am trying to tell you.

This process is literally endless. The abundance of energy at your command is more vast than you suppose. Conscious projections are journeys into other nonintervals, and they are extremely valuable to the whole personality.

They relieve the physical organism for one thing. They refresh it immeasurably for another. We will deal with dream projections in detail, and then we shall discuss conscious projections literally from the waking state. I will give you my directions for projections from within the dream state first.

You may take a break, and we shall continue.

(Break at 9:52. Jane said she was far-out. Her pace was a bit faster, her eyes open often, etc. As Seth talked she had feelings of concepts, of things "opening up." She felt herself rushing in various directions, she said, inspired by these concepts, then giving voice to them one by one as she reached them. She called it a process of returning.

(She resumed in the same active manner at 10:00.)

We have not <u>really</u> begun full discussions of the types and kinds and degrees of dream experiences.

Some dreams as you know are more closely allied with physical reality than others. Some however are excellent as thresholds for conscious projection. What Fox called awake-seeming dreams are excellent. These can be produced during relatively brief naps also.

Our instructions will begin with the use of these dreams whenever they occur. You will know them by their intense vividness. These are dreams when at first you are certain that you are awake. It is sufficient to keep this in mind, so that in the middle of a dream you can realize what it is.

The pure and brilliant quality of the surroundings have much in common with the appearance physical reality has for children. The physical senses seem to operate with such efficiency that you think you are awake, but their brilliancy is superperfect. As soon as you realize what type of dream this is, then with practice you can project within it consciously, and explore your environment.

Now. Do you have an envelope for me?

("Yes."

(Jane paused at 10:09, then took the sealed envelope for our 64th experiment from me without opening her eyes. She of course knew that envelope experiments were scheduled for Mondays now, and asked out of formality. She pressed the envelope to her forehead in a vertical position.)

Give us a moment, please. These are impressions.

A connection with a flower or flowers, and with lace or material. Something suitable for an occasion.

A small round object in a lower corner, rather balanced by another round object in a diagonal corner. *(Jane gestured with the envelope; she indicated first the bottom half, then the top.)*

A center, as the center of spokes. As the spokes of a wheel, for example.

A connection with the number 5. This could refer to a date or to five people. At an affair or a gathering, and this is a distant connection.

The impression of a chain, or chain of events. An A and a G or J. Also the letters D O L, perhaps followed by another L *(pause)* and the number 63.

Eleven, or perhaps the month of November. The color red. Circular red. Green and an off-blue. A cross designation.

Tree shapes and an arch. A note that was not answered. This leads Ruburt to think, for his own reasons, of his ESP book notices. I tell you this for your own information.

<u>6</u> plus 1, or 7 times. A printed note. Action. I suggest your break unless you have questions. *(Pause at 10:17.*

("Are you saying there are two objects in the envelope?")

Or represented on a single object.

("Can you say something more about G or J or A?")

The initials or the letters seem to be connected with a square item, or package.

("Can you say something about the five people?")

(Pause.) Three females and two males.

("Where was this group?")

Outdoors, rather than indoors in this particular instance.

("Do you want to name the object?"

(Pause.) We are getting two separate impressions. One is of a blanket, and one is of a note. The blanket on grass.

I suggest your break.

(Break at 10:21. Jane was out as usual. Her eyes remained closed throughout. She had some images and these will be mentioned in sequence.

(See the tracing of the object and the notes on page 284. As stated we obtained the parking ticket used as object on July 12,1966 at Robert Treman State Park, Ithaca, NY, and I kept track of this date by attaching a note to the ticket. Other visits to the same park later in the week enter into the data, and these will be discussed as the need arises. Seth also helps out after break. In the meantime Jane and I began making our own connections with the object.

("A connection with a flower or flowers", immediately reminded Jane of our

visits to Enfield Glen, or Robert Treman State Park. Jane was subjectively sure of this, she said. I remember our specifically commenting on the flowers there, on all our visits. Objectively however there is nothing in this data to connect it to Enfield.

("and with lace or material. Something suitable for an occasion." We made no connections.

("A small round object in a lower corner, rather balanced by another round object in a diagonal corner." Jane, her eyes closed, indicated both ends of the envelope. There was of course but one object, the parking ticket, in the envelopes. Two of its corners are beveled but hardly round. The object however is small in comparison to the envelopes. Jane had one of her images here, seeing mentally two small objects in a space resembling the usual envelopes; she saw no detail however.

("A center, as the center of spokes. As the spokes of a wheel, for example." In a free manner Seth uses associations of Jane's to get at the idea of a car, or travel. The parking ticket was obtained at the state park as a result of a 60-mile round trip by automobile, as were the two subsequent parking tickets for the same state park. But again no mention of either a car or the park in specific terms.

("A connection with the number five. This could refer to a date or to five people. At an affair or a gathering, and this is a distant connection." A somewhat distant connection, but a good one, we believe. As stated Jane and I visited Enfield Glen, or Robert Treman State Park, three times—July 12 for Tuesday, July 14 for Thursday, and July 16 for Saturday. The envelope object contained the ticket for the visit of July 12. We also obtained like objects for the other two visits, and Seth evidently uses this fact to lead to related connections. The above data concerns our visit to Enfield Glen on Saturday, July 16.

(At Saturday's visit there was indeed a gathering and an affair—an outdoor picnic involving 15 people, either relatives or close friends. Five of these people were my brother Dick and his family, including three children, from Rochester, NY. The above data is developed further in two of the questions Seth answers later, and will be furnished then for convenience's sake.

(The people at the gathering were 4 Joe Korens, 5 Dick Buttses, my parents, Jane and me, and 2 Crosbys.

(The object also contains the number 5 twice, in the serial number and the price. I didn't ask Seth about this, but perhaps the number 5 at the beginning of the above data was used to lead to the rest of it involving the gathering, etc.

("The impression of a chain, or chain of events." Jane felt subjectively that this referred to the mention on the back of the parking ticket regarding the Finger Lakes State Parks Commission, which includes several parks of course in its territory.

("An A and a G or J." Too vague to be of help. If initials for instance, there were two Ann's at the gathering, a Jane and a Joe, etc.

("Also the letters D O L, followed perhaps by another L," Here is another instance of Seth trying something new in the way of association, as he did with the D E L for delivery data in the last envelope experiment. See page 276 of the 273rd session. It appears to be a good system and promises much. Jane was quite vexed at break to realize the implications of this method, and that she hadn't followed through as Seth evidently intended her to.

(At break she now recalled that in addition to the D O L L which she had given voice to, and which she had seen mentally within, she had also seen the letters A R, but hadn't spoken them aloud. The word of course being dollar. Jane now said this word was Seth's way of leading her to the price on the object, 50¢; she thought that if she voiced the word dollar, Seth might have tried to get the 50¢ through.

(Jane said this method is new and she is not used to taking advantage of it. Mentally she first saw the D O L. She was aware of a "space," she said, then she saw the second L, there was another space and she saw the A R. Each segment as described vanished before the next came along. She now added that in the D E L for delivery data in the 273rd session, she had seen only the D E L.

("and the number 63." We made no connections.

("Eleven, or perhaps the month of November." No connections.

("The color red. Circular red. Green and an off-blue. A cross designation. Tree shapes and an arch. A note that was not answered. This leads Ruburt to think, for his own reasons, of his ESP book notices. I tell you this for your own information. <u>6</u> plus 1, or 7 times." Most of these led us to consider various connections, some probably correct enough had we asked Seth to verify them. Since we didn't take the time we cannot claim them.

("A printed note." Here Jane was subjectively sure that this refers to the envelope object. The back of the parking ticket bears 15 lines of fine print pertaining to automobiles, loss or damage, etc. Jane said this data is the way she would refer to such an object.

("Action." No connections since not specific enough.

(First Question: "Are you saying there are two objects in the envelope?" Answer: "Or represented on a single object." Only one item comprised the envelope object, but we don't know how particularly to break down this single item to comprise two objects. See the tracings on page 284.

(Second Question: Can you say something more about G or J or A? "The initials or the letters seem to be connected with a square item, or package." As stated, there were two Anns at the gathering Saturday, and a Jane and a Joe, etc. See page 284. This would connect such initials with the fact that the envelope object is a square item, [although not a package]. However, remember that the object came from our visit of Tuesday July 12, whereas the gathering was held on Saturday July

16. The link here being that a parking ticket was also obtained, and saved by me, during Saturday's visit; this ticket was the same except for the serial number as the ticket used as object.

(Question: "Can you say something about the five people?" "Three females and two males." See the five and gathering data on page 289, concerning my brother Dick and his family. The next two questions also develop this particular data begun on page 289. And again, the link here being parking tickets for both our July 12 and July 16 visits to Enfield Glen/Robert Treman State Park.

(What could have been a serious incident developed at the park and gathering during our Saturday visit. Dick's young son David fell from a high slide and injured his back. At first it was thought seriously. David naturally cried loudly. As it happened five people tended to David, and their action was witnessed by Jane and myself from some distance away. Three females and two males did the attending: My mother; David's mother Ida; Ann Crosby; David's father Dick; and my father.

(Jane and I thought the strong emotional content of this experience accounted for its cropping up in the data, since the incident took place at the location designated by the object; although on a different day, it still took place within the same week. Seth concurs after break.

(Question: "Where was this group?" "Outdoors, rather than indoors in this particular instance." Very good, the incident involving David did take place outdoors in the park.

(Question: "Do you want to name the object?" "We are getting two separate impressions. One is of a blanket, and one is of a note. The blanket on grass." Again, very good. In view of the printed note data on page 290, we believe Jane came very close to allowing Seth to name the envelope object.

(Both impressions here are valid. The blanket data because of David. After he took his fall a blanket was hunted for among the members of the gathering. One was finally taken from a car, and David was made to lie quietly on it for a while to make sure no delayed injury showed up. None did. The interesting bit of information here is that a deliberate effort was made to spread the blanket on a grassy spot near the picnic tables, so that a softer bed would be furnished.

(Jane resumed at 10:50; her eyes again open. She left her glasses on for perhaps a third of the delivery.)

We will end our session.

We have been making attempts in the direction of more specific material, and giving it to Ruburt in a slightly different fashion. For example, the D O L L. Your interpretation was correct. I was leading him to dollar, and then to half dollar.

I gave him a visual image of the letters, and this is fairly new for him. He will catch on however rather quickly, and then our data should be better than it was before.

The blanket incident overshadowed the other data because of the emotional content of the child's fall. There is no need to go further in interpreting the material now. My heartiest regards to you both. Again, my concern for your time limitations. The D O L L you see, followed by the A R, would have required little interpretation. I was leading him to half dollar. We are coming along. Good night, my friends.

("Good night, Seth.")

(End at 10:59. Actually, now, Jane sat very still, in trance, for over two minutes. Her eyes were closed, her head bowed. She was smiling, somewhat expectantly, I thought. I could see that Seth was in a fond mood. When she did leave trance Jane said Seth "spoke to us silently," and debated as to whether to speak further this evening without notes on my part. He decided not to.)

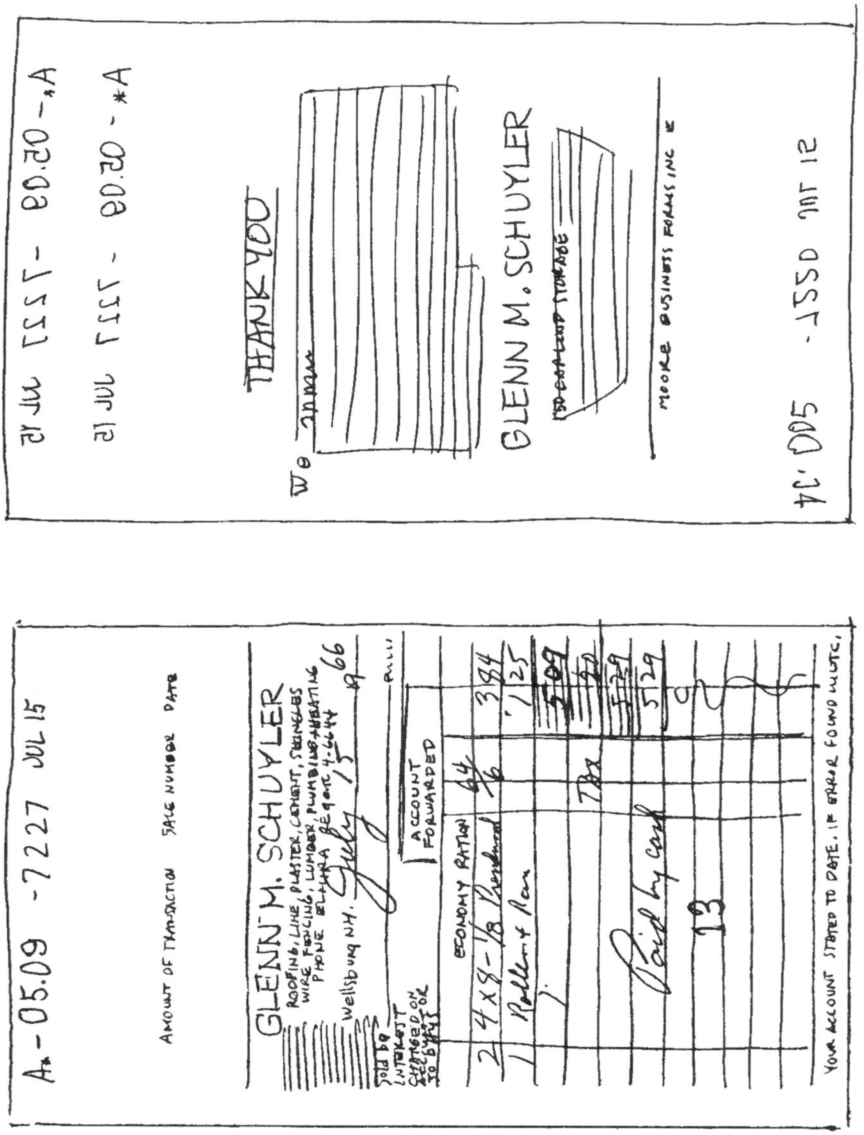

(Reduced front and back tracings of the bill used as the object in the 65th envelope experiment, in the 276th session for August 1, 1966.)

SESSION 276
AUGUST 1, 1966 9 PM MONDAY

(The regularly scheduled session for last Wednesday, July 27,1966, was not held because Jane was ill for several days. Her pendulum told her the illness was brought on by a case of nerves and panic over the forthcoming publication of her ESP book. Jane hadn't been working or sleeping well for some days prior to her illness.

(Shortly after this our new cat, Catherine, fell ill with distemper, and received a shot at the veterinarian's Friday evening, July 29, along with some pills for subsequent days. By tonight it appeared the cat would be all right. Jane wanted me to be sure to ask Seth about the cat in case that personality failed to mention it voluntarily.

(The 65th envelope experiment was held. The object was the bill I received for the purchase of Masonite in Wellsburg, NY, on Friday, July 15,1966. As usual I placed the bill between two pieces of Bristol, then sealed the sandwich in two envelopes. Jane was present at the lumber company in Wellsburg when the bill was made out, but like me at the time she paid no particular attention to it, and hadn't seen it since then.

(Jane began speaking while sitting down and with her eyes open and dark at the start. She was also smoking. Her pace was average, so was her voice.)

Good evening.

("Good evening, Seth.")

Now. If Ruburt were in danger of any serious illness, I would know it. And I would warn you, though I am aware of the power of suggestion you see, and would be under such circumstances extremely careful less the warning itself act as a negative suggestion.

If it appeared necessary however I would warn you, and give instructions as to how it could be best avoided. I was not aware of Ruburt's approaching indisposition at our last session, although I knew his <u>overall</u> condition was not of the best.

His condition was not severe enough to strike me. Had you asked however I could have explored his state and given you some warning. The proper mental attitude could have prevented the indisposition. On the other hand, better solutions not having been used, the indisposition served a purpose and a desired end was gained.

(Jane had been somewhat restless while speaking. Now without pausing in particular she got up from her favorite Kennedy rocker and sat in a chair across the table from me. She does such things extremely seldom, usually confining herself to the rocker.)

The overall psychic and mental problems were concentrated into physical symptoms—

(We were interrupted by a knock on the door at 9:08. The neighbor left us within a couple of minutes. Jane was not bothered by the noise or distraction. She resumed while sitting in the rocker again, but almost at once got up and returned to the chair across from me. 9:10.)

Now. The mental and psychic difficulties were concentrated into physical symptoms, and the system was rid of the difficulty in this manner. The problem was dealt with physically in other words—always, incidentally, the last resort.

There is always the initial attempt to handle problems on a mental and psychic level. Physical illness represents the failure to deal with these sufficiently or effectively, and in all cases the intensity and severity of physical illness is in proportion to the severity and intensity of the inner problem.

A chronic and longlasting physical symptom therefore represents for example a chronic, fairly enduring inner problem. There is of course subconscious symbolism involved in the course of the illness itself. There is also a deeper psychic symbolism.

Ruburt was sick to his stomach because he had not been able to work properly. He acted this out physically. The enforced rest also gave him time to gain back his psychic resources. All of this could have been dealt with on mental and psychic levels. In the past the physical conditions under comparable circumstances would have been far worse.

Now. The particular virus that attacked your cat had actually been in his system for some time. His own native resiliency and your combined psychic reinforcement protected him. Now. Ruburt picked up the cat's virus and became ill. With his illness he was not able to reinforce the cat's condition by his own psychic creativity.

You used your psychic energies to aid Ruburt, and the animal was left to his own resiliency, and it was not enough. You need have no worries now concerning the animal's survival. The antibiotics serve as a physical reinforcement, you see, since the condition now appears in physical terms.

The cat needs all the reinforcements you can give it now. If he is to survive as a fully effective and fully healthy animal. There is no reason why he will not, as long as you maintain your present course.

I intend to give you some more material this evening on projections. However I wanted to make these and a few other personal comments. Are your fingers tired?

("No." At 9:26.)

Now. Your party, at which I was present occasionally *(sitting across from me still, Jane tapped on the table, her eyes very dark and wide)* was of great benefit, as you know. But you do not know some important facts.

You chose, both of you, the two people who are the most psychically gifted of your acquaintance, and you called them here. You called them because the illness of the animal served to tell you that some extra reinforcement would be helpful. The whole affair was psychically logical, and followed inner patterns that aided all of you.

(The party, Saturday night, with Bill Macdonnel, his friend Tom, and Jane and me, lasted until 4:45 AM Sunday, July 31.)

You understand the therapeutic results of explosive laughter. I will not dwell on this then. The explosive laughter however was in direct proportion to the inner tensions. From the first signs of Ruburt's illness you both took precisely the correct steps. The illness itself was a regrettable, but on the whole beneficial act, for if it had not occurred, and if the inner problems had not been worked out psychically, then a more serious illness could have been the result.

Ruburt took, all in all, a wise course under the circumstances. It was not the best course, which would have been a psychic one. I suggest your break.

(Break at 9:32. Jane was well dissociated. Her eyes had opened often, her voice had grown a bit stronger. She had been aware of leaving her rocker to sit opposite me at the table, where she remained until break, and had been surprised at her doing so.

(Jane resumed in the same rather active manner, again sitting at the table with me, at 9:44.)

Now. One further point. Your friend Mark *(Bill Macdonnel)* was subconsciously trying to pay you back, to repay you, for your help to him, and particularly for the meals.

He is particularly appreciative, and feels that with the food he eats he also receives other benefits, as indeed he does. This is a point aside, yet an important one: Food is indeed sacred. Its preparation is more a psychic matter than a physical one. The preparer of food puts more into it than spices. A food can be contaminated, poisoned, by a cook, with no physical elements involved at all. When ten people are poisoned for example by a food, it is no coincidence, and more is involved than mayonnaise left in the sun. Ruburt's healing nature protects and enriches your meals, and this is an important and constant element in your well-being.

In many households steady small illnesses often result because the preparer of foods has an unhealthy psychic nature. These are often the carriers of disease. This is meant as a general statement however, for you are all subject to fluctuating circumstances, and are more or less able to use your abilities.

For Ruburt once more: Yes, you are perfectly safe with your cat, if you both proceed with your present course.

Now, unless you have any questions we will go to other material.

("Go ahead." 9:52.)

Projections actually involve a change of atomic structure.

Consciousness simply changes its form. The physical body is maintained, yet certain chemical changes occur in it also. Initially when projection is first accomplished, there is a strong charge of adrenaline. There is high activity of the thyroid gland. There is a charge of sexual hormones, which are utilized also for projection.

After projection is accomplished however there is a marked decline of chemical activity and hormone action, a drop in temperature, sometimes very low, and a drop in blood pressure. There are changes also in the eye mechanisms. The rapid eyes movements noted in the dream state by investigators, cease entirely.

The eyes muscles are not used, the normal muscular activity that usually occurs in sleep vanishes. The physical body is in a deep trance state. The trance may be masked also by sleep, if the projection occurs from a dream state. According to the intensity of the projection and according to the systems visited, the physical body becomes more or less rigid when consciousness <u>returns</u> to it.

This is simply a reaction to returning consciousness. There is a subtle difference in the way sugar molecules are utilized. Momentarily the physical body uses less sugar. However the sugar is important in fueling the consciousness on its journey. It aids in connecting the consciousness <u>to</u> the body, and without it under some conditions consciousness could be cut off from return. In other words, there is indeed a connection that is and must be partially physical, between the body and the traveling consciousness, and it is based upon a certain sugar molecule in a form not normally seen.

Before conscious projection I would therefore recommend you take a small amount of starchy or sugar food. This molecular structure thins out, so to speak, and while not physically visible has a physical basis. For projections within other systems, another transformation must and does take place. The physical connection will only allow you to go so far. What amounts to another projection from this first form then occurs.

To return then under such circumstances requires an entry from this second form back into the first, and then into the physical body. You may take your break.

(Break at 10:06. Jane out as usual, eyes open often. She again sat at the table for the delivery. She resumed, seated in the rocker and with her eyes closed, at 10:15.)

I had intended to begin my practical suggestions this evening, for I will give you a complete set of instructions.

A small snack before bed is a good one you see from this standpoint. Alcohol is of some benefit, though not to any great degree. Excellent results can be achieved in dream-based projections during the day, in a nap. When these are good they will perhaps be the best of any dream-based projections.

They are also exceedingly safe. The body itself is well stocked, so to speak, and it is possible to maintain projections for a longer period than usual in night projections. I am speaking now only of dream-based projections.

The morning hours are better than the afternoon hours. The period just before the menstruation cycle is a good one for Ruburt for this purpose. *(Pause.)*

Do you have an envelope for me?

("Yes.")

(At 10:22, her eyes closed, Jane took the envelope for our 65th experiment from me and pressed it to her forehead in a more or less vertical position.)

Give us a moment, please. These are impressions.

Stern. I do not know if this refers to stern as severe, or stern as a ship.

Connection with a March date, and three. Either March third *(pause)* or an event involving three people in March. Connection with an event not repeated. Numbers, perhaps 01913.

Connection with black, and a small square. This could be symbolic of a death connection, or it could be literal. A word beginning with an M. I do not know—massage, mucilage—leave it for now.

Soothing music perhaps. Four square, or four and four squares.

A tree, or tall tree shape. Straight. A word with M again, perhaps this time a name or initial. Ruburt thinks of Marie or Mary. It is a large M, and belongs with a name. This seems very vivid in itself, but it could simply stand for Miss so-and-so you see, or Mrs. A woman connection.

An E and a B. A tournament, perhaps symbolic. A crossing, as of swords. Connection with transportation, and perhaps with water. Rectangular object, with some dark coloring, perhaps dark blue. The color reminds me of water at night.

An implied border. Writing or printing in a lower left-hand corner perhaps, very small, holding the object horizontally. *(Jane gestured with the envelope, which she now held horizontally.)*

Something on the back also. An oval shape, or eye shape—that is, this kind of an eye, you see *(her eyes closed, Jane pointed to one of her own)* inside of a rectangle or triangle.

The feeling of something hanging over, threatening or overhanging, on the upper half of the object, and dark. Something small and bright also, beneath this overhanging or threatening portion.

1966, also looking forward to 1967. Connection with a photograph I believe, or other object with triangular corners that photographs usually fit into in an album.

Two people. You and Ruburt, I believe.

Do you have any questions? *(10:35.*

("Can you say something more about the March date?")

March, progress, march along. An event in March, that led to similar events while the original one was not repeated. I believe the letter G is somehow connected with this event.

I suggest your break. Unless you have questions?

(Jane lowered the envelope to her lap, her eyes closed.

("Well, suppose you try naming the object, then.")

I came as close as I can, in the data given.

("Can you say something more about four squares?")

I believe not.

("I guess that's it, then."

(Break at 10:39. Jane had been dissociated as usual, and her eyes had remained closed. She had images and these will be noted as the material unfolds.

(We made our own connections and Seth verified some of them. Once again Jane's associations seemed to flow in a freer manner, this being the third experiment in which this is apparent. We think more data was obtained on this envelope than in previous ones.

("Stern. I do not know if this refers to stern as severe, or stern as a ship." At first this stumped us. Jane said then that the connection referred to Enfield Glen, which we visited three times during our vacation from July 9-17. See the notes on page 294 and the tracing on the previous page. The object was obtained July 15, during our vacation, on Friday. Jane recalled that she had wanted to visit the Glen instead of drive to Wellsburg. The connection would be the Glen, where there is a beautiful pool and stream, leading to stern "as a ship."

(I believe the "well" in Wellsburg, also implying water and thus stern, worked in the same manner here. In addition the first name of the owner of the lumberyard in Wellsburg, which furnished the object, is named Glenn; associating thus with Enfield Glen, or Robert H. Treman State Park near Ithaca, NY.

("Connection with a March date, and three. Either March third or an event involving three people in March." We could make no connection here, although Seth was quite positive. Because of the length of the session we did not ask for elaboration.

("Connection with an event not repeated." I bought two sheets, 4 x 8 feet, at the lumberyard in Wellsburg on July 15. Since this particular kind of Masonite is hard to find and the Schuyler lumberyard had a good supply, I decided to return to

Wellsburg on Saturday, July 23, to buy two more full sheets. But in the interim I figured out a method to coat the Masonite for paintings that obviated the use of any special kind of Masonite, and thus did not return to Wellsburg.

("Numbers, perhaps 01913." Since the object is a bill, many numbers appear on it. See page 293. The sequence 01913 does not appear in whole, but the sequence beginning with 0 does appear, in .09. This shows twice on the front of the bill; once via bleedthrough on the back, also. There are two other sets of numbers visible as ghost images on the back of the bill, and both evidently begin with a zero, but are hard to decipher.

("Connection with black, and a small square. This could be symbolic of a death connection, or it could be literal." Perhaps it is both. The back of the bill is printed in heavy black ink, the front in red. The arrangement on the back is not square, being more rectangular.

(The death connection enters in because the bill was filled out by the worker at the lumberyard who obtained and cut the Masonite so it would fit into our station wagon. The worker—whose name we do not know, but could easily learn—became quite talkative when he learned I planned to use the Masonite as support for paintings. He described to us in some detail how he had a portrait of himself drawn during the Second World War, when he was overseas. War...death. The conversation was unusual in that the worker explained how the artist drew his face as though it was symmetrical, whereas in reality it is quite asymmetrical, with an impaired eye.

("A word beginning with an M." The middle initial of the proprietor of the lumberyard: Glenn M. Schuyler, shown in large red type on the bill. Another M enters in later. There is a chance here that Seth did not mean an initial. In this event, it can be said we made the trip to Wellsburg for the express purpose of buying Masonite.

(Jane however had an image of a large capital M, she said, in which case the first interpretation applies above. Seth mentions an initial specifically later but not above. Jane was aware of no color in her image; she saw the M alone.

(Seth continues the above data, and gives another instance of the freer association employed, all stemming from the letter M: "I do not know—massage, mucilage—leave it for now." Jane said the mucilage connection referred to the word cement on the bill heading, beneath the Schuyler name.

("Soothing music perhaps." Jane said this is a distortion of the massage data above, massage and music both being soothing.

("Four square, or four and four squares." This I regard as excellent data pertaining to the object, whereas Jane said it had no particular meaning for her because she didn't know the specifics concerning the way I usually buy Masonite.

(The object shows I bought two full sheets of Masonite, each one 4 x 8 feet in dimension. The worker previously mentioned at the lumberyard cut the sheets in half so that we could load them into the car. This gave <u>four</u> pieces of Masonite, each one of which was <u>four feet square</u>.

("A tree, or tall tree shape." The bill's heading contains the word lumber, a product of trees. Masonite of course is a lumber product, but the connection is farther removed from the object, perhaps, in this case.

("Straight." We associate this with the tree data above. Lumber usually being straight as opposed to crooked.

("A word with M again, perhaps this time a name or initial." Ruburt thinks of Marie or Mary. It is a <u>large</u> M, and belongs with a name. This seems very vivid in itself, but it could simply stand for Miss So-and-So, you see, or Mrs. A woman connection." Seth here evidently refers to a different name this time than that shown on the bill, Glenn M. Schuyler. Jane is subjectively sure Seth was getting at the name of Mrs. Marilyn Wilbur, who lives with her husband Don in Wellsburg; the Wilburs are good friends of ours. The Marie or Mary is very suggestive of Marilyn.

("An E and a B." There are words beginning with E and B on the object, but the data is too general.

("A tournament, perhaps symbolic. A crossing, as of swords." Jane was sure this referred to the story told us by the worker at the lumberyard, who procured the Masonite for me, concerning his war service, his portrait, etc., done while he was in the service. The worker made out the bill which served as object.

("Connection with transportation." This could be our trip to Wellsburg, specifically to buy the Masonite. A distance of perhaps ten miles each way.

("And perhaps with water." This could stem from the wells in Wellsburg, as explained earlier, or from the fact that Jane would have preferred going to Enfield Glen to swim, instead of buying Masonite. Also, we planned to go swimming locally after getting the Masonite, but became so busy we did not do so.

("Rectangular object, with some dark coloring, perhaps dark blue. The color reminds me of water at night." The bill used as object is rectangular in shape. The back of it is printed in black. The price and date applied automatically by the register at the top of the bill is in a medium blue ink. Since we have the carbon copy, the handwriting on the bill is in a dark blue or gray. These three points can all be included in the "dark coloring" category, and blue is given specifically by Seth.

("An implied border." The object has an implied border on both the front and back. See the tracings on page 293.

("Writing or printing in a lower left-hand corner perhaps, very small, holding the object horizontally." Jane at this time held the envelope horizontally. We did not mark the envelopes or the object to verify this data. However if she held the object so

that its head, or top, pointed to the right as she faced it, then there would be printing along the left-hand side of the bill. This being the fine print at the bottom of the front of the bill.

(If Jane held the object with its head pointing to the left as she faced it, then the price and date would be at the left edge of the bill. This copy is larger however.

("Something on the back also." There is black printing on the back of the object, plus a bleedthrough of the price and date at the top, and a couple of ghost images of other price-and-date data beneath, in reverse.

("An oval shape, or eye shape—that is, this kind of an eye, you see, inside of a rectangle or triangle." Jane pointed to her own eye while giving this data. It is very good. As stated earlier the worker at the lumberyard who procured the Masonite for me, then made out the bill used as object, had a bad eye. It will be recalled that the worker described a portrait drawn of him while he was in the service; and that the artist making the portrait drew him with a symmetrical face, whereas his face is decidedly not symmetrical.

(The rectangle or triangle data refers to the fact that the worker wears glasses.

("The feeling of something hanging over, threatening or overhanging, on the upper half of the object, and dark." This is most interesting, and is an example of the new method in which Seth gives Jane some of her data now. Jane said it was difficult to describe, but she had the very definite impression, or feeling or image, within, of a large dark overhanging mass above her, as a roof might be, for instance. This impression was strong, and she believes the overhanging feeling led her to attach the threatening data to it.

(On the object, the first word in the heading beneath the name is Roofing. This ties in neatly with the next data. Note also that the word Roofing is located on the upper half of the object; that is, high up on the object, as a roof would usually be over the head of an observer.

("Something bright and small also, beneath this overhanging or threatening portion." Again, very interesting when the bill is studied. Note that the 1 Roller Pan is written on the bill <u>directly beneath</u> the word Roofing, which is referred to in the data above. Thus, the position of the roller pan is interpreted literally by Seth as being under a roof—quite a logical position. The roller pan, which I never used, is of course bright and shiny, tin coated probably, and is small in comparison to a roof size.

("1966, also looking to 1967." Note the box on the front of the bill bearing the words Account forwarded. Since I bought the Masonite in 1966, and presumably would keep an account going at the lumberyard, any sum due would be carried over into 1967.

("Connection with a photograph, I <u>believe</u>, or other object with triangular corners that photographs usually fit into in an album." As stated earlier the worker at

the lumberyard described a portrait drawn of him overseas. This basic information perhaps led to the above data, but we believe the following is more likely correct.

(Jane had an image of a photo of the two of us, taken at Enfield Glen. Remember that she wanted to go to the Glen on July 15, rather than to the lumberyard in Wellsburg to buy Masonite. No photos of us have been taken at the Glen in recent years. Also, the Glen idea links up with the proprietor of the lumberyard, Glenn M. Schuyler.

("Two people. You and Ruburt, I believe." Jane and I of course made the trip to Wellsburg for the Masonite, etc.; although contacting others on this mission in the usual routine fashion.

(First Question: "Can you say something about the March date?" "March, progress, march along. An event in March, that led to similar events while the original one was not repeated. I believe the letter G is somehow connected with this event." We still could make no connections for this data, and I did not ask Seth to explain. Jane had a mental image of a single G, nothing else. There is Glenn on the bill used as object, but this wouldn't refer back to March; our July visit was our first ever to this particular lumberyard.

(Question: "Well, suppose you try naming the object, then." "I came as close as I can, in the data given."

(Question: "Can you say something more about four squares?" "I believe not." See the four square data on page 301, referring to the Masonite I bought and had cut to size. I wanted to see if Jane could be more specific here, since she had already given excellent data, but she could not. As stated, the four squares data meant nothing to her, but quite a lot to me. Perhaps her lack of conscious interest prevented more information here.

(Jane resumed with her eyes closed and her glasses on at 11:27.)

We will close. If it were not so late I would discuss this experiment, as there are some interesting connections.

The tournament did refer to a war. The swords were bayonets.

My heartiest regards. Advances are being made that will begin to show themselves rather clearly. Ruburt was correct as far as he went, in describing the way in which he received the information regarding the roof. This is also something quite new. We will attempt to mix it also with visual data. It will serve finally to round out and pinpoint information more concisely. I will briefly discuss this particular point at our next session. It regards a method of perception that you use subconsciously but never recognize—a sense that is something like the way you register temperature.

And now good evening, my dear friends. I enjoy our sessions. I regret the limitations that necessarily prevent longer sessions. I am with you both often, and regard you highly. You are good students. I hope I am as good a teacher.

("Good night, Seth.")

(End at 11:30. Jane was pretty far-out. She had a strong awareness of Seth's benevolent emotional feeling.)

SESSION 277
AUGUST 3, 1966 9 PM WEDNESDAY

(Jane began speaking while sitting down and with her eyes closed, in a voice a bit deeper than usual and with pauses.)

Now. Good evening.

("Good evening, Seth.")

Your waking consciousness only participates in projections as a rule when you are in a period of high vitality, and exceptional health.

On occasion the waking consciousness does participate during other usually very depressed periods. But generally speaking high energy is needed in order to maintain overall stability, and in order that the ego is not overstrained. Such conscious projections are automatically spaced out. In this way there is little danger that problems will arise.

It is the same with the conscious retention of dreams in general. You are indeed exercising what amounts to an added ability. You are learning to manipulate within other dimensions of consciousness. Automatic controls are therefore used. *(Voice somewhat deeper.)* You proceed as your abilities and control develop.

Suggestion given before sleep will greatly add to your chances of conscious projections from the dream state. It is not necessary, basically speaking, that you notice some small incongruous detail in order to realize while dreaming that you are dreaming. There is however one good method to use. The suggestion "I will realize while dreaming that I am dreaming" can also be used, as another method, or both of these may be utilized together.

At your stage it is of course easier if the actual separation of consciousness from the physical body occurs without your awareness. However the experience itself is excellent training. I have told you that these projections may carry you to different systems. In the beginning you are safer perhaps in those projections that involve your own reality.

There is not any great matter of danger, only that you could fall into blunders. The north-south position is most beneficial. It might be of benefit if you concentrate before sleep upon a simple projection that involves leaving the body, walking out into this room, for example, *(the living room)* or perhaps strolling around the block.

When falling off to sleep for example, imagine that you are in your yard, in another room of your apartment, or in front of the house. When this method is effective you will not be consciously aware of the actual separation however. I do not suggest at this point that you or Ruburt attempt to contact me during any projection. Later, when you have more training.

If by chance you blunder *(smile, eyes open)* into my territory, then I will know it, and seek you out. Whenever you find yourself in any potentially dangerous dream situation during a projection, immediately terminate the dream. You will then return to an ordinary state of consciousness.

Now. Mr. Fox is quite correct. When you know you are in a projection do not be tempted to tamper. There are forces that you do not yet understand. You will find that these projections become more vivid. I must repeat that these are quite valid. They are not hallucinations. Conscious projections do not occur with any frequency as far as a large percentage of humanity is concerned. Note that I speak only now of projections in which you are self-consciously aware.

The reasons are somewhat obvious. Conscious projections are dependent upon abilities and control. Also this ability and control presupposes a fairly disciplined personality. Otherwise we would have explosive outbursts of suddenly released aggressions in systems where they do not belong.

It is quite possible to meet survival personalities, incidentally, during such projections. This does not happen often, because so many other issues are necessary. It is also possible of course to move into your own future. This occurs regularly, though not always with awareness. Projections into the past are also frequent.

Because of some matters we have not yet discussed, at any rate deeply, it is possible to meet your own projection. You are accountable for acts committed during projections, of course, and these alter the personality as any acts do. If you have your wits about you, you can gain information concerning the future by studying your projection environment, if for any reason you suppose it to be ahead of you in time.

Some of this is extremely complicated. You may for example request before sleep that you project into your own future, to see what occurs there. This is legitimate enough, if you are willing to accept the results of your projections. For what you see will influence what you do in the present. You will be projecting of course into the probable future as it exists for you at this point.

The very act of projecting will alter these probabilities. I am not saying that this future environment is not real, however. It is as real as your present environment indeed, you understand this.

("Yes." Jane stared at me, then took a long pause with her eyes closed.)

Do not touch another figure if you have reason to believe that it is a traveling form like your own. You will have to learn to distinguish. When you realize that you are dreaming, and if in the dream you are with another person, then tell him that you are both dreaming, and note his response.

You may now take your break.

(Break at 9:40. Jane had been dissociated as usual. Her eyes had come to open often. She had spoken with many short pauses, sipped iced tea and smoked. Her voice had been average.

(She resumed in the same manner at 9:52.)

During projection you are dealing with environments and realities with which you are not acquainted on a conscious level. Yet during projections you will be consciously aware of them.

(Long pause.) You understand how physical matter is formed. You will be dealing with realities in which the durability of images is far different. You will be much more aware of the shifting guise of materialized images. You will be aware of the mental energy and psychic force that gives all objects their existence.

I suggest you take a cat break. I will wait.

("Okay." Our cat Willy had been kicking up a fuss, so at 9:56 I got up to put him in a back room. Jane sat waiting quietly, still in trance, then resumed when I sat down.)

You will to some degree learn control amid a conglomeration of energy forces that have no objective form. All objects as you know are energy. If the energy is focused in a particular manner, then you have physical objects within your system.

There are also potential objects. The energy is focusing toward materialization. There is also energy that will never focus in this way. The bulk of this energy is mental, or exists in such a way that you will never perceive it as form. It has motion. This motion follows certain laws which we will not discuss at this time.

You may experience this in your projections. Perhaps as a barrier to your own motion, or perhaps as a propelling agent, over which you have little control. It is not harmful but may surprise you. It is not correct precisely to call this a current, although spiritualistic literature speaks of it as such.

It is very simply the energy that composes your universe, only you are usually familiar with it when it is formed into matter exclusively. Now it is this that may carry you to other systems, though the word carry seems to imply a motion backward or forward. The motion may feel backward or forward, but instead there is an immersion into various depths.

On very few occasions you may, if you are lucky, travel or project so effectively that you are aware of the spacious present, in which case you will sense the reality of all systems simultaneously. But here there is a strong possibility that memory of the experience in its entirety will not be retained.

All projections involve literally an extension of identity and self. The usual limitations set upon the self by the ego vanish. Now. This gives some hint of the abilities that exist for the individual in future existences. *(Long pause, head down, eyes closed.)* Whether or not projections are conscious, they occur in any case, and the personality learns from them. The conscious projection however involves a much higher achievement. *(Long pause.)*

One point: There is involved here a freedom from your physical time that can be gained in no other way. This freedom is extremely refreshing, and has therapeutic results unless the experience is overindulged in. There is a benefit for the physical body also. It is momentarily free of any irritating demands put upon it by a divided personality, automatically for example free from aggressions and unhealthy aspects of this nature. I mentioned that double and even triple projections can occur as you adopt forms. These forms represent forms that your personality will take in future existences.

They are adopted to meet the particular requirements of the environment in which they are used. In some dreams individuals see what they imagine to be the image of their own dead self. Instead they have been projecting, and see one of their own projected forms that they have themselves just vacated.

These forms do exist, as your physical body does. They are fused however with your inner self. They are not physical, but they do exist in the whole package of the self, perhaps like the skins of an onion, you see. They are merely the forms that your own consciousness takes in different dreams.

You may take a break.

(Break at 10:25. Jane out more than usual. She had some little difficulty getting her eyes open at break; also, her eyes had remained closed during the delivery except for a couple of short intervals. She did remember the disturbance Willy had created however. She used many pauses.

(She resumed in a more active manner, her pace faster, at 10:36.)

This energy may carry you, then, with startling rapidity away to another environment.

When you become proficient this can be avoided to some extent, but never entirely. Because of the nature of such projections you are not stationed, so to speak, within any of the systems through which you may pass. Therefore you cannot expect any great permanence for yourself within them.

The perceptions of those who exist within them are basically different than your own, and many of them will not perceive you. Those who do are apt to be projecting also, you see. I told you that if you can you should mention the fact that you are dreaming. If the other individual realizes this also, then you are both projecting. He may on the other hand be projecting and not be aware of the fact.

Again, make no effort to touch any other individual you meet, particularly if there is reason to believe he is also projecting. This will be uncomfortable for you both.

Now, as always regretfully, I will close our session. My heartiest wishes to you both.

("Good night, Seth.")

(End at 10:42. Jane out as usual. Eyes open and closed, voice okay, she smoked a cigarette. Again her eyes opened slowly.)

FRONT

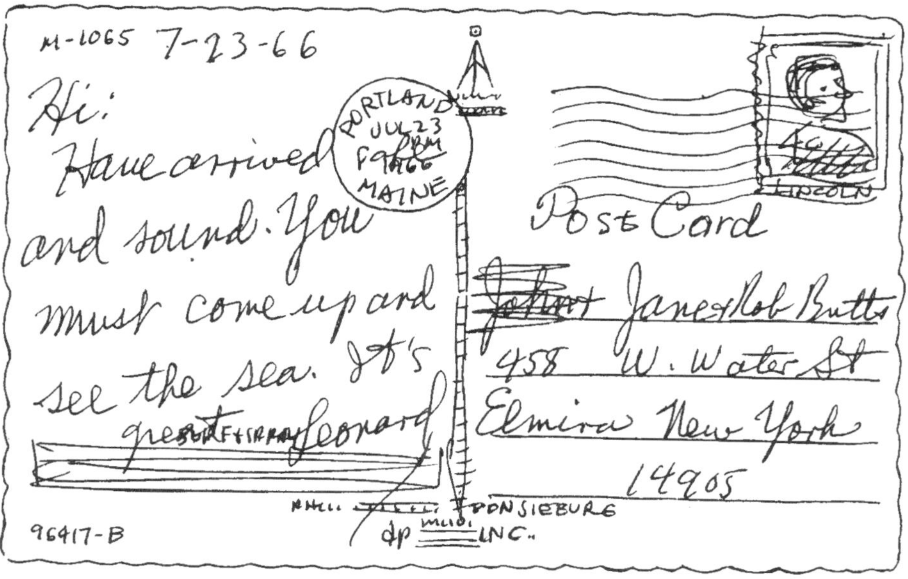

BACK

(Tracings of the postcard used as object in the 66th envelope experiment, in the 278th session for August 8,1966.)

SESSION 278
AUGUST 8, 1966 9 PM MONDAY

(The 66th envelope object was a postcard mailed to us by our neighbor across the hall, Leonard Yaudes, from Portland, Maine, on July 23,1966. I sealed it in the usual double envelopes after placing it between two pieces of Bristol.

(Jane woke up Sunday morning, August 7, with a stiff neck. We attributed a mental cause to it, probably concern over the forthcoming publication of her ESP book.

(Jane began speaking while sitting down and with her eyes open. She was smoking. Her voice was good, with pauses.)

Now dear friends, good evening.

("Good evening, Seth.")

In your present existence the <u>large</u> area of mental activity is translated into physical terms.

This you can hardly escape, for it is the means by which you exist physically. This means that your positive and healthy attitudes are physically manifest, as well as your unhealthy or negative attitudes. It is almost impossible for you to weed out <u>all</u> negative attitudes, for by these you understand the difference between positive and negative. And by seeing physically the results of your inner activity, you better understand the nature of inner activity itself.

You can of course improve to a much higher degree than you believe possible. It is natural that at a point such as this, Ruburt's activities should show in great contrasts. He is not upset basically *(Jane got up from her rocker and walked about the room as she spoke, looking for her cigarettes)* believe it or not, with the delay in his book publication, though this is the conscious rationalization.

(Laugh.) He is concerned, you see, over the publication of his book, period. He is concerned simply because these strong inner efforts will now become exteriorized to some extent. This is the point that bothers him.

Subconsciously he exaggerates the dangers that will beset him as a result of the publication, and the actual facts will be a relief. He is in many ways extremely individualistic. He fights for what he believes in, but he also has strong docile tendencies, which are usually rather effectively controlled. These rise up, you see however, in <u>direct proportion</u> to the degree of his independent accomplishments, so that he then fears the accumulated results, social results, of what he has done. It is therefore fairly natural that when this accomplishment is being exteriorized he would become frightened of the opinion of his brethren. These are two faces of the same coin.

The delay bothers him simply because he is in suspense of the <u>imagined</u>

rebuffs. The facts will prove otherwise, and he will be able to relax.

A business representative is a good idea, for his relationships will be tinged otherwise with these difficulties. You have more to gain than to lose by any visit from Ruburt's aunt.

Now Joseph, I will see that you are both adequately protected psychically, and therefore physically, during any such visit. And you have my word on this issue.

I will also see to it that Ruburt's condition improves, and immediately. I am doing this simply as a good and kind gesture. I do not make such gestures lightly however, for there is something to be gained by understanding reactions. I do not like to interfere as a rule. *(Long pause.)* I will however, because I do sympathize, see to it that Ruburt's condition immediately changes for the better, in all ways.

He has himself built up psychic energies that allow this to be done. The delays themselves are normal ones, indeed a part of the trade. Were he better known he would be informed of them, or if he lived nearby for example. It is his reactions rather than the delays which are important.

I suggest a brief break and we shall continue.

(Break at 9:21. Jane was dissociated a little more than usual, she said. After she had gotten up to get her cigarettes, she sat down opposite me at the table again, and spoke from there until break. Her eyes had been open much of the time.

(She resumed in the same manner, again from the same chair, at 9:26.)

Part of Ruburt's difficulty is based upon precognitive knowledge.

I told you that this book would change your lives. Not only would it represent the beginning of financial changes for the better, but it will affect your dealings with your fellow man, and put you in a different relationship with them. Ruburt knows this and becomes frightened. There is not need to be fearful. The means and the energy will be given to you both, or you would not have progressed to this stage.

There will be a rather sudden change of fortune, of which Ruburt is well aware. It is not immediate, but it is inevitable with the publication of the book, and he fears having money, even though he wants it.

He is indeed being stiff-necked about the affair. I can help him, and you, simply because you have earned such aid by your own efforts. I could not give it to you otherwise, for you would be unable to accept it. You will mark my words, these words, well, in the future.

Now. Your projection attempts, Joseph, have been most successful, though you are not consciously aware of them as yet. Ruburt did well today. He saw, in part, a future dwelling which you will both temporarily inhabit. You were within this system in your projection dream. You will shortly, I believe, allow yourself more freedom as far as conscious levitation within a projection.

(See my dream of August 4 in my dream notebook.)

Your original inspiration is captured in your painting. It is there. *(Smile.)* The desire for creative accomplishment brings forth the opposite fear of accomplishment. One does not exist without the other. At the point of highest accomplishment, often, you fear that nothing has been accomplished.

I am giving you the rules by which accomplishment can truly be achieved. See that you heed them, both of you.

In your dream you were afraid of falling, Joseph. You were legitimately projecting. To rid yourself of your fear you formed the image of a man falling, but you gave him a parachute.

(Long pause, eyes closed.) It will be easiest for you, Joseph, to attain and remember projections on the 2nd, 12th and 24th nights of a month; and Ruburt on the 3rd, 9th and 27th. These dates have to do with your general overall peaks of psychic activity.

(Long pause, eyes still closed.) An event in a week and a half, that will be beneficial for you both.

Do you have an envelope for me?

("Yes.")

Would you prefer a break?

("No." At 9:43 Jane took the envelope for our 66th experiment from me without opening her eyes. She pressed it to her forehead in a horizontal manner.)

Give us a moment, please. These are impressions.

Fur. Eight. A small square. A geometrical figure.

The color red. 414. Three people. The busts rather than full figures, as three heads for example. *(Pause.)* I only see the tops of these figures.

Vertical objects close together, as a woods. *(Jane was now gesturing often with the envelope, though still mainly holding it horizontally.)* Five plus one. A small circular object with something on top of it, perhaps like a stem.

Invitation of sorts, or implied. Grass. An oval shape or scene.

J B. Connection with a fortunate circumstance. 1963 and 1966. A turnabout or change of mind or plan.

Small squares, not in line. April. Four. Connection with a letter or note, and a male. A distant religious connection. *(Pause.)*

The object a card. A design like a flower or stem.

Your initials.

You may ask a question or take a break. *(At 9:51.*

("Can you be more specific about the three people?")

For some reason the impression is chopped off, so that only the top portion is seen. Heads.

("Are they male or female, for instance?")

Impression of light-colored hair on two, and a similarity. These I believe males. Perhaps a family resemblance, but a definite similarity in any case.

("Well, you're correct, the object is a card.")

A grouping.

("What's that about a geometrical figure?")

Please repeat.

(I did so. Traffic noise was loud.)

No. An equality, a balance. A balanced arrangement.

("What's the color red connected to?")

I believe a circular object, though perhaps a dress.

("Can you elaborate on a turnabout?")

Having to do with a change of plan. An event not taking place when originally planned. Put off. *(Pause.*

("What's that about the oval shape?")

I am not clear here. This, perhaps: To a completed plan, as distinct from the incomplete one. A coming together.

(This data evidently refers to turnabout rather than the oval shape. I had thought it okay to ask the next question, since Seth had taken a rather lengthy pause.)

I suggest your break. The color purple I believe also. And small dark lettering, perhaps I N C.

(Break at 9:58. Jane was out as usual. Her eyes remained closed. She felt no particular reaction, she said, when I told her she had been correct in calling the object a card. She also said she would recall any images when we went over the data.

(See the tracings of the object on page 309. Pertinent data connected to it will be brought out as we list our connections. We were able to make some, and Seth did not help us out after break.

("Fur." I wrote this as fur, rather than fir, when Jane gave it, not knowing which she meant. I saw no connection, but as soon as she saw the scene on the postcard used as object, Jane said fur had been a reference to the white foamy water spray and surf. To her it had a definite resemblance to the white thick fur of our longhaired cat, Willy. As soon as Jane mentioned this resemblance I agreed with her.

("Eight." Possibly the numeral 8 in 458 W. Water Street, our address. The only 8 on the object, although there are 28 other numbers on the object, including the denomination on the stamp.

("A small square." See the back of the object. Just to the right and above of the circular postmark is a geometrical triangular symbol. This small symbol is topped by

a very small square, with a dot in it. The square about 1/16" on a side.

(Jane mentioned the 4¢ postage stamp on the object; strictly speaking the stamp is not quite square, but if the stamp had been perceived clairvoyantly perhaps its shape was interpreted as a square.

("A geometrical figure." Again, the triangular design, topped by the square containing a dot, just to the right and above the postmark on back of the card. Also—are circles, regarding the postmark itself, geometrical figures? Such a definition also includes the rectangular postage stamp.

("The color red." The only thing close to red on the object is the 4¢ postage stamp, current series, bearing Lincoln's bust. This is a predominant red with a bluish tint. Seth hints at another possible meaning later, but we believe the stamp is the object referred to.

("414." There is no 414, numbers in this sequence, on the object. There are several groups of numbers however. Among them are 417, bottom left corner on the back of the card, and 149 as part of the ZIP code number of our address.

("Three people. The busts rather than full figures, as three heads for example. I only see the tops of these figures." Our interpretation: Note that Leonard Yaudes addressed the object to Jane and me, after crossing out the name John. [John happens to be a good friend of Leonard's, though merely an acquaintance of ours; Leonard evidently made an absentminded mistake in addressing the card.] The address line of the card thus contains three names. Above this line is the postage stamp, bearing the head and shoulders of Lincoln.

(Some confusion of clairvoyant images here could have led Jane to assign the bust attribute of Lincoln to the three people on the line below the stamp.

(There are actually 6 personal names on the back of the object: Leonard, John, Jane and myself, Lincoln, and the photographer who took the pictures used on the front of the postcard, Don Sieburg.

("Vertical objects close together, as a woods." In giving the data Jane gestured often with the envelope, her eyes closed; she would then return it to her forehead in mainly a horizontal position. At times she held it briefly in other positions. The wavy lines of the cancellation are close together, and in the abstract could symbolize anything such as trees, etc. Perhaps Jane perceived this while the envelope was in a vertical position, or the data is simply somewhat distorted.

(Another valid connection is that Leonard mailed the card to us from the state of Maine, where he was vacationing on a camping trip; implying woods in the state parks where he did stay, as we later learned.

("Five plus one." There are two combinations of numbers containing five and one on the back of the object: M-1065 in the upper left corner, and 14905, the ZIP code on the lower right.

(It can also be said that five plus one makes six. There are, thus, 6 sixes on the back of the object. And as stated earlier there are 6 personal names there also.

("A small circular object with something on top of it, perhaps like a stem." See the tracings on page 309. The postmark on the back of the object is of course small and circular. The small triangular design mentioned earlier is just above the postmark, to the right, and is of a line, or stemlike, design. The triangular design does not quite touch the postmark, but the two words just beneath it, Natural Color, do run into the postmark, uniting the two designs.

("Invitation of sorts, or implied." Leonard's message to us on the back of the card contains such an invitation: "Hi: Have arrived safe and sound. You must come up and see the sea. It's great. Leonard."

("Grass." We don't know. Grass of course is implied through the object in many ways: Campgrounds for one; also, before leaving for Maine Leonard had his new tent set up on the grass in the backyard of the apartment house for several days, checking it out. He lives in the apartment across the hall from us, on the second floor.

("An oval shape or scene." See the tracings on page 309. The scene on the front of the postcard consists almost entirely of oval components in the abstract: The sea spray, the clouds, even the rocks in the foreground. We believe this applies since Seth used the word scene in the data.

("J B." Jane [and Rob] Butts—J B—appears in the address line on the back of the object.

(Although this interpretation seems obvious, Jane said that J B also reminded her of our friend John Bradley, who had witnessed some sessions. Note that the name John, although crossed out, appears on the object. Jane thinks she could have also thought of John Bradley as well as Jane Butts, and not wanting to commit herself spoke aloud the initials instead of one or the other full name.

("Connection with a fortunate circumstance." We don't know, unless the fact that Leonard going on vacation was a fortunate circumstance. Leonard's girl also accompanied him.

("1963 and 1966." The 1966 appears within the postmark, as well as the date July 23,1966, in Leonard's handwriting. We are not sure of 1963. We know Leonard for instance has made other trips to Maine and other New England states in recent years, and could have done so perhaps in 1963. There may be other connections.

("A turnabout or change of mind or plan." We speculate: Before leaving for Maine with his girl, Leonard talked often to us of marriage to her. Since his return he has not mentioned the subject, and as far as we know has not seen the girl. I wanted to ask Seth more about turnabout.

(More speculation: Leonard told us that while in Maine cold weather forced

them to change their plans on occasion and take cabins, since tents were too cold.

("Small squares, not in line." It might be said the abstract shapes of the letters in Portland, Maine, within the circular postmark, are angular. Of course the letters are not in line, being confined within the circle shape. There could be other connections. The rest of the copy on the back of the postcard, whether printed or handwritten, is in line.

("April." We don't know. April is the fourth month.

("Four." The numeral 4 appears four times on the object's back. Was the April data a method of leading up to the four data? Also—there are four handwritten names on the back of the object. There are a total of six personal names on the object, the other two, Don Sieburg and Lincoln, being printed.

("Connection with a letter or note," See the tracings on page 309. The object, a postcard, bears a note to Jane and me.

("and a male." The obvious connection being that a male, Leonard Yaudes, wrote the note on the object, and signed it. Once again, there are six personal names on the object, and five of them are male.)

("A distant religious connection." We don't know.

("The object a card." The object is a card. I did not push Jane to be more specific as to what kind of card, etc.

("A design like a flower or stem." Again, the small triangular design on the back of the object, just above and to the right of the circular postmark. We believe the stem data, mentioned by Seth earlier, led Jane to the flower mention here.

("Your initials." Jane gestured at me, her eyes closed, as she gave this data. My name on the back of the object, Rob Butts, contains my initials.

(First Question: "Can you be more specific about the <u>three</u> people?" "For some reason the impression is chopped off, so that only the top portion is seen. Heads." See the data under three people on page 314. The data here, and consequently the answer we give, being the same as the other given earlier.

(Question: "Are they male or female, for instance?" "Impression of light-colored hair on two, and a similarity. These I believe males. Perhaps a family resemblance, but a definite similarity in any case." This was of little help to us, and since we didn't ask Seth to explain after break we cannot decipher the data. We are not related to Leonard, of course. The other male on the address line of the object, John, crossed out by Leonard, is a close friend of Leonard's but not a relative. None of us—Jane, Leonard, John or myself—are blond or light-haired.

(Leonard does have a brother, Ken, who also lives here in Elmira, but as far as we know Ken was not involved in the Maine trip, which inspired the envelope object. Leonard's girl, who went to Maine with him, is also dark-haired. Leonard and Ken look much alike; there is little resemblance between Leonard and John, and

I do not look like either one of them.

(I then said: "Well, you're correct, the object is a card." I wanted to note Jane's reaction, while in trance, to being told she had named the envelope object at least in a general way. There was none, and she told me later she felt no particular reaction. At the time she said, as Seth: "A grouping". I took this to mean she was still concerned with the three people data already cited, even though I had waited until she paused in a definite manner before making the comment.

(Question: "What's that about a geometrical figure?" "No. An equality. A balance. A balanced arrangement." This data came after I had to repeat the question because of traffic noise. See the interpretation of the geometrical data on page 313. All of the geometrical figures on the back of the object are balanced—the circular postmark, the small triangle and square just above and to the right of the postmark, and the rectangle of the postage stamp.

(Question: "What's the color red connected to?" "I believe a circular object, though perhaps a dress." As far as the object is concerned, it could be said the circular postmark is connected to the reddish postage stamp via the typical wavy lines of the cancellation.

(The mention of a dress is interesting, implying a female—and a female did accompany Leonard to Maine, from where he mailed us the object. We do not know whether Leonard's girl had a red dress with her on the trip.

(Question: "Can you elaborate on a turnabout?" "Having to do with a change of plan. An event not taking place when originally planned. Put off." See the interpretation of the turnabout data on page 315. The above adds no more to that interpretation. Note that Seth's answers to the questions this evening seem to add little that is more specific to the data originally given.

(Question: "What's that about the oval shape?" "I am not clear here. This, perhaps: To a completed plan, as distinct from the incomplete one. A coming together." Once again, Seth appears to be still considering the previous question, although as before I had waited until Jane had taken a definite pause before asking the next question. Even so, this data did not help us.

(Jane, or Seth, now added two pieces of information that I hadn't asked for: "The color purple I believe also." We think this applies to the 4¢ Lincoln U.S. postage stamp on the object. As stated earlier the stamp is printed in red ink with blue added. The resultant color can be called a purple, a violet, etc.

("And small dark lettering, perhaps I N C." Very good indeed. See the tracings of the object on page 309. At bottom center on the back of the object, in small capital lettering, is the logo and address of: DP—Dexter Press, Inc., West Nyack, New York. Printed in a dark blue.

(Jane resumed, once again sitting across from me at the table instead of in her

rocker, at 10:30.)

We will close our session. Had Ruburt been at his best, the results would have been better. As it is, we progress.

My heartiest wishes to you both. I am fully willing and capable of carrying on for some time. It is only in deference to your time schedule that I close.

("Good night, Seth."

(End at 10:32. Jane out as usual, eyes open, voice quiet.

(Note on August 14. Jane and I talked with Leonard today, Sunday, and learned that he appears to have put off marriage to the girl in question—see Turnabout—because of her "attitude about money." It seems he thinks she is somewhat overbearing regarding the subject, since her parents are wealthy. Leonard made the remark, "I don't think I'll ever get married," etc.)

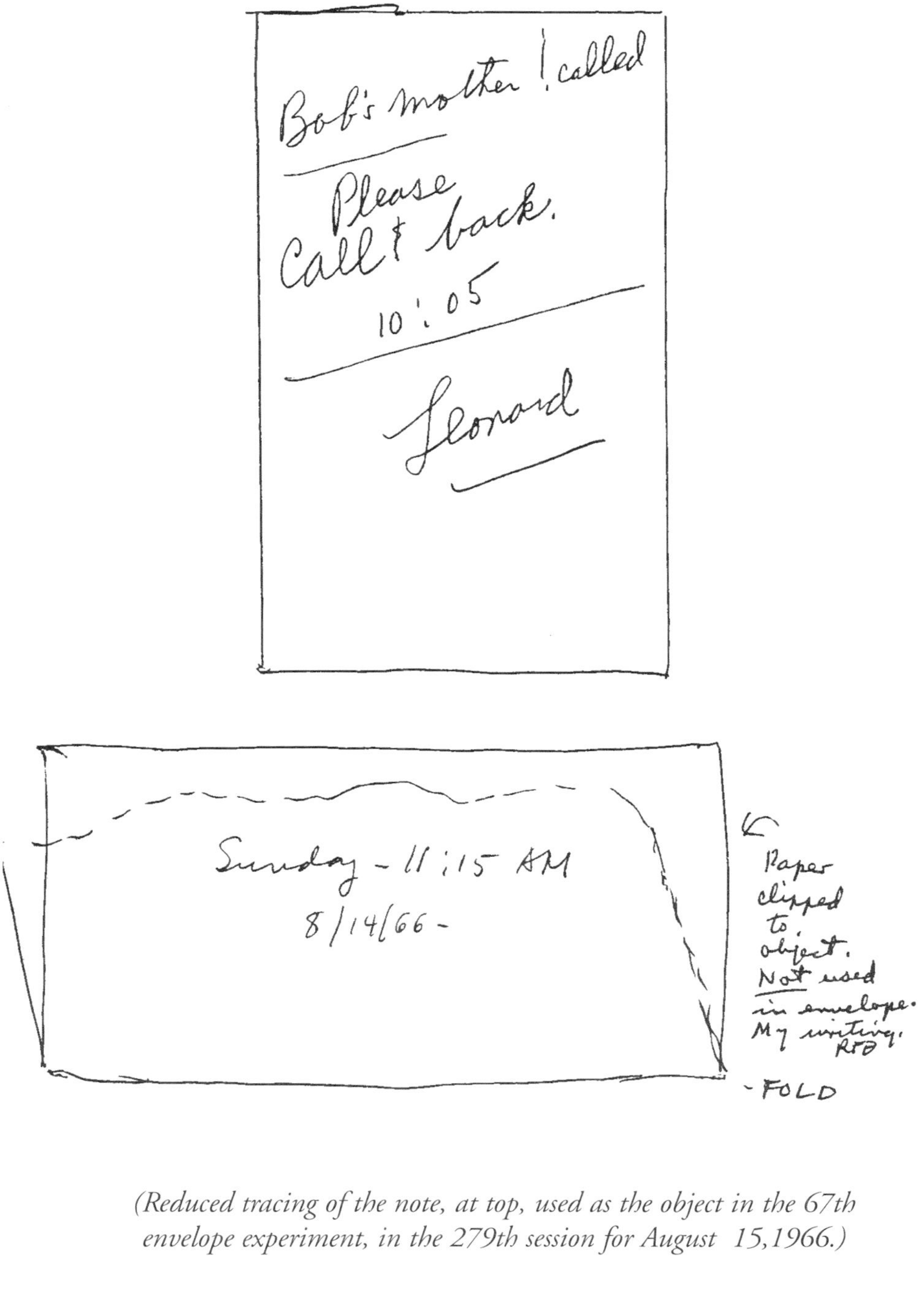

(Reduced tracing of the note, at top, used as the object in the 67th envelope experiment, in the 279th session for August 15,1966.)

(Reduced tracing of the outside of the greeting card which also figures in the 67th envelope data. It was mailed to Jane and me on August 11,1966 by my mother, but was not used as envelope object.)

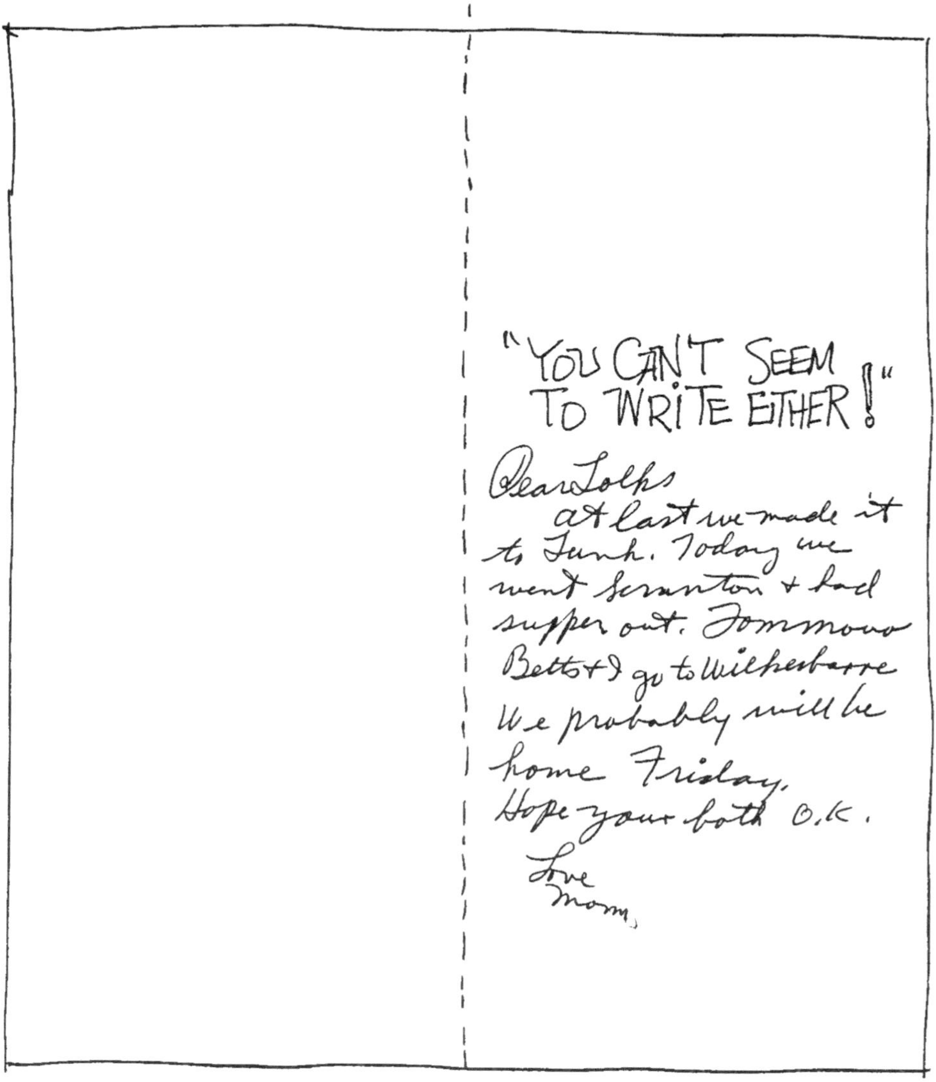

(Tracing of the inside of the greeting card which also figures in the 67th envelope data. It was mailed to Jane and me on August 11,1966 by my mother, but was not used as envelope object.)

SESSION 279
AUGUST 15, 1966 9 PM MONDAY

(The regularly scheduled session due Wednesday, August 10, was not held because Jane was indisposed.

(The 67th envelope object was a penciled note written on one side of a piece of white paper by our neighbor, Leonard Yaudes. See page 319. The folded note shown below the object is my own, made at the time I discovered Leonard's note stuck in our door on Sunday morning. Thus Leonard wrote his note in answer to a phone call by my mother at 10:05 Sunday morning, August 14. We do not have a phone.

(The greeting card represented on pages 320-21 figures in the envelope data, and so is shown also. It was not used in the envelope. The card was mailed to Jane and me by my mother from Tunkhannock, PA, on August 11,1966. It is on file along with the envelope, bearing date, ZIP code, etc.

(My own note, bearing the time and date, shown at the bottom of page 319, was clipped to the envelope object. I removed it before enclosing the object between two pieces of Bristol, then sealing the sandwich in the usual double envelopes.

(Jane began speaking while sitting down, in an average voice and with pauses at the beginning. Her eyes soon opened; she was smoking.)

Good evening.

("Good evening, Seth.")

My instructions concerning projection should tell you a good deal about the true nature of the self.

All limitations, basically, are self-adopted. They may be necessary at one time or another, but they can never be primary realities. Limitations, in other words, are illusion. You have to deal with them only because you have created them. Your exterior circumstances are the materializations of inner climate.

We are all existing in many dimensions at once. The primary difference between us is that I am aware of my existence in many dimensions, and you are not aware of yours. We form a new dimension in our sessions. I give voice to ideas that are known to various levels of your personalities, yet I am not at the level of your personalities.

There are no limits to the types of projections that can occur, basically speaking, for there are no limitations to the self, and a projection is an extension of the self. Your present existence is of course a projection. Activities based upon the framework of your present existence must be initiated within a system of chemicals and physical properties which make physical existence possible.

If life within the physical organism is to be maintained, then consciousness must return to it. This does not mean that consciousness is dependent upon the physical organism. There will be [an] endless series of projections in other existences, and these will have no chemical basis as you know it. Your traveling consciousness appears as an apparition within some other systems.

Your own thoughts have a reality that you do not understand, and their own kind of form, or psychic content, and this content exists not as pure energy, but as energy with form and shape. And when it is perceived by you, then it has bulk. The bulk is the result of your own perception. The bulk, or mass, is perceived whether or not the ideas have ever been materialized as physical matter. Whenever you come in contact with a particular idea form, and this will only happen in projections, then you will automatically perceive that form with bulk or mass.

In other systems the same energy idea will be transformed in a different way entirely, even as the physical objects within your universe are perceived in entirely different ways to others not within your system. Any given physical object exists in the manner in which you are accustomed to perceiving it. This *(Jane struck the arm of the rocker in which she sat)* for example exists as a chair. It also exists as sound. It has a counterpart that can, under given conditions, be perceived exclusively in terms of any of your senses.

You can hear the chair as a musical note in a trance state, for example, or with the use of drugs. You are still dealing in terms of your senses, however. You are seeing—or perceiving, rather—separately, the various components that are usually organized to form the solid object.

With the full use of the inner senses, however, it is theoretically possible to perceive all the shapes and forms that have ever been, or will ever be, adopted by the atoms and molecules that compose the particular chair. This kind of experience is beyond the power of drugs. It is true to say that in one sense both you and Ruburt are a part of the table and the chair, and the room in which they sit.

You organize yourselves out of other matter, you see. The difference is a psychic one, and not a physical one as it appears. The inner identity extends itself over larger and larger groups of energy forms, and acts as an overall psychic pattern. But all is connected.

Now. Projections further extend the self and the identity, only this time in realms where the physical self cannot follow. Now this kind of projection, this extension of identity, is the true nature and the creative aspect of aggression. This and not war, is the meaning of aggression. It is a forward thrust of creative activity, forever extending itself in this manner, and instantly changed, and no longer what it was.

Projection then is aggression. The self thrusts forward into new dimensions, and this is creative. Painting a picture is aggressive. You are thrusting energy into new forms. All this you see implies a destruction, but only in your limited terms. Each projection, for example, is the death, in one way, of the limited self that stood earlier.

Each painting that you create represents the death of the self that you were before you created it. The changing self forever dies in this manner, and yet only this symbolic death insures psychic survival. There is no basic moral problem then when you consider the true nature of aggression, for it is highly creative, and without destruction there would be no existence. These are two faces of the same coin.

Are your fingers tired?

("No." 9:35.)

A projection, an out-of-body experience, is a creative act, and again all creative acts are basically aggressive. Now, you change those dimensions in which your projections take place. You cannot visit them and leave no mark.

The ego, as a rule, is frightfully leery of such action, since to it an out-of-body experience always symbolizes physical death. At the same time the ego becomes more assured after successful projections, since it discovers itself not only intact but immeasurably enriched. Indeed, the ego both fights, fears and desires any creative act. Any creative act, including the production of any art, necessitates a momentary release from the ego, an escape from it, which the ego fears.

Yet again, the ego is enriched and therefore allows the self more freedom. Successful projections therefore will ultimately lead to more projections, and they will be more easily executed.

For the benefit of your fingers, we should perhaps take a break, though we are doing very well. We will leave our friend as he is.

("Okay."

(Break at 9:40. As she had done during the 274th session, Jane remained in trance at break. This didn't mean she confined herself to her chair, sitting with her eyes closed. Instead she too paced about the room, her eyes open and very dark, and spoke to me as I stretched. We discussed briefly the similarity between projections and my paintings. She lit a cigarette and said she'd let me tell her when I was ready to resume.

(Her manner had been quite active and expressive during delivery, her eyes open more often than not. She had smoked and sipped wine. We resumed in about the same fashion, with a few pauses interspersed, at 9:45.)

Now, you see, when you paint a picture you use your physical body as a tool to create your inner idea. When you create physical matter you are not aware of doing so, but you affect energy directly in such an execution, your own attention being focused primarily in the physical system.

You can only do so much in your painting. You can only create it as a reality in so many dimensions. You cannot appreciate, for that matter, all the systems of reality in which the painting does have reality. This is a very simple analogy: However, in some aspects a projection to another system could be likened to a situation in which you entered the landscape of one of your own paintings.

(One of our cats now scratched at the hall door for admittance, as is customary. Without pausing, her eyes open and dark, Jane rose and went to the door and let the cat in. She resumed her seat in the rocker without interruption.)

You would have so much freedom within, and no more. You would be different from the inhabitants who you might encounter there. But in one way or another your existence would be perceived.

Now. Most systems have more reality than a painting, but not all of them. The very nature of some would be frightening to you. Your paintings are a creation, and yet by their nature they are limitations. They are limitations because their reality is necessarily limited by the elements you have chosen. You paint one house within a landscape for example. This is a creation. But two houses will never appear.

Now in the realities of other systems another house, you see, could appear *(smile)* and another person could appear, and the projecting consciousness would be such a person. He must instantly adapt to the new surroundings.

Now. Do you have an envelope?

("Yes." 10:05. Jane's eyes now closed, and remained so.)

Do you want to rest your hand before we begin?

("No."

(Jane now took the sealed double envelope from me without opening her eyes. This is our 67th such experiment. She pressed the envelope to her forehead horizontally.)

Give us a moment, please. These are impressions.

A grave. Something grave. Three. *(Pause.)* A card with a cartoon. Connection with a disturbance. The color white. Something misplaced.

A connection with a closet. I do not understand as yet to what this particular image refers.

A connection with a monument. Something misplaced again. Four plus one. This month. I L I A. *(Spelled out. Shakes head, puzzled.)*

Distant connection with a cat. Perhaps black.

A very distant connection with a foreign land and a person. *(Pause, briefly.)* A woman. A Butts, I believe.

Monumental. A monumental occasion. A folded card. Writing on the inside. Printed matter and handwriting.

The number 4. Several events happening together, or a series of objects strung together on the object. *(Pause.)* This leading Ruburt to think of Christmas. *(Gesture with envelope.)*

Several colors. White, orange, red perhaps, this being circular, and a yellow. Plus dark printing.

I N C again, and perhaps 1418. Something sent through the mail in an envelope. Long and narrow in shape.

Apples. 73. Perhaps a connection with your parents. The word Ensenada.

Do you have any questions?

(Jane paused at about 10:15. She had been speaking rapidly. Before I could ask a question she continued:)

Something favorite, or favored, here. Some one favored.

("Can you be more specific about the I L I A?")

No. Perhaps it could be a reference to Illinois, but that is all I see.

("Can you elaborate upon the closet data?")

Ruburt thinks of your mother's sewing room. To me a reference to some shape, dark and narrow, with the feeling of motion involved, as a falling through or a falling out. Downward motion, with some speed.

("What's that about a black cat?")

A distant connection. *(Pause.)* A loss of an advantage, or <u>period</u> of poor luck.

("What's the shape of the object?"

(Jane sat with the envelope resting in her lap, eyes still closed.)

Roughly rectangular, in itself.

("Can you elaborate on the grave data?")

A connection with someone, dead or in poor health. Perhaps a male.

("How about the number 4?")

Four boxes, I believe. Box shapes.

("Can you tell me anything about what the handwriting says on the object?"

(Pause.) Not an invitation precisely at all, but reference to an occasion or visit. *(Pause.)*

("Was that word you mentioned Ensenada?")

An incident primarily involving four people, I believe. *(Pause.)* This is in continued answer to your previous question.

("Well, why don't you tell me something about the four people?"

(Jane paused again. Briefly her eyes opened—something that seldom happens during envelope experiments.)

These are further general impressions. An S. Perhaps a C. The object, a card with a note. An out-of-town connection.

("Well, that's correct. The object does involve a note.")

A very definite connection with illness however. I suggest your break.

(Break at 10:25. Jane said she was "way-out." Seth hadn't wanted to take a break at the regular time, and had wanted to keep her under for the experiment also. He also had Jane let the cat in so she wouldn't get upset by the animal's scratching at the door. Her eyes had remained closed during the experiment and her pace had been quite rapid except where indicated.

(See the tracing of the actual object on page 319, and the copies of the greeting card on page 320-21. Notes pertaining to both are found on page 322, and will be developed as we run through the connections we make with the envelope object. Seth adds a few comments after break.

(Jane had one predominant image during the data, and this was of the greeting card. This is the reason for its inclusion with the actual object, since much of the following data actually deals with the greeting card. This is a case where the actual object, Leonard's note to us, served as a springboard. The connection between the object and the greeting card is a legitimate and close one, and presumably would not have developed had Jane not correctly divined the nature of the object itself to begin with. The connection between the two being the fact that the object concerned a phone call to us from my mother; and that my mother was also the sender of the card to us.

(Jane of course had seen the card upon arrival, on August 12 or 13,1966. It had become mislaid after arrival and we hadn't seen it since. We saw the envelope object on August 14. As soon as Jane began giving the envelope data I realized she referred to Mother's card as well as the object. At break we launched a search for the card. It was fruitless; we had given up on finding it until I looked through a stack of old magazines as a last resort.

(Of course the emotional involvement and reaction between us and my parents is strong, and would tend to override more specific details of the envelope object itself, once Jane had picked up the idea of my mother. Jane had the idea of Mother's greeting card in mind from the start of the envelope data, she said. She tried not to let this color the data. She mentally dropped it, deciding to let Seth speak in his own way. But the card plays a large part in the data nevertheless.

("A grave. Something grave." Jane had a strong ill or grave feeling, meaning burial, here, and it is applicable. My mother made the phone call that resulted in the object; my father is in poor health, and she talked of this when Jane returned the phone call at about noon on Sunday, August 14. In addition, the greeting card was mailed to us by Mother from Tunkhannock, PA, where she visited my brother and

his wife. My sister-in-law's father is also very ill, having nearly died recently.

("Three." We could make many connections here, with no real idea of which applied.

("A card with a cartoon." Yes. See pages 320-21. Again, this is not the object, but the card and the object are strongly related both in emotional content and in our physical time.

("Connection with a disturbance." My mother's call, represented by the object, reflected her own disturbance, and this in turn affected Jane and me when we made the return call later in the morning, August 14,1966.

("The color white." The object is a note on white paper. Also the greeting card is printed on white paper.

("Something misplaced." Leonard Yaudes, the author of the object, has recently lost a pair of garden shears. Jane subjectively feels this is the correct interpretation. I wondered if it might not refer to our search for the greeting card, described on page 327. Jane might have had subconscious knowledge that the card was lost. She was well aware that she was giving data concerning this card. I did not think of this possibility at the time and so did not ask Seth.

("A connection with a closet. I do not understand as yet to what <u>this</u> *particular image refers." This is legitimate data and is explained when Seth answers the second question.*

("A connection with a monument." This is, we think, developed further below with the monumental occasion data.

("Something misplaced again." See something misplaced above.

("Four plus one." Usually one can make a connection with a number, without knowing whether it is correct. Four plus one could apply to the date Leonard wrote the note used as object. See the copy of the folded slip I clipped to the object, on page 319. This slip bore the date, August14,1966. Other connections could be made if one chooses to interpret the data as four plus one means five, etc. Thus there is a five on the object itself in the time noted: 10:05. Also: The card was mailed to us from 54 Slocum Avenue, Tunkhannock, PA.

("This month." The object was produced this month, August 14,1966.

("I L I A." Jane was puzzled at this data at the time she gave it, as though she didn't have it right. Seth deals with it when he answers the first question.

("Distant connection with a cat. Perhaps black." A black cat is connected to my mother in perhaps more than a casual way. My mother's next-door neighbor acquired a black kitten a few months ago; the animal has made quite an impression on my parents, who enjoy watching its antics in their own yard as well as the neighbors'.

(Thus much of the data can be connected to my mother in a direct way,

bespeaking strong emotional connections. These connections seem to spring out of the original perception of the envelope object, more or less leaving the object behind.

("A very distant connection with a foreign land and a person. A woman. A Butts, I believe." This is another example growing out of my mother's connection with the object. The key is a mention of a Butts. Jane said that when giving the data she knew she meant the A as an initial A, standing for Alice Butts. I of course did not know this. Alice Butts is a retired cousin of my mother's whom my mother admires very much. Alice served in Korea as a missionary for many years. In addition, Leonard Yaudes, author of the envelope object, knows Alice Butts.

("Monumental. A monumental occasion." See the copy my mother wrote inside the greeting card, shown on page 321, in which she refers to finally arriving in Tunkhannock to visit my brother and his family. My parents live in Sayre, 50-some miles north of Tunkhannock. My father does not drive much anymore, and traveling is difficult for them. We think that in my mother's eyes the visit to Tunkhannock can legitimately be called a monumental occasion. Her copy begins: "At last we made it to Tunk..."

(The above could also have been intended to lead into the next data.

("A folded card. Writing on the inside. Printed matter and handwriting." All of this refers to the greeting card shown on pages 320-21, and sent to Jane and me by Mother on August 14,1966. The envelope object itself is not folded.

("The number 4." We don't know. Many connections possible.

("Several events happening together, or a series of objects strung together on the object." Probably a reference to the contents of my mother's writing on the greeting card, since this deals with several events. The objects strung together being words. This could apply to the envelope object, but this data is sandwiched in with others applying to the greeting card.

("Several colors. White, orange, red perhaps, this being circular, and a yellow. Plus dark printing." All of this applies to the greeting card, which we received in the mail either on August 12 or 13, and was of course seen by Jane. The envelope object came into being August 14. All of the above is accurate with the exception that there is no yellow on the card. The orange, red applies to the red halftone used on the cartoon figure, as indicated on page 319.

("I N C again, and perhaps 1418." This is interesting data. No I N C appears on the greeting card, although a company logo and address does on the back. However I N C did appear on the envelope used in the last experiment, the 66th. That was a postcard, and this evening's object is a greeting card. In addition, both are related to Leonard Yaudes; who sent us the postcard, and who authored tonight's object. The connection being Leonard, and the fact that Jane picked up Leonard's involvement in both experiments.

(The exact sequence, 1418, does not appear either on the envelope object or the greeting card. When we located the greeting card we also found its envelope. Tunkhannock's zip code is 18657. On the back of the envelope my mother wrote my brother-in-law's return address, which she should have. However she absent-mindedly wrote her own ZIP code, for Sayre, PA, after the address—18840. This is closer to 1418.

(See the tracing of the penciled slip I had attached to the envelope object when I first obtained it, reminding me of the date. The sequence, 8/14/66, is also close to 1418. Jane had never seen this slip, but it had been attached to the object for some time and perhaps was clairvoyantly divined. She had seen the envelope containing the greeting card in a casual way, of course, as had I. I did not discover the discrepancy in ZIP codes on the envelope until examining it after the session—several days after.

("Something sent through the mail in an envelope. Long and narrow in shape." An obvious reference to the greeting card.

("Apples." Another reference to my parents and their home in Sayre, PA. A large, old and beautiful apple tree sits in the backyard. We are all fond of sitting beneath it.

("73." My mother is 73 years old. Are there other connections?

("Perhaps a connection with your parents." Yes, both the object and the greeting card.

(In reference to the Apples data above, I should add that an apple tree in the backyard of our place here in Elmira can also furnish connections. Leonard Yaudes, the author of the envelope object, irritated Jane somewhat in July by cutting some of the limbs from this tree. He also talked of cutting the tree itself down, and Jane asked him not to.

("The word Ensenada." We thought this referred to a camping trip Jane and I made to Baja California with Jane's father. This being a distant connection with my parents, who also camped in years past.

("Something favorite, or favored, here. Some one favored." Jane said she was subjectively sure this was another reference to my mother, who caused Leonard to author the object. Me being my mother's favorite son.

(First Question: "Can you be more specific about the I L I A?" "No. Perhaps it could be a reference to Illinois, but that is all I see." The greeting card was manufactured in Illinois, as shown in small print to the right of the logo on page 4.

(2nd Question: "Can you elaborate upon the closet data?" "Ruburt thinks of your mother's sewing room. To me a reference to some shape, dark and narrow, with the feeling of motion involved, as a falling through or a falling out. Downward motion, with some speed." The sewing room of my mother is a legitimate connection.

We aren't so sure of Seth's interpretation, unless it pertains to the motion of the sewing machine. Could the dark and narrow, etc., be another grave or illness reference?

(3rd Question: "What's that about a black cat?" "A distant connection. [Pause.] A loss of an advantage, or <u>*period*</u> *of poor luck." See the explanation re the black cat on page 328. Seth's additional data here conjures up the thought that the neighbor's black cat also serves as the classic symbol of bad or poor luck; the connection here being the failing health of my father, and the failing health in a more drastic way of Mr. Meeker, the father-in-law of my brother Loren. It was while at Loren's that my mother sent us the greeting card. When she called us on August 14, she, of course, discussed the health both of my father and Mr. Meeker.*

(4th Question: "What's the shape of the object?" "Roughly rectangular, in itself." Correct. The envelope object is rectangular. So is the greeting card.

(5th Question: "Can you elaborate upon the grave data?" "A connection with someone, dead or in poor health. Perhaps a male." See the interpretation of the 3rd question, above.

(6th Question: "How about that number four?" "Four boxes, I believe. Box shapes." This still didn't help us.

(7th Question: "Can you tell me anything about what the handwriting says on the object?" "Not an invitation precisely at all, but reference to an occasion or visit." I thought it okay to ask this question since Seth had already mentioned handwriting in connection with the data. Seth's answer here is a good reference to the note Mother wrote inside the greeting card. It can actually apply just as well to the envelope object itself. The phone call on August 14 from my mother concerned a visit by us to Sayre, and one by her to us in Elmira. During this call arrangements were made for her to visit us here next weekend, on Saturday, August 20.

(8th Question: "Was that word you mentioned Ensenada?" "An incident primarily involving four people, I believe. This is in continued answer to your previous question." This data seems to emphasize the first of the two possibilities mentioned in the 7th Question. The four people thus, presumably, would be my parents, and my brother and his wife in Tunkhannock.

(9th Question: "Well, why don't you tell me something about the four people?" "These are further general impressions. An <u>*S*</u>*. Perhaps a C. The object, a card with a note. An out-of-town connection." As can be seen Seth did not answer the last two questions directly. A connection with S? Perhaps Sayre, my parents' home... We see none offhand for C.*

(Once again the greeting card shoulders its way into the data ahead of the actual envelope object. As explained both are related closely, but the greeting card with note, referred to above, and with an out-of-town connection, is of course not the object itself.

(Comment, meant to encourage Jane: "Well, that's correct. The object does involve a note." "A very definite connection with illness however." As explained, both the envelope object and the greeting card have connections with the illness of my father and Mr. Meeker.

(Jane resumed at 11:03.)

We will now close our session.

The one impression of which Ruburt was aware was a greeting card—quite legitimate, but it was meant only to lead him further.

My heartiest wishes to you both. I am as usual quite capable of carrying on further. However I bow to the necessary time limitations.

("Was that word you gave in the envelope data, Ensenada?")

It was.

("Why did that crop up?")

It was a very distant connection, and not very useful at all. Ruburt camped with his parent you see at Ensenada *(in Baja, California)*, and your parents' camp. There were two illnesses however referred to, the severe one, and your own father's. The illness of both men gave a strong impression and that is all.

I look forward to our Wednesday session, and though I feel in high spirits myself, I will here take pity upon you both and terminate our visit.

("Good night, Seth."

(End at 11:09. Jane was out as usual, her eyes open part of the time. She said Seth was quite capable of going on for hours.

(Note that I asked Seth 9 questions concerning the envelope data—the most so far.)

SESSION 280
AUGUST 24, 1966 9 PM WEDNESDAY

(The last two regularly scheduled sessions due, for Wednesday, August 17 and Monday, August 22, were not held because of my own illness.

(In the 278th session for Monday, August 8,1966, Seth said: "An event in a week and a half, that will be beneficial for you both." Exactly a week and a half later, on Wednesday, August 17, Jane received a letter from Don Wollheim, of Ace Books. He is to visit us on September 1. Jane is particularly interested to talk business with him. The Wollheim letter was entirely unexpected, no correspondence having passed between Jane and Mr. Wollheim, or business, for a long time.

(On Saturday, August 20, Jane received her first press copy of her book from her publisher, F. Fell: How to Develop Your ESP Power.

(Our landlady, Marian Spaziani, visiting with us this evening, left at 9 PM. Jane began speaking in an average voice, with her eyes closed and while sitting down, at 9:09.)

Now, good evening.

("Good evening, Seth.")

First of all, some personal comments.

We will begin with Ruburt. His past indispositions, from an overall viewpoint, have been most necessary and beneficial. You cannot afford to keep knowledge at an intellectual level, and not use it practically, for when you do so it is useless to you. His indispositions taught him this is a way that he will not forget. His inner and unthinking reactions literally immobilized him.

This immobilization was in itself a lesson, and he has learned it. He conquered mentally and emotionally, and therefore he conquered finally in physical terms. The immobile foot was a direct translation of the following: "I am exhausted and I will go no further at this point." The exhaustion was a natural result of his own reactions. He is fond of saying that if you cannot control events, you can control your reactions. He did not do so well here, however, and he is considering only a half-truth in the above statement.

Actually reactions to events do control other events. You see what I mean here. The hip was simply a panic reaction. It was also the result of negative suggestion given by your chiropractor. There are ways of protecting yourself. You know them, and must use them.

Fortunately Ruburt benefited, for he learned. I have given you important and practical suggestions concerning health measures, and I take it for granted that you use them.

(Once again one of our cats scratched at the door for admittance. As she has done before Jane got up while speaking, and without interrupting her delivery let the cat in. She then sat back down.)

Again, I did not foresee this difficulty. And again, your purposes will be served if you make a habit in our sessions of asking me to check into immediate probabilities as far as health is concerned.

It is a matter of focus on my part. If the overall developments are not dangerous, I will not automatically sense them, but only the end result. On Ruburt's part this time it was additional knowledge. Specific questions will cause me to turn my attention to such matters.

We can then change the probabilities, or manipulate them to your advantage. It many cases proper suggestions given immediately may well suffice. You cannot expect however a steady and unchanging state of exuberant happiness. *(Smile.)* It is not practical in your terms. You would learn nothing, or very little.

In the main physical existence means a translation of inner mood and psychological climate into physical terms, and no consciousness is constantly in a state of bliss. There is always effort involved, for this is the meaning of consciousness. It is the meaning of creative effort. You should not accept a barrage of illness as natural, however, for it is not. On the other hand neither should you blame yourselves for various small and separated indispositions.

In a state of excellent health there will still be small, infrequent but definite indispositions. You can be sure of adequate protection if you daily suggest that you will be open to constructive and healthful suggestions and influences. Also suggest that you will be automatically protected against negative suggestions and influences.

It is important that influences also be included.

We will rest whenever you prefer, Joseph.

("Go ahead for a while." 9:29.)

Now. The cat episode, my dear friend, *(laugh)* was not connected with either of your indispositions, except for your own negative expectations. Ruburt picked these up from you. You learned quickly, saving your cat.

Some harm was done, of course. You can command yourself protection from such viruses through the suggestions given earlier. You may rest.

(Jane paused while I sneezed.)

We will have a short session if you prefer, for your convenience.

("No, I'm all right. Please continue.")

The suggestions mentioned, had you used them consistently, would have changed your own reactions to the Miss Callahan incidents, and allowed you greater freedom. Not only did the incidents upset you, but unwittingly you prevented Ruburt himself from giving some aid in the later stages that he could have provided.

It was your reactions that should have been changed, as it was Ruburt's reactions concerning his book that should have been changed. His attitude toward his book and publisher largely were responsible for the delays.

You should have made a positive and enlightened effort to help Miss Callahan, once you realized your predicament. If you had done so, dear friend, you would not have become ill. And this material is quite undistorted.

Help those you are free to help. It will make up for many things.

Now you may take a more relaxing rest.

(Break at 9:39. Jane was pretty well dissociated, she said. She wasn't aware, really, that she had let the cat in until she was back in the chair. She likened the experience to manipulated dream images; none of them had bothered her.

(Her pace had become quite active, her eyes open often; she had smoked and

sipped wine. She resumed in the same manner at 9:44.)

Your hay fever situation will be greatly benefited if you particularly suggest that you be free of past (underlined) negative influences and suggestions. Do not drink as much milk as usual.

Stay away from cheese. *(Pause.)* There is some confusion regarding wheat products. I am not sure if it is white or brown wheat bread that has a tendency to bother you during this season. *(Pause.)*

Coffee with milk is not good. Coffee alone is satisfactory if it is fresh, and is a benefit to you. Your habit of drinking old, cold, settled coffee is not good. There is a change in the acid which disturbs your system, and adds to the allergic symptoms.

Margarine, however, although a dairy product, is beneficial in this context. I am speaking now mainly of the hay fever allergy. *(Pause.)* Mints, not chocolate covered, will be of benefit. I am not speaking of your indigestion remedies here.

Give us a moment longer on these points.

(Jane took a long pause, sitting with her eyes closed.)

Clorox in your clothes is not good, or in your bedding. Ruburt uses this I believe in laundry. Its use should be disregarded for now. *(Pause.)*

The animal hair is not an irritant in your case, though there are some associations of the past concerning your mother that may lead you to think so. The perfumed soap should be exchanged for another variety. The particular kind you are using is not good in your particular circumstances.

These instructions apply only during hay fever season. In your room keep some cotton in a saucer. The cotton to be saturated with ink. The ink will draw certain alloids from the atmosphere of the house. The cotton should be daily discarded and a new piece put in its place.

These measures will greatly benefit you, but they would not be necessary if you conquered the condition from the subjective end. Now you have not asked me, but if you give me a moment I will look into your probable health situation, and see what we find.

(Long pause, eyes closed, at 9:57.)

If you go to your landlord's, do not use the apples if they are given to you. You will not break down the acids in them properly, judging from past performance. If you follow my suggestions and use what you know, then you should have a very light hay fever season. If you do an excellent job of it, then you would experience no symptoms.

I do not see any too-annoying symptoms in any case. Ruburt is clear also. He frightened himself into some sense. During hay fever season Ruburt should use a diluted (underlined) ammonia household cleaner.

When possible a window facing the north should be opened in your room, in the morning particularly. These past episodes, again, have been beneficial to you both. You are quite correct, Joseph. You ended your illness however not twice as quickly, but three times as quickly, as it would have been otherwise.

Now Ruburt utilized his abilities in helping you, but he did not mobilize them with any vigor in helping himself, until panic drove him to do so.

I have told you that his book will sell well—very well, and so it shall.

If the Wollheim meeting takes place, it will prove highly beneficial to all parties concerned, but at a later date and at a time when it will be highly needed. The association will continue, and in other places. Within I believe three years there will be a much closer and significant relationship between the two families.

I have taken this session to give you healthful suggestions. Take advantage of them. There seems to be something about a Wednesday, significant within I believe a month, but I cannot pin it down.

Ruburt should wash his dust mop.

Stay away also, Joseph, from peanut butter, for a while only. You may take a break, or end the session as you prefer.

("Well, we can take the break."

(Break at 10:15. Jane had been well dissociated. At first she could remember nothing except the last sentence or two she had delivered; then bits of the material began to return. Her pace had been good, her eyes open often, etc.

(At break we tried looking up the word "alloid" in the dictionary, without success. Nor did approximations yield anything. I was sure of the word Jane had given, as far as sound goes, although my spelling was phonetic. We thought Seth would comment later.

(Jane resumed in the same manner at 10:25.)

We will shortly close.

The difficulties over the word have to do with Ruburt's vocabulary. The word I mean is one connected with trace minerals of metallic base.

There is an interchange of acids between metallic traces. During the season you do not utilize some acids properly, and excesses sometimes build up. The ink arrangement takes care of these.

(Long pause, eyes closed.) I am quiet simply because I am searching for future suggestions here. Do not drink milk in your parents' home, particularly at this time. Cottage cheese is advisable to replace other cheeses.

Your Formosan tea is excellent for you. Avoid orange pekoe for now.

Our next session will be concerned with the discussion which we earlier began, rather than with personal concerns. I suggest however that you make a habit of questioning me concerning health probabilities as you go along.

Ruburt's ankle was sprained originally in your home. A very simple sprain, suffered in the kitchen. It was mending nicely until the evening at your dancing establishment, when it was again bruised. He kept on dancing however, a mistake.

("How did Jane sprain it in the kitchen?")

I believe moving the refrigerator out to clean. The weight was poorly distributed. It is now on the mend, and he should experience no further difficulties. He should automatically now give himself the suggestions mentioned in this session, before he reads a letter from his mother. This alone will save him from many indispositions. Your cat should be inoculated. There is no great danger here, but since you know he is not inoculated, it should be done. Do you have any questions?

("What did you think of my dream experience involving the back windows of the studio? Did this involve a projection?" See my dream notebook for August 20,1966.)

It was indeed, as you suspected; you were afraid to carry on however. It could have been quite interesting. Ruburt's sudden propulsions, so far, have saved him from having to make that kind of decision, you see. All in all you did well. There is no rush. All of those dreams, grouped during your illness, were projections, and the result of suggestion. If you have no more questions, we will end our session.

("I guess not.")

My heartiest regards. And to Ruburt my congratulations on his book.

("You're in it.")

I am indeed. *(Smile, eyes closed.)* I am its inspiration.

(End at 10:42. Jane was again far-out. Eyes open at times, etc.)

Books by Jane Roberts from Amber-Allen Publishing

Seth Speaks: The Eternal Validity of the Soul. This essential guide to conscious living clearly and powerfully articulates the furthest reaches of human potential, and the concept that each of us creates our own reality.

The Nature of Personal Reality: Specific, Practical Techniques for Solving Everyday Problems and Enriching the Life You Know.. In this perennial bestseller, Seth challenges our assumptions about the nature of reality and stresses the individual's capacity for conscious action.

The Individual and the Nature of Mass Events. Seth explores the connection between personal beliefs and world events, how our realities merge and combine "to form mass reactions such as the overthrow of governments, the birth of a new religion, wars, epidemics, earthquakes, and new periods of art, architecture, and technology."

The Magical Approach: Seth Speaks About the Art of Creative Living. Seth reveals the true, magical nature of our deepest levels of being, and explains how to live our lives spontaneously, creatively, and according to our own natural rhythms.

The Oversoul Seven Trilogy (The Education of Oversoul Seven, The Further Education of Oversoul Seven, Oversoul Seven and the Museum of Time). Inspired by Jane's own experiences with the Seth Material, the adventures of Oversoul Seven are an intriguing fantasy, a mind-altering exploration of our inner being, and a vibrant celebration of life.

The Nature of the Psyche. Seth reveals a startling new concept of self, answering questions about the inner reality that exists apart from time, the origins and powers of dreams, human sexuality, and how we choose our physical death.

The "Unknown" Reality, Volumes One and Two. Seth reveals the multidimensional nature of the human soul, the dazzling labyrinths of unseen probabilities involved in any decision, and how probable realities combine to create the waking life we know.

Dreams, "Evolution," and Value Fulfillment, Volumes One and Two. Seth discusses the material world as an ongoing self-creation—the product of a conscious, self-aware and thoroughly animate universe, where virtually every possibility not only exists, but is constantly encouraged to achieve its highest potential.

The Way Toward Health. Woven through the poignant story of Jane Roberts' final days are Seth's teachings about self-healing and the mind's effect upon physical health.

Available in bookstores everywhere.